General Manuel Roxas, First President of
the Republic of the Philippines.

FIRST MALAYAN REPUBLIC

FIRST MALAYAN REPUBLIC

The Story of the Philippines

ILLUSTRATED

BY

GEORGE A. MALCOLM

Dean, College of Law, University of the Philippines, 1912-17; Justice, Supreme Court of the Philippines, 1917-36; Staff Member, Office of the U. S. High Commissioner to the Philippines, 1936-40; Professorial Lecturer, University of the Philippines, 1948-49.

THE CHRISTOPHER PUBLISHING HOUSE
BOSTON, U.S.A.

COPYRIGHT 1951
BY THE CHRISTOPHER PUBLISHING HOUSE

PRINTED IN
THE UNITED STATES OF AMERICA

This volume is dedicated to my former students, builders of the Christian, Democratic, Malayan Republic of the Philippines, the first in all history.

These worthy Filipinos include:

The first and second Presidents of the Republic, and numerous Cabinet officers and heads of offices;

Three Speakers of the House of Representatives, and many Senators and Congressmen;

Ten Justices of the Supreme Court;

Leaders in professional and business life.

All, whether of high or low degree, retain my respect and affection.

The Author

AUTOBIOGRAPHICAL PREFACE

It is possible that I am the only American who deliberately entered the American counterpart of what in other lands would be termed "the Colonial Service" for a career. At any rate, from September 25, 1906 to November 10, 1942, a span of over thirty-six years, I held various positions in the American administration of the Philippines and Puerto Rico. In 1948-49 I returned to the Philippines at the invitation of the University of the Philippines to deliver lectures in the College of Law.

My arrival in Manila on the Army Transport *Logan,* shortly after the San Francisco Quake of 1906, naturally went unheralded. I was a callow graduate of the University of Michigan, with a law degree to be sure, but no job awaited me and less than ten dollars jingled in my pockets. Eventually I was able to secure a temporary clerkship that no one else wanted, at seventy-five dollars a month, in the Bureau of Health, of which the efficient Dr. Victor G. Heiser was the Director. Then, having squeezed through the first grade civil service examination, I was appointed by Executive Secretary Frank W. Carpenter, one of America's most capable administrators, to help edit the Philippine Reports. About the same time, Director of Education David P. Barrows, later to become President of the University of California, named me a night school teacher in the Philippine Normal School at three pesos per class.

Heiser, Carpenter and Barrows were splendid Americans who, at the time they served in the Philippines, may not have been as well known as their Governor General superiors, but who were to receive international acclaim.

At this point in my career I became associated with such Filipino dignitaries as Judge Ignacio Villamor who was the Attorney General, later was chosen President of the University of the Philippines, and finally joined me on the Supreme Bench; and Judge Ramon Avanceña, Attorney General and subsequently Chief Justice and likewise my colleague on the Court. These fine Christian gentlemen and other Filipino leaders with whom I was brought into intimate contact, like Secretary of Finance and Justice Gregorio Araneta, Chief Justices Cayetano Arellano, Victorina Mapa, Manuel Araullo, and Jose Abad Santos, not to mention political leaders like Sergio Osmeña, Manuel L. Quezon, Rafael Palma, and Juan Sumulong, brought me a realization of their many admirable qualities.

7

In 1910 when I had risen step by step to the position of Assistant Attorney General in the Bureau of Justice, an event occurred which was to turn the current of my life and at the same time affect the future history of the Philippines.

I had maintained loose connections with the Philippine Normal School. There young Filipinos were able to finish a preparatory law course in English, but no modern law school existed in the Philippines in which to continue their educations in the English language. I proposed the establishment of a law school in the University of the Philippines, only to meet with blunt refusal from Secretary of Public Instruction and Chairman of the University Board of Regents Newton W. Gilbert and other influential Regents. Nevertheless, with the audacity of youth, I went ahead to organize law courses in connection with the Y. M. C. A. of Manila. At the end of the first year, the University capitulated and authorized the organization of a College of Law. I continued as Dean of this institution until 1917 when President Wilson named me an Associate Justice of the Supreme Court of the Philippines. Just about ten years after my arrival in the Philippines I had reached what could be the legitimate goal of any lawyer.

I remained on the Supreme Court for over eighteen years and eventually became the senior member and the Presiding Justice of the Civil Division. I left the Court shortly after the inauguration of the Commonwealth of the Philippines in January, 1936 to join the staff of the United States High Commissioner to the Philippines. After four enjoyable years with High Commissioners Frank Murphy and Paul V. McNutt, I left the Philippines to become Attorney General of Puerto Rico—which is another story.

Of my various experiences in the Philippines, I would like to emphasize two. The first was my contact with what was then called "the rising generation" of English-speaking and democratically-trained Filipinos. The second was the interest which I developed in Philippine research, resulting in the production of books in Philippine political science and law.

There was drawn to the College of Law, University of the Philippines, the best of the youth of the Islands—not all to be sure, but a goodly portion. They were taught to dig for the law and the facts with untiring industry, to think and reason for themselves, and to understand democracy in all its phases. Moreover, they acquired the confidence and stature that goes with success—so much so, those law graduates became Presidents of the Philippines, Speakers of the House of Representatives, Justices of the Supreme Court, and Members of the Cabinet. Knowing these men intimately as former students and being familiar with their careers, I can affirm that they were and are fully capable of holding the reins of state of the first Malayan Republic.

As for the books which I have written on the Philippines, they were originally associated with the Government of the Philippine Islands in existence from 1901 to 1935. More recently my research was related to the successor government, the Commonwealth of the Philippines. And now, if all goes well, these studies will be climaxed by this volume on the Republic of the Philippines.

My point of view in bringing together and solidifying the experience of nearly half a century's association with the Philippines is simple. I would deal with warm sympathy, and I hope understanding and tolerance, with the problems facing the Filipino people. I would avoid the pitfall of maintaining and fortifying a predetermined point of view. I would have this volume, while it cannot be a catchall or the counterpart of an encyclopedia, encompass as much as possible of the Philippine scene in all its phases, in order to offer a clear picture of the whole. I have tried to be fair, not sensational.

As originally prepared, the manuscript included a sixty typewritten page appendix of acknowledgments, representative authorities, and notes. Therein my debt to the persons who checked sections of the volume and to the authors listed in a select bibliography was recorded, and corroborative material was added. The need to reduce the size of the book has compelled the elimination of the appendix. Accordingly I must limit myself to a blanket expression of thanks to all who helped.

George A. Malcolm

Manila, Republic of the Philippines,
and Hollywood, California, United States,
December 1, 1950.

CONTENTS

CHAPTER V

American Philippine policy. The Government established. Pro-Consuls of the United States. The Colonial
Service. Carpenter and Hayden. The American record
in the Philippines.

CHAPTER VI

Development. Dr. Jose Rizal. Revolts. The ephemeral
Philippine Republic. General Emilio Aguinaldo. Nationalist leaders. Progress toward autonomy. Philippine independence. Nationalist fervor under the Republic.

CHAPTER VII

Passage by the Congress of two Philippine Independence
Acts. First rejection and then acceptance by the Philip-
pine Legislature. Status of the Commonwealth of the
Philippines. The Commonwealth election. President
Quezon takes office. The Commonwealth in operation.
The Resident Commissioner of the Philippines to the
United States. The United States High Commissioner
to the Philippines.

CHAPTER VIII

Bataan and Corregidor. Japanese Occupation. Guerrilla
resistance. Chief Justice Abad Santos and General Lim—
Philippine heroes. Santo Tomas Internment Camp. The
Government-In-Exile. President Quezon Wages the
Good Fight. General MacArthur returns. Statesman
Osmeña becomes President.

CHAPTER IX

Pre-independence election. Birth of a Nation. President Roxas charts his course. Ordeal of the Republic. Graft, rackets, thievery. The collaboration issue. America's tardy help. The almost forgotten veteran. A Nation mourns the death of Manuel Roxas, first President of the Republic. His Excellency Elpidio Quirino, second President of the Republic. State of the Nation.

CHAPTER X

Philippine Constitutional history. The Constitutional Convention. Submission of the Constitution for approval. Amendments to the Constitution. New features. A Republican State. A commentary.

CHAPTER XI

A strong executive. Presidential powers and perquisites. The Vice President. The Council of State. Presidential tenure. Defenses against dictatorship. The Cabinet. Executive bureaus and offices. The Civil Service. Malacañan Palace.

CHAPTER XII

Legislative bodies of the former Government of the Philippine Islands. The Unicameral National Assembly of the former Commonwealth. The Bicameral Congress of the Republic. Legislative power. Congressional Commissions. Impeachment. The Speaker of the House. The President of the Senate. Legislative practices.

CHAPTER XIII

Philippine justice. The Supreme Court of the Philippines. A galaxy of Filipino jurists. Inferior courts. Administering justice. The N.B.I. Philippine law. Land titles.

CHAPTER XIV

The Foreign Service. Philippine affairs in Washington. Membership in the United Nations. Southeast Asia or Pacific Union. The Diplomatic and Consular Corps in Manila. Privileges and disabilities of resident aliens. Foreign communities in the Philippines. American pioneers. Cultural connections with Spain. The Chinese conquest of the Philippines. *Sayonara* Japan. The yellow peril. Pinoys abroad.

CHAPTER XV

Manila, the metropolis. Quezon, the official capital. Baguio, the summer capital. The Chartered Cities, including Cebu. Zamboanga, the beautiful. Pagsanjan, the progressive. Occidental Negros, the sugar province.

CHAPTER XVI

Suffrage and elections. The Commission on Elections. The Federal Party. The *Nacionalista* Majority. The *Democrata* Minority. One party government under the Commonwealth. The two party system for the Republic. Realignments for the 1949 election. Practical politics.

CHAPTER XVII

CHAPTER XXII

The public schools. The University of the Philippines. The University of Santo Tomas and the private schools. Literacy. English and a national language. Health. Quarantine. Hansen's disease. Social service.

CHAPTER XXIII

Paganism. Mohammedanism. The Roman Catholic Church. The Filipino Independent Church. The Protestant Churches. Separation of Church and State.

CHAPTER XXIV

Filipino attainments. Philippine Literature. Philippine classics and near classics. Science. Art. Music. Public opinion.

CHAPTER XXV

Filipino capacity for self-government. Will the first Malayan Republic survive? *Mabuhay*.

ILLUSTRATIONS

Modern Personages in the Development of Philippine Nationalism

17

FIRST MALAYAN REPUBLIC

FIRST MALAYAN REPUBLIC

THE STORY OF THE PHILIPPINES

CHAPTER I

THE PHILIPPINES

SHOW WINDOW OF DEMOCRACY IN THE FAR EAST

High-placed representatives of the foreign services of the Philippines and the United States are agreed that the Philippines is the show window of democracy in the Far East. If the Philippines is thus to serve as a successful demonstration area, Philippine-American cooperation is essential.

It is, however, lamentably the truth that the American people have evinced only a spasmodic interest in Philippine affairs. This lack of understanding of the Filipinos and their problems following half a century of American association with them is particularly regrettable, even hazardous, to both parties.

Before the Spanish-American War in 1898, the Philippine Islands were not even a recognizable geographical expression to the United States. Until then, American relations with the Islands had been confined to desultory commerce carried on by clipper ships which occasionally came into the port of Manila and to the trade that had been fostered by two American houses under the protective blessing of an American Consul. When Commodore George Dewey was appointed Commander of the Asiatic Squadron of the United States Navy prior to the outbreak of war with Spain, he found that the latest official report relative to the Philippines on file in the Office of Naval Intelligence bore the date 1876. Senator John Sharp Williams enjoyed telling how, as a member of the House Committee on Foreign Relations during the Spanish-American War, it was one of his arduous tasks to climb upon a stool and point out the Islands on a map for the benefit of his colleagues. The ignorance was reciprocal. The Filipinos knew just as little about the "North Americans," as the Americans did about the "Phili-pine-os."

In the course of time the Americans learned more about the Philippines, and the Filipinos more about the United States. The agitation for Philippine independence focused attention on American relations in the Far East. Missions—the disrespectful called them junkets—have come and gone: American missions to the Philippines to investigate conditions and render reports; Filipino missions to the United States to plead for liberty and trade concessions and render reports. The efforts of American Governors General, High Commissioners, and Ambassadors have done much to acquaint the world with the facts relating to the Philippine Islands. Returning Filipino students and travellers from the United States have helped to disabuse the public of false notions regarding their respective countries.

With the advent of the Second World War there was a surge of personal interest on the part of the American public in everything Philippine. Their boys were fighting on Philippine soil, which suddenly became sacred, and relatives and friends wanted information about places and islands and conditions as never before. With the cessation of hostilities, however, there was all too strong an inclination to return to the complacence of prewar days, thus adding ingratitude to indifference and ignorance.

The debacle in China and the fighting war in Korea have again focused American attention on the Philippines. In effect the islands constituting the Republic of the Philippines have become outposts in a security zone, extending from the Aleutians to the Philippines, to be defended by the United States against communism in Asia. The Filipinos have taken advantage of this situation to tap the reservoir of good will and thus to gain more aid for the rehabilitation and defense of their country.

What is needed above all else is accurate information about the Philippines. Unfortunately, dependable facts cannot be acquired from sensational articles prepared after a few days sojourn in the Islands and presenting the bizarre in vivid colors. Preconceived ideas, part true, part fantasy, about the "South Seas" of which the Philippine Archipelago is not technically a part, must be disregarded if one is to obtain a correct picture of actual conditions. Superficial judgments formed over a highball at the club bar are likewise hardly to be relied upon. Knowledge grounded on facts will tend to promote mutual understanding between the people of the United States and the people of the Philippines.

The Filipinos do not lack in anything of interest to the statesman and the student, or even to the casual visitor. They offer a background of fascinating history. The Islands comprising the Republic of the Philippines, and the people of Malay extraction inhabiting these Islands are of the Orient. Culturally, however, because of Spanish and American influence, the Filipino people are of the Occident. The Republic, proclaimed by the Filipinos under American auspices, is the first Malay State of the modern world, the only Christian and truly democratic nation of the Orient. Thus placed at the crossroads between the East and the West, the Christian, democratic Malayan Republic of the Philippines is certain to play a significant role in world affairs.

The purpose of this volume will be to try to give you as nearly as is possible an approximation of the truth about the Philippines and the Filipinos as they have been and are today.

LOCATION[1]

The average American has a very hazy idea of the geographical location of the Philippine Islands. He is likely to confuse them with the Hawaiian Islands and thinks them possibly a five-day journey by ship from San Francisco. He might even place the Philippine Islands in the Caribbean Sea somewhere in the West Indies near Cuba, instead of in the East Indies near Borneo. Returning residents of the Philippines report amusing experiences of this nature.

In order to set the matter straight, let it be known that the Philippines is an important part of the general region which anthropologists call "Malaysia" in the far western Pacific. More specifically, the Philippine Archipelago lies southeast of Asia, and for a thousand miles and more fronts on the coast of that continent. The islands composing the Philippines are bounded on the north by Formosa and Japan, on the east by the islands under the trusteeship of the United States—the nearest land in this direction being the Palau Islands, on the south by Borneo and Celebes Islands, and on the west by China, the British colony of Hongkong, and French Indo China. The most northerly island of the Archipelago is but sixty-one miles from Sho Antau Su Island, lying east of Formosa, which may be seen from the Philippines on a clear day. Along its southern boundary are islands which lie within a short one mile of British territory and forty-three miles of the nearest land in the Netherlands Indies. Sibitu in the Sulu group of the Philippines is just north of the equator and but a step from Borneo.

From the Philippines to Hongkong direct is six hundred and thirty-one miles. From the Philippines by way of the usual ports of call to San Francisco is 8,094 miles. The voyage from San Francisco or Los

[1] This section and the following section were checked and brought up to date by Capt. Andres O. Hizon, Director of the Bureau of Coast and Geodetic Survey, Republic of the Philippines.

Angeles to Manila is of seventeen or twenty-three days duration depending on the route. Giant airway clippers starting at San Francisco, Los Angeles, and Seattle, and on the southern route proceeding by way of Honolulu and Guam, and on the northern route by way of Alaska and Japan, have shortened the trip to hours. Excellent air connections on around the world are available.

The Philippines comprises the territory ceded to the United States by the Treaty of Paris concluded between the United States and Spain on December 10, 1898, together with the group of islands known as Cagayan Sulu and Sibitu embraced in a supplemental treaty between the same parties. The Turtle and Mangsee Islands, situated between Britain's North Borneo and the Philippines' Sulu, were taken over by the Philippine Republic on October 16, 1947, after Great Britain had relinquished administration of the islands.

Geographically speaking, therefore, the islands which go to make up the Republic of the Philippines are of the Orient. The Filipinos inhabiting those islands have as near neighbors Chinese, Japanese, Formosans, Americans, British, and Indonesians. Farther away "down under" are the Australians and New Zealanders. From the north falls the shadow of the Russians in Siberia, Manchuria, Mongolia and Korea.

PHYSICAL FEATURES

The number of islands and islets in the Philippine Archipelago that have been charted total approximately 7,100. Of these, about eight hundred are large and fertile enough to be inhabited. The two large islands are Luzon and Mindanao with areas approaching that of the State of New York. No other archipelago contains as many islands so compactly grouped.

The combined land area of all the islands composing the Philippines is 115,600 square miles.[2] This is considerably less than the area of the State of California, but is more than the area of the neighboring States of Oregon and Washington. In size the Philippines ranks slightly above New Zealand, slightly below Italy, and contains three-fourths the area of Japan.

The salient characteristics of the Philippine group have been outlined as follows: 1. The rugged and irregular features of the islands; 2. the fertility of the soil; 3. the great extent of coast line almost as long as that of the United States; 4. the mountainous character of the

[2] Based upon surveys made up to January 1, 1939. This area of 115,600 square miles is 1,200 square miles greater than the 114,400 square miles formerly determined. See Census Atlas of the Philippines, 1939 Census Vol. V, p. 11.

country, with the mountain ranges generally following the coast; 5. the relatively few large rivers and lakes; and 6. the number of active and dormant volcanoes. Generally speaking, the prevailing physical features are heavily forested mountain ranges with alternating valleys or plains.

The mountains rise to considerable elevations. Mount Apo in Mindanao is nearly 10,000 feet in height, and Mount Pulog in Northern Luzon is only a little less in height. While the highest peaks in the Philippines fall short of the elevations of mountains in other parts of the world, it should be noted that Philippine mountain ranges rise more or less abruptly from the seashore and present a striking picture of contrasting ruggedness.

The three best known volcanoes are Taal, located in Taal Lake, about two hours by automobile from Manila, Mayon on the southern end of the Island of Luzon, and Hibok-hibok on little Camiguin Island in the Southern Philippines. The first is said to be the lowest volcano in the world, the second is supposed to possess the most symmetrically beautiful volcanic cone, and the third is the most recent to bring death to those in its molten path. Taal and Hibok-hibok are classified by experts as of the explosive, man-killing type, in contrast to Mayon of the gradually-erupting category.

Taal Volcano was last in eruption in 1911, when it eclipsed all previous records by putting on a pyrotechnic display of vast proportions and causing great loss of life. Mount Mayon, with a base of eighty miles in circumference, sweeps up sheer from the seashore and a large cultivated plain to an elevation of 8,000 feet, and occasionally shows signs of activity. When Mayon was in eruption in 1928, it was estimated by government observers that the vapor column reached a height of twenty miles. Long dormant Hibok-hibok began eruption in September, 1948, driving more than 35,000 persons off the island. The volcano has since built around itself a gigantic wall over 1,100 feet high.

Ocean depths, called "deeps," are found in many sections within or bordering the Archipelago. The greatest known ocean depth is the famous "Mindanao Deep," only forty-five miles to the eastward of Northern Mindanao, where the whole of Mount Everest could be sunk with a mile of water to spare.

The Philippines has been pronounced by experts—who ought to know whereof they speak—to be the most favored group of tropical islands in the world. On the fertile land of these islands nature has bestowed her riches with a generous hand and her beauties in harmonious combination. The latent possibilities in agriculture, forestry, and mining are unsurpassed. The natural resources of the Philippines are so varied and represent so much wealth as hardly to be within the comprehension of mere man.

CLIMATE

The newcomer to Manila in the Philippines finds the tropical climate hard to endure. He or she may be dressed in heavy stateside clothes, may overindulge in stimulating beverages causing excessive perspiration, may rush madly hither and yon in the middle of the day, or may combine all these heat-provoking habits during a stay, and usually a brief one. So it is written, "Manila is hot, stickily, depressingly, incredibly hot." [3] Or synonyms of similar import are viciously thrown together to punctuate thoughts about the pestilential climate.

The oldtimer and the Filipino, who dress in white or khaki, drink in moderation, and stay out of the sun, find Manila comfortable. They live to ripe old ages, forgetful of the much-maligned climate. For the common, superficial belief that the heat in Manila and other lowland cities is unbearable does not accord with the facts.

Comparatively speaking, the torrid temperatures experienced in Washington are seldom approached in Manila. The mean average daily temperature of the Philippines metropolis is 80°F. Rarely does the thermometer fall to 60°F. or below. On the other hand, just as rarely does the mercury reach or pass the 100°F. mark. [4] Air conditioning is a boon of which an increasing number of offices and homes are availing themselves.

Close to the low-lying port of Manila, but on a higher level of land, is the recently authorized capitol, Quezon City. There, with less crowding and more air, the days and nights can be lived pleasantly.

About forty miles from the Cities of Manila and Quezon is Tagaytay City, located on a lovely ridge overlooking Lake Taal, 2,000 feet above sea level. In Tagaytay the temperature is several degrees cooler than in Manila.

The Philippine Islands as a whole are entirely within the tropic zone. Nevertheless, in the lowlands the climate is merely mildly

---

[3] Florence Horn, *Orphans of the Pacific*, p. 27 (New York, 1941). See Rev. Jose Coronas, S. J., *The Climate and Weather of the Philippine Islands* (Manila, 1920).

[4] The highest temperature ever recorded in Manila was 103.5°F., and this was in May, 1878; again in May, 1912, April and May, 1915, and May, 1942 the mercury shot past the 100°F. mark. The all-time low of 58.1°F. was recorded on January 11, 1914. Figures were checked with the records of the Weather Bureau by Director C. del Rosario.

tropical, while in the higher altitudes the air is cool and bracing. Snow, of course, is unknown, and frost and ice occur only on the mountain peaks. The land around Lake Lanao and the uplands of Bukidnon in Mindanao represent types of agreeable mountain climates of the Phillipines. Baguio, the summer capital, over 5,000 feet above sea level and only an hour by air from Manila, permits the person oppressed by the heat to seek relaxation before a log fire or to find refreshing sleep in pine-laden air.

The year is popularly divided into three seasons. There is the hot season, which begins about the first of March and lasts until about the first of July, when the rainy season starts, to be followed about the first of November by the so-called cool season of four months duration. April and May are the hottest months, August and September the most humid. Even then the heat is never extreme, and sunstroke is unknown.

The rainfall is heavy. In certain regions it amounts to as much as two hundred and fifty inches annually. The world record for a twenty-four hour rainfall is forty-seven inches, and occurred on July 14-15, 1911, at Baguio, the mountain resort in the Philippines.

The Islands, excepting the southern portion, are in the typhoon belt. The typhoon appears to be a phenomenon peculiar to the waters in and about the Philippine Archipelago. A destructive typhoon, like a destructive cyclone, is a great calamity causing terrible disasters on land and sea and enormous material damage. On the other hand, ordinary depressions owing to the beneficial rains they produce, are often rather a blessing to the Islands than otherwise.

The Philippines is situated in the seismic belt, but certain islands, as Bohol and Palawan, have been proved to be relatively earthquake-immune areas. In Manila the average of seismic disturbances throughout a long course of years has been one a month, but of the feeble tremors only slight notice is taken by the populace. The most devastating earthquake was the one on June 3, 1863, which demolished the Cathedral, the palace of the Governor General, and other public buildings in Manila.

Fortunately for the Philippines, weather forecasts are made accurately by the Weather Bureau. The Manila Observatory, the central office of the Weather Bureau, was founded by the Jesuit Order in 1865. Notable scientists, including Fathers Federico Faura and Jose Algue, have been in charge of it, and their contributions to meteorology brought them international renown. The Philippine Republic, while transferring control of the Weather Bureau to non-sectarian hands, wisely follows the policy set by the Jesuit Fathers.

Broadly and truthfully speaking, the climate of the Philippines is the most healthful and comfortable of any portion of the tropics inhabited by man.

LIFE IN THE PHILIPPINE TROPICS

If the reader retains a movie-fostered picture of an American in the tropics sweltering in terrific heat and wearing, à la Stanley in Africa, a cork helmet, or if he has a vision of scantily-clad maidens doing a hula in the moonlight, let him get these notions out of his head. The Philippines is not India, where a helmet or double felt hats are vital necessities to give protection from the rays of the sun. The Philippines is not Hawaii, where native dances are arranged for the edification of the tourists. Life in the Philippines runs along different, if less fanciful, channels.

In "the days of the Empire," Americans suffered real hardships in the Philippines. A Constabulary officer might be directed to proceed to an isolated post, or a teacher might be assigned to organize a school in a remote municipality. Life in such primitive surroundings, even among hospitable Filipino neighbors, was a test of the physical and moral fibre of a man or woman. In course of time, living conditions gradually and steadily improved. Before the outbreak of the Second World War, Americans could live comfortably and even luxuriously in Manila and the larger towns.

War transformed the peaceful scene. Manila, with its contrasting Spanish and American architecture, was eighty percent destroyed. Cebu and numerous other provincial cities were wiped out. Life was difficult for everyone during those trying days.

With the war's end came momentary jubilation followed by a moral letdown, black markets, soaring prices. But slowly streets were cleared, buildings were patched, and new structures appeared. Now everyone can really live again. By current world standards, there is an air of relative well-being about Manila and other centers of population.

With the emergence of the Republic of the Philippines, those days which the oldtimers were wont to extoll were at an end. Homes are not as easy to find. Prices are higher. Servants are more demanding and cost more. Yet Americans can live happily in their adopted land. Modern refrigeration brings in standard products from the United States and other countries. During the hot season the cool breezes of the mountain resort of Baguio beckon.

The Philippine Four Hundred is pretty well determined by what has been called the license plate aristocracy. The earnest endeavor of most everyone seems to be to secure a low number for his automobile. The mad scramble thus generated has provided numerous instances of vanity gone wild. One Vice Governor scaled the social heights by usurping the then Governor General's Number 1 with a letter added. A national crisis was narrowly averted when the Speaker and the Speaker *Pro Tempore* of the House of Representatives clashed over the use of the number three. The United States High Commissioner to the Philippines diplomatically compromised rank by accepting U. S. I, while the President of the Philippines sported P. I. I.

At present, of course, the President of the Philippines ranks Number I in all respects. That does not deter others of the anointed who ride in low-numbered cars from accepting the policeman's salute with a condescending nod, their souls flooding with the glowing warmth of smug egotism.

Even under post-war conditions and in their new status of aliens under an independent regime, the American family, resident in the Philippines, not only lives comfortably but pleasurably. Clothes, white and khaki for the men, summer and evening apparel for the women, can be had. There are clubs where friends can be entertained and cocktails can be taken. There are night spots of every description—all too many of them—for the gay of heart. There are theatres where the latest movies and occasionally symphonic music can be enjoyed. There are sports like golf, tennis and swimming for the athletic. Altogether, plenty of facilities for recreation are available.

Some Filipinos live on a magnificent scale. Their homes are large and elegantly furnished with antiques or importations from China and Europe. Their servants are practically numberless and are paid much less than Americans pay their help. Most Filipinos, however, are forced to subsist on a lower scale, in nipa-thatched houses. Their food is good and substantial, rice being the main item on the menu. With friendly neighbors, life moves on smoothly for them.

So waste no pity on the poor American doomed to a dreary existence in the Oriental Seas, and forget your sympathy over the plight of the poor Filipino who has been placed by fate in the Philippines.

ATTRACTIONS FOR THE VISITOR

The traveller planning a trip to the Philippines needs to be warned of the exasperating red tape in which he will be entangled. He will, of course, need a passport with a Philippine *visa* and a smallpox vaccination certificate. In addition he will be assessed a head tax for the privilege of entering the country and will be required to fill out various forms including a money declaration. If the tourist remains more than a month in the Philippines, he must be prepared to spend a day obtaining necessary exit forms.

In all fairness it should be added that government agencies are conscious of the fact that travel restrictions and limited facilities in the country are siphoning away money that should be retained in the Philippines. Steps are being taken to remove the sources of irritation by centralizing clearance and inspection at the points of entry. Even with the legal requirements imposed on people entering or leaving the country thus reduced, enough official pestering and gouging will remain to act as a deterrent to the development of the tourist "industry."

If not already led to postpone his visit to the Islands, the prospective visitor must be ready to endure a tropical climate and, much worse, the snarled up traffic of Manila. Precautions against the heat can be taken. Precautions against the juvenile masters of a miscellaneous lot of vehicles are another matter. The dare-devil driving of a Parisian jehu has nothing on the unpredictable antics of a youthful Filipino driver of a "jeepney." Manila, with one-half the total motor vehicles in the Philippines, must accommodate them in an eighteenth century street system and on improvised bridges, which means temper-trying traffic jams.

The foregoing is inserted in an attempt to be honest with the visitor. Nevertheless, people do disembark in Manila and do enjoy their stay. So do not be discouraged, but retain the Philippines on your itinerary.

To continue in more optimistic vein, the traveller entering the large expanse of Manila Bay is coming to a pleasant land. True the scars of war remain. True many of the ancient landmarks are gone. True the souls of the people have been seared with hate. Yet the Islands still have much to offer the visitor. And the people, in the main, are as happy and hospitable as of yore.

Sailing by Mount Mariveles, the headland at the north of the bay entrance, the traveller will be reminded of Bataan and the tragic battles fought there. He will next pass Corregidor, once mistakenly called America's Island Gibraltar, now a peaceful national defense zone in Filipino hands, on which it is proposed to construct a war memorial shrine. His ship comes to anchor just outside the breakwater which protects the waterfront of Manila. From the ship can be seen vessels flying the flags of many nations, the rebuilt and modern Manila Hotel, and the Luneta with its adjacent clubs. He steps ashore, not on to Pier 7 of which it was formerly the boast that it was "the longest and finest covered pier under the American flag," but on to Pier 13, a modest counterpart of the same, to be received by Filipino customs officials.

The visitor may care to hasten his arrival. If he does, he will come by air to land at the International Airport operated by the Philippine administration for the use of all airlines. Automobiles will carry him the short distances to the business center of Manila. On the way he will pass over the route which American troops took in capturing Manila in 1898, and through the fashionable bay front district pretty well destroyed during World War II, now again alive with activity.

Manila, the largest city in the Islands, is toured in an automobile which keeps to the right. (Formerly all vehicles followed the European rule of road which was to the left.) The driver of the car will understand English.

Historic *Intramuros* (Walled City) was leveled by war operations and is a desolate no man's land, except that the Church and Convent of San Agustin stands only partly scarred among the ruins. The Church, on account of its hoary age and unique construction, is well worth a visit. Fort Santiago very properly is a hallowed shrine.

Crossing a bridge with some difficulty because of the dense traffic, the visitor comes to the shops on the Escolta and Rizal Avenue. Then he can continue, if he so desires by the Presidential Malacañan Palace to the University of Santo Tomas. The University, the oldest ever under the American Flag, was transformed into an internment camp for Americans and Europeans during the war with Japan.

Beyond the boundaries of Manila, the visitor passes into Quezon City, the newly planned capitol of the Philippines. On his return route he may care to inspect a sanitary cigar or cigarette factory or a brewery. Or he may prefer just to watch the passing scenes from his car as he is driven through a colorful panorama, interesting even to the most satiated of travellers. In late afternoon, he will be treated to the indescribably gorgeous sunset over Manila Bay, painting a flaming background for mountains and sea.

The cosmopolitan character of the population will be noticed, because it is in marked contrast to what one finds in some nearby lands. The streets over which the people pass will not, however, encourage peans of praise. The debris of war, the dust from reconstruction projects, and the letdown of the masses are not conducive to cleanliness.

Decent automobile roads, a car of the Manila Railroad, or a modern plane will take the traveller north from Manila to Baguio, the summer capital nestling 5,000 feet above sea level in pine-clad mountains. After having to acknowledge that blankets are a necessity in Baguio, tramping over the verdant hills while playing a round of golf, sauntering through the native market, or visiting a nearby gold mine, reluctant departure for even higher regions may be taken. On the way the wonderful rice terraces of the Ifugaos, begun long before the Spaniards or Americans came to the Islands and one of the scenic wonders of the world, draw forth admiration for native ingenuity and culture.

South from Manila the traveller goes through coconut groves to the exquisite little city of Pagsanjan to get the thrill of a lifetime in shooting the falls, or, in the Island of Luzon, through the hemp region to Mount Mayon, whose beautiful volcanic cone is unexcelled by any and equalled only in loveliness by the far-famed Fujiyama of Japan. Returning to Manila, the visitor is taken by inter-island ships or fast air lines to the cities of Iloilo and Bacolod, the center of the sugar region, or to Cebu, the second largest city in the Islands, or farther south to languorous Zamboanga or busy Davao, the former Japanese-developed city of Moroland. All the time the traveller delights in the people; the school children speaking an English patois, the elders rarely failing to display courtesy, and the picturesque non-Christians.

The Philippines has much indeed to offer the vacationist!

POPULATION [5]

The population of the Philippines is 20,000,000. Compared with the hordes of China or the millions of Japan, this number of inhabitants is not large. The Philippine population, however, is greater than that of any state of the American Union. It exceeds that of Australia and of a number of European and Latin American nations.

The population of the Islands has shown a steady increase. At the time of the conquest of the Philippines by the Spaniards in the latter part of the sixteenth century, the number of people in the Islands was estimated at half a million. After American occupation the first official census in 1903 gave the population as 7,635,426. Succeeding 1918, 1939 and 1948 censuses have indicated an upward

---

[5] Data furnished by Dr. Leon Ma. Gonzales, Director of the Bureau of Census and Statistics. See Philippine Censuses of 1903, 1918, 1939 and 1948, particularly the last. Also note C. C. Cruz, "Population and Land Utilization in the Philippines," included in Lasker and Holland, Editors, *Problems of the Pacific*, and Warren S. Thompson, *Population and Peace in the Pacific*, pp. 274 *et. seq.* (University of Chicago Press, 1946).

curve in depicting the number of persons in the Philippines. The 20,000,000 figure, representing the 1948 tabulation of 19,234,182, plus the normal increase since then, shows a population nearly three times as large as when the United States acquired the Islands.

The density of the population may be estimated at approximately one hundred sixty-six per square mile. This figure stands out favorably in comparison with four hundred eighty-eight per square mile in Japan and nine hundred sixty in Java, and signifies that the Philippines as a whole is sparsely inhabited. Many hectares of arable land are as yet untilled. The great Island of Mindanao, except in spots, is thinly populated. Other regions, however, like the crowded Ilocano provinces in the northwestern part of the Island of Luzon, and the densely populated Island of Cebu to the south are faced with a growing problem of population pressure.

The overall problem is to achieve a better distribution of the people. The government is wisely encouraging suitable families to pioneer homes in newly opened districts.

Various estimates of the number of inhabitants that the Philippines could sustain have been made. It is reasonable to expect the customary increase in population to continue. On this basis and taking into account the available amount of uncultivated farm land, the Philippine census statement that, from the agricultural standpoint, the Philippines is capable of supporting a population of from 70,000,000 to 80,000,000 may be accepted as substantially correct. If to this be added employment to come from the contemplated industrialization, we can look forward to a Philippines of 100,000,000 inhabitants. That would give the Philippines of the future equality of manpower with neighboring Japan, but in the former case it would be backed by immeasurably richer natural resources.

The Philippine population is a cosmopolitan one. Americans, not including the armed forces, number at least 15,000, or practically double the prewar figure. This is plain evidence of the incorrectness of prognostications that with the coming of Philippine independence Americans would withdraw from the scene. Other aliens, including 175,000 Chinese and 3,000 Spaniards who have the largest communities, bring the grand total to 200,000. The Japanese colonies of Davao, Baguio and Manila are gone. Only about one hundred Russian nationals have been listed.

The main elements in the population, generally but mistakenly classified by religion, are the Christians, who are the Filipinos proper, and the non-Christians, who include the minority groups. These people will be described in the two succeeding chapters.

CHAPTER II

THE FILIPINO PEOPLE[1]

ORIGIN: LEGENDARY AND SCIENTIFIC

"The people," wrote Mencius, the Chinese sage, "are the most important element in a nation; the spirit of the land and grain are next; the sovereign is the least in importance." And it is with the people, the Filipino people—their origin, race, social system, traits, and nationality—that we are concerned.

A legend in the northern Philippines and one quite similar in the southern islands purports to tell how man was created. A very long time ago—so the tale runs—a god and a goddess inhabited the earth. Because they were lonesome, they took clay, moulded it, and baked it. At the first attempt, the inexperienced deities did not bake the clay long enough. At the second attempt, they baked it too long. At the third attempt, the clay was baked just right. When life was breathed into the figures, produced in each of the three bakings, they became the white race, the black race, and the brown race. The Filipinos, who belong to the brown race, were thus the perfect product of the gods.

The anthropologists and ethnologists offer a more scientific, if less traditional, explanation of the ancestry of the Filipino people. They inform us that at least six migrations reached the islands composing the Philippine group. Three varieties of man—the Negritos, the Indonesians, and the Malays—have left their mark.[2]

The most primitive culture was that of the aboriginal inhabitants, the Negritos. They were kinky-haired, black dwarfs of low intelligence who settled near the coast. In connection with the origin

---

[1] Any number of anthropologists have written books based on personal research on the peoples of the Philippines. Among others can be noted A. L. Kroeber, *Peoples of the Philippines*, Handbook of the American Museum of Natural History (Revised Edition, 1928); Felix M. Keesing, *Native Peoples of the Pacific World* (New York, 1945); and Fay-Cooper Cole, *The Peoples of Malaysia* (New York, 1947). Also see Dr. Najeeb M. Saleeby, *Origin of the Malayan Filipinos* (Manila, 1912).

[2] Beyer Table of Philippine Racial Ancestry: Negrito and Proto-Malay, 10%; Indonesian, 30%; Malayan, 40%; Chinese, 10%; Hindu, 5%; European and American 3%; Arab, 2%. Dr. H. Otley Beyer, originally prepared for the Census of 1918 and finally revised in 1942.

of this civilization-shy people, one theory has it that the Philippine Archipelago once formed a part of Asia and that they spread over land bridges to the Philippines. A small number of Negritos are now found living in remote mountainous regions.

Some 6,000 years ago the Indonesians arrived by boat and drove the Negritos into the interior. Remnants of this wave of immigrants are found in the mountain peoples of Luzon and elsewhere. They blend pretty much into the predominant Malay strain.

Finally there was a gradual infiltration of Malays from the south and southwest to push out of the way their Negrito and Indonesian predecessors. The Malays now represent the greater portion of the racial stock of the Philippines.

Asia, then, and Malaysia, which may have been the cradle of mankind, can be pointed out with reasonable assurance as the birthplaces of the ancestors of the Filipinos.

THE FILIPINO RACE

The primary stocks of mankind as commonly classified are: 1. Caucasoid, white people; 2. Mongoloid, yellow people; and 3. Negroid, black people. Now recall that the color of the Filipinos is not white, yellow or black, but rather brown, and you gain a glimpse of the racial problem to be solved.

Are the Filipinos Caucasians? H. G. Wells in his *Outline of History* suggests that the Malays—and the Filipinos are Malays—are cousins of the dark people of Southern Europe and North-Central India. In this view, the Filipinos are Caucasians or near-Caucasians. But now it is the august United States Supreme Court speaking and judicially holding that the term "Caucasians" excludes Filipinos.[3] Until further proof is adduced, the Caucasian theory will have to be rejected.

Are the Filipinos Mongolians? This question likewise has reached the courts and there has been variously answered. A well-documented decision coming from the State of California, where the race problem has been violently agitated, found correctly that the Filipinos are not of the Mongolian race.[4]

Just as the Filipinos were once judicially pronounced neither American citizens nor aliens, so at first blush do they appear to have no race which they can claim for their own. Further study discloses that a place can be found for the Filipinos in the ethnological

---

[3] Morrison *v* U. S., 291 U. S. 82.
[4] Roldan *v* Los Angeles County, 129 Cal. App. 267, 18 Pac. 2nd S. 706.

table. The solution is to accept the standard classification of races by Blumenbach who adds to the three divisions of mankind already mentioned two more: 4. American, red people; and 5. Malay, brown people. Of if this view is disputed by ethnologists, the Mongoloid type can be subdivided into (a) Asiatic Mongoloids, (b) American Indians, and (c) Malays.

The Filipino's viewpoint on this subject is simple. He is content to be included among the Malays, and is not honored by having his people considered a branch either of the Caucasian or Mongolian races. In other words, the Filipino prefers brown to white or yellow in the color scheme of the universe.

Whether as a race or a sub-race, the Filipinos are Malays. The term "Malay" is now popularly and properly applied to the bulk of the inhabitants of the Philippines.

SOCIAL SYSTEM

The Filipino social system divides among class lines. On the lower level are the *taos*. On the higher level are the *caciques* or *ilustrados*. Sandwiched between the two widely separated extremes is the middle class.

The *taos* are peasants who constitute the rural laborers of the Islands. They are the largest group in number, but provide the smallest count in the matter of educations. Hard workers in the fields, although often paid barely living wages, they are resigned to their lot, if not stirred by leaders into violence. The sad fate of the *taos* has been that from time immemorial they have all too often been oppressed by their employers and preyed upon by usurers. It would be too sweeping a statement to affirm that their life is not much different from what it was centuries ago. At least it will not be prudent for the government to give no constructive attention to the needs of the peasants.

The *caciques* are large landowners or persons of influence. Small in number, but wealthy, well educated, and cultured, they constitute the ruling class. Generally these men have used their influence and riches for the development of the country. Again it cannot be denied that their power has at times been exercised arbitrarily to the still further debasement of the defenseless poor. Rizal in his novel *Noli Me Tangere* ("The Social Cancer") drew a dark picture of the life and character of the *cacique* of his day. Such unscrupulous individuals are still to be found.

The middle class is made up of the small landowners, the tradespeople, the professionals, the teachers, the government employees in the lower brackets, and others similarly circumstanced. They are the men and women who are neither rich nor poor, who neither oppress anyone nor are oppressed by anyone, but who live in comfortable surroundings and have educations that permit them to take advantage of cultural enjoyments. Generally the sturdy middle class is independent in politics and opinions. It is a pleasure to report that the men and women who make up this type of happy people are increasing in number and influence. They can be expected to become the stabilizing factor in the life of the young Republic.

From another angle, there are in the Philippines the Filipinos proper and the *mestizos* (half castes). The Filipinos proper are the products of diverse ancestors of which the prevailing physical type is the Malay blend. The *mestizos* are Filipinos of mixed Malay and other blood. They are the products of intermarriage of the Malay Filipinos with the Chinese, the Spaniards, the Americans, and other foreigners. Just how many *mestizos* there are cannot be exactly determined, but possibly the number of native-born inhabitants having appreciable alien blood represents fifteen percent of the population. The *mestizos* with their admixture of lighter blood are inclined to look down upon their dark-skinned brothers, and in turn the full-blooded Filipinos have little love for the "Castillas."

The type of Filipino with Chinese blood, as for example the student class and the merchant class, have proved themselves to be leaders in scholarship and commerce. Many common Filipino surnames are merely Chinese names combined to constitute new Filipino names. Spanish and American men in considerable numbers have married Filipino women, and many of these unions have proved happy.

The *compadre* and *comadre* (godfather and godmother) system permeates all classes. It is *compadre* this and *comadre* that, and the relationship is taken very seriously. So not only are the people bound by natural blood ties but by voluntary religious ones.

FILIPINO TRAITS

To a youthful Spanish priest was assigned the task—so the story goes—of preparing a tome dealing with the Filipinos, and he was given big blank books on which to write his findings. Years went by and the priest died. The books were found and cautiously and reverently the covers of the *magnum opus* were opened. Lo and behold, the pages were blank except the first page of the first volume on which was written a single line: "Here is all that I have found about the Filipinos."

Rudyard Kipling in vivid verse wrote, "Oh, East is East and West is West and never the twain shall meet."

The anecdote has been taken literally. The lines of the famous poem have been ripped out of their setting to spread a poisonous falsehood of narrow prejudice. The Oriental people, and the Filipinos are loosely thus classified, have been set apart as being entirely distinct from their Occidental brothers.

In the specific case of the Filipinos, theirs is an Oriental country, geographically and racially speaking, but the Filipinos religious and political beliefs reflect the culture of the Occident. Basically the modern Filipinos are the product of three influences—the Malayan, the Spanish and the American. The result is an unusual social and cultural pattern that fits into neither an Oriental nor an Occidental straight jacket. In the Philippines East and West *have* met and blended.

Authorities of more or less repute have asserted that they cannot understand the Filipinos. Some have lamented that they could comprehend nothing of the Filipino mind. Others have attempted an analysis of the character of the Filipinos and have found it most mysterious. That the Filipino has not displayed emotion when held up before the microscope as a wondrous enigma has been due to his innate courtesy.

Certain authors have purported to tell "the truth about the Philippines"[5] and the Filipinos, but in such a grotesque manner as not to be recognizable as truth by those who have lived for years among the kindly people who inhabit the Islands. Theodore Roosevelt, Jr., after he had left the gubernatorial chair in the Philippines, offered a ready explanation of the reason for the dissemination of misinformation. It made no sort of story, said the former Governor General, to tell of the metropolitan City of Manila and the Filipinos who formed the greater part of the population. It did give a thrill of adventure to speak of savage tribes who had lately been headhunters.[6] In the post-war Philippines, reputable journalists have by their own admission emphasized the negative elements because they over shadow the positive elements. Thus abnormal happenings have been given currency to present an unbalanced view of the Philippine scene.

---

[5] Katherine Mayo, *The Isles of Fear, the Truth About the Philippines* (New York, 1925).

[6] Theodore Roosevelt, *Colonial Policies of the United States,* pp. 168, 169 (Garden City, 1937). Note William Gray, *Time,* June 5, 1950, and Blake Clark, *Readers Digest,* June, 1950.

In one instance, the Filipinos made an international issue of an alleged slander on their character. President Hoover named Nicolas Roosevelt to be Vice Governor of the Philippines. Unfortunately for the nominee, he had written a book about the Philippines [7], and a readable book at that, in which misunderstandings between Americans and Filipinos were highlighted. Mr. Roosevelt was now to furnish a real ground for misunderstanding, for the Filipinos objected strenuously to pages in the book. A mammoth mass meeting was held. The offending volume was burned on the sacrificial pyre, that is, it was claimed that it was burned, but those "in the know" say that no Roosevelt book could be found and that another, anonymous, book was substituted. At any rate, Filipino feeling was calmed, and Mr. Roosevelt was quietly shifted to the innocuous post of Minister to Hungary.

The Filipinos have naturally resented what to them were unjust reflections on their nation. Filipino leaders of thought, like Supreme Court Justices Villamor and Romualdez, have judicially conceded that it is difficult for the Occidental to understand the idiosyncrasies of the Filipinos. "Perhaps no race has been so much misunderstood and as poorly studied as the Filipinos," wrote the first-named jurist.[8] Understandably, these men have felt impelled to defend their people from unfair criticism. Brigadier General Carlos P. Romulo, who possesses an American education and has had long and close contacts with the American public, during which he has continuously run up against the misconceptions about the Filipinos which are prevalent in the United States, has countered with an offensive against the white man's sense of superiority and the few Americans in Manila who are "as greedy as the worst." [9]

With this as a background, perhaps we can skeletonize the subjects "The Filipino People: A Study in National Character"; "The Philippines Through American Eyes"; and "Why Are the Filipinos Different?" The quoted words are paraphrased from recent books written about the American people. The author's approach to an attempt to explain the Filipinos is from the vantage point of a normal mode of life in the Philippines and an acquaintance with many Filipinos of all types.

In the first place, let it be emphasized that, like other races, the Filipino possesses particular characteristics. He *is* different.

---

[7] Nicolas Roosevelt, *The Philippines, A Treasure and a Problem* (London, 1926).

[8] Justice Ignacio Villamor, *Industrious Men*, p. X (Manila, 1930).

[9] Carlos P. Romulo, *Mother America*, Ch. X and p. 9 (Garden City, 1943).

What has been said a moment ago brings to notice one dominant trait of the Filipino. He is sensitive—extremely so. Why? He feels that he merits racial and social equality. Therefore, he is ever on the alert to note slights, fancied or real. He rather resents the use of the word "native" as conveying a derogatory meaning; on the other hand, the term "mestizo" carries with it no particularly sinister connotation. Also, in the Filipino, delicacy of sentiment predominates and his natural reserve is all too often rudely jarred by blunt Americans.

Dating back to the time of Magellan, a remark often made about the Filipino is to say of him that he is lazy. In reality the myth rests on superficial observation of his work habits. The truth is that the Filipino laborer is anything but lazy. Given the right incentive he will work hard.

Employers in the Philippines and Hawaii speak well of their Filipino employees who, they state, are good workers when left alone by unscrupulous agitators. In the provinces of the Philippines, the sturdy farmer arises with the dawn and stays in the fields for long hours, but usually not in the heat of the day, which is using good judgment. In other words, the Filipino fits into the environment in which he must live under tropical conditions.

A candid look at the less admirable customs and habits of the Filipino spotlights his proneness to blind imitation, his deficient business thrift, his easygoing ways, his evasion of refusal through indirection, his lack of civic spirit, and his love of gambling. Without intending to extenuate these traits, they are readily explainable. The Filipino copies standards set by foreigners, for otherwise he feels he might be ridiculed. The Filipino is a poor business man because nature provides his necessities, and the Chinaman is omnipresent to buy his products and to sell him what he needs. The Filipino's serenity is a combination of fatalism, natural dignity, and a protest against haste; it contrasts sharply with the behavior of those Americans who try to hustle the East and soon rest beneath a few feet of sod. The Filipino when he answers with a shading of the truth does not intend it as a falsehood; he is only giving expression to a desire to be courteous and says what he thinks might please the listener. The Filipino is finding it much less difficult to get together with his fellows in civic enterprises; community service is being stressed in many localities by private organizations.

The Filipino is an inveterate gambler, for thus he varies a rather monotonous existence. Laws against gambling have been passed, and intermittent attempts at enforcement have been made. Now the

Government has surrendered to the passion for gambling, and, like other countries, has taken advantage of it to help legitimate causes by sanctioning the holding of sweepstakes with large prizes.

The admirable traits of the Filipinos have often been stressed, and some of them are deserved and some are not. In the first place, the people are naturally gentle and kindly. Their inbred courtesy on which has been overlaid the politeness of Spain has given to the Filipinos unfailing decorum and charming manners. This was literally true of what is known as the old-time Filipinos. Either a false imitation of American ways or wrong notions engendered by a too free educational system have broken down this characteristic virtue. It has given way to exaggerated boldness bordering on insolence which is the opposite of good manners. Regrettable as this is, the change exists and will probably continue.

The sobriety of the Filipinos is also given as a conspicuous characteristic. It is undeniable that they are abstemious in the matter of liquors. Either they do not drink at all or they drink in moderation, and then do not indulge in the hard liquors favored by foreigners. While this is the general impression and admittedly it is correct, judicial experience has brought to notice cases in which the underlying cause of a tragedy was the immoderate use of native intoxicants. A laborer in the provinces goes to a *tienda* (a small store) and begins to drink *tuba* (palm liquor). It makes him crazy drunk, and without knowing what he is doing he engages in a bolo fight with disastrous results. When, therefore, we say that the Filipinos are not given to alcoholism, the truth is stated with the proviso that drunkenness does occur in occasional instances.

The ready hospitality of the Filipino has been much commented upon. He is most considerate of all persons, including strangers. Everything the Filipino host possesses is at the guest's disposal. However, the guest is not expected to take literally the kindly proffer of a costly gift as some Americans have done, for the proffer is generally intended merely as a gesture of good will. To show her appreciation of her guests, the hostess is also likely to serve a banquet with many meat courses, and if the guest is not accustomed to Spanish or Filipino cookery, with garlic used lavishly, the result is sometimes dangerous to digestion.

The Filipinos have long respected authority and its outward forms. This was due to their experience with Spanish and American rulers and with their own officials. It meant general peace in the Philippines. This admirable virtue persists, except that since the conclusion of World War II banditry and disorders bordering on insurrection have prevailed in certain regions.

One could run on indefinitely enumerating the desirable qualities of the Filipinos. Mention should be made of the lowland Filipino's personal cleanliness. In speech, however, he may not be so clean, for remarks are made and jokes bandied which are realistically frank. Indubitably the most commendable of all Filipino traits is his attachment to his family and his home.

Perspicacity might well be displayed by drawing a blue pencil through everything written in an attempt to explain the Filipino. Writing in 1940, Lord Tweedsmuir (better known as John Buchan) made a sharp observation about Americans and those who write about America. He said: "It is foolish to generalize about America. You no sooner construct a rule than it is shattered by the exception." Substitute the name of any country for "America" and the aphorism holds true for that country. As for the Filipinos, one of their brilliant journalists has put into words what this author has long suspected, namely: "The Filipinos are one kind of people when they are among themselves, and another when there is present, for instance, an American."[10]

As a consequence, Filipino readers may not recognize themselves from the incomplete dissection of their good and bad points, here attempted. If they do not, their experience will coincide with that of the author, who could never discover himself in the description by foreign writers of the typical American, portrayed as an uncouth, hurrying, money-mad, gum-chewing specimen of the *genus homo*. But whatever their reaction, Filipinos will continue to receive an American friend in their homes, and never by word or deed will they let on that they disagree with the appraisal. For that is the Filipino, ever courteous, gracious and hospitable.

The concluding thought is that the Filipinos, individually and collectively, possess the full biological and cultural potentials for development and progress.

Juan de la Cruz

The favorite name in the Philippines is Juan de la Cruz, literally, in English, John of the Cross. It is as common in the Philippines as John Smith is in the United States.

---

[10] Teodoro M. Locsin, Staff Member in the *Philippines Free Press* of June 21, 1947. In the succeeding July 19, 1947 issue Mr. Locsin asks: "What's the matter with us?" and proceeds to cast a candid look at the less admirable traits, customs and habits of Filipinos.

Juan de la Cruz is a national character who typifies the Filipinos just as Uncle Sam does the Americans and John Bull the Britons. He is usually pictured or cartooned garbed in *barong tagalog*, wearing a broad-brimmed coolie hat, a shirt of native material and nondescript color, with the tail left hanging outside of knee-length red pants, and with his feet in *chinelas* (heel-less slippers).

Juan, a typical Filipino of the common people, is small in stature, for to be over five feet four inches in height is the exception. His figure is lithe and well muscled. His skin is unlined. His eyes are dark and luminous. His nose is short and flat. He bathes frequently and is scrupulously clean. He dresses modestly, but on occasion yields to a fondness for fine raiment. He is temperate in most of his habits, except in an overfondness for gambling. He is an honest, peaceful, hard-working citizen and possesses the Filipino's dominant trait of hospitality.

Juan lives in a small nipa hut, simply furnished, and with him are his wife and children. As if this were not sufficient, *parientes* (relatives) add themselves to his already large family. One of his dearest possessions is his rooster, which he trains for the coming fight in the cockpit. If he has capital enough, he keeps one or more pigs which are left to roam under the house, and if he is more fortunate, he has as his richest heritage a faithful carabao. At night every aperture of the house will be closed to keep out the evil spirits.

Juan de la Cruz is the rock on whose solid character Filipino nationalism is grounded.

FILIPINO WOMEN[11]

Any unbiased judge or jury would hand down a verdict based on overwhelming evidence that the greatest blessing of the Philippines is the Filipino woman. Nor would a judgment to this effect come about because of masculine gallantry. It would rather stem from the Filipino woman's acknowledged social and political equality with men and her innate ability and sense of responsibility. As has been aptly remarked, the Filipino woman "is the best man in the country."

The position of Filipino women in the family and in the community is that of the Occident rather than the Orient. They are as highly honored and well treated as are the women of America. This

[11] See Dr. Maria Paz Mendoza-Guazon, *The Development and Progress of Filipino Women* (Manila, 1928); and Encarnacion Alzona, *The Filipino Woman*, the social, economic and political status of the Filipino women from 1565 to 1937 (Manila, 1937).

was relatively and uniquely true even before the arrival of the Spaniards centuries ago. Unlike their Oriental sisters, Filipino women were never confined to a life of sheltered seclusion. On the contrary, they participated freely in industrial, social, and religious activities.

Changes in Philippine life brought about by American influences were as a whole favorable to women. Social customs show the unmistakable evidence of American contacts. Filipino women have taken full advantage of the newly acquired freedom. Their public welfare activities have assumed varied aspects in their clubs and societies. The National Federation of Women's Clubs is an active organization that plays a leading role in community life.

Filipino girls are afforded opportunities to obtain good educations. Some institutions are in the nature of exclusive finishing schools. The public schools, the University of the Philippines, and most private universities and colleges are co-educational. On graduation the fair sex have invaded the various professions. They practice pharmacy in large numbers, and medicine, dentistry, and law to a lesser but increasing degree. Filipino women are particularly adept at nursing.

Unabashed and confident, Filipino women have entered the political arena to contest with men. They were the first women in the Orient to win the right of equal suffrage. Two lady solons, Mrs. Geronima Pecson in the Senate and Mrs. Remedios Ozamis Fortich in the House, have been influential members of the Congress of the Philippines. Senator Pecson fathered, or should we say mothered, the far reaching educational reform bill. Congresswoman Fortich succeeded her legislator husband who died violently at the hands of a demented soldier whom he was trying to disarm. This charming and energetic lady represented Bukidnon, the wildly beautiful province in the heart of Mindanao. And she did so honorably, for she and her husband risked death daily as they supplied and sheltered the guerrillas throughout the war.[12] More recently Mrs. Medina Lacson de Leon became the lone woman member of the House.

Like the women in the United States, Filipino women have campaigned to secure a grant of full civil rights. With the approval of the new Civil Code the decisive battle was won, for by its provisions the women of the Philippines were emancipated.

Just as Juan de la Cruz has typified the common Filipino man, so has Maria Clara, the heroine of Rizal's *Noli Me Tangere*, been taken as personifying the best in Filipino womanhood. Maria Clara

[12] The role of Filipino women in politics was described by a talented Filipino lady, Mrs. Maria Kalaw-Katigbak, in the *Christian Science Monitor* of June 3, 1948.

is pictured in tasteful native dress and with a singularly modest demeanor. Today, however, Maria Clara would have to undergo some changes. She is no longer the appealingly timid young thing who answered in monosyllables when addressed. The modern Filipina, though still lovely and outwardly demure, is more outspoken and is the mainstay of her family. She is mistress of her home and safekeeper of her husband's income. She likes to take part in social entertainment. With keen enjoyment, the Filipino girls participate in modern dances and make graceful partners.

The Filipino women are comely. In youth they are often young goddesses, erect in carriage, with clean golden-brown skin and dark flashing eyes, and possessed of black tresses long enough to reach to the ground. The *mestizas*, who are Filipino-Chinese, Filipino-Spanish, or Filipino-American, frequently present pleasing combinations of the good points of both races.

The native costume of the Filipino women is very becoming to them. It is a dress uniquely their own and considered one of the most beautiful in the world. The materials vary, with colors vivid and strikingly blended. The skirts are long and the sleeves of the waists are large and loose to show smooth-skinned arms. About the neck is often placed a starched and folded *panuelo* which flatters the shoulders and face.

The native costumes are not likely to disappear because they are so appropriate for the Filipino type of womanhood. Instead they have been modernized. The costumier's genius often produces models costing hundreds of pesos. Great is the competition among the socialites to be acclaimed the best dressed lady present at exclusive gatherings.

The modern figures of active womanhood in the Philippines have come a long way from the Maria Clara of book fame. The late Mrs. Aurora A. Quezon, widow of the President, was highly respected in her own right for her interest in philanthropy. Mrs. Sophie R. de Veyra has long been active in feminist movements, as likewise have been Mrs. Pilar H. Lim, Mrs. Trinidad F. Legarda, Cabinet member Asuncion A. Perez, and others. However, all would without doubt yield precedence to heroines of the war of whom there were many.[18] Typical of these dauntless patriots were Mrs. Josefa L. Escoda and Mrs. Josefina ("Joey") Guerrero.

Mrs. Escoda with her husband gave aid to the internees and the guerrillas only to be apprehended and liquidated by the Japanese.

[18] George Hagar in the *National Catholic Monthly* of March, 1948 tells the occupation adventures of Miss Lulu Reyes.

In honor of this dauntless couple a scholarship fund to educate the Escoda children has been provided by grateful friends. The Escoda Memorial Building, named after the occupation heroine and Federation President at the time of her death, is the club house of the National Federation of Women's Clubs.

Mrs. Guerrero's case is equally impressive. The wife of a faculty member of the School of Medicine at the University of Santo Tomas, she smuggled food to American and Filipino soldiers on Bataan in the darkest days of the war. She contracted leprosy while engaged in humanitarian work and was granted special permission to enter the United States Leprosarium at Carville, Louisiana for treatment. An ovation welcomed the Filipina heroine when she landed in the United States. Bands played the National Anthem of the Philippines; army officers and dignitaries stood at attention as Mrs. Guerrero walked down the gangplank; soldiers whom she had aided greeted their benefactress. The winner of the U. S. Medal of Freedom was overwhelmed by the esteem which was so much deserved.

The Filipino Nation

The inhabitants of the Philippines are collectively known as Filipinos. Theirs is a composite race, possibly eighty-five percent Malay and fifteen percent intrusive foreign elements. The Filipinos are a people who think of themselves as Filipinos and dislike being taken for other Orientals, for whom they have little feeling of brotherhood. They are bound together by common ties, problems and aspirations. And these are the prime tests of nationalism.

The Filipinos are of fairly uniform type. They are of medium size, about two inches shorter and twenty pounds lighter than the average Caucasian. The men and women are well developed physically.

The dissimilarities among the people inhabiting the various regions are principally induced by linguistic differences. The three most important of the ethnographic groups are the Tagalogs, the Visayans, and the Ilocanos. The Tagalogs found in Manila and surrounding provinces are the best known and the most aggressive. The Visayans, who inhabit the islands farther south are the largest in number, are in many ways the gentlest, and are the best liked. The Ilocanos reflect the rugged terrain which they occupy in Northern Luzon as evidenced by equally strong characters molded in the school of hard work.

The Ilocanos are often dubbed the Yankees of the Philippines. They enjoy a deserved reputation for restlessness, industry and thrift. Many of them migrated to Hawaii and there saved their earnings. In one year, more than 6,000,000 pesos ($3,000,000) were sent from Hawaii to the Ilocano provinces to help support relatives or to buy property. The Ilocanos also constitute the pioneers who spread out into neighboring provinces or who venture into Mindanao to develop homesteads.

On the one hand, it is the practice of some Filipinos to minimize regional antagonism, and, on the other hand, of some Americans to argue that the Filipinos are not one people. The author is unable to subscribe fully to either viewpoint.

Racial and social differences among the major groups are readily discernible. Group and provincial loyalty is evident. Place a number of Tagalog, Visayan and Ilocano laborers together and they will gravitate into factions representing their varying languages. Antagonize an individual from a certain province and he will gain the sympathy and support of the people of his province. But these are more in the nature of family squabbles. Against the rest of the world, the people are unitedly Filipino.

The Filipinos of today are Malays by lineage, which means that, like the Americans, they are a blend of a number of races. By blood they are as much one people distinct from all others as are the inhabitants of the United States. Based on such homogeneity, national unity has come about through the influence of religion, education, culture, the bond of English as an official language, and the joining of all classes and groups to attain independence. Add to these factors the physical data of area, population and resources which place the Philippines among the middle-sized countries of the world, and all the elements needed to form a nation are present.

There is far greater unity among all groups in the Philippines than surface diversities would seem to indicate. The patriotic sense of identity as a distinct people and loyalty to a common cause have brought the Filipinos far along in the welding process. There is no reason why they cannot steadily advance in economic status to attain more complete political stability.

CHAPTER III

MINORITY GROUPS

THE SO-CALLED NON-CHRISTIANS

The awkward and unsatisfactory term "non-Christian" was coined in the early days of American occupation for blanket coverage of minority groups in the Philippines. It has neither a literal nor a religious significance. Rather, it has historical and political meaning. Given practical application, the so-called non-Christians are natives of the Philippines living in specified geographical areas.

The Bureau of non-Christian Tribes exercised general supervision over the public affairs of the non-Christians between 1917 and 1936, pursuant to a specific provision in the Act of Congress known as the Jones Law. The Bureau was abolished in the latter year by the Filipino-controlled Commonwealth Government. The reasons back of this action were obvious. The terms "non-Christian" and "Tribes" were particularly distasteful to the Filipinos and in fact were misnomers. What was desired to be emphasized was unity, and not misleading disunity.

The most important element among the minority groups are the Mohammedan Moros who inhabit the Sulu Archipelago and certain areas in Mindanao and Palawan. Other groups include the Igorots and associated peoples found in the Mountain Province of Luzon and the primitive Negritos who roam remote regions.

THE MOROS[1]

Conjure up, if you can, a picture of the barbaric Huns, the terrible Mongols, or, better yet, of the fierce Moors, attacking, killing and pillaging, and you will have a picture of the Moros as they fought, and harried and plundered during past ages. Commander Charles Wilkes in his narrative of the United States Exploring Expedition during the years 1838 to 1842,[2] one of the few early accounts of the Philippines written by an American, tells of his visit to conclude a treaty with the Sultan of Sulu and gives no pretty account of the

---

[1] See Vic Hurley, *Swish of the Kris* (New York, 1936). The story of the Moros is told by an author who lived among them.

[2] Found in Blair and Robertson, *The Philippine Islands*, Vol. XLIII, pp. 148-188.

Moros. Describing the scene when the audience with the ranking Datu was held, the Commander writes: "The whole was a strange mixture of tragedy and farce; and the group of natives were not far removed in appearance from the supernumeraries that a Turkish tragedy might have brought together in the green-room of a theatre." Continuing, he thus describes the Joloanos: "A set of more cowardly looking miscreants I never saw. They appeared ready either to trade with us, pick our pockets, or cut our throats, as an opportunity might offer."

Truth compels one to state that today the Moros reputation for blood-thirstiness is not what it was of yore. Tardily and grudgingly they are learning how to live at peace among themselves and with their neighbors.

The word "Moro" is the Spanish equivalent of "Moor" and was applied indiscriminately to the Mohammedan peoples by the Spaniards when they arrived in the Islands. The name has remained and is used as descriptive of the Mohammedan Filipinos. Do not get the impression that the Moros are racially of different stock than the rest of the inhabitants of the Philippines. The Moros are Filipinos just as much as the people of the Philippines commonly referred to as Filipinos. The chief difference is one of religion. The Filipinos proper are Christians, while the Moros are Mohammedans.

Originally pagans of Indonesian origin, the ancestors of the Moros came under Mohammedan influence in the fifteenth century. A century later, when the Spaniards entered the Philippines, they found the Moros in complete control in the south and rapidly spreading their influence in the north. The fierce Moros became the pet abomination of the Spaniards. They raided Manila and other towns, captured slaves, and looted vessels, while the Spaniards attempted reprisals without permanent success. Never were the Spaniards able to subjugate the Moros. As for the Americans, they too found that bloody lessons were needed to teach the Moro recalcitrants the ways of peace.

The Moros are the predominating group in the Sulu Archipelago and in limited areas in the large island of Mindanao and the smaller island of Palawan.

The Sultan Of Sulu[3]

The Sultan of Sulu here described is not the Sultan of Sulu made famous by the musical comedy of that name. The Sulus are not the

---

[3] Facts were furnished by Ysup Abubakar, Philippine Vice Consul of Los Angeles. See Dr. Sixto Y. Orosa, *The Sulu Archipelago and Its People* (New York, 1923).

Zulus of Africa. The Sultan of Sulu is a man of flesh and blood who holds court like any potentate. His subjects are Moros living in the Sulu Archipelago in the Philippines.

Prior to the advent of the Americans, the Sultan of Sulu had been an independent sovereign. He was an absolute and hereditary monarch whose word was law in temporal and spiritual matters. At its height, his power extended throughout the Sulu Archipelago to parts of Basilan and Palawan Islands in the Philippines, and to North Borneo in Borneo.

From the date of American occupation of the Philippines until his death in 1936, the Sultan of Sulu was His Highness Padukka Mahasari Manulana Hadji Mohammed Jamalul Kiram II. Although a colorful figure, he saw most of his actual power fade away until eventually he retained but a tithe of his former influence. General Bates made a so-called treaty with the Sultan in 1899, an arrangement later abrogated for cause, and Governor Carpenter of the Department of Mindanao and Sulu, concluded an agreement with the Sultan in 1915. By this formal agreement, the Sultan renounced pretensions to temporal power and in return was recognized as the spiritual head of Mohammedanism in Sulu. He also received a grant of land and a life pension.

Sultan Jamalul II was the scion of a dynasty that dates back to Mohammed with a genealogy of fully five hundred years. His material wants were fairly well provided for by his government allowance, payments for various services by his subjects, and the rental for land in Borneo from the British North Borneo Company. He made a valiant attempt to keep alive a show of petty royalty, but the truth is that the Sultan was an unimpressive personality who displayed no particular talent for leadership.

The Sultan's domestic life was gladdened by many wives, but saddened because they presented him with no heir. Current rumor had it that the Sultan asked the hand in marriage of "Princess" Alice Roosevelt Longworth. Once he visited the United States and had a gay time on New York's Broadway.

The strong man in Sulu during these long years was the Sultan's grand vizier, Hadji Butu. He was a descendant of Mantiri Asip, the great minister of Raja Baginda, the first Malay Prince to rule Sulu. Hadji Butu was the adviser of the Sultan and the spiritual mentor of the Moros. Also he held many appointive positions, finally becoming a member of the Philippine Senate. By precept and example he encouraged the people to keep to the path of progress.

Hadji Butu was rightly regarded as the best educated and ablest of his people, a Moro patriarch of whom the Philippines could well be proud. He was alike the symbol of Sulu's turbulent past and of the spirit of cooperation of the present. Hadji Butu passed on in 1938. His grandson, Yusup Abubakar, is carrying on in accordance with the family tradition in the Philippine Service.

Two factions have long contested for supremacy in Sulu. The death of Sultan Jamalul II brought confusion over the succession. Datu Jainal Abirin II was accepted by most Moros as the Sultan of Sulu. Following the demise of the latter in 1950, two Sultans of Sulu were proclaimed, the son, Datu Jamalul Abirin by the council of datus and Datu Esmail Kiram by the Moro priests.

This arrangement does not make for a contented family in Sulu-land. But the Moros love trouble and so, judged from that angle, must be happy.

The people of Sulu still have with them the amazing Princess Tarhata Atik Kiram, niece of the former Sultan. She was the one of the royal house chosen by Governor Carpenter to be American-educated and then to return to lead the untractable Moros to the ways of peace. Only the great plan did not work out as the good Governor expected.

Princess Tarhata did indeed become a full-fledged co-ed in the University of Illinois. Then back to Manila she came with the dress and slang of the typical sophisticated college girl. Her picture was taken, she gave out an interview, and all seemed well. Down to Jolo she went and almost immediately discarded her modish clothes for a Moro *sarong*, married already-married, middle-aged Datu Tahil, and with the Datu became involved in a revolt against the Government. While the Datu was in prison serving his sentence, the petite Princess divorced him and married Datu Buyongan, a fifty year old widower.

In Jolo, in the Sulu Archipelago, lives the Princess Tarhata, who is now a widow, gone Moro, disdainful of her college days, but perhaps happier in the life she prefers than she would ever have been as an Americanized Moro, a missionary of good deeds, and the delegate of Philippine unity.

The inhabitants of the Sulu Archipelago are interesting in every sense of the word.

THE MINDANAO MOROS AND THEIR RULERS[4]

Before the Spaniards came to the Philippines, Sharif Mohammed Kabungsuwan, an Arabian priest, had converted the Maguindanaws

[4] See Dr. Najeeb M. Saleeby, *Studies in Moro History, Law, and Religion* (Manila, 1905).

to Mohammedanism and had become their ruler. The Maguindanaws were the largest tribe of Moros in Mindanao, living in the Northern Cotabato region. Not only was Kabungsuwan responsible for the successful introduction of Mohammedanism into Mindanao, but he founded the Sultanate of Maguindanaw and reformed the whole system of government. Dr. Najeeb M. Saleeby, the most eminent authority on Moro history, states that Kabungsuwan was without doubt the greatest Mohammedan adventurer to trod the soil of Mindanao. In the fullness of his glory, the Sultan of Maguindanaw ruled over almost the entire island. His children succeeded to the Sultanate, but gradually its power declined.

Of modern figures in Mindanao, Datu Piang was the most picturesque. He possessed a hundred or more wives and sired a hundred or more children; the prolific Datu could never recall exactly how many. Friend alike of Moros, Chinese, Spaniards, Americans, and Filipinos, he was progressive in his ways and the loyal supporter of the Government. The grand old man of Cotabato was the wealthiest Moro of his day and the most powerful chief in Mindanao.

In the early part of the nineteenth century, Tan Toy (Toya), an Amoy Chinese, wandered into Dulawan in Northern Mindanao. To the Chinaman and a Moro woman of the vicinity six sons were born. Piang was the youngest. After the death of his father, and despite his youth, he took upon himself the family responsibilities. His Chinese blood contributed the sagacity and industry that brought him wealth and influence, and his Moro blood made him a Mohammedan, to which faith he was loyal to the last. For more than half a century Datu Piang exercised a power that was unchallenged in Cotabato. Fortunately he exercised that power to the great advantage of his people. The Datu set the example by sending his children to the public schools, and he encouraged the children of his followers to do likewise.

About fifty miles up the Cotabato River was the large Maguindanaw village of Kuduarangan (Dulawan) where Datu Piang reigned. There he entertained on a grand scale. To greet him came lowly Moros and Governors General, neighboring Datus and Generals of the United States Army, all certain of a cordial welcome. To most of his visitors, certainly to all American officers, Piang made presents. Colonel John R. White reported that the Datu had a carefully graduated scale of gifts that ran from an engraved *lantaka* (brass cannon) or valuable piece of brass for a general down to half a dozen eggs for a second lieutenant.[5]

[5] John R. White, *Bullets and Bolos*, p. 235 (New York, 1928).

Datu Piang died in 1933 at about ninety years of age. He now rests in eternal sleep near the remains of his Chinese father in Cotabato. Over the grave his children and grandchildren have placed a *lantaka*, a gift from the Spaniards to the Moro leader. It will be a long time before Mindanao has another figure as colorful and powerful as Datu Piang.

After Datu Piang, no figure of approximate influence arose. Instead numerous Sultans and Datus with their followers are to be found.

In the course of time the Japanese pretty well took over the Davao region in Mindanao. Americans came also to develop plantations, and Filipino settlers crowded in to find homes. The Moros were not exactly pushed out, but what happened was that the uncultivated parts of the island were occupied by more aggressive elements. The time is not far distant when Mindanao, conceded to be the rich storehouse of the Philippines, will find its wealth utilized, and in this process it is likely that little regard will be paid to the protests of the Moros.

Of present day Moro leaders, the most conspicuous are those who have thrown in their lot with the Republic. Salipada Pendatun is an example of a Moro who after giving a good account of himself in guerrilla activities during the war crowned his record with active service as a member of the Philippine Senate.

The Moros of Mindanao figured prominently in the history of the Philippines. It is within their power to do so again, without giving up their identity or forsaking ther religion, by cooperating with the Republic in the development of their island.

MORO CUSTOMS

It is not easy to give in a few sentences the facts about the Moros and their characteristic customs and idiosyncrasies.

Physically the Moros are very much like other Filipinos. In dress, however, they are different, with a costume that is gaudy and picturesque. The dress of the Moro men at times consists of nothing except a *sarong*, a long piece of cloth joined at the ends and tied around the waist. More often they wear trousers that fit close to the skin from the hip to the ankle and a tight jacket. A handkerchief loosely wound around the head serves as a turban. In the folds of the *sarong* are invariably carried a brass box for betelnut and a short dagger. Women also wear jackets, but with them they use wide loose trousers not unlike those worn by Chinese women.

Like the Guaymis of Central America and the Dyaks of Borneo, the Moros file the teeth to points. Betelnut juice gives their lips a nearly perpetual vermilion hue.

The Moro girls are particularly careful of their honor, and it is the outraging of Moro women that has most often caused trouble in Mindanao and Sulu. The Moros marry very young, boys of fifteen and girls even younger not infrequently assuming the responsibilities of married life. The Moro practices polygamy as this is sanctioned by his religion, a man having as many wives as he cares to support.

The principal occupations of the Moros are agriculture and fishing. They have shown considerable skill in the manufacture of articles of hammered brass. They are also expert weavers and silversmiths.

As has been said, the Moros profess the Mohammedan religion. The over-observance of their religion makes of the Moros fanatics and assumes peculiar forms in two aspects. They *"run amuck"* and they *"go juramentado."* A Moro *amuck* is simply a crazed, frenzied man violently and indiscriminately killing until he himself is slain. The *juramentado* Moro, on the other hand, makes careful preparation, quietly and treacherously seeks a spot where Christians are wont to gather, and then begins the business of beheading and disemboweling. The fanatical *juramentado* Moro believes that if he meets his death as a result of killing a Christian he goes to a Mohammedan paradise.

The Moros are governed by numerous petty Datus. Within the land under the Datu's more or less vague jurisdiction, he and his subjects construct a fortress called a *cotta*, and inside and around the *cotta* he and his retainers live. The Datu's word is practically absolute as to ordinary questions arising among his people.

The Moros never go abroad without a weapon. The *kris* is said to be their God, and Mohammed his prophet. This is readily understandable, for above all else the Moro is a fighter. Proud and touchy, the Moro is quick to resent any intrusion on his rights and customs and is prone to vindicate himself by the skillful use of beautiful blades of the type of the *kris, kampilan,* or *barong.*

GOVERNMENT POLICY TOWARDS THE MOROS

Varied have been the forms which governmental policy has assumed for the Moros: extermination, as at Bud Dajo and Mount Bagsak; negotiations, like the Bates treaty and the Carpenter agreement; and, in later years, attraction and conciliation.

Originally it was thought that the only good Moro was the dead Moro. Numerous punitive expeditions by the Military or Constabulary, or both, were organized and ordered to overcome opposing Moro elements in Lanao and Sulu. In 1906, on Bud Dajo, a bluff-sided and extinct volcano, troops sent by General Leonard Wood were forced to kill six hundred Moro men, women and children who resisted to the last, and one-fourth of the troops actively engaged were killed or wounded. Seven years later, General John J. Pershing repeated the lesson at Mount Bagsak. Three hundred Moros were killed and organized resistance was broken.

From time to time the press is enlivened by dispatches of sporadic Moro uprisings. In 1933 a Constabulary patrol was ambushed and nearly exterminated by the Moro marauders whom they were hunting. In 1949, when all efforts at peaceful negotiations failed, a major offensive against lawless elements in Sulu was begun and successfully concluded. Gradually, however, such occurrences are becoming fewer and when they do take place are not on the same scale as before.

The Moro Province was created in 1903 with General Wood as the governor. Ten years later Frank W. Carpenter relieved General Pershing and became the first civilian governor of the Department of Mindanao and Sulu. In turn the Department gave way to a government under the Bureau of non-Christian Tribes. With the disappearance of this Bureau and its temporary successor, the Commissioner for Mindanao and Sulu, no special agency is entrusted with supervision of the Moro region.

Two civilian administrators of the Moro country, one American and the other Filipino, accomplished more for the Moros in a few years than Spanish, American, and Filipino troops had in many years. They did so by incredible patience, by understanding Moro customs, and by gaining Moro respect through fair dealing. The two administrators here referred to were Governor Carpenter and Governor Teopisto Guingona, who subsequently became Chief of the Bureau of non-Christian Tribes and Commissioner for Mindanao and Sulu.

The prophecies of some Americans that when freedom came to the Filipinos, the Moros would again take up arms and ravage the country have not been fulfilled. During the recent war years, Mindanao and Sulu were the scenes of battles and skirmishes between the Japanese and the guerrilla forces. Unsettled conditions naturally appealed to the turbulent instincts of many of the Moros, which mostly took the form of opposition to the Japanese invaders. With peace, outlawry in the Moro region is no more prevalent than in prewar days. The Philippine Armed Forces and the Constabulary, because of better training and equipment, should experience no particular difficulty in maintaining order over combative bands of Moros.

One cardinal point in the policy toward Moros has consistently been not to interfere with their religion. With rare understanding, officialdom felt that the Moros should be left alone in their religious practices. This policy has meant tacit recognition of polygamy and even slavery, but this could not be helped. The Government has also respected Mohammedan law based on the Koran. The attitude thus assumed by the Government has been wise, considering how touchy the Moros are on religious questions.

To emphasize the desire for unity, self-government has been partially accorded the Moros. The Datus and Sultans have not been molested when they have settled the disputes of their followers. The Moros have been permitted to elect their local officials, and their advice has been sought in the selection of higher officials. To the Philippine Legislature have come Moro senators and representatives.

Moro children have been educated in the public schools and have been graduated from the higher courses. At times, however, the Moros have not taken very kindly to the practices of the school. The reason has been that the children have learned methods incompatible with the Mohammedan customs. One most excellent institution was the Indanan Farm School in the heart of the Island of Jolo, founded by an estimable American lady, Mrs. Lorillard Spencer, who largely maintained the school at her own expense.

The effort of the Government during the last few years has been to improve relations between the Moros and the Filipinos. Filipino officials have been sent to Moroland, and most of them have given good accounts of themselves. Occasionally a Filipino teacher or Constabulary officer has grossly offended the Moros, but these have fortunately been the exception and not the rule. In such cases the Moros have an effective way of retaliating, but with bloodshed at the end of the trail. Filipino settlers have been encouraged to migrate to Mindanao to develop the land. Most of these immigrants have been permitted to live peaceably, but once in a while they have been attacked by the Moros in the neighborhood who have resented their intrusion.

The government policy of understanding, attraction and recognition of the right of self-government appears to be working out fairly well.

THE MOUNTAIN PEOPLES[6]

The whole experiment in the control of the peoples found in

[6] See Dean C. Worcester, *The Philippines, Past and Present*, Hayden edition of 1930, Chs. XX-XXIII; Felix and Marie Keesing, *Taming Philippine Headhunters* (Stanford University Press, 1934); and Samuel E. Kane, *Life or Death in Luzon* (Indianapolis, 1933).

the Moutain Province of Northern Luzon has been successful. The Spaniards left them pretty much alone. The Americans obtained spectacular results. Many Filipino officials have performed excellent administrative work in these remote regions.

The mountain peoples of Luzon are the largest in number among the 600,000 pagans who live mostly in the hinterland of the Philippines. They constitute a picturesque group. Loosely but inaccurately referred to as a whole by the name Igorot, the Philippine highlanders retain no traditions of migration from Asia or Malaysia. Nor can they furnish any clue to the origin of their wonderful rice terraces.

The clothing problem of these peoples is easily solved. The men usually wear a gee-string, while for women a brief *tapis*, large enough to girdle the waist and reach the knees, suffices. If the men put on more than a gee-string, it will be a coat and a hat, but never trousers. If the women use more than a *tapis*, you will find them removing their jackets when they are out of sight of settlements. One social institution rather unique and extremely modern is a form of trial marriage.

In Baguio a scene unlike that to be encountered in any part of the world is afforded on Sunday mornings when the Igorots come in from the hills carrying their burdens on their heads and backs, to offer their articles for sale in the public market. Dogs are no longer permitted to be sold there, but outside Baguio the dog market continues, for the favorite dish of these mountain dwellers is roast dog. Civilization has come to the Igorots in the form of the taxi, and it is no uncommon sight to see a near-naked pagan riding in a bantam jitney.

If you are at all familiar with the American Indians, you will rub your eyes and wonder if after all you are in the Philippines. To a surprising extent the Igorots and other mountaineers of the Philippines resemble certain tribes of American Indians. Color, a copperish brown; hair, coarse and black; high cheek bones; none too clean; the women carrying their babies on their backs—that is the Igorot.

To the simple mountaineers the American was an *apo* or chief who could be looked to for protection and for the settlement of all problems. And they did not look in vain. Head-hunting, their favorite sport, was checked through the influence of the schools and by substituting athletic contests and grand *canaos* (ceremonial feasts at which dancing takes place) for the ferocious practice. In possibly no other phase of endeavor were so many Americans so conspicuously successful. Secretary Dean C. Worcester; W. F. Pack,

Governor of Benguet and first Governor of the Mountain Province; Samuel E. Kane (who resided for thirty odd years in the mountain country), Governor of Bontoc; John E. Early, practical teacher and Governor of the Mountain Province; Colonel William E. Dosser, also Governor of the same province; and Judge Charles Burritt (who startled even his scantily attired audience by holding court in a full dress suit)—the list of these sturdy pioneers is long, the tales of their exploits are many and lurid.

A considerable number of the mountain peoples have proved adaptable to education. The possibilities for advancement of at least a portion of the erstwhile headhunters and of their absorption into the general body politic as fully participating citizens are good.

The Aboriginal Negritos

The Negritos found in the Philippines belong to what was probably the oldest living race. They constitute the disappearing remnants of the aborigines who once populated the Archipelago.

The Negritos are truly pygmy Negros—black, with thick wooly hair, and with a stature of less than five feet. Few in number, they roam the forests of the Philippines in scattered bands. While some of them have made acceptable servants, the great mass are of low intelligence, and attempts to educate them have usually failed.

The pagans of the southern islands, like the Mangyans of Mindoro and the Bajaos or sea gypsies of Mindanao and Sulu, are not very much farther advanced in civilization than the Negritos. On the other hand, the Bagobos and others like them are a handsome people with many fine qualities.

Solvable Problems

Responsibility for bridging the gulf between the Filipinos proper and their Moro brothers rests with the Filipino leaders. Responsibility for governing the backward mountain peoples must likewise be assumed. These are complicated but not unsolvable problems.

The representatives of the Philippine Republic can utilize the reservoir of good will stored up by previous American and Filipino administrators. They have it within their power to break down the social line drawn between Christians and non-Christians, to show by example that there is no reason for the Moros and pagans to distrust or fear the men in power, and to protect their wards from all forms of exploitation. Patiently and deliberately the task of assimilation can be carried forward.

Otherwise stated, the minority groups in the Philippines can be exploited for the gain of the more powerful. Or the groups that have displayed unmistakable aptitude when given a chance can be afforded opportunities for betterment. The policy of assimilation by education and attraction will pay off in the long run in a closer approach to national unity. The special problems that make up that general policy, however, will remain with the Republic of the Philippines for a long time to come.

CHAPTER IV

HISTORICAL BACKGROUND

DISCOVERY OF THE PHILIPPINE ISLANDS

The Philippine Islands have been "discovered" many times. They were first "discovered" by the inhabitants of Asia and Oceania during ages shrouded in antiquity. They were next "discovered" on the near circumnavigation of the globe by Ferdinand Magellan. The Islands were again "discovered" when Commodore George Dewey fought the Battle of Manila Bay and brought the Philippines within the geographical ken of America. And there was "self-discovery" of the Philippines by the Filipinos when within recent years they became race-conscious and began to move about and know their own country.

The characteristic statement to be found in the books is that the Philippine Islands were "discovered" by Ferdinand Magellan on March 16, 1521. If by this is meant that the Philippines was then brought to the notice of Europe, the statement is correct. But long before Magellan set eyes on the Island of Samar and entered into a blood compact with the chief of Cebu in the Philippines, the Islands were known to other countries, and particularly to China. Just as old Nankin porcelain has been found in the Zimbabwe ruins in South Africa, so has ancient Chinese porcelain been dug up in the Philippines. It is reasonably certain that for centuries before the coming of the Spaniards, certainly from the late ninth century, the Islands were in communication with China.[1]

Magellan called the land that he had discovered "Saint Lazarus." Afterwards the archipelago was officially christened "Filipinas" (Philippines) in honor "of our fortunate Prince" Philip, later King Philip II of Spain. The names "Philippines" or "Philippine Islands," have since been current. The shorter form, "Philippines," is favored by the people inhabiting the island group.

The various discoveries of the Philippines furnish the dividing lines of its history. The three great formative periods were the pre-

---

[1] Dr. H. Otley Beyer, *Early History of Philippine Relations With Foreign Countries, Especially China* (Manila, 1948).

Photo by EDGARDO DEBAS
Madrid—1890

Dr. Jose Rizal
Filipino Author, Patriot and Martyr.

Spanish, the era of Spanish rule dating from their entrance into the Archipelago and continuing to Dewey's victory in Manila Bay on May 1, 1898, and the American period commencing soon after that date and ending on July 4, 1946 when the Republic of the Philippines was inaugurated. Overlapping both Spanish and American administrations in point of time was a fourth division, Philippine Nationalism, which is at present being carried forward into a new epoch.

The first period was mainly Filipino, the second combined Spanish and Filipino, the third combined American and Filipino, and the last aspires to be strictly Filipino. It is noteworthy that the Philippines has thus been touched by various civilizations—by the aboriginal and Oriental, by the Latin and European, and by the Anglo-Saxon and distinctly American.

PHILIPPINE SAGA[2]

The task is not here essayed of telling in full the epic story of the Philippines. Not but that the Philippines is a land of adventure, for it is. No country possesses a more romantic history. The reason an attempt is not made to unfold the fascinating narrative is that the answers to many questions must be left to surmise. The best that can be done is to join the fragments of human knowledge to make a mosaic of Philippine history.

We proceed to set down a few of the many intriguing and questioned points pertaining to the Filipinos and the Philippines.

Whence came the pygmy Negritos, the aboriginal inhabitants of the Philippines, and the equally wild Mangyans? Whence came the mountain peoples of Northern Luzon with their Indonesian features? Whence came the Malay ancestors of the present-day Filipinos?

Is the Philippines a remnant of the vast continent of Mu located in mid-Pacific, which, like its mythological rival Atlantis of the Atlantic, has long since sunk beneath the waves? Or did the Philippines once form part of the Continent of Asia? Or was the Philippines attached to the Australian continental mass? Or did the islands constituting the Philippines arise by violent geological upthrusts?

Were the Islands in ages past known as "Ophir," the country that supplied King Solomon with precious gold? Was the Philippines a part of the great Sumatran State, Sri-Vishaya, a part of the

---

[2] Note Professors H. Otley Beyer and Jaime C. de Veyra, *Philippine Saga,* a Pictorial History of the Archipelago since time began, published by the *Evening News,* Manila, in 1947.

equally great Javanese State, Madjapahit, or a part of a vast Chinese Empire under the Ming dynasty? Or are these theories untenable? Instead, was the Philippines, together with Borneo, an independent state ruled by an imperial Philippine family which traced its descent from Philip of Macedon?

And the names linked by legend to the Philippines—Sinbad, Marco Polo, Alexander the Great, and Mohammed—were they really authentic figures in Philippine history?

Sinbad! According to an early myth, Sinbad the Sailor of the Arabian Nights visited Malaysia and Mindanao in the Philippines on one of his voyages. Strictly fiction?

Marco Polo! When Marco Polo, the Venetian, returned to Europe after a lengthy stay in China and Japan, and possibly other distant regions, he was thrown into prison for his supposed lies concerning these far-away countries. Persons endowed with sufficient imagination have conjectured that Marco Polo may have explored the coasts of Mindanao and Sulu in the Philippines in his travels. Fact or fiction?

Alexander the Great! It is commonly believed in Sulu that the Macedonian conqueror once ruled in Jolo. When the Spaniards arrived, Manila was a Moro outpost, and its royal family boasted of descent from King Alexander. Fact or fiction?

Mohammed! The Sultan of Sulu is the last of a dynasty which has as the base of its genealogical tree the prophet Mohammed. Across the sea in Mindanao, Sharif Kabungsuwan, the Sultan of Maguindanaw, claimed descent from Mohammed. Fact or fiction?

From this point on, we are on surer ground. First, a few inadequate words are in order about the unrivaled exploit of the expedition under the command of Ferdinand Magellan, a Portugese in the service of Spain, in circumnavigating the world. After an absence of three years one ship of the fleet returned home to Seville. Magellan's feat excelled that of the Argonauts. His voyage must be deemed the most notable single human achievement on the sea. Of Magellan it can be said with assurance that he ranks as the first navigator of ancient and modern times.[3]

The word "Lapu-Lapu" is widely known to residents of the Philippines as a fish popular with epicures, but it also has historical significance. Lapu-Lapu was the first Filipino chieftain to resist European invasion after the discovery of the Philippines by Spain, and this he did successfully when the intrepid Magellan was killed.

---

[3] An author who eulogizes the courageous Magellan in a late book is Christopher Lloyd, *Pacific Horizons* (London, 1946).

Regardless of how much we may lament that the worthy Magellan was the victim of this encounter, we must concede that it took courage of a high order for Lapu-Lapu to attack strange foreigners protected by armor and equipped with superior weapons.

Of the same fibre as Magellan were Miguel Lopez de Legaspi and Andres de Urdaneta, whose expedition daringly set forth from Mexico to colonize and Christianize the unknown Philippines. The work of Legaspi during his crowded years in the Islands entitles him to a place as a colonizer without a peer.

Time passes. The sun of the Spanish day is setting. Commodore Dewey sails from Hongkong for the Philippines and after a brief but daring engagement sinks the Spanish fleet and writes his name large in American annals. About the same time the Filipino insurgents are eliminating the last vestiges of Spanish power. A detachment of Spanish troops is located in Baler, since made famous as the birthplace of President Manuel Quezon. Besieged, the small group of courageous soldiers refuses to surrender even after Spanish sovereignty has passed, furnishing an inspiring example of Spanish bravery.

In 1899 the Filipinos and the Americans are no longer comrades, but are pitted against each other in war. The fratricidal feud takes its ghastly toll. Among the dead lies Henry W. Lawton, a soldier who never lost a fight, America's greatest campaigner in the Philippines, and a titan of courage and strength. Another sacrifice to war is Gregorio H. del Pilar, the youngest and bravest Filipino leader of a lost cause.

General Lawton had been the terror of the Indian marauders of the Northwest. In the Philippines he had become the "General of the Night," feared with superstitious dread by the Filipinos. In middle December he left Manila on his last scout. Disdainful as usual of the bullets spattering about him, his towering frame and conspicuous garb made him a target for the insurgents. He was shot through the lungs and died almost immediately. General Lawton now rests at Arlington, the national cemetery, among the valiant dead.

In the same fatal month of December, General Aguinaldo's insurgents were in retreat. The rear-guard was formed of sixty men under the command of the young General Gregorio H. del Pilar. Up the trail at lonely Tirad Pass[4] a battalion of the 33rd Volunteer Infantry attacked on three sides, but the little band refused to surrender. When the fight was over the defenders of the pass were annihilated. Among them was found the body of the brave com-

---

[4] Also erroneously called "Tila Pass" and "Tilad Pass." *Tirad* is an Ilocano word meaning "pointed."

mander, who had welcomed death and who was proud to die fighting for his country. As a tribute to the hero of Tirad Pass, he was buried with full military honors.

The peaceful years are again broken by two terrible holocausts. In the Second World War, the Philippines becomes a decisive battleground. Feats of epic bravery on the part of American and Filipino comrades are so common as not to permit of the signaling out of any one exploit for description. The American and the Filipino had once more demonstrated that they must be accounted men of courage, of the heroic mould of their great commander, General of the Army Douglas MacArthur, and his fearless Filipino associate, General Vicente Lim.

Sinbad, Marco Polo, Alexander, Mohammed—names about which to speculate. Magellan and Legaspi, Dewey and Lawton, Lapu-Lapu and del Pilar, MacArthur and Lim—names among a myriad of others worthy of honor. All are enshrined in the golden pages of Philippine history.

The Ancient Philippines

Human life existed in the Philippines 25,000 years ago, or so it has been affirmed.[5] This statement does not partake of exaggeration when placed alongside a broader one to the effect that a primitive type of man lived in Malaysia half a million years ago. And the latter deduction does not pass into the realm of fantasy when scientific findings show that the neighboring island of Java has harbored a succession of races which bridge the gap to manlike characteristics. These peoples of the dim past were the ancestors of the primitive Negritos.

Of the antiquity of the Philippines no one can speak with exact authority. Yet, though the historical data are by no means complete, Dr. H. Otley Beyer, eminent archaeologist and ethnologist, ventures the statement that the Philippines can claim 250,000 years of existence. It is certain that shortly before the Christian era, the Philippines came in contact with the civilization developed in India which left a profound impress on the people. From the third century A. D., parts of the Philippines were successively dominated by the colorful Indo-Malayan Empire of Sri-Vishaya, with its seat of power in Sumatra, and the later Javanese Empire of Madjapahit.

Contemporaneous with these Hindu-Malayan relations were con-

---

5 Dr. H. Otley Beyer, introduction to *Philippine Saga*, corrected version, *Manila Bulletin*, Fiftieth Anniversary Edition, 1950; Vic Hurley, *Swish of the Kris*, p. 2; Raymond Kennedy, *The Ageless Indies*, pp. 27 *et. seq.*; Findings of Dr. G. H. R. von Koenugswald, reported in *Newsweek*.

tacts with China. The Chinese gained a shadowy control of the Islands for a time and exacted tribute. However, the Chinese influence was principally felt through the channels of trade. In addition the Philippine peoples traded with merchants from other lands.

The Mohammedan movement spreading eastward from Arabia finally engulfed the peoples of the Sulu Archipelago and Mindanao in the Philippine group. The advance of Moslem power was only stopped by the coming of the Christian Spaniards in the sixteenth century. The southern islands remained Mohammedan in religion and sentiment.

When the Spaniards arrived they found the Filipinos scattered over the Islands in groups called "barangays." In Manila, the chieftain Rajah Soliman had his stronghold on the south bank of the Pasig River, and Rajah Lakandola had his town on the north bank. Curiously enough when Manila was taken by assault by the Spanish forces, a Portuguese gunner was found among the dead. Apparently unnamed Portuguese sailors had adventured to this far off land even before the Spaniards.

The early Filipinos were a highly literate people. They had a peculiar phonetic alphabet and form of writing similar to the Arabic. Their laws, stories, poems and proverbs were written on scrolls, bamboo and the bark of trees. Standard weights and measures were in use. The year was divided into lunar months. Agriculture was in a prosperous condition. Fishing, weaving, and metal-working were among the common occupations. The material wealth was considerable.

In short, it can be positively stated that long before the Spanish conquest, the inhabitants of the Philippines had acquired a culture distinctly their own and were living in a state of comparative well being and contentment.

Unfortunately the missionaries in their mistaken zeal ruthlessly destroyed practically every vestige of the writings of the early Filipinos. One Spanish priest in Southern Luzon boasted that he had destroyed more than three hundred scrolls written in native characters. As a result only a few fragments of pre-Spanish Filipino literature survive, to the vexation of modern scholars. Accordingly it has been necessary to search the chronicles of neighboring countries for the history of the Philippines before the arrival of Magellan. The isolated facts thus disclosed have then had to be carefully tested for authenticity and pieced together to make a connected narrative.

When the Spaniards took over control of the major portion of the Philippines from the Filipinos, the latter were divided politically. In the degree of their civilization, however, they were at a stage of development fairly comparable with other progressive races of the equivalent period in history. What would have happened in the Philippines had it not been for the conquest by the Spaniards is problematical. Probably the Moro invasion from the south would have persisted, and eventually the Philippines would have been consolidated into one or more Mohammedan states. But that was not to be the fate of the Filipinos. To them was to come not only the crescent of the Moslems but the cross of the Spaniards and the democracy of the Americans.

Spanish Rule

Except for a brief interval during the Seven Years' War when the British occupied the Islands, the Spaniards were in control of the Philippines for over three centuries. The Philippines was a part of a far flung Spanish empire which in its heyday included South America and a goodly portion of North America.

From Mexico, in 1564, there sailed for the Philippines an expedition commanded by Miguel Lopez de Legaspi, with the soldier-priest, Andres de Urdaneta, as his chief adviser and navigating officer. Legaspi effected permanent settlements in Cebu in 1569 and in Manila in 1571. Thereafter, with but slight resistance, the peoples of the lowlands were brought under subjection.

During all these years the soldier and priest were supreme. As has been so aptly said, Spain carried the sword in one hand and the cross in the other.

Governors General with vice-regal powers represented the Spanish crown in the Philippines. Bishops of the Roman Catholic Church with scarcely less authority and sometimes with more authority than the Spanish viceroys carried out the missionary plans of Rome. Practically the only restriction on the Governors and other officials was an institution known as the *residencia*, devised by the Spaniards to secure an investigation into the conduct of the Philippine officials during their entire term of office.

The Philippines was primarily a Spanish colony. The Spaniard was the ruler, the Filipino the ruled. With the exception of a limited number of minor offices which the Spaniards permitted the Filipinos to fill, the government was administered by Spain for Spain. Only during three short periods, due to governmental upheavals in Spain, was the Philippines allowed nominal representation in the Spanish Cortes. True, there was a ponderous collection of Laws of the Indies designed to protect the natives, but unfortunately they were not enforced.

The legitimate criticism of Spanish colonial policy is practically self-evident and needs little elucidation. The thought was ever of the mother country and of securing the most from the Filipinos for the benefit of Spain and her numerous officials. That corruption existed has never been denied. It was to be found not only in the executive department but in the judiciary, where it is most detestable.

It serves no good purpose to belittle Spain and to underrate her solid contributions to the Philippines. Spanish rule made a definite impress on the life of the people. The laws, customs and culture, and to some extent the language, of one of the most advanced nations of Europe were introduced. The seeds of Latin civilization were planted and occasionally came to fruition. Hand in hand with the secular administration went religious zeal, with the result that the Filipinos acquired the blessings of a common Christian faith. The Spaniards did indeed influence the Filipinos for the better.

In one respect the impact of Spanish rule was particularly beneficial. The heterogeneous system of native government was abolished and the rights of the petty royal families were extinguished. Spain encouraged community loyalty and brought nearer to national unity peoples previously lacking in those prime requisites for self-government. Where Spain failed was in not going forward to prepare the Philippine people for freedom.

Only once during the years of Spanish domination did an official speak up in behalf of the rights of the Filipinos to say that if Spain did not liberalize her policy, she would not be able to retain the Philippines. This was in 1843, but Sinalbaldo de Mas' report to the home government was quietly pigeonholed. Only two men, one the German naturalist Feodor Jagor, and the other the Filipino Jose Rizal, the most famous of his race, foresaw Spain's inevitable loss of the Philippines and predicted that the Philippines would sooner or later succumb to the American influence.[6]

THE AMERICAN FLAG ARRIVES[7]

The eventful year 1898 found Fernando Primo de Rivera, uncle

---

[6] Feodor Jagor, *Reisen in den Philippinen* ("Travels in the Philippines"), 1873, concluding paragraphs; and Jose Rizal, *Filipinas Dentro de Cien Anos* ("The Philippines a Century Hence"), 1889.

[7] See *Autobiography of George Dewey* (New York, 1913); and Karl Irving Faust, *Campaigning in the Philippines* (1898). The Spanish version of the Battle of Manila Bay appeared in the *Diario de Manila* of May 4, 1898.

of the future dictator of Spain, as the Spanish Governor General of the Philippines, although shortly thereafter he was succeeded by Governor General Basilio Augustin, with Admiral Montojo in command of the fleet. The same year found General Emilio Aguinaldo in Singapore, whence he had gone after the Pact of Biak-na-bato, which concluded peace between the Filipino insurgents and the Spaniards. And 1898 also found Commodore Dewey in command of the American fleet in Hongkong. A condition of comparative quiet prevailed in the Philippines. The United States declared war on Spain and there was activity on all fronts.

On April 25, a laconic message, inspired by Assistant Secretary of the Navy Theodore Roosevelt, instructed Dewey to proceed at once to the Philippines and to "capture vessels" of the Spanish fleet "or destroy" them. Aguinaldo, on hearing of the war, rushed from Singapore to Hongkong and was conveyed on an American vessel to the Philippines, where he renewed operations against the Spaniards. Governor General Augustin in Manila issued a bombastic manifesto calling on the Filipinos to fight the "uncultured, undisciplined crew" who have "dared to come to these shores for the insane purpose of depriving you of all that means life, honor, and liberty." A few days later Archbishop Nozaleda added his mite by urging the people to "subscribe to this holy war."

At about dawn on May 1, 1898, the American fleet under the command of Commodore Dewey entered Manila Bay, and, after navigating safely the mines planted by the Spaniards and avoiding the fire of the shore batteries, passed in battle array before the Spanish fleet. When at a distance of 5,000 yards, Dewey turned to Captain Gridley and said, "You may fire when you are ready, Gridley." In a decisive naval combat, the Spanish fleet was destroyed and the American flag brought to Philippine shores.

Manila capitulated to the American forces, which arrived in the Islands after the Battle of Manila Bay, on August 13 of the same year. By a coincidence, a protocol of peace between the United States and Spain had been signed on August 12 (August 13, 5:30 A. M., Manila time), or a few hours before the capture of Manila. The Treaty of Paris concluding the Spanish-American War was agreed to on December 10, 1898, and later was ratified by both signatories. By the treaty Spain ceded the Philippine Islands and Puerto Rico to the United States, and the United States paid Spain $20,000,000, but there was no stated connection between the two transactions. The treaty provided that "the civil rights and political status of the native inhabitants of the territories hereby ceded to the United States shall be determined by the Congress."

After eliminating the Spaniards, it became necessary for the American troops to pacify the Islands. Who started the trouble between the Americans and the Filipinos has long been debated. Did a Filipino insurgent at San Juan bridge just outside of Manila fire on an American sentry, or did an over-zealous American soldier prematurely fire on the Filipino lines? Whatever the cause, war was on, and before it was concluded Filipino and American lives had been sacrificed. With the capture of General Aguinaldo by Frederick Funston, the insurrection was broken and peace brought to the Archipelago. By 1902 allegiance to the United States had been won.

Military rule was first instituted in the Islands. Civil administration was begun in 1901 and a government was organized which was to continue for over thirty years.

The status of the Philippines was determined by the United States Supreme Court in nearly evenly divided decisions in what are known as the Insular Cases. In popular phrase the high Court ruled that the American Constitution had not followed the flag to the Philippines. Practically speaking, the doctrine proved no handicap, for the Philippine Government was closely patterned after American institutions. Excepting the right to trial by jury, which was withheld because it was deemed unsuitable to conditions in the Islands, all the important provisions of the American Bill of Rights were extended to the Philippines.

For four decades the American flag floated proudly in the Philippine breezes. On July 4, 1946 it was honorably lowered, and the Philippine flag honorably raised to take its place among the free nations of the world. This unprecedented action in world history was taken voluntarily by the American people, with the grateful concurrence of the Filipino people.

CHAPTER V

THE GOVERNMENT OF THE PHILIPPINE ISLANDS[1]

American Philippine Policy[2]

The Philippine policy of the United States was begun haltingly and reluctantly. At the council table to formulate the Treaty of Peace between Spain and the United States, the American Commissioners were unable to state whether the United States wanted the Philippines at all, desired the Island of Luzon alone, or claimed the entire archipelago. The higher authorities at Washington could give no more definite instructions. Even after President William McKinley on bended knees had sought divine guidance and had decided to place the Philippines on the American map, the opinion of the country was no better formed than that of its officials. By the closest of margins, the treaty received the necessary two-thirds vote in the United States Senate. The issue of anti-imperialism was threshed out before the American electorate, and the President was given a vote of confidence.

Having decided to keep the Philippine Islands, the question was what to do with them. Because the original ambiguity and uncertainty of American policy permitted of readjustment, what may be termed the compromise plan was given practical application in the Philippines. The first and simplest policy, that of the anti-imperialists and their successors, advocated that the Americans get out of the Philippines as soon as possible and hand over everything to the Filipinos; this was rejected. The policy advanced by the imperialists and their successors was that the Philippines was a possession fairly acquired and worth retaining permanently; this was likewise foresworn. It was the middle course between the two extreme schools of thought

---

[1] This chapter was originally read by the late Colonel Louis J. Van Schaick, Governor of Mindoro and Cavite in the early years of American occupation, later on the staff of Governors General Roosevelt and Murphy. See W. Cameron Forbes, *The Philippine Islands* (Harvard University Press, 1945), revised and abridged copy of the two volume edition of 1928.

[2] See William Howard Taft, *Present Day Problems* (1908). This is a collection of addresses by Mr. Taft, including inaugural address as Civil Governor and address at the inauguration of the Philippine Assembly. Also note Francis Burton Harrison, *The Cornerstone of Philippine Independence* (New York, 1922).

First Civil Governor William H. Taft and Mrs. Taft.

that was approved. In legal parlance, this signified that the Philippines was not to be considered as either a foreign country or a colony, but was to be a dependency temporarily held by the United States.

The United States thereafter consistently pursued a policy leading to eventual independence for the Philippines. President Herbert Hoover in his veto message of the Hare-Hawes-Cutting Independence Bill frankly admitted that the Filipino people had been encouraged in their aspiration for a separate nationality "by every President of the United States during the years of our association with the Philippines and by declarations of the Congress." The much-debated question was: When and how should independence be granted?

Generally speaking, American policy in the Philippines was determined by no more than seven or eight men. Until 1913 it was influenced by Elihu Root and William H. Taft; from 1913 to 1921 by Woodrow Wilson; from 1921 to 1933 by Leonard Wood and Henry L. Stimson; and from 1933 to 1946 by Franklin D. Roosevelt (until his death) and Millard E. Tydings.

Mr. Taft publicly acclaimed Secretary Root as the man who more than any other person initiated the Philippine policy of the United States and "was responsible for its success from the standpoint of statesmanship and farsightedness." Root, said Taft, drafted the Instructions of April 7, 1900, which President McKinley gave the Second Philippine Commission.[3] This great state paper, besides outlining a form of government, laid down a reasonable and tolerant basis for that government.

Taft was overly modest in giving Root sole credit for the formulation and execution of a Philippine policy. Taft is at least entitled to recognition as a co-author. He was mainly responsible for the inauguration of the Philippine Government, for the dictum "the Philippines for the Filipinos," and for the provisions of the Philippine Bill of July 1, 1902 that paved the way for an elective Philippine Assembly. Taft declared that the national policy was to govern the Philippines for the benefit and welfare of the people of the Islands and gradually to extend to them, as they showed themselves fit to exercise it, a greater measure of popular self-government. This meant in practice the evolution of a government of Americans assisted by Filipinos into a government of Filipinos assisted by Americans and preparation for future independence.

With the election of President Woodrow Wilson and with the

[3] Address by Mr. Taft after leaving the Presidency before the Brooklyn Institute of Arts and Sciences on November 19, 1913.

inauguration of Francis Burton Harrison as Governor General of the Philippine Islands, American policy took a turn toward the left of center. The President appointed a majority of Filipinos to the Philippine Commission and so *Filipinized* the Philippine Legislature. Governor General Harrison on the day of his arrival in Manila delivered to the satisfaction of the Filipinos a message from the President which began, "We regard ourselves as trustees, acting, not for the advantage of the United States, but for the benefit of the people of the Philippine Islands. Every step we take will be taken with a view to ultimate independence, and we hope to move towards that end as rapidly as the safety and the permanent interests of the Islands will permit." Governor General Harrison, continuing his Inaugural Address, coined a phrase of his own which became historical: "People of the Philippine Islands, a new era is dawning." Thereafter, the Jones Law of August 29, 1916 was enacted with a preamble in President Wilson's own hand in which it was stated that "it is, as it has always been, the purpose of the people of the United States to withdraw their sovereignty over the Philippine Islands and to recognize their independence as soon as a stable government can be established therein."

Secretary of War Newton D. Baker addressed to Governor General Harrison a covering letter relating to the administration of the Philippines under the Jones Law. The purpose of the letter was to forestall too radical developments, but apparently it was disregarded. At least the Baker letter was kept secret, for it was not until December, 1925 that it was read into the *Congressional Record* by Congressman Robert Bacon.

With the passing of the Democratic administration, there was a tendency for the pendulum to swing back towards the center. Despite the stand of Governor General Wood, and of Henry L. Stimson in the capacity of Governor General and later of Secretary of State, this only amounted to a tendency. It is axiomatic that when any advance in self-government for a dependent people has been sanctioned, it can only be reclaimed with the utmost difficulty.

The Democrats returned to power. The Philippine Commonwealth and Independence Act of 1934 put the stamp of approval and accomplishment on the principles previously announced in the President's Instructions, the Philippine Bill, and the Jones Law, by providing "for the complete independence of the Philippines." The moving spirit in the enactment of this law and of the implementing Trade and War Damage Acts of 1946 was Senator Tydings.

The much debated question of independence for the Philippines had been definitely settled. How well and how satisfactorily it was settled only time can judge. However, this much can be said—American policy was begun as a noble experiment in altruism. It was to be "the Philippines for the Filipinos," the Americans acting as "trustees" for the benefit of the Filipino people, and a gradual development of self-government, step by step, to culminate in Philippine independence. In the greater part, these principles were adhered to. In a lesser degree, the record was not one of unmixed benevolence. A depression gripped the United States. Lobbies for powerful interests became insistent. A considerable portion of the support for Philippine independence was motivated by mercenary considerations.

Aside from the not wholly unexpected manifestations of the might of selfishness over the right of principle, American policy for the Philippines was otherwise guided by a sincere desire to do the most possible for the Filipino people and in the way desired by the people. This policy was most vulnerable to criticism in that it concentrated on political independence to the exclusion of consideration of the need for economic independence for the Philippines.

The Government Established

Space does not permit of a description in all its phases of the government established by the United States in the Philippines. Only the most general outlines of the development and structure of the Philippine Government can be sketched.

General Wesley Merritt assumed the duties of Military Governor of the Philippines on August 26, 1898, but left almost immediately for Paris to attend the Peace Conference with Spain. He was ultimately succeeded by General Arthur MacArthur. To the latter was transferred all of the war powers of the President.

Not long after, the First Philippine Commission, of which Jacob Gould Schurman, President of Cornell University, was chairman, was sent out to the Philippines by the President to investigate conditions and make recommendations. In due time the Commission submitted a report. The President thereupon appointed the Second Philippine Commission, headed by William H. Taft, then a Federal Judge of Ohio, to establish a civil administration. In obedience to the instructions given the Commission, the first task was the organization of local governments. Next, the legislative branch was taken over from the military, and finally the executive branch. On July 4, 1901, Mr. Taft was inaugurated Civil Governor with simple but impressive ceremonies.

The administration of the government by the Philippine Commission extended until the creation of the Philippine Assembly. The Commission first made the laws and then executed them. After 1907, the legislative power in the parts of the Islands not inhabited by the Moros and other non-Christians was shared by the Philippine Assembly. With the creation of the Philippine Senate in 1916, all legislative power was transferred to a Philippine Legislature exclusively Filipino.

The title Civil Governor was almost immediately changed to Governor General and thus remained. The executive departments acting under the direction of the Governor General were first manned by American officials. It was not long, however, until all of these executive positions, with the sole exception of Secretary of Public Instruction, were administered by capable Filipinos.

As the old Philippine Government went out and the new Philippine Commonwealth came in, the latter found a government administered by an executive power at the head of which was an American Governor General, assisted by an American Insular Auditor and by seven department secretaries, six Filipinos and one American, the latter being the Vice Governor. It found a Philippine Legislature to which had been delegated general legislative power, restricted only by the regulatory authority vested in a few instances in the President and the right to veto of the Governor General. All the courts had been *Filipinized*, with the exception of the Supreme Court, over which a Filipino Chief Justice presided, with a majority of its members Filipinos.

When America, by the accident of war, was forced to set up a new government in the far-away Philippines, there was no light to guide its officials save the experience of European nations that had colonies in the Far East. But the generally accepted principles of colonization were repugnant to liberty-loving Americans. The only other model with which the Americans were acquainted was to be found in their early history in the Territory of Louisiana and in other acquisitions. Accordingly, the Philippine Government was patterned after a form of government with which Americans were most familiar. In many respects, the institutions provided for the Philippines were the same as those to be found in the United States. Where the Philippine Government differed from a typical American Government of equivalent time was in the concentration of power in the Governor General, in the creation of a Council of State combining legislative and executive functions, and in the appointment of legislators to cabinet posts.

Pro-Consuls Of The United States[4]

Spanning three and a half centuries, the Philippine Islands had over one hundred Spanish and American Chief Executives. Although seldom if ever recalled, the Philippines under Spanish rule also had one Filipino Governor in the person of Bishop Miguel Lino de Éspeleta and one English Governor, Mr. Dawsonne Drake, whose troubled experiences as Deputy and Provisional Governor of Manila featured a brief stay during the Seven Years' War. The eleven Governors General under the American regime were William H. Taft, 1901-1904; Luke E. Wright, 1904-1906; Henry C. Ide, 1906; James F. Smith, 1906-1909; W. Cameron Forbes, 1909-1913; Francis Burton Harrison, 1913-1921; Leonard Wood, 1921-1927; Henry L. Stimson, 1928-1929; Dwight F. Davis, 1929-1932; Theodore Roosevelt, Jr., 1932-1933; and Frank Murphy, 1933-1935. Various Vice Governors served as Chief Executives of the Islands in an *ad interim* capacity.

The acquaintance of the author with Governors General of the Philippine Islands began in 1906, and by accident, when General Smith was compelled at Honolulu to transfer from the liner on which he was a passenger to the Army Transport *Logan* bound for Manila. The association ended with Mayor Murphy of Detroit, whose trans-Pacific journey was shared when he came over to be the Island's last Chief Executive. The author was privileged to listen to the inaugural addresses of the Governors General and all, without exception, breathed a spirit of good will and good intentions. The American Pro-Consuls were found to be estimable gentlemen actuated by a sincere desire to advance the interests of the Philippines.

If into the gold of the makeup of the American Chief Executives there entered a baser alloy of personal ambition, and if they used their Philippine records to further preferment, one could hardly blame them, for this is a natural manifestation of human desire. Taft left the Philippines to be successively Secretary of War, President of the United States, and Chief Justice of the United States Supreme Court; Wright to be Ambassador to Japan and Secretary of War; Ide to be Minister to Spain: Smith to be Judge of the United States Court of Customs Appeals; Forbes, after a quiet interval, to be Ambassador to

---

[4] For the experiences of the wife of a Civil Governor, see Mrs. William Howard Taft, *Recollection of Full Years* (1915). For an authoritative Filipino estimate of the American Governors General, see Manuel Luis Quezon, *The Good Fight* (New York, 1946). For the impressions made by the Governors General on an American businessman of Manila, see Major Wm. H. Anderson, *The Philippine Problem*, Ch. IV (New York, 1939).

Japan; Harrison to become an adviser to the Presidents of the Philippine Commonwealth and Republic; Stimson to be Secretary of State and later to be recalled to active service as Secretary of War throughout World War II; Davis to support the war effort in responsible positions; Roosevelt to command combat teams in the North African, Sicily, and Italian campaigns, and finally, with the rank of Brigadier General, to lead the first assault wave in the invasion of Normandy, where he gave his life to his country; and Murphy to receive appointments as Attorney General and Justice of the Supreme Court of the United States.

Nor should one be too critical if a Governor General showed exaggerated deference to the Filipino leaders, for thereby a record of accomplishment was made and excellent publicity was obtained for American consumption. Indeed, American Governors General and Filipino leaders were literally forced into close cooperation. Forbes made the then Speaker of the Philippine Assembly, Sergio Osmeña, his confidant, and a warm friendship was fostered. Harrison frankly admitted that he owed his appointment to Manuel Quezon. Roosevelt greeted Quezon familiarly as "Manuel." Quezon in turn leaned heavily on the counsel of Justice Murphy.

Of the American Governors General, seven were Republicans and four Democrats, but two of the Democrats were named by Republican Presidents. In religion, nine of the Governors General were Protestants and two Catholics, but the two latter, Smith and Murphy, deeply resented any effort by Catholic elements to make use of a common religious belief to advance sectarian interests. The same ratio persisted in marital status, for nine were married (the courtly Harrison six times), and two, Forbes and Murphy, were eligible bachelors. In wealth, it could be said that only three Governors General—Forbes, Harrison, and Davis—were so fixed financially as to be lavish in their expenditures.

The average length of gubernatorial service was three years. Ide served the shortest period, barely five months, and Harrison the longest, over seven years. In contrast, Caesar was in Gaul eight years, Clive in India six years, Raffles in Malaya five years, while England kept Cromer in Egypt many years. The constant shifting of Spanish Governors General drew from Rizal a bitter complaint in his novel, *Noli Me Tangere*. A continuation of the same system in American times resulted in much loss of momentum and was detrimental to the service.

If one were to attempt pen-pictures, in large strokes, of the American Viceroys, the following might appear:

Taft was the constructive organizer of the civil government of the Philippines. He displayed courage—that rare quality in a public man—when, to advance the welfare of the Filipino people, he dared to antagonize American business interests in the Islands. He displayed the same consistent adherence to principle when he was content to see his popularity with the Filipinos wane by sharply advising them not to rush Philippine independence.

Wright, a former General of the Confederacy, swung to the other extreme from Taft by advocating an equal chance for all. His administration was pointed to as a model tested by colonial standards.

Ide was a good man who was not left in office long enough to display his talents.

Smith, a Colonel of California Volunteers, had an understanding of Filipino ways and gave the Islands a calm, uneventful administration.

Forbes, grandson of Ralph Waldo Emerson, was the Boston business man heeding the call of public service. He was known as "Caminero Forbes," a pun on his middle name and a testimonial to his fame as a road builder. As befitted his background and temperament, he concentrated on economic advancement, fostered it by various methods, and left the Islands with a splendid system of highways.

Harrison was a liberal who put into practise the doctrines of the Democratic Party by permitting the Filipino leaders to give a practical demonstration of their aptitude for self-government. In so doing he contributed to the policy which won for the United States the loyalty of the Filipino people. He combined the qualities of a gracious host and an administrator devoid of race prejudice.

Wood was the typical pro-consul. He was Cuba's liberator and had served many years in the Philippines while in the Army. As a consequence, he was thoroughly experienced in colonial administration. He brought the Philippines back to financial stability, recaptured the powers of his office, and laid down his life in harness, as he would have wished.

Stimson was a lawyer and public servant of the Elihu Root type, keen and analytical, who never left anyone in doubt as to his meaning or stand. He succeeded in persuading the Filipino leaders to call off their vendetta with the Governor General. He won the respect of those leaders as he did of the American people, for he was the great statesman of his generation.

Davis was known as the donor of the famous trophy in tennis that bears his name. He was also known as the gentleman personified, with a Mona Lisa smile. In addition to his support of athletics and his charm and amiability, he carried on the administration in a scrupulous manner and initiated a crusade against graft.

Roosevelt, son of the former President of the same name, exuded characteristic family energy. He brought to the office experience in a similar position in Puerto Rico. He travelled extensively over the Islands, displayed a genuine liking for the common *tao*, spoke to the people in Spanish or Tagalog, and organized Village Council Meetings. Prior to departure he was acclaimed "the most popular Governor General the Islands ever had."

Murphy came from the elective office of Mayor of Detroit to the appointive office of Governor General through a combination of fateful incidents: the death of Senator Thomas J. Walsh on the eve of induction as Attorney General and the shift of Homer Cummings from prospective Governor General to become Attorney General. Murphy made the financial stability of the government and social service the keynotes of his administration. Also, as the last Governor General, he implemented the policy of preparing the Philippines for self-government in a deliberate and conscientious manner.

The two administrations most debated and most in contrast were those of Governor General Harrison and Governor General Wood.

Harrison was at outs with most local Americans in the Philippines from the very start. To begin with, although this was without Harrison's knowledge, the following remarkable cable came from Washington:

Washington
August 23, 1913

FORBES, MANILA
Confidential. Harrison confirmed August 21st. The President desires him to sail September 10th. Will it be convenient to have your resignation accepted September 1st? Harrison to accept and take oath of office September 2nd. The President desires to meet your convenience. Should Harrison take linen, silver, glass, china, and automobiles? What else would you suggest? Wife and children will accompany him. Please engage for him servants you leave.

McIntyre.

Following this *faux pas*, the announcement was cabled from Japan that the new Governor General would appear at the ceremonies attendant on his arrival in a cutaway coat and top hat. Great was the consternation among Manila officials who hastily resurrected formal dress of ancient vintage from mothballs and funeral parlors. Anxiety was relieved when the reception committee dared to greet His Excellency attired in the plain white drill of the tropics.

On Harrison's arrival, the political guillotine was quickly put in commission, and official heads fell right and left. Undeterred by the cries of anguish or the obstacles put in his way, the Governor General steadfastly carried out his policy of turning over the administration of the Philippines to the Filipinos. Under such conditions it was to be expected that from Americans in the Islands Governor General Harrison would receive very little support. To the same extent he became a prime favorite with the Filipinos.

Harrison went out. The Wood-Forbes Mission composed of General Leonard Wood and former Governor General Forbes came in and reported to the President on Philippine conditions. General Wood remained as Governor General. First he straightened out the monetary problem of the Philippine Government. Next, and at frequent intervals, he visited all parts of the Archipelago. He labored earnestly to give the Islands a clean and efficient administration.

Then a member of the Secret Service of Manila by the name of Conley became involved in serious charges. Before the case was concluded, Secretary of the Interior Laurel asked for Conley's removal, but General Wood espoused the latter's cause. The Filipino members of the Council of State dramatically presented their resignations. They were immediately accepted by the Governor General. Later, the dispute reached a legal head in the Board of Control Cases which concerned the question of the authority, respectively, of the Governor General and of the President of the Senate and the Speaker of the House. The author was assigned to write the opinion of the Supreme Court of the Philippines. In view of the explicit wording of the Organic Act, the decision was in favor of the Governor General. The United States Supreme Court sustained the Philippine Supreme Court.[5]

All will now concede that Governor General Wood gave loyal and disinterested service to the Philippines. He deserved the tribute of Lord Cromer that he was the man best fitted to untangle the problems of a colony or possession.

A trait of the Filipinos generally recognized is that they yield their truest loyalty when there is at the head of affairs one man in supreme power. The Spaniards sensed this fact and accordingly gave to their Governors General practically all the influence and

---

[5] Springer v. Philippine Islands, 277 U. S. 189.

standing of the Spanish monarch. With the change of sovereignty, the office of Governor General remained, and the authority pertaining thereto was but slightly reduced. The Governor General fulfilled the popular conception of a Roman Pro-Consul or British Viceroy. The tendency persisted to the last to look upon the Governor General as possessing regal powers.

The Governor General received a salary of ₱36,000 ($18,000) a year payable from the Philippine treasury. In addition, Malacañan Palace in Manila and Mansion House in Baguio were set aside for his use. While these emoluments seemed attractive to Americans, in reality they were much less than what the British and Dutch allotted the Governors of their colonies. However, it was axiomatic that no Governor General of the Philippines ever left the office voluntarily unless to advance to a post of even greater allurement. The Chief Executive needed a cast-iron digestive apparatus capable of withstanding a banquet at any hour. He had to shoulder heavy responsibility. Yet Governors General have frankly admitted that the vice-royal privileges that were theirs were not unpleasant.[6]

Sic transit gloria mundi! The king is dead; long live the king! No longer is there an American Governor General in Malacañan Palace. Instead to the President of the Republic of the Philippines has gone the glory of high office and the burdens that formerly rested on American shoulders. May His Excellency, the President, prove as capable as His Excellency, the Governor General.

THE COLONIAL SERVICE

The United States has had no "Colonial Service" in the sense in which the Britons trained a Colonial Service of career men who administered the outposts of the Empire. Possibly this was because Americans generally rejected the use of the words "Colony" and "Colonial" as inconsistent with a policy that meant eventual independence for the Philippines, and independence, statehood, or dominion status for Puerto Rico. Possibly it was because "Colony" and "Colonial" conveyed the distasteful connotation of exploitation of a native population for the benefit of the home country. Whatever the basic reason, no effort was made to develop a permanent body of men and women for service in the American Dependencies.

The American policy, or shall we say lack of policy, in practice did not signify that American personnel was not provided to fill offices in the Philippines. For instance, teachers were contracted

6 Henry L. Stimson and McGeorge Bundy, *On Active Service In Peace and War,* p. 143 (New York, 1948).

in the United States for two year periods of Philippine service. Some merely fulfilled their contracts, while others remained in the Philippines for long periods of time. Selections of officials were, as a rule, little influenced by partisan politics.

Competent men were found to become Directors of Bureaus and to fill equally important posts. They became not mere "buck passing" bureaucrats but, as a body, constituted the backbone of an efficient administration. A number of bureau chiefs of this type who contributed largely to Philippine progress under American Governors General won the respect of the Filipinos to such degree that they were retained as advisers to Filipino Presidents. These experts included Dr. Luther B. Bewley, formerly Director of Education; Colonel Arthur F. Fischer, formerly Director of Forestry, who later was to make a conspicuous war record on Bataan and elsewhere; and Mr. A. D. Williams, formerly Director of Public Works.

From the earliest days the Governor General needed technical advisers in administering the Philippines. For a number of years he was able to obtain this help from American cabinet officers and special assistants. Governor General Forbes' fondness for polo and his importation of polo ponies and young Harvard graduates caused the public to speak of his closest confidants as the "Polo Cabinet." With the *Filipinizing* of the executive departments during the Harrison administration, it was thought imperative that there be suitable American advisers for the Governor General. The only available source of supply was the War Department, and so officers were detached from the Army to assist the Governor General. These men, mostly experts in Philippine affairs by virtue of years of experience, were termed the "Cavalry Cabinet" of Governor General Wood. The best known was General Frank R. McCoy who was genuinely liked by all classes in the Philippines.

A policy of this sort smacked too much, at least in name, of military government. At the behest of Governor General Stimson and with the cooperation of the Filipino leaders, legislation was railroaded through the Philippine Legislature that alloted the Governor General the sum of ₱250,000 annually to be expended according to his best judgment in the employment of American assistants.

Thereafter the coterie of advisers of the Governor General were colloquially and irreverently spoken of as "Belo Boys." The first word was acquired from Senator Antonio Belo, who won undying fame by introducing the bill which provided funds for the payment of a secretarial and technical staff for the Governor General. The second word was coined by someone with a sense of sardonic humor, to typify the messenger-like services occasionally required of those in the inner circle about the Chief Executive.

As a matter of strict truth, the members of the "Polo Cabinet" of Forbes and the "Cavalry Cabinet" of Wood, and the "Belo Boys" of Stimson, Davis, Roosevelt, and Murphy were the eyes, ears, and even the noses of their chiefs. To their credit be it added that while ferreting and smelling out information, they did so in such a discreet way that no friction resulted with Filipino officials. These fine American gentlemen—men of the stature of General Blanton Winship, later to become Governor of Puerto Rico, and Attorney Edward G. Kemp, the right hand man of Governor General Murphy—while possessed of "a passion for anonymity" that thrust their superior alone into the spotlight, gave full measure of loyal and intelligent service.

CARPENTER AND HAYDEN

Two officials, typical of the able American administrators, who did as much for the Philippines as any Governor General, were Frank W. Carpenter and Joseph Ralston Hayden. The author was privileged to know them both. When as a needy young University of Michigan graduate, he favored Manila with his unobtrusive presence, Carpenter was the one person to extend a helping hand. This he did by foisting inexperience on to Dr. Victor G. Heiser, Director of Health, in the role of an inefficient voucher clerk. Because of connections in Michigan and the Philippines, Hayden and the author became intimate associates and friends.

If one could take the time to write the biographies of Carpenter and Hayden from beginning to end, the output would be the story of the entire period of the American administration of the Philippines. Carpenter's association with the Philippines began with the Spanish American War in 1898 and continued through the formative period. Hayden became interested in the Philippines about the time that Carpenter left the scene, and his contact with Philippine affairs was only severed by death just as World War II was concluding.

Both of these representative Americans loyally adhered to the basic American policy that was laid down in the Instructions of the President to the Second Philippine Commission. They did indeed "bear in mind" that the government being established was designed "for the happiness, peace, and prosperity of the people of the Philippines" and that "the measures adopted should be made to conform to their customs, their habits, and even their prejudices." That was why Carpenter and Hayden gained the esteem of Americans and Filipinos alike.

In other respects, too, the lives of Carpenter and Hayden were similar. Carpenter was a soldier in the Spanish-American War; Hayden an officer in the first World War. Carpenter, although without benefit of college training, conducted the research for former Governor General Forbes' standard work, *The Philippine Islands;* Hayden, University-educated and an occupant of professorial posts, was the scholar who built his own monument by the production of *The Philippines, A Study in National Development.* Carpenter and Hayden included in their assets engaging personalities that made friends easily.

Frank W. Carpenter came out to the Philippines with General Lawton in the days of the empire. Not long after, he became private secretary to the Military Governor. After the organization of civil government, he was appointed Assistant Executive Secretary. On the death of Executive Secretary Arthur W. Fergusson, Carpenter succeeded him in that office.

In those days the Executive Bureau exercised a power that one unfamiliar with the administrative structure can hardly appreciate. It operated as the clearing house for the entire Philippine Government; it exercised close supervision over provincial and municipal governments; it maintained relations with foreign representatives; it kept an eye on insular and local finances; it prepared the budget; and it acted as an outer office for the Governor General. To these important and multifarious duties Carpenter brought marked ability, a proficiency in languages, and an industry that knew no office hours. Carpenter was the *alter ego* of various Governors General and by his tact bridged many a painful breach.

Carpenter was a familiar figure in Manila. Ordinarily he was dressed in white, his high-collared coat opened at the throat, a cheap straw hat resting obliquely and jauntily on his head. His one dissipation was indulging in innumerable cigarettes. He shunned formal society, but every afternoon found him at the round table at Clarke's Restaurant where gathered Manila's men-about-town. Then back to his office he went to receive the endless stream of callers of all classes with whom he was able to converse interchangeably in English, Spanish, or Tagalog.

In 1913 General Pershing was superseded as Governor of Mindanao and Sulu by Carpenter, who became the first civilian Governor of the newly created Department of Mindanao and Sulu. To his new work Governor Carpenter brought a natural aptitude for administration which he used to good purpose. He inaugurated a policy of attraction, which meant in practice leaving the Moros to their own devices as to customs and religious beliefs, but otherwise governing

them with a firm hand. It has been said of Carpenter's work in Moroland that what had not been attained by hundreds of years of warfare
he accomplished in a few years by wise administration. In a short
time, Carpenter brought the Moros and the Filipinos amicably together and substituted order and trust for bloodshed and suspicion.
No other official was ever so successful in handling the Moros as
was Frank W. Carpenter.

That Carpenter had won the esteem of the Filipinos was shown
when the Philippine Legislature granted him special remuneration
"in recognition of the outstanding services rendered by him to the
Government of the Philippine Islands." That gratuity, along with
his health, was lost in an unfortunate business venture. Righting himself, he became associated with W. Cameron Forbes, his former Chief.
Carpenter died in retirement at Salem, Massachusetts in 1945.

Joseph Ralston Hayden[7] was the last of a long line of Michigan
men, either graduates of the State University or members of its faculty, who left their imprint on the Philippines. Dean C. Worcester,
Secretary of Interior in the Philippine Government; E. Finley Johnson, a Justice of the Supreme Court; Dr. Paul Freer, Director of
Science; Frank Murphy, Governor General and United States High
Commissioner—the list could be extended indefinitely—all contributed
to making the American experiment in colonial government the success that it was in the Philippines. To this roll of honor can be
added the name of Dr. Hayden, fittingly termed the "scholar in
government."

Joseph Ralston Hayden was born in Quincy, Illinois on September 24, 1887. Upon graduation from Knox College in 1910, he accepted an offer to join the faculty of the University of Michigan.
Except for the years spent in the Navy during World War I, and
later in the Philippines, Hayden was continuously associated with
the University until his death. He was made Chairman of the Department of Political Science of the University in 1937, and four
years later was named James Orin Murfin Professor of Political
Science.

Hayden first visited the Philippines in 1922 as an exchange Professor to the University of the Philippines. In 1926 he returned in the
capacity of adviser to Colonel Carmi A. Thompson, who had been
named by President Coolidge to make a survey of conditions in the
Islands. In 1930-31 Hayden was once more a visiting Professor. A

---

[7] Biographical data on the life of Dr. Hayden was taken from the excellent article
entitled "Joseph Ralston Hayden: Scholar in Government," by Edward W. Mill,
which appeared in the *Michigan Alumnus* of May 8, 1948.

background of Philippine experience made logical his appointment in November, 1933 as Vice Governor and Secretary of Public Instruction in the Philippine Government. He remained as Vice Governor until the inauguration of the Commonwealth of the Philippines two years later.

Dr. Hayden's return to the peaceful life of a university professor was interrupted once more with the outbreak of World War II. Again it was the Philippines calling. After serving for some time with the Offices of Coordination of Information and Strategic Services, he became adviser on Philippine Affairs to General MacArthur. Hayden perfected the plans for the administration of civil affairs in the Philippines. With liberation of the Philippines under way, he continued to serve President Osmeña in an advisory capacity. It was while on a special mission to Washington in 1945 that the war's ordeal took its toll in his collapse.

The close association of Dr. Hayden with the Philippines and the varied nature of his experiences were put to good account by him in two major contributions to literature.

No two men were more unlike than Dean C. Worcester and Joseph Ralston Hayden. Where Worcester was brusque, Hayden was tactful. Where Worcester rubbed the Filipinos the wrong way, Hayden was accepted as an understanding friend. Yet it was Hayden who brought out in 1930 a revision of Worcester's book, *The Philippines: Past and Present*.

Scholarship at its best was displayed in Dr. Hayden's work, *The Philippines, A Study in National Development*. It is a completely documented book. It is marked by discriminating fairness, restraint and understanding. In effect, Dr. Hayden has written a convincing brief in support of his country's case in applying sound, if historically different, principles to the government of the Philippine possession.

Frank W. Carpenter and Joseph Ralston Hayden had served their country well, and in so doing had become the bearers to the Philippines of "the richest blessings of a liberating rather than a conquering nation." They were content with the credit which goes with tasks well done.

The American Record in the Philippines

We may be too close to passing events to form a just estimate of the defects and merits of the American administration of the Philippines. Further, the author may be prejudiced in favor of a government of which he was a part for over thirty years, and may be inclined to look with too kindly an eye on errors of omission or commission.

So for the benefit of some future historian, an attempt will only be made to provide a rough inventory of the bad and good points of the American-administered government.

Tested by the colonial standards of other governments, the United States failed miserably in her Philippine adventure. In 1898 the United States was afforded an opportunity to give the Islands a good government, to develop their resources, and to eschew politics. Instead, ranking American officials encouraged the Filipinos to expect ultimate independence, gradually shifted control from American hands into Filipino hands, and partially neglected economic development. The only adequate answer to criticism of this sort is to reiterate the platitude that the United States saw fit to set up a new ethical standard in dealing with a dependent people and to guide that people along the path to self-sufficiency.

As was to be expected, there were a few dark spots on the American record in the Philippines. Some things were done which might better have been left undone. Other things were neglected. Errors of judgment expensive to the taxpayers were committed. Injustices and wrongs were occasionally perpetrated. All this is undeniable.

Along with the good in American life, the bad was propagated in the Philippines. The standard of living was raised, but with it went extravagance not at all in accord with income. Luxury instead of self-denial was tacitly sanctioned. Too frank an imitation of American customs caused a loosening of the Filipino moral code. Jazz and hot spot music usurped the place of native music and dances; cheap literature flooded the news stands to the exclusion of serious books; girls forsook traditional chaperonage to seek lax pleasures. These are a few of the things that have corrupted Philippine life and for which partial blame must be laid at America's door. Fortunately these ephemeral expressions of present day tendencies are not impossible to eradicate.

A government may be one of laws, but it has to be administered by men. In the early days of the Philippines and occasionally in later days, the public servants were not always honest. Some occupying positions of trust had to be prosecuted criminally. That was to be expected when untried men were put in offices of responsibility and weakly yielded to temptation. Except for these isolated exceptions, the Americans in the service of the Philippine Government were high-grade men and women, inspired by pioneer motives. They were far above the personnel of the State governments in character, ideals and efficiency.

What America did in the Philippines is an open book which all may read. American accomplishments are so numerous as to defy exact enumeration. With apologies for necessary omissions, there is written down on the credit side a few of the most notable triumphs of the government.

It is puzzling to know exactly where to begin. Possibly education would be as proper a topic as any, for whatever else the American does, he invariably feels that it is necessary to afford an opportunity for instruction to all. An educational system was established which furnished Filipino children with the chance to obtain a schooling. This was one of the most important and permanent American legacies to the Filipino people. The improvement of health and sanitation is another typical American policy. Health and quarantine services were established; smallpox and cholera were stamped out; the lepers were isolated and cared for; and the insane were afforded considerate treatment. Pages could be written in laudatory terms based on the facts that are here mentioned.

Passing on to equally important matters, the islands were given a sound and convenient currency to replace the fluctuating medium which had made a gamble of business operations. A civil service free from politics and broader in scope than the American civil service was established. An admirable state of public order was brought about, and brigandage and lawlessness were suppressed. To accomplish this, a native constabulary was trained which succeeded in an excellent manner in policing the Islands. The legal system was reformed, procedure was simplified, and an independent judiciary was provided in which the people could have confidence. The uncertainty with reference to land titles was eradicated by adopting the Torrens land-registration system.

Politically, the people were afforded an opportunity to receive training in a system of popular government. Economically, America contributed largely to progress in the Philippines, particularly by throwing open the American market to Philippine exports.

One could go on indefinitely naming and analyzing American contributions to Philippine progress. With reference to this progress, every American official would, of course, generously concede that it could not have been obtained without Filipino cooperation. Had the Filipino leaders balked, little could have been done for their people. It was by combined American incentive and Filipino backing that so much was accomplished for the good of the Islands within a comparatively short span of years.

American actions in the Philippines during the Commonwealth

period when much of their authority was abdicated in favor of Filipino responsibility did no harm to the record previously made. Even American mistakes and delays in the post-war period have not permanently undermined the prestige of the United States in the Philippines.

The American and the Filipino have been associated as partners for half a century. That is a brief period as time is counted in universal history. Yet no one can review the achievements of America's stay in the Philippines without granting it to be a signal triumph over unusual difficulties. The American regime was immeasurably the best government that the Philippines has ever known.

Results in the Philippines will appear more clearly if contrasted with results elsewhere, for example in Puerto Rico. It will be recalled that by the treaty of peace that concluded the Spanish-American War, Spain ceded these two possessions to the United States.

American policy towards the Philippines—after that phrase can be written the one word "Success." American policy towards Puerto Rico—after that phrase can be written the two words "Partial Failure." That is the definite conclusion of the author, one of the few privileged to serve the United States in both the Philippines and Puerto Rico. Naturally it is a conclusion with provisos and explanations.

American policy towards the Philippines—Success. American policy towards Puerto Rico—Partial Failure. Why?

Firstly, the United States had for the Philippines a policy of eventual independence. A promise to withdraw American sovereignty from the Islands was made and was kept. In contrast, the United States has had no Puerto Rican Policy. A half century after the acquisition of Puerto Rico, the United States has not selected a goal towards which a policy could be shaped, whether statehood, independence, or some kind of dominion status.

Secondly, the United States chose outstanding Americans for the Office of Governor General of the Philippine Islands. Puerto Rico has had but few distinguished Governors. Only in 1948 were the Puerto Ricans permitted to elect a Governor, which they did by choosing popular, brilliant Luis Munoz Marin.

Thirdly, the Philippines was fortunate in being located thousands of miles from Washington. The Governors General were left free to administer the Islands in their own way. Puerto Rico was unfortunate in being situated all too close to the national capitol. The result for Puerto Rico was that Federal higher-ups inflicted their opinions on the Island's Governor on the slightest provocation, and that the Puerto Ricans learned to lay their complaints, big and little, before Washington bureaucrats.

Fourthly, the Filipinos were educated in the ways of democracy. They responded by the adoption of a Constitution that set up a Republican state. The Puerto Ricans were also democratically trained, but it was not until 1950 that they were accorded an opportunity to frame an organic law.

Fifthly, both the Filipinos and the Puerto Ricans have moved far along the path toward state socialism. The Filipinos are free to nationalize as much as they please. The Puerto Ricans are American citizens and form a part of the United States. A special committee of the House of Representatives of the United States Congress headed by Judge C. Jasper Bell, after conducting a study of political, economic and social conditions in Puerto Rico reported in 1945 as follows: "It requires only a brief and cursory study of the pattern created by this new control through authorities and governmental agencies to understand that it is quite comparable to the pattern used by the Fascists in Italy to control every avenue of business life. . . . The trend of government in Puerto Rico is very obviously headed toward total state control."[8] The "trend" last emphasized was halted by elective Governor Munoz Marin by the simple method of offering to free enterprise opportunities for investment. A tax holiday for new industries up to June 30, 1959 was the lure to business.[9] At last a long range policy, leading to economic self-sufficiency and full self-government under a locally drafted constitution, was taking form in Puerto Rico.

The record that the United States made in the Philippines can, however, best be evaluated by placing it alongside of past and contemporary governments in the Far East. By comparison with the condition of the Filipinos at the end of Spanish rule, the progress that had been made was phenomenal. By comparison with the administration of the Dutch in the Netherlands Indies, the French in Indo-China, and the English in India, Burma, and Malaya, the United States had set a pattern for self-government in the Philippines for the other powers to copy. And by comparison with the

---

[8] Report of the Committee on Insular Affairs, House of Representatives, of May 1, 1945; Judge Welburn Mayock in an independent survey; Emmet Crozier in an article in the *New York Herald Tribune* in 1945, reprinted in *Readers Digest.*

[9] Lloyd Stouffer, "Puerto Rico Fights Back," *Future*, January, 1949, reprinted in *Readers Digest;* William A. Krauss, "Opportunity in Puerto Rico," *Rotarian*, September, 1949. Note Vincenzo Petrullo, *Puerto Rican Paradox* (University of Pennsylvania Press, 1947).

current state of other nations in the Orient, the Philippines counts many blessings for which the United States can be thanked.

The United States had greatly benefited the Filipino people politically, economically and culturally. They had been prepared for nationhood.[10]

---

[10] Representative authorities reinforcing conclusion include: Theodore Roosevelt, *Colonial Policies of the United States*, p. 29; Joseph Ralston Hayden, *The Philippines, A Study in National Development*, concluding paragraph, pp. 804, 805 (New York, 1942); and Frank Murphy, *Last Message of the Last Governor General of the Philippine Islands*, November 14, 1935, a factual review of American achievements and Philippine progress.

General Emilio Aguinaldo, as President of the short lived "Philippine Republic."

CHAPTER VI

PHILIPPINE NATIONALISM

DEVELOPMENT

At the time of the conquest of the Philippines by the Spaniards, the people had no common government, religion or language. Racial consciousness had not asserted itself. National solidarity was lacking. Even for centuries after the Spaniards arrived, bringing with them their religion, language and culture, any betterment that occurred in the Philippines was individualistic and not nationalistic in nature. The individual might improve his own condition, but was not acquainted with the people residing beyond the confines of his hamlet and might even be on unfriendly terms with them. It was not until the opening of the nineteenth century that changes took place in the relations of the Filipinos with each other and in their outlook on life.

As the system imposed by Spain altered gradually the life of the people, so did it likewise cause grievances. The enlarged commercial contact with the outer world, the construction of the Suez Canal, and the increasing number of Filipino youths who secured educations in Europe apprized the few of their nationality, and they in turn enlightened their less fortunate countrymen. The liberal tendencies of the nineteenth century were reflected in the Philippines. In the late eighties and early nineties of that century a number of young men, among whom Dr. Jose Rizal and Marcelo H. del Pilar were the leading spirits, organized the Filipinos residing in Europe. Rizal with almost divine vision was inspired to write his crusading novels depicting the social cancer in the Philippines.

La Liga Filipina ("The Filipino League"), founded by Rizal in 1892, developed the patriotic spirit of the Filipinos and encouraged petitions for governmental changes. The reforms desired beat against the inertia of Spanish officialdom, only to be thrown back and to lead the petitioners to espouse more drastic measures. The *Katipunan*, organized by Andres Bonifacio and other patriots with more radical purposes including secession from Spain, succeeded the Filipino League. Revolts unified the people by giving them a common purpose, and provided leaders to extend the movement.

Too late Spain dimly realized her mistake in denying justice to the Filipino people. The Maura Law, taking its name from the Spanish minister of the colonies, was provided to liberalize municipal government in the Philippines, but was never made effective. Again during Spain's declining years in the Philippines, a Consultative Assembly was decreed, but this attempted reform likewise came too tardily to serve any purpose. The only effect of these belated measures was to solidify Filipino opinion and to accentuate the vacillating and compromising attitude of the Spanish officials.

After American occupation, Filipino aspirations originally met with disappointment. However, education of the masses was begun and proved to be a prime factor in moulding nationalism. Every teacher automatically became an apostle of independence when he taught the stories of American history. What school-child could read of Patrick Henry and his "Give me liberty or give me death," and of Washington, the father of his country, and not apply the lessons to Philippine conditions? With the inauguration of the Philippine Assembly in 1907, Filipino unity was effectively achieved and has been militantly aggressive ever since.

DR. JOSE RIZAL[1]

No account of the Philippines, whether of Philippine nationalism or Philippine culture, would be complete without special mention of the life of Dr. Jose Rizal. A product of his times and of his exceptional opportunities, Rizal has been canonized by the Filipinos as their national hero. As will presently appear, Rizal was in many respects worthy of the adulation of his people.

Jose Rizal-Mercado y Alonso, known throughout his life as Jose Rizal, was of Malay extraction with strains of Chinese and Spanish blood. He was born in Calamba, Laguna, on June 19, 1861, the son of common people who were tenants on the Friar Lands Estate. His education was obtained in the Ateneo de Manila of the Jesuits and the University of Santo Tomas of the Dominicans, with postgraduate work in Europe. In his youth he was influenced by two books by foreign authors: Jagor, *Travels in the Philippines*, and Morga, *Sucesos de las Filipinas* ("Events in the Philippines"). His admiration for

---

[1] This section was originally read by Dr. Austin Craig, outstanding Philippine historian. See Austin Craig, *Rizal's Life and Minor Writings* (1927); W. E. Retana, *Vida y Escritos del Dr. Jose Rizal* (Madrid, 1907); Camilo Osias, *Jose Rizal: His Life and Times* (1948); Rafael Palma, *The Pride of the Malay Race*, a biography of Rizal translated from the Spanish by Justice Roman Ozaeta (1949); and Jose Batungbacal, *The Mistrial of Dr. Jose Rizal* (1949).

the latter caused him to spend some time editing the work, with notes intended to show that the Filipinos had been possessed of considerable culture before the Spanish conquest. While in Europe he prepared and published the novels *"Noli Me Tangere"* ("The Social Cancer") and *"El Filibusterismo"* ("The Reign of Greed"), and other works. Returning to the Philippines, he inspired the formation of the Filipino League, which had the peaceful purpose of obtaining governmental reforms and economic improvement.

The foregoing biographical data fail to bring forth the dramatic incidents in Rizal's life. To comprehend his place in history, one has to form a picture of the Philippines in the eighteen nineties under absolute Spanish domination. In such a setting it was treasonable for any Filipino publicly to criticize officialdom for allowing an oppressive administration to continue, and far more was it treasonable even to hint at a desire to see his country free. A Spanish Governor General was accordingly only too ready to consider suspicions as proven facts.

Rizal was arrested and banished to Dapitan in the Southern Philippines, although later he was permitted to sail for Spain. A pretext for again arresting him was found, and he was returned to Manila to stand trial before a military court. The charge laid against him was the formation of an illegal society, the Filipino League, and being responsible because of his writings for the existing rebellion. No trained lawyer was there to defend him, and he was already convicted before trial. The tribunal imposed the death sentence.

The date was December 30, 1896. In the early morning, as the dawn was breaking out of the horizon, Rizal made the journey on foot from Fort Santiago to the place of execution, the Bagumbayan field, now called the Luneta. His arms were tied tightly behind his back and he was surrounded by guards. A gay crowd of Spanish Army officers and civilians and their womenfolk awaited him. Rizal asked to be allowed to face the firing squad, but the request was refused. With a normal pulse, which drew forth an involuntary expression of admiration from the attending military surgeon, he stood there alone, not blind-folded, and was able to work one hand sufficiently free from his bonds to indicate the place at which the soldiers should fire. The captain of the guard gave the signal. A volley rang out. With a last tremendous effort of will Rizal turned so as to fall with his face upward. The body was removed in a hospital dead-wagon to Paco Cemetery.

In 1912, with solemn ceremonies, the remains were honorably and reverently deposited in the mausoleum specially erected for the purpose on the Luneta, close to the spot where Rizal had given his life for his country. On the monument was engraved this inscription: "To the memory of Jose Rizal, patriot and martyr, executed on Bagumbayan field December 30, 1896, this monument is dedicated by the people of the Philippines."

Rizal was a conspicuous figure in many fields. His versatility was almost incredible. He was at home in a score of languages, and used at least five of them effectively: English for travel, French for *belles lettres*, German for science, Spanish for politics, and Tagalog for the vernacular. He was a doctor of medicine, an ethnologist, a naturalist, an artist, a sculptor, a novelist, and a poet. Rizal's two novels, *Noli Me Tangere* and *El Filibusterismo*, were instructive political sermons, written to expose the sufferings of the Filipino people to the end that generous souls might counsel and apply the proper remedies. They were intended to be exact mirrors of Philippine life.

Some nights before the day of execution, in his cell by the light of a little alcohol lamp, Rizal had written his final message to his family and country. That poem was the beautiful and tender elegy entitled *"Mi Ultimo Adios"* ("My Last Farewell"). It has become the national classic of the Philippines.

The memory of Rizal is kept alive in the Philippines in many ways. The anniversary of his death is a public holiday. Throughout the country there is scarcely a town without a statue or bust of Rizal. A province bordering on Manila was created to bear his name. Rizal's home in Calamba has been restored, and his home in exile in Dapitan has been made a national park. The Filipino people feel that by honoring the name of Rizal they pay tribute to their heritage.

REVOLTS

Many revolts featured the Spanish rule. A few were serious enough to leave enduring records. For instance, in 1872 Fathers Gomez, Burgos, and Zamora were garroted for supposedly seditious activities. Nevertheless, until 1896 Filipino uprisings were local in nature. But in that year the peaceful campaign for a more liberal government suddenly shifted to a bloody war to secure independence for the Philippines. Rizal bravely faced a firing squad and became the national hero. About the same time the *Katipunan* started a widespread revolt among the masses. General Emilio Aguinaldo, who had become the Filipino leader, proclaimed independence as his purpose. After being temporarily checked by the Pact of Biak-na-bato, which was an agreement for a truce between the Spanish Governor General and General Aguinaldo, revolt broke out anew in the Philippines.

Unfortunate misunderstandings of the Filipinos and Americans brought about three years of struggle between their forces. In March, 1901, General Aguinaldo was captured by Funston and his Macabebe scouts. Soon after, Aguinaldo took the oath of allegiance to the United States and issued a proclamation to the Filipino people in favor of peace. Still the insurgents carried on for a year longer. Then General Miguel Malvar, signing as commander-in-chief and supreme head of the Filipino Government, issued a manifesto in which he made known to all concerned that the war carried on against the authority of the United States by the Filipino people had ended. On July 4, 1902, amnesty was proclaimed by President Theodore Roosevelt and the military regime was terminated.

Even such a serious matter as an insurrection against Spain had its ludicrous side. Pedro A. Paterno acted as the peacemaker between the Filipino rebels and the Spanish officials. He was a man of ability through which, unfortunately, radiated overly-developed egotism. Don Pedro was sorely disappointed when, in his opinion, the Spanish Government failed to remunerate him for his valuable services. Very modestly he addressed a letter to a high authority which concluded: "For family reasons, I want a title of Castille, that of Prince or Duke, if possible, and to be a Grandee of the first class, free of nobility patent fees and the sum of . . . once for all."

The Philippine insurrection against the United States furnished an example of patriotism carried to the extreme in General Artemio Ricarte, an unreconstructed Filipino. During the war Ricarte had assumed the title of "The Viper." He was captured by the Americans, and when he refused to take the oath of allegiance was deported to Guam. When it was decided to release the political prisoners, Ricarte was brought back to Manila. When he still refused to acknowledge American sovereignty, he was again deported. For years General Ricarte with his family resided in Japan, stubbornly adhering to his original attitude of non-comformity to the established regime. The aged general finally returned to his native land with the Japanese invaders.

The Filipinos in their revolts against Spain and the United States proved their mettle as brave fighters. The Spanish forces were practically eliminated from the Philippines. Against the Americans the Filipinos fought valiantly, as veterans of the Spanish-American War have repeatedly and generously testified. But as General Aguinaldo said when he laid down his arms, the Filipinos found their advance along the path of their aspirations for freedom impeded by an irresistible force. Wisely, therefore, the Filipino leaders sought to obtain by peaceful methods what could never have been obtained by force, and won in this game by adroit and skillful moves.

The Ephemeral Philippine Republic[2]

Due to the collapse of the insurrection of 1896-1902, the "Philippine Republic" of that period was little more than a name. It was notable only because it afforded an opportunity for the display of forceful leadership, promulgated valuable state papers, and consolidated individual Filipinos into a nation with a common ideal—the independence of their country.

Soon after General Aguinaldo returned to the Philippines from Hongkong to take up the fight against the Spaniards, he proclaimed a dictatorial government. Within a month, that is, on June 23, 1898, he changed from a dictatorship to a revolutionary government. In turn, the revolutionary government evolved into the "Philippine Republic." The pressure of the American forces permitted of little concrete accomplishment by the short-lived republic.

General Aguinaldo, it should be stated, was the Captain General of the Filipino forces, the supreme head of the dictatorial government, and the President of the "Philippine Republic." He performed his duties with the assistance of army officers and a civilian cabinet. The capitol of the revolutionary government was at Malolos, Bulacan. There a Congress assembled and drafted what is known as the Malolos Constitution for the "Philippine Republic."

The character of the "Philippine Republic" has been much debated. On the one hand, various gratuitous epithets were used to delineate the revolutionary government as "a bouffe government," "a tinhorn government," "the paper government of the Filipinos." On the other extreme were those who wildly exaggerated Filipino capacity during this period in order to substantiate present capacity. To them it would seem that the only Republic in Asia, set up by the only Christian people in the Far East, was crushed—a genuine government of promise extinguished.

Judicially weighing the facts, only a few deductions capable of being substantiated are possible. In the first place, the Filipino Government was principally a Tagalog enterprise; nevertheless it was recognized in other portions of the Archipelago. In the second

---

[2] See Emilio Aguinaldo, *Riseña Veridica de la Revolucion Filipina* ("True Version of the Philippine Revolution") (Manila, 1899); and Apolinario Mabini, *La Revolucion Filipina* ("The Philippine Revolution") (Manila, 1902).

place, from the standpoint of international law, the Filipino Government was of the class known as "*de facto* government," And, in the third place, the "Philippine Republic" during the short time it existed gave indications of an earnest desire to furnish a government for the people fitted to their needs and progressively beneficial. However, it was only in the Malolos Congress that the ablest Filipinos were afforded an opportunity to make use of their talents, and this they did, according to observers, with great decorum and display of parliamentary law.

The ephemeral "Philippine Republic" has been too long dead to be resuscitated. It now serves simply as a lesson in patriotism. The real Philippine Republic has been forced to lay down its foundations anew.

General Emilio Aguinaldo

Aguinaldo is a name written large on the pages of American-Philippine history. Successively he has been foe and friend of the United States, and in the latter case, if not an actual foe, at least a doubtful friend.

Emilio Aguinaldo was born March 22, 1869, in Kawit, Cavite of well-to-do parents. From his mother he derived a strain of Chinese blood. At an early age his education was interrupted by the death of his father. Returning to Kawit, the boy took up farming and business. Hardly was he of age before he became the *Capitan Municipal* of his home town. About the same time, young Aguinaldo joined the *Katipunan*, and though relatively an obscure member rose rapidly to prominence because of his successes in the field. At an assembly of high officials and other citizens who took part in the Revolution in 1896, at which Aguinaldo was not present, he was elected President, thereby defeating Andres Bonifacio. At this time, it should be recalled, Aguinaldo was barely twenty-eight years of age.

General Aguinaldo caused the Spaniards so much trouble that they were glad to make peace with him, which they did by signing the Pact of Biak-na-bato. Thereafter Admiral Dewey brought Aguinaldo from Hongkong to Manila and sanctioned his cooperation with the American forces. After the split between the Americans and the Filipinos, resulting in sanguinary battles in which the Filipinos were defeated, and after Aguinaldo's capture, the latter issued a proclamation inviting his countrymen to lay down their arms. His dignity of manner and his attractive personality under trying circumstances made a favorable impression on all who came in contact with him.

On two occasions as leader of revolts against Spain and subsequently against the United States, Aguinaldo took effective measures to maintain his position. In the case of Andres Bonifacio who had been defeated for the presidency of the Filipino government, the death penalty imposed by a military court could be justified by military expediency. The mysterious death of General Antonio Luna, admittedly the skilled strategist of the Filipino forces, occurred at the hands of Aguinaldo's own bodyguard. The veil of charity will have to be drawn over these tragedies—the byproducts of war and of a desire to maintain a unified front against the enemy.

Followed the days of peace. General Aguinaldo was content with the life of a farmer. Aside from his private business, his activities centered on the Filipino Veterans Association, of which he was the President. Only once in this period was the General drawn into the spotlight, and this was when he sided with Governor General Wood in the latter's dispute with Senate President Quezon.

During all the years in which the American administration was in control, Aguinaldo consistently shunned public office. But when the time came to elect the first President of the Commonwealth of the Philippines, he apparently felt that as the former President of the "Philippine Republic" the right to head an autonomous Filipino regime was his due. Aguinaldo, on entering the political arena, had to contest for the presidency with Senate President Quezon. It was an unequal battle: on one side Aguinaldo, an ineffective public speaker, inexperienced in the ways of politics, and without an organization; on the other side Quezon, a gifted orator who did not need to campaign, a master politician backed by a coalition of the two principal parties. Aguinaldo went down to defeat.

Aguinaldo proved himself a poor loser. Even revolt was threatened. Apparently his dislike of Quezon, who had been a young officer on his staff, for the latter's temerity in claiming an office that Aguinaldo believed should be his by right, was ineradicable. Ten years later, however, Aguinaldo chivalrously supported President-elect Roxas.

In contrast to this unfortunate excursion into politics, Aguinaldo's gameness won him the admiration of countless Americans—at least it had until World War II. He had fought bravely against great odds. Following capture his bearing was manly. In those days it was a pleasing sight to see General Aguinaldo foregather with American veterans of the Spanish-American War and the Philippine Insurrection.

General Aguinaldo's home has remained in Kawit, Cavite. That is a small town midway between the Cities of Manila and Cavite on

Manila Bay. Historic memories cluster about the Aguinaldo residence. In that building more than any other was Philippine independence formed. Even the walls furnish mute evidence of the struggles against the Spaniards and the Americans. General Aguinaldo's home has not alone been a Mecca for Filipinos, but to it have been attracted many Americans and foreigners. His wife, Mrs. Maria Agoncillo Aguinaldo, and his daughters, Mrs. Carmen Aguinaldo Melencio and Mrs. Cristina Aguinaldo Suntay, have proved charming hostesses to a long list of notable callers. Every Governor General and every Commanding General of the United States Army in the Philippines has been a guest of General Aguinaldo and has considered it a rare privilege to be thus honored.

Now comes a disagreeable duty for the author, by custom a member of the Aguinaldo family in his capacity of godfather to General Aguinaldo's grandchild Ameurfina. But the narrative must be completed.

During the early and tragic weeks of World War II, Aguinaldo hailed the promise of "prompt independence with honor" made by Prime Minister Tojo before the Japanese Diet, and invited his countrymen to lend "whole-hearted cooperation to Japan." A few days later he broadcast a plea to MacArthur on Corregidor, advising surrender to the Japanese.[3] Whether these speeches were made voluntarily or under duress is a moot question. At least when MacArthur returned in triumph to the Philippines, and Aguinaldo presented himself for confinement, the latter was told to return to his home. Subsequently Aguinaldo was indicted along with other prominent Filipinos and charged with collaboration. President Roxas' amnesty proclamation wiped the slate clean. The question of whether Aguinaldo did indeed violate the oath of allegiance to the United States which he had taken years before under dramatic circumstances remains.

Of Aguinaldo's place in history this can be said. As leader of the Filipino revolution, he was no mere figurehead. He represented cohesion and unity at a time when these qualities were sadly lacking among the Filipinos. He proved himself genuinely honest and sincere, for he carefully conserved the money paid him by the Spaniards to gain a truce, and kept it as a trust fund to finance a new revolt.

[3] General Aguinaldo's statement urging the people to lend wholehearted cooperation to Japan appeared the *The Tribune*, a publication of Manila then controlled by the Japanese Army of Occupation in the Philippines, on January 24, 1942. General Aguinaldo's broadcast to General MacArthur on Corregidor was published by the same newspaper on February 2, 1942.

It was no small thing for a young man, with scant education, living in a provincial town, in the face of every disadvantage, to weld together a people who had never been unified, and to maintain himself as the acknowledged leader of a popular uprising which when unsuccessful is stigmatized as an insurrection, but which when successful bears the honored title of a revolution.

NATIONALIST LEADERS

It was previously remarked that seven or eight men charted the Philippine policy of the United States. A similar observation holds good with reference to the development of Philippine nationalism. In addition, by coincidence or otherwise, it is worthy of note that leaders of Philippine thought appeared on the scene by pairs. Marcelo H. del Pilar and Jose Rizal, Andres Bonifacio and Emilio Aguinaldo, Sergio Osmeña and Manuel Quezon, Manuel Roxas and with him possibly some present day leader—to these seven men goes the chief credit for the progress made in the forward march to the attainment of the independence of their country.

As powerful personalities ever will, the Filipino leaders had their differences and misunderstandings. Del Pilar and Rizal, members of a brilliant group of youthful Filipinos, worked together in Europe for Philippine benefits only later to go their separate ways. Contemporaries of the two considered del Pilar the more intelligent leader, the soul of the separatist movement, and the real founder of Philippine nationalism. Yet though Rizal was moderate in his political views and never advocated armed revolt, his death more than any other one event moved the people to engage in a general insurrection against Spain. Rizal by his courageous exposure of Spain's maladministration of the Philippines and by his dramatic martyrdom was to typify in his name all that was noble in Philippine aspirations. When yearly on December 30th the Filipinos at home and in foreign lands gather to honor the memory of Rizal, there is a stupendous outpouring of patriotic fervor.

In all governmental upheavals, agitation passes from stage to stage, from peaceful petition for reform to armed demands for the changes desired. Just as del Pilar and Rizal made their exits from the Philippine scene, their successors appeared. As del Pilar and Rizal laid down their pens, Andres Bonifacio and Emilio Aguinaldo took up the weapons of revolt. Bonifacio organized the *Katipunan*, an insurrectionary society, while Aguinaldo led the forces in the field in his home province of Cavite. Inevitably the two strong wills had to clash. When they did "the great Plebian" was eliminated and Aguinaldo held undisputed sway. Aguinaldo became as magnetic a rallying point for his fellow countrymen as Rizal had been.

From 1907 when representative government was inaugurated in the Philippines by the Americans to 1945 when the latter prepared to leave, the Philippines recognized two leaders, Sergio Osmeña and Manuel Quezon. Until the split in the *Nacionalista* Party in 1922, Osmeña was the undisputed boss of the Filipino element in the government. After that date Quezon came into power, and despite the handicap of ill health retained supremacy until his death just before the end of World War II.

Sergio Osmeña and Manuel Quezon together formed an invincible team. Then the experience of del Pilar and Rizal and of Bonifacio and Aguinaldo, repeated itself. Whether because of real differences of opinion or because of a clash in ambitions—most likely the latter was the true reason—Osmeña and Quezon became heads of rival political parties. Later they were reconciled, again parted and contested for supremacy before the electorate, and finally were reunited in a coalition. At all times it was an uneasy alliance. Osmeña shrouded his feelings in Oriental reticence, but Quezon in explosive asides to intimates, made no secret of his contempt for his rival. Impartially weighing their careers in the balance, there is glory enough for each of them.

The mantle of leadership fell from the shoulders of President of the Commonwealth Quezon to pass on to Manuel Roxas, the heir he had tacitly chosen. The gigantic task cast upon the latter after his election as first President of the Philippine Republic would have apalled a less courageous man. His was the obligation not to lose independence just as it was won, to unite a people torn apart by collaboration charges, to secure American aid in rehabilitation, and to evolve an economy sufficiently robust to maintain political cohesion. That Roxas met the patriotic test in every way, that he labored constantly for the common good, that he was the Filipino best fitted to meet the emergency, and that he ranked in statesmanship with the heads of other states, even his political opponents have conceded. Roxas represented in his person Philippine nationalism brought to fruition.

With Roxas borne down to death by responsibilities too heavy for any man to carry, other leaders have taken over where he left off. President Elpidio Quirino is an experienced administrator. Dr. Jose P. Laurel's indisputable talents can again be utilized to help his country. Possibly we should be tolerant enough to recognize Luis Taruc, the leader of the dissident forces, as a true, if ill-advised patriot. More conservatively considered, other Filipinos who deserve recognition for their help in forging statehood for the Philippines include all the distinguished men who filled the post of Resident Commissioner at Washington.

Worthy exponents of Philippine nationalism were del Pilar, Rizal, Bonifacio, Aguinaldo, Osmeña, Quezon, and Roxas. Their dominant personalities welded a nation and made it free.

Progress Toward Autonomy

A corollary of the American Philippine policy, nay more than that, the paramount plank, was to make available the institutions of self-government for the Filipino people. As the Jones Law, enacted by the Congress in 1916, expressed the thought, "it was desirable to place in the hands of the people of the Philippines as large a control of their domestic affairs as can be given them, without in the meantime impairing the exercise of the right of sovereignty by the people of the United States."

At first municipal governments were established; then provincial governments. In both, the important officers were chosen by suffrage of the people.

The plan of progressive *Filipinization* (replacements of Americans by Filipinos) was carried out more slowly in the executive departments of the central government. Gregorio Araneta became the first Filipino head of an executive department, that of Finance and Justice, and Manuel Tiño the first Filipino chief of a bureau, that of Labor. This process continued until, instead of one Filipino cabinet officer, all the members of the cabinet were Filipinos, with the exception of an American Secretary of Public Instruction. Little by little, portions of the powers lodged in the Governor General were chipped off to fall into the hands of Filipino officials. In the Council of State, the heads of the executive departments and the leaders of the Legislature shared with the Governor General the responsibility of formulating general policies.

The legislative power was partially handed over to the representatives of the Filipino people when the Philippine Assembly was organized. The same power was more completely granted the representatives of the people when the Philippine Legislature was made to consist of the House of Representatives and the Philippine Senate. As the Philippine Legislature thus had a direct grant of authority, efforts were continuously made to extend its influence. To this end the principle of partial cabinet responsibility to the Legislature received practical application. But there were those who ironically referred to the Council of State as the fourth side of the triangle, and who pointed to an extra-legal development of Filipino self-government through the predominating influence of the Legislature and the identification of party leadership with government leadership.

Immediately on the inauguration of the American Government in the Philippines, Filipino judges were chosen for the bench. These included a Filipino Chief Justice of the Supreme Court, a number of Associate Justices of that Court, and Judges of First Instance. The practice was continued of having a Filipino Chief Justice of the Supreme Court, but not until 1935 were the Filipinos given a majority of its members. In the lower courts, there resulted the gradual elimination of all American judges.

Beginning with the President's Instructions to the Second Philippine Commission, it became the consistent governmental policy to give preference to the Filipinos in the selection of officers and employees. The rapid progress in the direction of *Filipinization* was borne out by the fact that while in 1903 the number of Americans and Filipinos in the service was about equal, thirty years later there were sixty Filipinos for every American in the service. To provide for competent Filipino officials in particular fields, what were known as *pensionados* were given scholarships in the United States and Europe. On the return of these specially trained Filipinos, they were expected to serve the government in repayment for their educations. The elimination of Americans from the government service was accelerated by a very ingenious device known as the Osmeña Law, by the terms of which those who applied for retirement before a certain date, later extended from year to year, became entitled to a gratuity. Large numbers of American officials availed themselves of this privilege because of the uncertainty of their tenure of office.

As the Government of the Philippine Islands passed out of existence, it was a government well prepared for the exercise of autonomous powers. Municipal, provincial and legislative officials were practically all Filipinos. Except for American Justices of the Supreme Court, the judiciary was Filipino-controlled. Except for an American Governor General, Vice Governor, Insular Auditor, and a few scattered American officials, the executive department was Filipino-administered. With an easy transition feasible, all powers residing in these American officers could be transferred to their Filipino successors and the government could be changed without stopping or injuring its machinery.

Philippine Independence[4]

No subject in American or Philippine politics has induced more heated and inconclusive debates than that of Philippine independence. The discussion was closed not by words but by action.

The continental American knew little of the Philippines and cared less. The insular American had a ready solution for the Philippine problem with which few others agreed. The Filipino clamored for liberty, thinking it the right thing to do, often without knowledge of what independence meant. Not until selfish forces intervened were the steps leading to the institution of the Republic of the Philippines and the withdrawal of American sovereignty over the Islands formalized.

When the Congress of the United States passed the Philippine Commonwealth and Independence Act in 1934, action came through strange alliances. Basically, a struggle existed between two competing spheres of sugar interests. The groups that exerted pressure for passage of the Independence Act included the organizations representing cane and beet sugar growers, the Cuban sugar lobby, the farm bloc, dairy and cottonseed oil interests, and organized labor of the Pacific coast. Joined in an unholy union with these formidable groups were the liberal thinkers and the Filipino missioners. On the other side, endeavoring to put a brake on precipitous action, were the exporters of American goods, capitalists with investments in the Islands, and conservative-minded men. With these forces, Philippine sugar magnates were in sympathy to the extent that they dreaded the loss of the American market for their product.

And so the Philippine problem was solved to the complete satisfaction of no one. Paradoxically, it was the United States that declared its independence from the Philippines and not the Philippines that gained independence.

It has just been remarked that the Philippine problem had been solved. During the course of World War II, it gained momentary attention. As an answer to Japanese propaganda, a Joint Resolution approved by the Congress of the United States provided for the advancement of the date of independence and its proclamation "as quickly as possible . . . prior to July 4, 1946" upon the restoration of "orderly and free democratic processes of government."[5] The realities of war blocked fulfillment of this commitment. As a matter of unemotional fact, if the pledge of independence on or before July

---

[4] See Grayson L. Kirk, *Philippine Independence* (New York, 1936).
[5] Joint Resolution of June 29, 1944, Public Law 380, 78th Congress.

4, 1946 had not stood in the way, it would have been to the overall advantage of the Filipino Nation to postpone redemption of the promise until the Philippine economy was better able to support political freedom.

Philippine independence had its beginnings in Chief Lapu Lapu's aggressive fight against Magellan. It had its out-croppings in revolts against foreign control. It received inspiration from del Pilar, Rizal, Bonifacio, and Aguinaldo. Formally the latter proclaimed independence at Cavite on June 12, 1898. It was a patriotic but inconclusive gesture.

The Philippine Assembly was organized and provided a fit forum for the expression of public opinion. At the close of its initial work and after it had demonstrated its willingness to cooperate with the American Government, Speaker Osmeña arose to deliver an address in which he said:

> Allow me, gentlemen of the House, following the dictates of my conscience as a delegate, as a representative of the country, under my responsibility as Speaker of this House, to declare solemnly as I do now before God and before the world, that we believe that our people aspire for their independence, that our people consider themselves capable of leading an orderly life, efficient for themselves and for others, in the concert of free and civilized nations, and that we believe that if the people of the United States were to decide at this moment the Philippine cause in favor of the Filipinos the latter could, in assuming the consequent responsibility, comply with their duties to themselves and to others, without detriment to liberty, to justice, and to right.

The statements of the Speaker were embodied in a formal resolution, although far from being unanimously adopted, and Resident Commissioner-elect Manuel Quezon was authorized to make known to the Congress of the United States Philippine aspirations for independence as expressed at the meeting of the Assembly. Regularly thereafter, as the Philippine Assembly or the Philippine Legislature annually convened, independence resolutions were approved without dissent and coursed on their way to Washington.

The campaign for Philippine independence had two aspects; the one Philippine, the other American. At home the purpose of the Filipino leaders was to encourage the development of public opinion solidly back of the movement for freedom, to furnish a practical demonstration of aptitude for self-government, and to support agitation in the United States. Away from the Philippines, the effort was to appeal to the justice of the American people to make good their promises of independence, to justify the statement that a stable government had been established, and to win assistance in any quarter where it could be obtained.

It can justly be said that the Filipino side of the independence question was effectively presented to the American people for the first time by Resident Commissioner Quezon. The sentiment fostered by him and others was so nearly completely successful that when the Clarke Amendment to the Jones Law, providing for the granting of quick independence, was offered in the United States Senate, it was adopted when the Vice President cast his deciding vote in favor. The Clarke Amendment was defeated in the House through the intervention of Cardinal Gibbons with the aid of Tammany Hall Congressmen. However, the Jones Law without the amendment was approved in 1916, and its preamble formally promised eventual independence.

In 1919 and periodically thereafter Philippine missions were sent to the United States. They emphasized over and over again the readiness of the Philippines for independence. Typical of the restraint shown by the Filipino leaders was the statement of Manuel Roxas before the House Committee on Insular Affairs, in which he said: "We do not contend that the Filipinos have reached the highest peak of progress and culture and economic advancement attainable, but we believe we have reached the limit of progress, advancement and education in democracy that we can achieve under American guardianship. The remainder we must learn by ourselves through the proven process of trial and error." By such unremitting Filipino efforts backed by American influences both sincere and insincere was Philippine independence won.

A question frequently asked in the past was: Do the Filipinos want independence? The query has now become academic. The Filipino people accepted their constitution by a vote of 30 to 1, a vote in favor meaning acceptance of independence. The Republic of the Philippines is now a fact. For whatever it may be worth, the statement can be added that the Woods-Forbes Mission, the Thompson Mission, and the Senator Hawes investigation, all reported that the Filipinos wanted independence. Among them, however, was found a minority more vocal in the early days than later who desired to maintain close relations with the United States.

It was true that certain Filipinos might tell an American in strict confidence that they did not favor independence. These assurances were often taken at face value by credulous newcomers. Back of answers of this nature was usually the desire of the Filipino to say the thing that pleases, and he assumed that Americans were not keen for independence.

While American sentiment in the United States was divided regarding the fitness of the Filipino people for the modern version of self-government, no such cleavage occurred among Americans in the Philippines. Undoubtedly a large majority of the Americans living in the Islands either actively opposed early independence or gave it no assistance. The formation of an adequate Philippine policy along liberal lines was for many years stoutly resisted by Americans with business interests in the Philippines. One of the arguments much favored was that since the Philippine Islands were a part of the American domain, they could only be alienated by a constitutional amendment. In one pamphlet distributed by the American Chamber of Commerce in 1924 it was said, "We are here by right, we are here by conquest and we have a title by conquest and a title by purchase. We are here as possessors, and we are here as sovereigns; we are here as owners and controllers of absolute sovereignty." The only manifest effect of this sort of fulmination was to irritate the Filipinos and to induce them to put forth greater efforts to secure their independence.

With the independence of the Philippines an actuality, the purpose should be to go beyond the name and the form to secure the substance and essence of liberty.[6]

Nationalist Fervor Under the Republic [7]

It should come as a surprise to no one that with the independence of the Philippines proclaimed, Filipino sentiment broke through restraints to express itself in all manner of ways.

Having won political independence, responsible Filipino leaders wanted to join with it financial and economic independence: hence creation of a Central Bank, and governmental aid for a vast industrialization program; hence an import control law; hence agitation begun by private business interests to secure modification of the Trade Act of 1946 and to minimize American competition in Philippine trade; hence revival of NEPA to foster and protect domestic in-

---

[6] President Quezon in *The Good Fight*.

[7] H. J. van Mook, in *The Stakes of Democracy in Southeast Asia*, ch. 9 (New York, 1950) describes the post war nationalist revolt.

dustry. All these moves were understandable. They simply meant that a young nation was flexing its muscles without any thought of asking for trouble.

The need of the Philippines to depend on the United States for a market and for defense, coming at a time when war had brought turmoil and left destruction in its wake, was a situation ready made for the ultranationalistic elements, and for the demagogue, the radical and the oppositionist. The independence issue was dead. In its place was raised the spectre of American colonial domination. With the return to more normal civilian life, with the aid of generous American help, and with the influence of Filipino leaders retarding unwise and unhealthy clamor against the nation which had just done the unprecedented in acclaiming the Philippine Republic, the better sense of the Filipinos reasserted itself.

Perfervid expressions of explosive Philippine Nationalism will continue. That is natural, is indeed inevitable. The young, whether as individuals or as a collection of individuals taking the pattern of a nation, are so inclined. The problem will be to curtail excesses in order not to injure normal relations with the countries upon which the Philippines depends for existence.

Justice Frank Murphy, last Governor General of the Philippine Islands, and Hon. Manuel L. Quezon, first President of the Commonwealth of the Philippines.

CHAPTER VII

THE COMMONWEALTH OF THE PHILIPPINES

Passage by the Congress of Two Philippine Independence Acts

In 1933 and again in 1934, the Congress of the United States approved two bills which would enable the Filipino people on acceptance to achieve eventual independence.

Congressional action was brought about by pressure exerted by members of a Philippine Mission who urged an early grant of independence, aided and abetted by diverse American separatist interests who sought to blunt the competititon afforded by Philippine industries and labor. Exhaustive hearings for months were held. The process of drafting a bill which would sanction the prime object of granting the Filipinos their independence, and at the same time appease the conflicting American claimants of economic advantage, was not easy. Eventually the Congressional Committees submitted nearly identical reports with recommendations for discharging American obligations in the Orient.

After three years of effort, the House of Representatives approved the Hare-Hawes-Cutting Bill, thus styled because of its principal authors, following forty minutes of inconsequential debate. In the Senate all opposition including attempted filibustering was crushed. The question then was: What would President Herbert Hoover do? The President did not leave anyone in doubt when he spoke. Advised by Henry L. Stimson, who not long since had left the post of Governor General of the Philippines to become Secretary of State, and by Secretary of War Patrick Hurley, who had jurisdiction over the Philippines, President Hoover returned the bill to the Congress with a vigorous message in which he set forth his most serious objections. Then, to the surprise of everyone, including ardent supporters of the Hare-Hawes-Cutting Bill, the Congress proceeded speedily and overwhelmingly to override the President's veto.

When the Philippine Legislature formally went on record as declining to accept the Hare-Hawes-Cutting Act, the scene shifted back to Washington. There, without blatant publicity and committee hearings of any sort, and with only brief committee reports and curtailed speechmaking, action was obtained. Quiet negotiations in which the participants were President Franklin D. Roosevelt, Senator Millard E. Tydings, Chairman of the Senate Committee on Territories and Insular Affairs, and Senator Manuel Quezon, President of the Philippine Senate and leader of the anti-group that had brought about rejection of the Hare-Hawes-Cutting Act, obtained quick results.

The Tydings-McDuffie Act, taking its name from the Chairmen of the Congressional Committees responsible for the introduction of the bill, revived, extended, amended, and superseded the Hare-Hawes-Cutting Act. This much maligned predecessor actually had been resurrected and rechristened and the expiration date extended in order to afford the Philippine Legislature another and last opportunity to accept the law. The right of the United States to retain military reservations scattered over the Islands was relinquished, coincident with the arrival of the date for independence. The question of naval bases was left for determination in future negotiations between the United States and the Republic of the Philippines. An alleged loophole in the law which it was charged made independence uncertain was closed, and the title to the act was changed so as to make it clear that the independence which the Islands would have at the expiration of the transition period would be "complete." With this last observation, one might be inclined to disagree, for there is no material difference between independence of the Philippines and complete independence of the Philippines. Otherwise the Tydings-McDuffie Act was simply a reenactment of the Hare-Hawes-Cutting Act.

The Tydings-McDuffie measure was approved by President Roosevelt on March 24, 1934. As he signed the bill the President said: "This is a great day in American-Philippine relations. It means the beginning of the Philippine Republic." Previously, and with even more significance, he had promised in effect that where imperfections or inequalities in the basic law were found to exist, they would be corrected after proper hearing and in fairness to both the American and Filipino peoples.

The Congressional Act represented a successful effort at all-around pacification. The law underwrote a many-sided, face-saving compromise. For the United States it sought to quiet agitation against Philippine products and to avoid stirring up quarrelsome issues. For the Philippines it sought to secure endorsement by the opposing camps. With good reason could Republican Senator Vandenberg taunt the Democrats and their allies with the fact that yesterday's anathema, referring to the Hare-Hawes-Cutting Act, had become the Tydings-McDuffie benediction.

First Rejection and then Acceptance by the Philippine Legislature

The concluding section of the Hare-Hawes-Cutting Act specified that the provisions of the Act were not to take effect until accepted by concurrent resolution of the Philippine Legislature, or by a convention called for the purpose of passing upon that question. This was an unusual stipulation, but one which placed responsibility for acceptance or non-acceptance of the proffer of independence squarely on the representatives of the Filipino people.

The question of whether to accept or not to accept set the whole Philippines agog with excitement. Those in favor were colloquially referred to as *Pros*, and those against as *Antis*. The *Pros* included the members of the Philippine Mission headed by Senator Osmeña and Speaker Roxas, who proudly presented their hard-won Independence Act for inspection and approval as the best law to be had. The undisputed chieftain of the *Antis* was President of the Senate Quezon, who pointedly stressed objectionable features of the Act as falling short of meeting national aspirations. In ability and standing the two groups were approximately equal. Although party lines were crossed, basically the struggle was a renewal of the Quezon-Osmeña fight for supremacy.

The Quezon group controlled the Legislature. With ruthless dispatch, the majority deposed members of the Mission from high legislative posts. Then came vacillation; a plebescite was authorized only to be disauthorized; an effort to postpone the day of reckoning was thwarted by an opinion of the Attorney General of the United States. Eventually the members of the Legislature had to toe the mark and vote either for or against the law. This they did when on October 17, 1933 the Philippine Legislature went on record as declining to accept the Hare-Hawes-Cutting Act.

The same resolution above referred to authorized a joint legislative mission and named its members. The missioners who made the trip were President of the Senate Quezon, Senator and Floor Leader Elpidio Quirino, and Former Resident Commissioner Isauro Gabaldon. In Washington, notwithstanding the none too friendly atmosphere, President Quezon was able through adroit negotiations to secure at least one modification of the Hare-Hawes-Cutting Act, the elimination of the Army base clauses. With the new law thus revised but in other respects practically identical with its predecessor, President

Quezon salved his conscience with the assurance of having driven the best possible bargain with Washington leaders for his people.

The day following President Quezon's triumphant return and appropriately on May 1st, the anniversary of America's arrival in the Philippines, the Philippine Legislature in joint session unanimously approved a resolution accepting the Tydings-McDuffie Act.

The Tydings-McDuffie Act was obtained not by one man or by one group of men, but through the efforts of many individuals. America's representatives had composed differences among conflicting interests sagaciously, had not given way to pique when what they considered a generous offer was rejected by the Filipinos, and had placed the stamp of approval on a solemn promise of independence pursuant to a definite schedule on a definite date. The Filipino missioners for their part had encountered a hard situation, but by their sincerity, aptitude and restraint had won through to success.

The way had been cleared for the steps designed to lead to an independent Philippines.

Status of the Commonwealth of the Philippines

The Act of Congress of March 24, 1934 we term the Philippine Commonwealth and Independence Act, because that title is indicative of its two main purposes. A transition period of ten years was contemplated, during which there was to be a Commonwealth of the Philippines. Thereafter, there was to be a Republic of the Philippines. The Act of Congress was in the nature of an enabling act to secure these two objectives.

The Philippine Commonwealth and Independence Act enumerated the steps leading to Philippine independence. The most significant of these steps was a grant to the Filipino people of the right to formulate their own constitution for both the preparatory commonwealth period and the independent republic. In due course a constitution was adopted in a constitutional convention, was accepted by the President of the United States as conforming to the terms of the Congressional Act, and was approved by the Filipino people by direct vote. An election and the inauguration of the Commonwealth Government followed.

During the Commonwealth period the Philippines was represented in the United States by a Resident Commissioner. The United States in turn was represented in the Philippines by a High Commissioner. A decade of economic readjustment was recognized as necessary, with trade relations between the two countries regulated by quotas set up for Philippine products entering the American market for five years, to be followed by gradually increasing export taxes.

The most significant fact in the whole political agreement was that the independence of the Philippines was to be proclaimed on the July 4th following the tenth year after the inauguration of the Commonwealth. The Republic of the Philippines was in fact recognized as in all respects a sovereign state on July 4, 1946.

The new government organized in the Philippines was officially christened "The Commonwealth of the Philippines." The word "commonwealth" signified self-government and autonomy. It did not, however, convey the idea of an independent state.

The true status of the Commonwealth of the Philippines was given point in an intriguing incident connected with the inauguration of the new regime. As President Quezon concluded taking his oath of office, a nineteen gun salute—not a twenty-one gun salute—boomed forth for him. The inside story involved in this seemingly trivial matter presented implications more serious than was evident to the casual observer.

General Douglas MacArthur, with the best of intentions, had arranged for a twenty-one gun salute for the President-elect. This meant, in diplomatic usage, recognition of the Philippines as a sovereign state, an untenable position. When Secretary of War Dern declined to change the order at the urgent request of Governor General Murphy, the latter cabled direct to the President of the United States. Immediately a directive came back ordering a nineteen gun salute and making it unmistakably clear that American sovereignty represented by the United States High Commissioner took precedence over the Commonwealth President.[1]

Anyone familiar with President Quezon's personality will realize that he was no mere onlooker to this maneuvering in protocol. There is good reason to believe that he threatened to stay away from his own inauguration. But his better judgment prevailed and he did appear. Years later in Washington, President Quezon was able to joke with his friend Justice Murphy about their one serious difference of opinion.

THE COMMONWEALTH ELECTION

On September 17, 1935, voters went to the polls to elect the first

---

[1] Information about the 21 or 19 gun salute episode was obtained from a source close to Justice Murphy.

set of executive and legislative officials under the Commonwealth Government. The officers to be voted for were President, Vice President, and ninety-eight members of the unicameral National Assembly.

Three tickets were in the field. Senate President Manuel Quezon and Senator Sergio Osmeña carried the colors of the coalition of the major political parties for President and Vice President. General Emilio Aguinaldo and former Supreme Court Justice Raymundo Melliza emerged from retirement to organize the National Socialist Party and to become its candidates for the Presidency and Vice Presidency. Bishop Gregorio Aglipay descended from the pulpit to the political arena as the standard bearer for President of the hastily-formed Republican Party, and later persuaded Norberto Nabong, communistically-inclined, to become a candidate for Vice President. From the start it was generally conceded that Quezon and Osmeña would win; the only question was as to their majority.

Stability and liberal idealism were the keynotes of the Quezon-Osmeña campaign. Their speeches of acceptance were acclaimed on all sides as outlining an attitude toward government and a program of administration which invited respect. Their campaign was front-porch conducted, without excursions into the provinces and without indulging in personalities. The radio was largely used to reach the remote regions.

General Aguinaldo and Bishop Aglipay were naturally forced to adopt different tactics from those of their opponents. They could and did take the offensive. Separately, of course, they toured as much of the country as they could cover, making numerous campaign speeches and meeting the people. The burden of their song was a shorter transition period before independence, the righting of the alleged wrongs suffered by the masses, and a critical lashing of existing leadership.

In the three-cornered political fight, the advantage was all with the Quezon-Osmeña coalition. Experienced and skillful politicians, behind them stood well-organized political parties and practically the whole force of the Government. Against them stood two venerable historical figures of the past: one, a former insurgent leader, coupled with a retired judge; the other, an octogenarian churchman teamed with an unknown citizen—all without political experience and without political organizations. The fight was over before it began.

As anticipated, the coalition ticket won by a landslide. For President, Quezon received over twice as many votes as Aguinaldo and Aglipay combined. For Vice President, Osmeña's victory was even more decisive. Aguinaldo and Aglipay had each carried only his home province and one other province.[2]

It was apparent that the country wanted Quezon and Osmeña as its leaders. The only discordant note was struck by Candidate Aguinaldo who persistently declined to congratulate President-elect Quezon on the ground that the victory of the coalition was due to manipulation and coercion, but who refused to tender proof of the commission of widespread frauds.

PRESIDENT QUEZON TAKES OFFICE[3]

For one day at least Manila was not only the center of interest of the Philippines but of the United States and the Orient. After centuries of foreign domination, a democratic government resting on the consent of the people was to be established. Rightly it was a colorful and momentous event.

Never before had such a large group of American solons—some forty Senators and Congressmen in all with their families—set out on such a long trek. It was the greatest trans-pacific Congressional journey in history. Also, it constituted one of the most glorious junkets *de luxe* on record—20,000 miles of travel and three months of superlative entertainment and sightseeing, all as guests of the Philippine Government.

Half a million pesos for ceremonial purposes and a display of unstinted hospitality for American officials and newspapermen was a large outlay. Its expenditure could not help but draw forth ironic and bitter comment in the United States and in the Philippines. In extenuation it could at least be said that the presence of these numerous guests testified to the good will of the Philippines toward the United States.

The induction into office of the first President of the Commonwealth of the Philippines, His Excellency Manuel Quezon, and along with him of the First Vice President, Hon. Sergio Osmeña, and the first members of the National Assembly took place in Manila on November 15, 1935. The ceremonies were held in a specially erected stand in front of the magnificent legislative building and facing the

---

[2] Election returns showed the following result:
For President: Quezon 695,279; Aguinaldo 179,401; Aglipay 148,006.
For Vice President: Osmeña 810,666; Melliza 70,891; Nabong 51,444.

[3] The Blue Book of the Inauguration of the Commonwealth of the Philippines and the induction into office of Manuel Quezon and Sergio Osmena on November 15, 1935 contains complete information about this historic event, including reproduction of the addresses delivered.

old Walled City. Among the distinguished visitors seated in the center of the stand were Secretary of War George H. Dern, the special envoy of the President of the United States and the fourth Secretary of War to visit the Islands, Vice President John N. Garner, Speaker Joseph W. Byrns, the remaining members of the Congressional party, General Douglas MacArthur, former Governor General Francis Burton Harrison, and William Allen White, Roy W. Howard, and other newspaper publishers and correspondents. General Emilio Aguinaldo and Bishop Gregorio Aglipay, defeated candidates for the Presidency, were conspicuously absent.

A large mass assembly, estimated by the police at a quarter of a million people, crowded the area around the ceremonial stand to view the inauguration and the parade. Millions of other Filipinos throughout the Islands enthusiastically celebrated the day. Radio broadcasts carried the proceedings to the United States and the neighboring Asiatic countries.

The program, which had been carefully planned, was carried out without a hitch. When the high dignitaries had entered and taken their seats, His Grace, the Most Reverend Gabriel Reyes, Archbishop of Cebu, gave the invocation. Secretary of War Dern, as the personal and official representative of the President of the United States, delivered an inspiring address in which he praised the progress of democracy in the Islands, laid emphasis on the fact that all the agencies of local government were passing to Filipino control, and pointed out the interdependency of the sovereign power and the autonomous Philippine Commonwealth. This was followed by the reading by Governor General Murphy of the proclamation of the President of the United States announcing the result of the election of the officers of the Commonwealth. The oaths of office were then administered to President-elect Quezon, Vice President-elect Osmeña and the members-elect of the National Assembly by Hon. Ramon Avanceña, Chief Justice of the Supreme Court.

The highlight of the day was the inaugural address delivered by President Quezon. It was not a long message. In fact it was constructed so as to take up exactly twenty minutes of time. Notwithstanding this self-imposed limitation, it was a well-phrased, well-balanced, and well-conceived address. Also, it was well-delivered by the President, who spoke firmly and forcefully, emphasizing the salient points with vigorous gestures.

With little prelude, except to make acknowledgement of gratitude to America and to pay tribute to the Filipino heroes, the President plunged into the exposition of his thought. First of all, he stated that

no violent changes from the established order of things were contemplated. Nevertheless, warning was given that the Government
would deal firmly with lawless individuals and subversive movements.
The point was made "that no man in this country from the Chief
Executive to the last citizen is above the law." Protection of labor
was promised. A balanced budget was to be insisted upon, but no
new taxes were contemplated. Economic plans were to be fostered,
and the hope was expressed "that the forthcoming trade conferences
between the representatives of the United States and of the Philippines
would result in more just and beneficial relations between the two
countries." The establishment of an economical, simple and efficient
government was pledged. Good will toward all nations was to be
the golden rule of the administration. An appeal was made to the
patriotism of all to unite in the common endeavor so that "we may
. . . once more dedicate ourselves to the realization of our national
destiny." The President concluded: "I face the future with hope and
fortitude, certain that God never abandons a people who ever follow
His unerring and guiding Hand. May He give me light, strength,
and courage evermore that I may not falter in the hour of service to
my people."

All who heard or read the inaugural address of President Quezon
pronounced it a great state document worthy of the occasion.

As a grand finale to the ceremonies, President Quezon was escorted
to Malacañan Palace. In significance this event equalled the more
elaborate inaugural display. The occupancy of Malacañan had there-
tofore been the symbol of alien domination. Henceforth that idea was
dissipated. As President Quezon entered the historic building, he became the first Filipino to do so by mandate of his fellow countrymen.

The Commonwealth In Operation[4]

The Commonwealth of the Philippines had been envisioned as
providing a ten year transition period during which the Filipinos
could prepare themselves for independence. The realities of war
rudely shattered the plan. Practically every tangible accomplishment
from late 1935, when the Filipinos took over an autonomous government, to late 1941, when the Japanese drove the heads of state into
exile, was lost in World War II.

The Commonwealth was launched under the best possible circumstances. Governor General Murphy and President Quezon jointly
and separately made ready for the momentous event.

---

[4] See Catherine Porter, *Crisis in the Philippines* (New York, 1942).

Governor General Murphy made it his purpose to close the books of one regime with all pending matters decided, and to open them for another regime with clean pages. Nor was this the work of the moment. On the contrary, it represented a hard two and a half years job. His main objectives had been the maintenance of financial stability and a contribution to social betterment to thwart unrest. The Chief Executive was entirely successful in keeping government finances in a sound condition. He was able to accomplish his purpose but partially in his effort to contribute to the contentment of the people, for it was a problem not soluble in a day or a year.

Governor General Murphy's last message to the Philippine Legislature was delivered the day before the Commonwealth Government got under way. It was a comprehensive document and displayed deep research and clear thinking. A brilliant factual review of American achievements and Philippine progress through American and Filipino cooperation was made. The state of the country was reported sound and its administration ready for the new regime. A fit valedictory of the American—guided and administered Government of the Philippine Islands had been delivered as it passed into history.

President Quezon at the start of the Commonwealth Government had to remove possible obstacles to plans laid down for a fruitful administration. He was endowed with great constitutional power. In addition he had to make his leadership secure and undisputed. To do this he had to be able to count on legislative as well as executive support. Against strong opposition, he was able to impose his will on a rather reluctant Legislature. As a result the Speaker of the National Assembly was divested of the traditional powers he had legally and extra-legally exercised to become principally a presiding officer, and the President of the Commonwealth was able to deal directly with legislative committees.

President Quezon thus was assured of a free hand in shaping the policies of the government and in carrying them out. He revealed his purpose to be "more government and less politics," an announcement which was greeted with wide public approbation. The President made full use of his powers.

The Chief Executive first busied himself with setting his house in order. Only imperative changes were made in personnel. The Cabinet was gradually reorganized. The Supreme Court was *Filipinized*. General MacArthur, former Governor General Harrison and others were brought in as advisers.

The Commonwealth Government had inherited a sound financial structure. It did nothing which fundamentally weakened the structure. Nevertheless it is undeniable that lavish expenditures were authorized. Some of the public works projects to which large sums were diverted appeared more in the nature of extravagant luxury than prime necessity. It was hard to justify them. Of a different nature are the matters next mentioned.

The defense program, indicative of a desire to make the people secure against internal and external dangers, ate up large appropriations. Estates were purchased and subdivided for resale in small lots, and agricultural colonies were started to alleviate agrarian unrest. The National Development Company was revitalized. Economic projects were begun. Money for such capital expenditures, to a considerable extent, came from windfalls provided by the coconut oil excise tax.

The net indebtedness of the Commonwealth at the time of the inauguration was some ₱95,000,000. By 1941 this amount had been markedly reduced. For a country as rich in resources as the Philippines, this was as if there were no outstanding fiscal charges against the government.

The flaws in the economic picture were all too evident. Dependence on income accruing from the coconut oil excise tax was bad enough. Worse, infinitely worse, would be the inevitable collapse of the entire economy on the closing of the American market to Philippine products, unless a program permitting of readjustments was authorized. The strain was eased somewhat by Congressional action taken in August, 1939, effective, however, only during the Commonwealth period. It was left to the eleventh hour, short weeks prior to the inauguration of the Republic of the Philippines, for definite legislation to take form in the shape of the Philippine Trade Act and the Philippine Rehabilitation Act.

It was too much to expect that provisions in the Philippine Constitution providing for a unicameral National Assembly and limiting the President to a term of six years with reelection barred, could long resist political pressure. By an amendment to the Constitution approved in 1940, the Islands reverted to the bicameral system with a Congress consisting of a Senate and a House of Representatives. By another constitutional amendment of the same date, the term of the President was reduced from six to four years, with one succeeding term permitted. The way had been cleared for the reelection of President Quezon.

Elections under the amended constitution were held less than a month before the war with Japan began. There was never any doubt of the result. The coalition in power was too well entrenched to be overthrown. The opposition offered by the Popular Front made up of numerous, poorly organized minority groups, with divergent aims and plagued by dissention from within, was ineffective. It was not necessary for Quezon or Osmeña to make a single campaign speech in their own behalf. Juan Sumulong, the Popular Front candidate for President, received only 298,000 odd votes to 1,340,000 for Quezon. Osmeña, the candidate for Vice President on the Coalition ticket, demonstrated his vote-getting ability by once again obtaining a larger vote than his running mate Quezon.

The first constructive action taken by the Commonwealth of the Philippines, by a curious shaking of the dice of fate, was reflected in its last years. The initial message of President Quezon to the National Assembly, showing careful study and thought, dwelt exclusively on the theme of national preparedness for defense. Act No. 1 of the Legislative body shaped the subject in a statute. It was this law as implemented by appropriations which provided for the training of the thousands of Filipinos who participated in the gallant defense of their homeland.

These matters were brought to mind when, after Pearl Harbor, a hastily-called Philippine Legislature delegated emergency powers to the President of the Philippines. Before he could make practical use of his authority, the exigencies of war forced him on to Corregidor with the Vice President and a few associates. The second inauguration ceremonies in the bleak shadow of the Island Fortress were in sharp contrast to the elaborate display of the first inauguration. Not long after, the President and the Vice President were evacuated to the Southern Philippines, and from there to Australia and the United States.

The Resident Commissioner of the Philippines to the United States

A single Resident Commissioner represented the Commonwealth of the Philippines in the United States. His salary and expenses were paid by the Commonwealth Government. This was in direct contrast to provisions in previous organic laws, which authorized two Resident Commissioners, and allowed them the same salary and perquisites received by members of the House of Representatives of the United States Congress, to be paid out of the Treasury of the United States.

The Resident Commissioner from the Commonwealth of the Philippines was appointed by the Commonwealth President with the consent of the Commission on Appointments. This sole Resident

Commissioner, like the two Resident Commissioners whom he succeeded, was granted a seat in the House of Representatives of the
United States Congress with the right to debate but without the
right to vote. The various Filipino Resident Commissioners took
full advantage of this parliamentary prerogative and were listened
to with respect by their Congressional colleagues. Outside the halls
of Congress the Resident Commissioners were the spokesmen of
their people and Government and the guardians of their interests both
personal and national.

The Commonwealth of the Philippines needed capable and well-
balanced men to handle the national interests in the United States.
Due to the special nature of the American-Philippine relationship,
the Resident Commissioner became a combined legislator, economist
and diplomat. During the war years, it became his obligation
to cooperate in the war effort in every possible way. With the war
over, new laws of benefit to the Philippines had to be guided through
the Congress.

From the first Resident Commissioners, Pablo Ocampo and Benito
Legarda, who arrived in Washington in 1907, down to the last Resident Commissioner in 1946, the Philippines was represented in the
United States by high class men. The most notable was Manuel
Quezon, who served from 1909 to 1916. He was responsible in large
part for the enactment of the Jones Law, conceding more self-government to the Islands and promising eventual independence.

The Philippines was fortunate in having former Speaker Quintin
Paredes as its first Resident Commissioner from the newly organized
Commonwealth. He was ultimately succeeded by Joaquin M. Elizalde,
an experienced business executive, who carried the burden of the
office throughout most of the war. The last Resident Commissioner
was Brigadier General Carlos P. Romulo, internationally renowned
journalist, orator and author.

The United States High Commissioner To The Philippines[5]

In the preparation of the Philippine Commonwealth and Independence Act, the Congress was confronted with the delicate problem
of providing for adequate American representation in the Philippines
and yet not incurring Filipino resentment. American sovereignty

---

[5] The seventh and final report of Hon. Paul V. McNutt, United States High Commissioner to the Philippines, dated June 30, 1946, House Document No. 389, is an
historical document. The report is well written, impartial and comprehensive. It
was prepared under the editorial direction of Commander Julius C. Edelstein.

was to continue during the transition period, and with American sovereignty went responsibility to safeguard a minimum of reserved powers. On the other hand, the Filipinos objected to any excessive lodgment of authority in an American representative, which would be destructive of maximum Filipino autonomy. The balance was struck by providing for an officer to be known as the United States High Commissioner to the Philippine Islands.

The United States High Commissioner was appointed by the President of the United States by and with the consent of the Senate. He was allowed the same compensation as had been received by the Governor General, that is, ₱36,000 ($18,000) annually.

The United States High Commissioner was made the representative of the President of the United States in the Philippines. This was important, for the basic law was careful to itemize the authority lodged in the President. As one example, the foreign affairs of the Commonwealth of the Philippines were placed under the direct control of the United States Secretary of State acting pursuant to the supervision of the President. As another example of potential authority which later was used, the President had the right to call into the service all armed forces organized by the Philippine Government.

While the title "High Commissioner" was understood in official circles as indicating a high ranking officer—frequently with the rank of Ambassador—and while the prestige of the President stood back of the actual occupant of the office, in reality the United States High Commissioner possessed little specific authority and had no precedents to follow. It is not strange, therefore, that confusion of thought existed even in the minds of those who should have known better.

Some were accustomed to speak of the High Commissioner as the Governor General of the Philippines. Not only was that not his title, but he did not possess a tithe of the power which the Governor General had formerly exercised. The High Commissioner was simply a Commissioner "to the Philippines." The use of the infinitive "to" gave eloquent proof of the true nature of the office.

Officials in the Commonwealth of the Philippines and foreign officials had to be taught the hard way that the United States High Commissioner was the representative of the sovereign authority of the United States which extended to the Philippines. Precedence was established at the very start of the Commonwealth Government by President Roosevelt. It was even more definitely determined for Commonwealth leaders, who were wont to confuse their status with that of an independent nation, by High Commissioner Paul V. Mc-

Nutt. Public recognition of protocol came when Commonwealth President Quezon graciously held a match for High Commissioner McNutt's cigarette.

The consular officers also had to be given a lesson in diplomatic usage. Whether by design or otherwise, messages began going direct from foreign consulates in Manila to the Commonwealth Government. High Commissioner McNutt abruptly put a stop to that practice by insisting that correspondence between Consuls and the Commonwealth be routed through his office. The same High Commissioner also put the Japanese in their place after they had snubbed him in toasts which ranked the Filipino Commonwealth President ahead of the American High Commissioner.

The so-called "toast me first" incident was made the butt of jokes by the unknowing. In truth it was no laughing matter. Behind the episode was discerned the start of the Japanese arrogance that was to become all too evident during the course of the war, and that sought to flatter nationalistic sensibilities to attain Japan's sinister purposes.

Over such seemingly trivial objects as cigarettes and cocktails is face in the Orient kept and lost and are diplomatic battles fought and won.

With Malacañan Palace in Manila and Mansion House in Baguio turned over to the President of the Philippines for his occupancy, it was necessary for the High Commissioner to seek office and residential quarters elsewhere. Eventually an establishment for the High Commissioner in Manila was erected on a large plot of land reclaimed from the waters of Manila Bay. A residence in Baguio was completed on a superb location commanding a magnificent view.[6]

Very little could truthfully be said in favor of the High Commissioner's establishment in Manila. As the mud was churned out of Manila Bay to make a site for the edifice next to the Army and Navy Club and the Elks Club, the American onlooker, sniffing the malodorous air, oft referred to what he saw and smelled as "Murphy's Mud Flat." Nor did the observer's sarcasm grow less as he viewed the finished product that an architect back in Washington had blueprinted. Whether the story that the plans originally provided for a fireplace and heating system be true or apocryphal, the fact remains that the building was architecturally unsuitable for the tropics. The structure was badly mauled during the war. As reconstructed

---

[6]The High Commissioner's residences in Manila and Baguio are piquantly described by Amea Willoughby in the forepart of her book, *I Was On Corregidor* (New York, 1943).

for the use of the American Ambassador, it is more in keeping with the facts of life in Manila.

The High Commissioner's establishment was used not only for living quarters but for offices. Originally a small staff mainly recruited from the Governor General's office force carried on the work. Just prior to the outbreak of the war in 1941, the number of assistants of the High Commissioner had risen to well over one hundred. Dr. Claude A. Buss, the Executive Assistant, deserves particular credit, for he stayed in Manila after the High Commissioner and others had left for Corregidor. He performed the disagreeable duty of meeting the victorious Japanese and did all possible for his compatriots.[7]

The United States High Commissioners during the transition period were Frank Murphy, Paul V. McNutt, and Francis B. Sayre. The author was privileged to serve on the staff of the two first-named. Unlike in personalities, they were alike in being representative Americans of ability who while protecting their country's interests were able to get along with the Filipino leaders.

Frank Murphy was the first United States High Commissioner who assumed office upon the inauguration of the Commonwealth. It was the logical choice. Mr. Murphy's outstanding record as the Island's last Governor General, his close relations with the Filipino leaders, and the confidence reposed in him by the President of the United States, were considerations which demanded that he continue on the job. He organized the High Commissioner's office and initiated policies for dealing wtih the Commonwealth. High Commissioner Murphy relinquished the office to heed other calls which finally landed him on the Supreme Court of the United States.

The second High Commissioner was Paul V. McNutt, who came into office in 1937 and served for two years. Then, after an interval as Federal Security Commissioner and Manpower Commissioner, he was drafted to return as High Commissioner during the last months of the Commonwealth. During his original tour of duty in the Islands he built a well-knit organization on what his predecessor had begun. In one instance, by threatening to use the President's reserved power of disapproval, the High Commissioner forced the Commonwealth to rescind action which would have done a grave injustice to American teachers. He labored as effectively for the relief of American taxpayers resident in the Philippines, who suddenly found themserves hounded for income taxes allegedly long past due, with demands for interest and threats of penalties. Notwithstanding the

---

[7] Clark Lee, *They Call It Pacific*, p. 148 (New York, 1943) pays tribute to the inspiring example of self-control given by Buss in the last nightmarish days.

fact that Mr. McNutt took strong measures on occasion, he held the esteem of the Filipinos and was popular with the American Community.

When Mr. McNutt returned to Manila, again to be high Commissioner, he had to begin from scratch in a reorganization of the office. He had also to bring the weight of his influence to bear on the Congress of the United States to secure much-needed legislation dealing with American-Philippine relations and problems. It was fit and proper that High Commissioner McNutt should become the first Ambassador from the United States to the Republic of the Philippines.

Between High Commissioner McNutt's resignation in 1939 and his return to the same post in 1945, Francis B. Sayre was High Commissioner for a portion of the time. He was in Manila during the trying prewar days, was on Corregidor during much of the bombardment, and was eventually evacuated by submarine. Dr. Sayre was an earnest man of high character, of professorial bearing and temperament. His lack of personal warmth and his methods did not particularly appeal to the effervescent Quezon, and there was a lack of understanding between them at a time when understanding was most needed. Following his Philippine experience, Dr. Sayre returned to service in the Department of State. Eventually he became a member of the United Nations Trusteeship Council, a position for which he was well qualified.

The office of United States High Commissioner is now extinct. The legacy of its personnel and policies was inherited by the American Ambassador to the Philippines.

CHAPTER VIII

THE WAR PERIOD

BATAAN AND CORREGIDOR [1]

For the United States, World War II began on Sunday, December 7, 1941 (Monday, December 8, in the Philippines) with the Japanese attack on Pearl Harbor. Comparable disasters for the Philippines were the occupation of Manila by the Japanese on January 2, 1942, followed by the fall of Bataan and the surrender of the island fortress of Corregidor on May 6, 1942.

The above is what is likely to appear in the history books. If so, it will neither accurately depict the origin of the conflict nor the tragic lack of preparation for war on the part of the United States.

In strict truth, the opening phase of the conflagration was touched off as far back as the fateful September 18, 1931, when the Japanese began their successful occupation of Manchuria. Secretary of State Henry L. Stimson lost out in his championship of international morality. Appeasement, permitting of the sale of scrap iron and other materials to build up the Japanese war machine, only led the Nipponese to continue their southward movement and to picture the Americans as a decadent race who could readily be defeated.

The Philippines had no part in the diplomatic maneuvering that led to war. Yet the Philippines had prepared much better for the conflict than had the United States.

President Manuel Quezon "with uncanny premonition," to use the words of General Douglas MacArthur, created during the first days of his administration the Philippines national defense program. The plan contemplated compulsory military training for Filipino youth to constitute a reserve force, supplementing a small, compact army of professional soldiers. Early in 1940 Quezon expressed doubts relative to the practicability of the plan, and there resulted a slackening in defense efforts, with corresponding cuts in appropria-

---

[1] First hand accounts by eye witnesses include: Carlos P. Romulo, *I Saw The Fall of the Philippines* (New York, 1942); Amea Willoughby, *I Was On Corregidor* (New York, 1943); and Sergeant Bob Reynolds, *Of Rice and Men* (Philadelphia, 1947).

General of the Army Douglas MacArthur,
Liberator of the Philippines.

tions. In a sense the President was right, for the kind of strength necessary for modern warfare could not be developed in the Philippines. That had to come from American arsenals. Nevertheless, the modest program had made considerable progress under the tutelage of MacArthur by the outbreak of the war. It accounted for the major portion of the forces with a top strength of 100,000 men that resisted the Japanese invasion.

From the start it was all-out war. Japanese bombers, naval units and troop ships converged on the Philippines. Simultaneous air attacks on Manila, Cavite, and Clark Field did not spare the capitol even after it had been declared an open city, laid waste the naval station, and destroyed scores of American planes on the ground. Only a masterfully conceived and executed plan permitted American and Filipino troops from the northern and southern lines to effect a junction on Bataan.

It was an unequal battle. The odds against the defenders of Bataan and Corregidor were terrific. Some 200,000 veteran Japanese troops were hurled against the American-Filipino forces. At the most, MacArthur had at his disposal 13,000 American troops. The remainder were some 30,000 Filipino soldiers, approximately one-half of whom were recruits who had received little or no training. The Asiatic fleet was not a factor. The air force, except for a token remnant, had been wiped out. Oft promised reinforcements never came. Yet many times outnumbered, lacking food, medicine and war material, with two-thirds of the survivors near the end suffering from wounds and disease, and without aërial and naval support, American and Filipino troops made a gallant, fighting stand. They held off the enemy for over three months, and in so doing wrote an imperishable saga of heroism.

The Bataan and Corregidor delaying action disrupted Japanese plans. General Tomoyuki Yamashita, who had blitzed Malaya and Singapore so daringly, did the same to the Philippine Fortress—but not on schedule. MacArthur in Australia, following his escape from Corregidor, had been given time to save the southern continent and to begin the march that was to take him back to Bataan, Corregidor, and Manila in triumph.

The Philippines had been drawn into the war largely because of association with the United States. Yet the Filipinos had not shown the slightest hesitation in choosing to join with the Americans in manning the dykes of defense against the oncoming flood of Japanese. Filipino soldiers had shown themselves the match of any other soldiers.

When heroic General Jonathan Wainwright surrendered the battered remnants of his starving, exhausted, grim garrison on the embattled rock of Corregidor, it did not mean the end—merely a tragic setback to be followed by bloody victory.

Over Corregidor, the Island at the entrance to Manila Bay, which had so oft been proclaimed the Pacific Gibraltar, a flag of the Republic of the Philippines now waves amidst the relative peace of a defense zone.

JAPANESE OCCUPATION [2]

For three years the Philippines was under Japanese domination—not entirely, of course, not even in the geographical sense, but Manila and all the principal centers were in Japanese hands; never voluntarily or spiritually, for only a small percentage of the people bowed low to the conquerors.

The Japanese, however, did not lack intelligence information nor want for help when their forces entered the Philippines. Thirty thousand of their nationals, two-thirds of them in Davao, resided in the Islands and busied themselves with other than commercial activities. Fishing boats operated by Japanese and registered in the name of Filipino "dummies" roamed the seas. Confirmed Filipino-Japanophiles were in evidence. General Artemio Ricarte, an *ex-insurrecto*, had lived in Japan for years, refusing to take the oath of allegiance to the United States. Benigno Ramos, who figured in subversive activities, had sought refuge in Japan. University-trained Pio Duran was most vocal in favoring a back-to-the-Orient movement. And there were others. Some were mere apologists for the Japanese; some were paid Japanese agents.

The Commander-in-Chief of the Imperial Japanese Forces in the Philippines was in effect a military dictator. Either through direct orders or by "advice," he ruled the portions of the Islands that his forces controlled. Yet, it was, of course, necessary to activate the customary functions of civil administration behind a Filipino façade of self-government.

President Quezon, on his departure for Corregidor, had left behind in Manila his personable Secretary Jorge B. Vargas with instructions to make the occupation as easy as possible for the people.

---

[2] The Japanese occupation described by Claude A. Buss, *The New World Of Southeast Asia*, pp. 44-59 (Univ. of Minnesota Press and Oxford University Press, 1949) and Manuel E. Buenafe, *Wartime Philippines* (Philippine Education Foundation, Manila, 1950).

Vargas was thus the natural choice of the Japanese to act as Chairman of an Executive Commission with power to govern under Japanese orders. Seven departments were created, headed by experienced Filipinos. This makeshift arrangement continued until October, 1943 when the Japanese-sponsored Republic came into being.

The successive steps leading to the proclamation of the puppet Republic were these: The Japanese Prime Minister promised that his country would "gladly enable" the Filipinos "to enjoy the honor of independence" if they would cooperate in the establishment of the Greater East Asia Co-Prosperity Sphere. A Preparatory Committee for Philippine Independence of appointive members was created. The Committee proceeded to draft and to approve a constitution. All political parties were abolished and in their place was set up the Japanese-sponsored *Kalibapi*. The President of the Republic was chosen without recourse to the people. On October 14, 1943, the Philippines became an "independent republic."

"Made in Japan" independence was foisted on the skeptical Filipino people. They were familiar with "Made in Japan" merchandise, mainly cheap and shoddy replicas of standard wares, that had flooded the world market before the war. The same process was adopted politically by the Japanese in occupied territory. But the Filipinos did not want an inferior imitation of liberty and democracy. They wanted the real thing.

The puppet Republic reflected totalitarian ideology. It was Japanese-created, with a constitution framed by appointed delegates and without ratification by the people. It was supported by the sole political party that was permitted, the *Kalibapi*. It contemplated a strong government with the President as virtual dictator.

On the same day that the so-called Republic was launched, a pact providing for a military alliance with Japan was signed.[3] About a year later the President of the "Republic," without obtaining the approval of the National Assembly, declared that "a state of war" existed between the Philippines and the United States and Great Britain. Except for the *Makapilis*, an irregular band of Filipino collaborationists, and the Philippine Constabulary, who with spies and informers made life miserable for the guerrillas and the patriots who

---

[3] TERMS OF UNDERSTANDING ATTACHED TO THE PACT OF ALLIANCE BETWEEN THE PHILIPPINES AND JAPAN. "The Philippines will afford all kinds of facilities for the military actions to be undertaken by Japan; the Philippines and Japan will closely cooperate with each other to safeguard the territorial integrity and independence of the Philippines." Official Gazette, Vol. 1, No. 1, p. 13.

aided them, the Philippines did not actively enter the war against the Allied Nations.

In the foreign field, the Philippines, along with other Japanese-occupied territories, was technically drawn within the Greater East Asia Co-Prosperity Sphere. Outside of this inglorious association with Japanese imperialism, the only other diplomatic success that was registered was apparent recognition granted by the Franco regime in Spain, later rather lamely excused as merely in the nature of routine diplomatic courtesy.[4]

The Japanese, from their standpoint, made the political weapon of puppetry a success. At the same time they allowed the condition of the Filipino people to go from bad to worse. Their liberties were curtailed. The cost of living rose six hundred to seven hundred times. Food was scarce or impossible to get. Unemployment was widespread. Debtors were paid off with worthless "Mickey Mouse" currency. In the face of such conditions, the Filipino people, with the exception of the comparatively few active collaborationists, resisted at least passively the blandishments of the Japanese.

Japanese policy followed an uneasy opportunist course. It had three phases. Initial victories by the Japanese were interspersed with barbarous cruelties. When it was found that this policy was making enemies of the Filipinos, the Japanese subtly shifted to friendly efforts to attract the Filipinos to join the Co-Prosperity Sphere. The last days of the war found the Japanese in the hysteria of defeat burning and bayoneting and murdering in a frenzy of sadistic atrocities.

The wonder is that Japanese propaganda did not influence the Filipino people, especially the less educated masses, more than it did. Japan and the United States had thrust the Philippines into a war without Filipino consent. The war could be pictured as not one between Japan and the United States, but as one between the races—between the yellow and the brown on the one side and the white on the other. The Japanese could pose "as a liberating army of fellow Orientals," to quote the words of a Filipino leader. Japanese propagandists could point to glaring instances of a white man's arrogance and show of crass superiority. The Japanese could foster friendship by means of magazine and newspaper articles, exaggerated radio scripts, and conducted tours to Japan. Withal, the Japanese could claim that they came as deliverers from colonial

---

[4] Spanish recognition of the Laurel government in the Philippines described by Emmet John Hughes, *Report From Spain* (New York, 1947).

enslavement, with a charter of independence effective earlier than America's promised liberty.

The Commissioners constituting the Executive Commission and the Director General of the *Kalibapi*, in an appeal to the Filipinos told of "the pledge of a noble people"—the Japanese—"that the independence of the Philippines will be granted in the shortest possible time, if the Filipinos actively and unreservedly cooperate with Japan in the establishment of the Greater East Asia Co-Prosperity Sphere." They dwelt on being "deluded into serving America with our blood, sweat, and treasure," when instead the people should "render to the Great Japanese Empire our fullest measure of support and cooperation for a prosecution to a victorious end of the Greater East Asia War." The appeal phrased in high-sounding words fell flat.[5]

The average Filipino, in the face of all such efforts to de-Americanize him, remained true to his Christian faith and his democratic training. He was unable to place out of mind Japanese atrocities and to accept the grinning Japanese bearing gifts as a brother. Just as the Germans could never understand the psychology of the Americans, so the Japanese could never understand the psychology of the Filipinos. The Japanese were utterly lacking in subtlety. Their crude directness was repulsive to the sensitive and understanding Filipinos. Except as an aftermath of the war furnishing ammunition to overcharged nationalists, Japanese propaganda failed of its purpose.

The Filipinos even managed to find satanic humor in the repetition of their age-long predicament. An anecdote current among the people of the Philippines during the occupation explains the Filipino's aversion to the Japanese in their midst. According to the storyteller:

The Spaniards came and they called us "Indio"; the Filipino was insulted. The Americans came and they called us "Gugu"; the Filipino was insulted. The Japanese came and they called us "Brother"; the Filipino was insulted the most of all.

The three Filipinos most prominent in the occupation government under the Japanese were Jorge B. Vargas, Jose P. Laurel, and Benigno Aquino. Vargas, Chairman of the Japanese-named Executive Commission, subsequently was appointed Ambassador to Japan; he was there picked up by the American forces. Laurel, like Vargas a member of the original Executive Commission and Commissioner of Justice as well as Commissioner of the Interior, later became Chairman of the Preparatory Committee for Independence, President of

---

[5] The appeal appeared in the *Tribune* on June 6, 1943.

the Puppet Republic, and Representative of the Philippines at a Greater East Asia Congress in Tokyo. As the hour of reckoning approached, he was hurried to Japan where he was taken into custody and confined in Sugamo Prison by the Americans. Aquino was Speaker and Director General of the *Kalibapi;* he fled to Japan where he was captured by the armed forces.

Aquino is dead. With amnesty proclaimed, charges against Vargas and Laurel were dismissed. They now occupy the same places in society that they did before the war. Without benefit of pertinent proof to justify conviction of collaboration, and without hearing the defense, it would be folly to judge their cases.

GUERRILLA RESISTANCE [6]

The Bataan and Corregidor disasters, followed by easy victories for the Japanese in other parts of the Philippines, did not end the war. A resistance movement rose spontaneously almost immediately all over the Islands. In many instances groups operated at cross-purposes under officers jealous of leaders of rival bands. Gradually, however, better discipline resulted in coordination of jungle fighters with the American forces at the zero hour of invasion.

The guerilla bands were made up of many and sometimes conflicting elements. There were those who, using the word "guerrilla" to foster their own ends, operated more like bandits. Seeing the war as a chance to equalize things, they exterminated the local rich under the pretext that the latter were collaborationists. To meet such hazards, the people of many municipalities policed themselves, only to acquiesce later in having their local organizations join the genuine guerrillas. Then, of course, there were a substantial number of army officers and soldiers who of their own volition had gone to the hills and there formed the hard core of a guerrilla band. The guerrilla forces were, on October 28, 1944, blanketed into the Commonwealth Army.

Beneath the whole guerrilla movement was either active resistance or passive non-cooperation on a nationalistic basis. Neither Japanese honeyed words, nor their brutal atrocities when disillusioned could

---

[6] Travis Ingham in *Rendezvous by Submarine* (New York, 1945) tells the story of "Chick" Parsons and the guerrilla soldiers. Numerous other books descriptive of guerrilla experiences have been published. Among them are Ira Wolfert, *American Guerilla in the Philippines* (New York, 1945) made into a motion picture; Edward Haggerty, *Guerrilla Padre in Mindanao* (New York, 1946); and Yay Marking, *The Crucible* (New York, 1949).

break down opposition, active or passive. Except for avowedly pro-Japanese spies and sympathizers, and the invariably to be found opportunist collaborators, the rest of the Filipino people had in fact or in spirit joined in resistance to Japanese domination. Even the pagan mountaineers considered the Americans "good people" in contrast to the Japanese who were "bad people."

By tradition and nature, the Filipinos were particularly effective in guerrilla warfare. Against the better-equipped Japanese forces, they fought a canny war which avoided pitched battles and instead attacked from ambush and dispersed only to attack another day. In time the Japanese learned from bloody experience to stay away from remote trails and to confine their activities to police duties in population centers. The agents of the guerrillas also performed a master job of espionage. All data thus gathered, when pieced together, gave the American forces the vital information which led them to strike at the heart of the Philippines in Leyte, instead of at Mindanao where the Japanese had prepared for an expected landing. Cebu guerrillas did a particularly useful job when they captured a Japanese admiral after his plane crashed and transmitted all his plans and papers to MacArthur's headquarters.

Any attempt to list the guerrilla leaders would fall short of just completeness because of omission of modest and unheralded patriots. Yet, at least, mention must be made of the more conspicuous of the chieftains of the resistance movement.

In Mindanao to the south was found the largest and best-organized guerrilla force in the Islands. The acknowledged leader was Wendell W. Fertig, a mining engineer, who, after serving on Bataan until it fell, escaped by plane to Mindanao and there set up mobile headquarters. Notable figures in the same region included Salipada Pendatun, a Cotabato Moro, more recently a member of the Philippine Senate; and Tomas Cabili, a Filipino of independent bent of mind, later Secretary of National Defense in the pre-Republic cabinet, and a Senator. Sam Wilson, Manila business executive, gave a romantic twist to an otherwise prosaically successful career by first escaping the Japanese net to find sanctuary among the fierce Bukidnons in the wilds of Mindanao, and then becoming the virtual civilian ruler of that large island. Father Edward Haggerty became a militant *padre* in every sense of the term. And there were others, many others, whose exploits adequately told would fill volumes.

Close by Mindanao, on Panay, Negros, and Leyte Islands were other closely-knit guerrilla movements. Tomas Confesor, resistance

Governor of Panay, distinguished himself for his uncompromising stand. His defiant response to an appeal to surrender, made by an emissary of the Japanese-sponsored occupation government, gave renewed strength to the weak of heart to fight on. Macario Peralta, Jr., military head of the guerrillas in the same Panay region, for three years made splendid use of his military training. Jesus A. Villamor, Filipino ace and hero, headed the vitally important resistance movement in Negros. Ruperto Kangleon, a professional soldier with many years of military experience, came forth from retirement after escaping from a Japanese prison, a tired, sick man, to prepare Leyte for the American landing; he later became the Secretary of National Defense in the Republic of the Philippines.

In regions on Luzon were guerrilla names to conjure with, like Adduru, Anderson, Boone, Cushing, Lapham, Ramsey, Straughan, and Thorpe. The "Markings"—the Colonel and his dauntless wife—fearlessly commanded Filipino underground units in Manila and adjoining territory. Governor Wenceslao Q. Vinzons became a legendary figure in the resistance movement in Southern Luzon. He was captured, tortured, and eventually liquidated by the Japanese.

MacArthur's personal representative in the Islands, who contacted the guerrilla groups, was Charles ("Chick") Parsons. Hardly anyone meeting the modest, jovial, polo-playing "Chick" before the war would have pictured him in the role of a hero. First he hoodwinked the Japanese by claiming and getting recognition as Consul of Panama in Manila, while discreetly failing to inform them that he was a reserve officer in the U. S. Navy. Once back in Washington following repatriation with his family, "Chick" reported to the Navy and became officially known as Lieutenant Charles Parsons. An obvious choice for assignment to the Australian theatre of operation, he was an equally obvious choice, because of his wide acquaintance in Mindanao and his linguistic ability, to contact the irregular forces operating there. This he did repeatedly by submarine, bringing in supplies and news, and taking out information. In the battle of Leyte Gulf, "Chick," who meanwhile had been promoted to Commander, nearly lost his life, but survived to help the Filipinos reestablish a normal civil administration. The saga of a mountain-born Tennessee boy is written deep in Philippine-American annals.

Linked with the history of guerrilla resistance during the war is the memory of nameless thousands of Filipinos who risked or lost their lives befriending the Americans in their midst. No reward would be too great to repay them for the heroism that not alone saved men and women of another race from sure death, but helped materially in beating down Japanese arrogance to ignominious defeat.

CHIEF JUSTICE ABAD SANTOS AND GENERAL LIM— PHILIPPINE HEROES

Heroes, countless heroes, there were in the war. The exploits of some of them have become known and have been fittingly eulogized. All too many, however, remain unheralded and unsung. Were that we were able to do justice to these conspicuously worthy patriots who laid down their lives on the altar of their country. As any attempt to list those brave men and women would fail, by omission of equally brave men and women whose remains lie in remote and forgotten graves, we have taken the only remaining course—the selection of a civilian who stayed true to his oath and paid with his life for a principle; and of a soldier who fought on Bataan and then, refusing to accept defeat, carried on the fight only to be captured and done away with by the enemy.

We dedicate these pages to the memory of Chief Justice Jose Abad Santos and General Vicente Lim. No one will challenge the appropriateness of the choice.

Chief Justice Abad Santos and General Lim were alike in that both had received a democratic training in the Philippines and the United States. They were similarly alike in their unblemished characters, in their abhorrence of the wrong, and in their devotion to the right. They were unlike in that Abad Santos chose a legal and public career, while Lim became a professional soldier.

Jose Abad Santos was a native of Pampanga, born in the capitol of the Province on February 19, 1886. He was sent as a *pensionado* to the United States, and graduated in law from Northwestern University Law School, and a year later from George Washington University Law School. Returning to the Philippines he entered on a career that raised him to the top of the legal profession as President of the Philippine Bar Association. His professional duties were repeatedly interrupted by calls to be attorney for the Philippine National Bank and the Manila Railroad and Secretary of Justice, which post he filled on three occasions. In 1932 Abad Santos was appointed an Associate Justice of the Supreme Court of the Philippines. The war found filling the position of Chief Justice.

Chief Justice Abad Santos accompanied President Quezon to Corregidor and later joined the Presidential party in the Southern Islands. The President desired Abad Santos to leave with him for Australia, but the Chief Justice preferred to remain behind. He was designated by the President as his delegate "with power to act on all matters of government."[7]

Chief Justice Abad Santos was made a prisoner near Carcar, Cebu.[8] The Japanese offered him his liberty on condition that he communicate with General Manuel Roxas in Mindanao and induce him to surrender and that he engage in pro-Japanese propaganda. Abad Santos refused, because to do so would be to violate his oath of allegiance to the United States. For some unfathomable reason the Japanese also blamed Abad Santos for the issuance of emergency currency and for the burning of Cebu.

The Japanese took Abad Santos to Malabang, Mindanao. There, on May 7, 1942, was enacted a scene reminiscent of another martyrdom on December 30, 1896 when Jose Rizal laid down his life for his country. Chief Justice Abad Santos, coming from the Japanese headquarters, called to his son who was with him to come down for he had something to tell him. Then casually he said to his son: "I have been sentenced to death. They will shoot me in a few minutes." As his son began to sob, the father continued: "Do not cry. Show these people that you are brave. This is a rare opportunity for me to die for our country; not everybody is given the chance."

Still calm, even smiling, Chief Justice Abad Santos was led away. Shots rang out. The Japanese executioners reported to the son: "Your father died a glorious death."

It has been repeatedly emphasized that Jose Abad Santos, in life and in death, was the perfect public servant. In peace, his were the ways of service; in war, his were the ways of courage. In peace and war, he had but one passion: Justice. He knew but one loyalty: Country.

Vicente Lim's life and death were equally as heroic and tragic. After receiving an education in the public schools of the Philippines, he entered West Point. As he was the first Filipino to graduate from the United States Military Academy and from the Command and General Staff School and Army War College, he set the standard for other young Filipinos who were to follow him into the Army.

It was the practice for the Filipino graduates of West Point to serve with the Philippine Scouts. This was a well-trained body of

---

[7] To clear doubts regarding the power actually delegated to Chief Justice Abad Santos, a certified copy of the letter from President Quezon was obtained from Serapio D. Canceran, Private Secretary to the President.

[8] The facts relative to the arrest and execution of Chief Justice Abad Santos were furnished the author by the son, Jose Abad Santos Jr., who was with his father at the time.

Filipinos who were a component part of the U. S. Army and who were officered by Americans and Filipinos. In this organization Lim rose steadily until at the time of the outbreak of war he was a Brigadier General.

It was on Bataan that General Lim particularly distinguished himself. He commanded the 41st Division during those terrible days. Not only did he command his men, he led them. Lim was to be found in the advance outposts and foxholes getting information and being an inspiration to his soldiers.

General Lim was taken prisoner with the rest of the gallant defenders of Bataan. Later with other Filipinos, under the policy of the Japanese which at one time was in evidence, he was released.

It was intended for General Lim, together with General Roxas, to be evacuated from the Philippines by Filipino and American agents, but somehow the mission miscarried. Instead General Lim was captured by the Japanese while attempting to escape to Australia. He has never been heard of since then. The presumption is that he was immediately liquidated.

A Filipino soldier had kept the soldier's faith. His ideals have been carried on by his widow, Pilar H. Lim, a charming and talented lady, who made an exceptionally fine impression on American audiences during a tour of the United States and who is a leader in civic movements in the Philippines.

Santo Tomas Internment Camp [9]

During the first days of January, 1942, some 3,500 people, most of them Americans, were rounded up by the Japanese and shunted into the compound of the University of Santo Tomas in Manila. A few of them were later fortunate enough to be repatriated on the exchange ships *Teia Maru* and *Gripsholm*. Others, from time to time, were let out to live elsewhere or to receive medical treatment. But for most of the internees in Santo Tomas, three long hard years were to pass before liberation.

Under the sudden and harsh measures imposed by the Japanese, no more than one or two suitcases of personal effects could be taken into the Santo Tomas Camp. Inevitably near-chaos resulted. Grad-

---

[9] Representative authorities include: Frederic H. Stevens, *Santo Tomas Internment Camp* (New York, 1946), a factual and detailed description of life in the Internment Camp by an internee; James E. McCall, *Santo Tomas Internment Camp* (Lincoln, Nebraska, 1945), humorous and statistical; and Shelley Smith Mydans, *Open City* (New York, 1947) a fictionized account of life in a Japanese internment camp near Manila.

ually, by means of internal organization of the internees themselves and relaxation of strict rules by the conquerors, living conditions improved. But when the Japanese found the war going against them, they took delight in venting their spleen on their helpless prisoners. All nationals who for one reason or another had been permitted to live outside the Camp were then crowded into its confines. Toward the end came grosser abuse on the part of the Japanese and greater privation and suffering on the part of the internees.

Before the outbreak of the war, an American Coordinating Committee had been formed in Manila to take care of American interests in the Philippines. It had been noted that there appeared to be a lack of cooperation between officials of the Commonwealth Government and the United States High Commissioner's office. The Committee, however, was not at all successful in combating public and private inertia and in preparing the community for possible adverse contingencies. The High Commissioner, in fact, refused to issue a statement advising American non-essentials, especially women and children, to return to the homeland.

With the Japanese on the outskirts of Manila, the New Year's Eve dances went merrily on. On January 2nd, the Japanese Army marched into Manila.

At the head of the Santo Tomas organization was the Japanese Commandant. Under him, a central committee composed of representative American and British business men was in charge of internee government. Earl Carroll became the first General Chairman by designation of the Japanese. He was succeeded by Carrol C. Grinnell, originally named to the position from a slate of elected Committeemen. Mr. Grinnell and Messrs. A. F. Duggleby, Ernest E. Johnson, and Clifford L. Larsen were arrested in early January, 1945, taken out of the Camp and liquidated. Thus died fine representative men, murdered for no reason unless it be that they acted like men.

While Santo Tomas may be termed the main internment camp because of its location, similar organizations were provided on sites in other parts of the Islands. The Camps at Davao, Iloilo, Cebu, and Bacolod were eventually abandoned and those interned in these places were transferred to Santo Tomas. The more permanent internee camps were those at Baguio, and at Los Baños, near the College of Agriculture of the University of the Philippines. The available statistics disclose that as of the day of liberation 3,785 persons were confined in Santo Tomas, 2,146 in Los Baños, and 468 in Baguio—making a total of 6,399.

Santo Tomas and the other internment camps, with all their

faults, were as heaven compared to the horrors of Fort Santiago Prison. There in crowded, stinking, and ancient dungeons, countless Americans and Filipinos were tortured and put to death. Three of those whose dauntless spirits overcame mental and physical abuse to survive were Frederic H. Stevens, President of the American Chamber of Commerce; Roy C. Bennett, Editor of the *Manila Daily Bulletin;* and R. McCulloch Dick, Publisher of the *Philippines Free Press.*

Santo Tomas was more thoroughly organized than many a small city. The organization served the double purpose of caring for the common good in a particular sphere and of keeping everyone employed in some useful task. So it came about that the general manager of a large commercial house could be seen gravely handing out the alloted four sheets of toilet paper to each solicitant hand. The main divisions of the Camp organization were Sanitation, Health, Education, Religion, Recreation, and Food-always Food.

Alleviation of the ever-recurring food problem was provided by various means. Certain firms made sums available when permitted to do so. Filipino friends on the outside furnished whatever they could manage. One Filipino, Luis de Alcuaz, Secretary to the Rector of Santo Tomas University, helped set up secret transmitter and receiving sets, smuggled in medicine, and during "the era of starvation" got thousands of cans of food and over a ton of beans into camp. Comfort kits were eventually received from the Red Cross. But the food problem was never licked.

Under the strain, all changed. Many, particularly the elderly, were unable to stand the privations, especially during the bleak last days when there was an average of twenty-one deaths per month. Even among the more hardy survivors, the average weight loss per person was forty-two pounds. This is understandable when a sample menu for one day in January, 1945 was:

Breakfast	*Lunch*
1 ladle mush (watery)	1 ladle soy bean soup
1 cup hot water	

Dinner

Camote — Beans — Rice Stew

Rescue came as a great surprise and in the nick of time. Word had somehow reached MacArthur's Headquarters that as a final gesture in refined barbarism, the Japanese losers planned a general massacre of the defenseless internees. A small but fiercely insistent force of veteran Americans from the 1st Cavalry Division fought through to the Camp on February 3, 1945. Followed harrowing hours as Japanese guards barricaded themselves in the education building of the Camp with unfortunate internees as hostages. A truce by means of which the Japanese were permitted to withdraw to their lines settled this matter, only to be followed by death for twenty-five internees and the wounding of many others as the Japanese guns got the range.

American armor and courage would not be denied. Manila was cleared of the enemy. Internees headed for the United States. On July 14, 1945 the Santo Tomas Internment Camp was closed.

It was not until four years after Japan's surrender that the United States was ready to tackle the job of paying off World War II claims against the government. Belatedly in 1948, the Congress of the United States finally got around to approve legislation to impound enemy assets and to make the fund thus created available for the relief of internees who were American citizens.[10] Another year elapsed before the members of the War Claims Commission which was to receive and adjudicate claims were appointed. Compensation at the rate of $60 for each month of detention for adults ($25 if under eighteen) and disability benefits were authorized. The Commission was directed to receive claims of all kinds from Americans or other nationals and report to the Congress with recommendation for possible action.

Efforts have been exerted to extend the benefits granted to civilian American citizens to civilian Filipino citizens who were held by the Japanese as prisoners or hostages.

THE GOVERNMENT-IN-EXILE [11]

The exigencies of war forced the regularly constituted Government of the Commonwealth of the Philippines to function outside the territorial limits of the Phillipines.

Of course it had not been planned that way. Early in November, 1941, Quezon and Osmeña had been returned to the offices of President and Vice President, respectively, by the overwhelming vote of the electorate. In December, the Congress of the Philippines, in extraordinary session, declared a total emergency and granted the President unlimited powers.[12] All the resources of the country were placed at

---

[10] War Claims Act of 1948, being Public Law 896 of the 80th Congress of July 3, 1948. Frank E. Wilson was the active spokesman for the internees in securing approval of this legislation.

[11] Note particularly David Bernstein, *The Philippine Story*, Chs. IX-XII (New York, 1947). Mr. Bernstein served as adviser to Presidents Quezon and Osmena, 1942-46.

[12] Commonwealth Act No. 671, approved December 16, 1941.

the disposal of the United States. Those were proper steps, but they fell short of meeting the national crisis. War did not wait on civilian convenience.

The afternoon before Christmas, President Quezon accompanied by his family and Vice President Osmeña, Chief Justice Abad Santos, Chief of Staff Major General Valdez, and the President's inseparable aide Colonel Manuel Nieto left Malacañan Palace in Manila for Corregidor.

The Philippine Government was still able to operate in reduced fashion on "unoccupied territory." In the mouth of Corregidor's Malinta tunnel, President Quezon was inaugurated for a second term under circumstances in strange contrast to the pomp attendant on the ceremonies that marked the beginning of his first term.

From the embattled rock, all that could be done to cooperate in the war effort was done. Efforts were continuously made to bolster the morale of the Filipino troops and the resistance spirit of the civilian populace. Only once did a defeatist frame of mind overwhelm President Quezon. This was when from gloomy Corregidor he impulsively proposed that independence for the Philippines be declared by the United States, with the Islands neutralized, and with both American and Japanese forces withdrawn. Washington soon convinced the President of the utter impracticability of such a scheme.[13] Ever afterwards Quezon never deviated from unflinching support of the war effort of the United Nations until the unholy alliance between Germany, Italy and Japan should be broken and defeated.

Confinement on Corregidor was like trying to function from a straight jacket. On February 20, Quezon was able to effect his escape to the Southern Islands of the Philippines, from there to Australia, and from Australia to Washington where he was met by President Roosevelt and every available former Governor General and High Commissioner. Three days after Quezon left Corregidor, High Commissioner Sayre and party, who had also retreated there, departed by submarine for the United States.

The Commonwealth Government was now a Government-In-Exile in every sense of the phrase.

The Government of the Commonwealth of the Philippines was reestablished in Washington early in 1942. Most of the Filipinos experienced in administration had been left behind in the Philippines,

---

[13] Henry L. Stimson and McGeorge Bundy, *On Active Service in Peace and War*, pp. 397 *et seq.*, including the quoted message of President Roosevelt to General MacArthur of February 9, 1942.

but such as were available in the United States were pressed into service. Major General Valdes and Colonel Nieto, who had accompanied the President, were named Secretary of National Defense and Secretary of Agriculture and Commerce, respectively. Jaime Hernandez, who happened to be in the United States when war broke out, handled most financial matters. Joaquin M. Elizalde continued as Resident Commissioner. Vice President Osmeña, apparently by design, was kept in the background.

It was at best a makeshift arrangement, yet with it President Quezon managed to carry on. He signed the agreement among the United Nations. He was a member of the Pacific War Council and objected to an overall strategy that made the Pacific a secondary theatre in the global war. He advocated advancing the date of independence for the Philippines to meet Japanese propaganda. He made it his policy to maintain the morale of the people at home. All this was accomplished under the handicap of steadily deteriorating health.

President Quezon was naturally disturbed about the ugly rumors as to the change of front and loyalty of the Filipino people which became widespread in the United States. He needed first-hand information on the real situation in the Islands. Dr. Emigdio Cruz, one of the President's personal physicians, volunteered for the hazardous secret mission. He was landed in Negros by submarine, worked his way northward to Manila, interviewed General Roxas, Chief Justice Yulo, and other leaders right under the noses of the Japanese, secured the information he was sent to get, and reported back to the President, who was ill in Miami, Florida. Dr. Cruz was awarded the Medal for Valor. If ever a man deserved it, Dr. Cruz did for personal courage and cool daring.[14]

Where the Government-In-Exile was least efficient was in the formulation of plans for a post-war program. There were a number of reasons for this weakness. One was the illness of President Quezon. Another was inability, readily understandable, to appreciate the nature and extent of war damage in the Philippines, coupled with the belief that the United States would be responsible for reconstruction and rehabilitation. Eventually, by Executive Order, a Post War Planning Board with Vice President Osmeña as Chairman was established. This body came into being too late, and received too little support, to become an effective agency.

14 The thrilling adventures of Lieutenant Colonel Emigdio Cruz, M. C., as told to Dr. Conrado Mata, are narrated under the title "Quezon's Secret Agent" in the Philippines Free Press of January 31, February 7, and February 14, 1948.

The Constitution of the Philippines, as amended, contemplated that the President should not serve for more than than eight consecutive years. The constitutionally provided period expired for President Quezon on November 15, 1943. He was expected on that date to relinquish the office of President to Vice President Osmeña. But the President loved power, and as others have done before him, found an excuse to retain power. It was pointed out that the Philippines was the battleground of the war, and that he was the symbol of Philippine resistance to the enemy. Vice President Osmeña, with the modest abstention so typical of him when the welfare of his country was at stake, gracefully yielded. The Congress of the United States approved a Joint Resolution extending the terms of office of the President and Vice President until the expulsion of the Japanese from the Philippines.[15] This action was constitutionally indefensible but perhaps was opportunely expedient.

President Quezon's prayer that he might be spared to see his native land again was not to be granted. He breathed his last on the first of August, 1944, as the American forces were gathering for the upward sweep that was to drive the enemy from the Philippines. Sergio Osmeña took office in Washington on the same day, as second President of the Commonwealth of the Philippines.

The Government-in-Exile became a *de jure* Government of the Philippines when President Osmeña landed in Leyte with General MacArthur on October 20, 1944.

PRESIDENT QUEZON WAGES THE GOOD FIGHT [16]

An autobiography of President Manuel Luis Quezon, regrettably in incomplete form, published posthumously, was called "The Good Fight." The title was well chosen. Courage was the predominant trait which took a boy from a humble home in an isolated municipality of the Philippines to the Presidency in Malacañan Palace and a seat among the mighty.

The former Province of Tayabas, recently and appropriately rechristened Quezon, occupies a long thin strip of land in the central part of the Island of Luzon. The most northernly town on the

---

[15] Joint Resolution 95, Public Law 186, 78th Congress, approved November 12, 1943.

[16] See Manuel Luis Quezon, *The Good Fight* (Appleton-Century, New York, 1946), an incomplete autobiography by the President of the Commonwealth of the Philippines, published posthumously. Biographies of President Quezon include: Carlos Quirino, *Quezon, Man of Destiny* (Manila, 1935), the winner of a prize contest, and Sol H. Gwekoh, *Manuel Quezon: His Life and Career* (Manila, 1948). All aspects of President Quezon's life are covered.

eastern coast of the province is Baler. Not only is the town remote and nearly inaccessible, but it is small. Since the heroic stand of the Spanish garrison during the Philippine Revolution, Baler's one claim to fame has been that it was the birthplace of Manuel Luis Quezon, first President of the Commonwealth of the Philippines.

Manuel Luis (from the patron Saint of Baler, Saint Luis, Bishop of Toulouse) Quezon was born on August 19, 1878. His father was a Tagalog school teacher and his mother a Spanish *mestiza*. They early discerned the promise in the boy and made every possible sacrifice so that he could secure an education. With such assistance as his father could give him and by working at menial tasks himself, Manuel was able to graduate from the San Juan de Letran College in Manila and was enrolled in the law course of the University of Santo Tomas when hostilities between the American and Filipino forces started. Thereupon young Quezon joined the Filipino Army and took part in the war. On surrender to the United States Army, Major Quezon (he had risen from 2nd Lieutenant to Major) was imprisoned for six months.

After being released from confinement, Quezon passed the bar examination with high marks and entered into the practice of his profession. But the public service was calling. From 1905 Quezon held public office without interruption until his death. His career was a variation of a single theme—to achieve independence for the Philippines and in so doing advance his personal ambition.

Attorney Quezon was induced to leave private practice to become provincial *fiscal* (district attorney) of Mindoro, and later of Tayabas. Soon thereafter he was elected Governor of Tayabas and won local renown as a vigorous executive. From the provincial governorship it was but a step to the first Philippine Assembly, wherein he became floor leader. Then he was sent as Resident Commissioner to the United States, where he remained until after the enactment of the Jones Law. On the constitution of the Philippine Senate as the upper House of the Philippine Legislature, he was elected Senator and President of the Senate. His position of leadership was made secure by election and reelection as the President of the Philippine Commonwealth.

The foregoing is the bare biographical data connected with the life of President Manuel Luis Quezon. Let us now fill in the outline.

There were three phases to the Quezon career. The first may be called preparatory. It was made up of sacrifices to secure an education, of rough experience in the Army, and of a start in politics which carried him to the Islands' legislative body. Had Quezon stopped there, he would have remained one of the crowd. Instead, he went forward to become the leader. In one phase of this part of Quezon's life, he took charge of the American end of the campaign for Philippine emancipation. In the other phase, he dominated Philippine politics.

Manuel Quezon was the accredited ambassador of his people to the United States. In the early part of that period, he was one of the two Resident Commissioners. In the latter part of that period, he headed various Philippine missions which journeyed to Washington to ask independence from the President and the Congress of the United States. In the dual role of astute diplomat and earnest advocate he presented his case skillfully and convincingly.

The marvel of it all was that Quezon was able to master his own emotions and prejudices and intuitively to comprehend the purposes of those arrayed against him. Quezon was Spanish-trained; but he learned English quickly and thoroughly. Quezon had had little acquaintance with Americans; but he soon grasped their psychology. Quezon was an *ex-insurrecto* and a firebrand; but his utterances were characterized by a restraint and tone that carried conviction. Quezon had rejected the Hare-Hawes-Cutting Act; but with amazing dexterity he extricated himself from an awkward position and convinced President Roosevelt and a doubting Congress that the same bill should be passed with Quezon-suggested changes.

In 1916 Quezon returned to the Philippines with the Jones Autonomy Act in his pocket. Eighteen years later he returned with the Tydings-McDuffie Commonwealth and Independence Act to his credit. These two simple statements constitute their own testimonials of work well done.

While Quezon kept watch over American developments with one eye, with the other he kept under observation events in his own country. In 1922, by a swift offensive, he overwhelmed his rival Osmeña. No sooner was he in power, than he gave battle to Governor General Wood and General Aguinaldo. No sooner was a truce effected, then there came another battle with Osmeña, who had allied with him Speaker Manuel Roxas and the other politically influential members of the mission who were bringing back with them an independence law. Quezon defeated them at the polls.

The mere statements of Quezon's political accomplishments fail to do justice to them. In Osmeña he had to meet the old master, and Osmeña, endowed with true Oriental guile and shrewdness, was no mean antagonist. In Roxas he had to meet a Quezon-trained protégé of great ability, and the idol of the Philippine youth. Quezon won out against the Osmeña-Roxas combination. If in the United States Quezon proved himself to be an earnest advocate, in the Philippines he proved himself to be a crafty and resourceful politician.

One reason for Quezon's political success was that as a public speaker he had no peer and was able to attract immense audiences. He was capable of speaking fluently in English, Spanish, or Tagalog, as the exigencies of the situation demanded. He was equally at home before critical listeners of the upper crust and a Tondo mass meeting of the common people. His voice was not strong; in fact it was grating. It was his dynamic force, earnestness and eloquence, coupled with an ability to coin daring phrases, that captured his listeners. When he pungently said, "Better a government run like hell by the Filipinos than one run like heaven by the Americans," it was a typical Quezonian remark intended to attract attention to his theme.

Enemies were not lacking to call Quezon neurotic and volatile, vain and unpredictable, an opportunist athirst for power. These attacks, of course, could only mean that Quezon with all his faults was versatile and brilliant. He was a great showman who thrived on a place in the limelight. He embarked on political pilgrimages all over the world, with a large entourage that entailed fabulous expense accounts. Nevertheless, he enjoyed the confidence of his people and commanded unrivalled prestige among them.

Manuel Quezon was essentially human. Indeed his weaknesses constituted some of his most lovable qualities. He enjoyed a good time, wanted to have entertaining people around him, was not above taking a drink, and was fond of dancing with pretty partners. Also, he liked to draw up his chair for a game of poker or bridge, and he played a good hand. He lived well, even luxuriously, but was not a multimillionaire. Mrs. Quezon was the capable manager of the family finances.

Quezon's relations with Americans were unique. Businessmen were mostly opponents of independence, and yet they were his friends and contributed to his campaign funds. Jake Rosenthal became his constant companion. Close bonds with the members of the United States Congress were established. Appointments of favored Governors General were wangled. Correct, even intimate, relations with most Chief Executives and High Commissioners were maintained. Certainly a many-sided man was Quezon.

In his prime, Quezon was a handsome man. Of middle height, his frame was lithe and erect. But it was his head that drew attention—the arched nose of the Spanish *Conquistador* which quivered when he was excited, dark flashing eyes, and abundant black hair flecked with gray. Set in the light-tinted skin of his Spanish forbears, his was a profile to admire. A gentleman of chivalrous bearing and faultlessly attired, he was at home in any company. When he entered a room, his attractive personality dominated the scene at once. No wonder a man like Manuel Quezon could hold the esteem of men and the admiration of women.

Quezon enjoyed his role of eligible bachelor. But when he chose a helpmate, he chose well. Unannounced, without pomp, and in Hongkong, Quezon married his first cousin, Aurora Aragon. She made him a good wife, one to raise his children, to be the head of the household, to comfort him in sickness, and to look tolerantly on his indiscretions. To the marriage four children were born; three girls—one still living—and one boy. The son, Manuel Jr., deeply religious in nature, studied for the priesthood.

It was intimated previously that courage should appear on the escutcheon of the Quezon family. It took courage for the youth Manuel to give up schooling to join the insurgents in the field. It took courage for the young Commissioner to journey to the United States to face a strange people and to speak to them in their own tongue. It took courage for the middle-aged Senator to fight Wood, Aguinaldo, Osmeña, and Roxas. It took courage for the aging President to come to grips with tuberculosis, appendicitis, and a kidney complaint, to curb a too-active spirit, and to will himself to retain some health. It took courage for President of the Philippines Quezon to assume the helm as the Philippine Ship of State put out into treacherous Oriental seas. And it took courage, with health steadily deteriorating, for him to carry on in the damp tunnels of Corregidor and in faraway Washington, as the ravages of war swept his homeland.

The same spirit of fortitude made Quezon inquisitive and adventurous. In religion particularly was an inconsistent quality displayed. He was brought up a Catholic, only to draw away from the Church to join the Masonic fraternity. He became Grand Master of Masons in the Philippines, only to renounce his apostasy to return to the Church. He died a devout Catholic.

Finis was written to the Good Fight for Manuel Luis Quezon at Saranac Lake on August 1, 1944 when he surrendered his spirit to a higher power.

A grateful and admiring people have expressed their love and respect for their President in many and diverse ways. Quezon City, close to old Manila, is the newly authorized capitol of the Republic. After him have been named Quezon Province, Quezon Bridge,

Quezon Institute, and Quezon Boulevards and Avenues. A Quezon Memorial is the latest project.

Someone has remarked that the history of the Philippines from 1906 to 1945 and the biography of Manuel Luis Quezon "are indissolubly one." That is correct. When, therefore, the Filipino people honor their beloved leader, they honor themselves.

GENERAL MACARTHUR RETURNS [17]

General MacArthur's pledge—"I Shall Return"—superb in simplicity and dramatic in appeal, became the slogan of American reoccupation of the Philippines. Matchboxes with wrappers displaying crossed American and Filipino flags and the words "I Shall Return—MacArthur" appeared as if by magic all over the Islands; such articles even cropped up on the desks of Japanese officers and did nothing to bolster their morale. MacArthur to the hard-pressed Filipino people typified America and hope.

General Douglas MacArthur kept his word. On October 20, 1944 he waded ashore at Red Beach on Leyte Island with the American forces. MacArthur had returned.

The Navy had wanted to leapfrog the islands in the Philippine group to attack Formosa for a final drive on Japan. President Roosevelt, at the urging of General MacArthur, vetoed the strategical project in favor of the invasion of the Philippines. This issue once settled, plans were made for a landing on Mindanao to be followed by an advance into Leyte. These plans were cancelled, when control of the air appeared assured, on recommendation of Admiral "Bull" Halsey, and were approved by General MacArthur, in favor of by-passing of Mindanao and a direct entrance into Leyte farther north. The war had been advanced two months or more.

While the element of surprise worked against the Japanese, it did not prevent them from putting up a bitter resistance on land, and from developing a cunningly conceived and desperate attempt to destroy the newly established Leyte beachhead from the sea.

The Battle of Leyte Gulf, between October 23-26, 1944, has been described by competent authorites, by any standard, "the greatest naval battle of history." [18] In reality this vast struggle was a series

---

[17] Note Fleet Admiral William F. Halsey and Lieutenant Commander Bryan, *Admiral Halsey's Story* (New York, 1947); *General Kenney Reports* (New York, 1949); and Lt. Gen. Robert L. Eichelberger, *Our Jungle Road to Tokyo* (New York, 1950).

[18] Note James A. Field, Jr., *The Japanese at Leyte Gulf, the Sho Operation* (Princeton University Press, 1947) — Valuable because based on Japanese source materials, and C. Vann Woodward, *The Battle for Leyte Gulf* (New York, 1947)— well documented.

of engagements fought over an area in encounters separated by as much as a thousand miles. The focus, however, of the entire combatant strength of the Japanese Navy, as it hurled itself from three directions against America's mightiest Armada, was on the transport area with its troop and supply ships in Leyte Gulf.

That the Japanese approached dangerously near to success can now offer little consolation to them. The outcome was the effective destruction of the Japanese Navy. While the actions of the Commanders at Leyte Gulf, American and Japanese, will be analysed and debated for years, the result remains the same—avoidance of disaster of incalculable proportions at the hands of the Japanese, overwhelming victory for the Americans.

After Leyte followed landings on Luzon to the north, the sealing off of Bataan and Corregidor in days—whereas it had taken the Japanese months to capture them—and the clean-up of Manila after a bloody struggle. With the Philippines lost to the Japanese, they had lost the war. The scene shifted to Japan and to the surrender of the Japanese to MacArthur.

Emphasis has perhaps unavoidably been laid on American victories. They were just as much Filipino victories. Filipinos in the Islands sought out information that paved the way for the invasion. Filipinos specially trained in Australia volunteered for the hazardous duties of landing close to Luzon, where the Japanese headquarters were located, and reported on the movements of the Japanese merchant marine, navy, and aircraft, and on weather conditions. Major Ricardo C. Galang's espionage work on a secret mission to the Philippines was typical of the unflinching devotion to duty of these men.[19] Filipino irregular forces cooperated effectively in the battles with the Japanese.

Many of those who participated in dangerous reconnaissance missions to the Islands were American or Hawaiian-resident Filipinos. They came from a larger group who demanded the right to take an active part in the liberation of the Philippines. Regiments of eager Filipino volunteers were trained to become a component unit of the United States Army.[20]

The dominant figure in the Pacific throughout the Second World War was General Douglas MacArthur.

The name MacArthur is writ large in the history of the Philippines.

[19] Described in *Secret Mission to the Philippines* by Major Ricardo C. Galang (Manila, 1948).

[20] Franc Shor, "See You In Manila," *American Legion Magazine*, March, 1943, condensed in *Readers Digest*.

Lieutenant General Arthur MacArthur was Military Governor of the Islands immediately after the Spanish-American War. His son Douglas spent much of his youth and middle age in the Philippines. Following the First World War in which General Douglas Mac-Arthur commanded the Rainbow Division, he returned to the Philippines to head the Philippine Division in Manila, and later the Philippine Department. He relinquished the post of Chief of Staff of the United States Army in 1935 to accept the position of Military Adviser of the newly inaugurated Commonwealth of the Philippines.

The outbreak of the Second World War found General Mac-Arthur with the national defense program of the Philippines well started. The President of the United States recalled him to active service as Commander in Chief of the American and Filipino forces during the invasion of the Philippines by the Japanese, and later as Supreme Commander of Allied Forces in the Southwest Pacific. The high moment of a brilliant career came when in August, 1945, General MacArthur accepted the surrender of the Japanese. Since that date he has commanded the occupational forces in Japan and the United Nations forces in Korea.

It was perhaps inevitable that Douglas MacArthur who, from the day he was graduated from West Point with an all-time scholastic record, invariably ranked Number One in everything he undertook, should become a controversial figure. His long and continuous sojourn in the Far East—fourteen consecutive years with vast responsibilities resting on his shoulders, without return to the homeland, and without a vacation—cast about him an aura of mystery. His dramatically phrased communiques incited comment and interest. Curiously, people either approved the General with an admiration approaching adulation or disliked him with an intensity akin to hate. But nothing could justify the wave of vilification, undoubtedly generated by unfriendly sources and certainly base slanders, that gained circulation.

As a matter of fact, there is nothing basically controversial or particularly mysterious about Douglas MacArthur. The author thus affirms on the strength of having been associated with Far Eastern affairs approximately the same length of time as General MacArthur and having been honored with his life-long friendship.

General Douglas MacArthur even in the sunset of life is a tall, erect and handsome man. He dresses meticulously—on occasion jauntily. He shuns formal social affairs when possible, but when protocol demands attendance he fulfills his obligations with geniality. In his own home, with his smiling, vivacious wife Jean, who exudes the hospitality of the South, General MacArthur is a charming host.

In any gathering he is an interesting conversationalist whose knowledge of history and world affairs is remarkable.

General MacArthur knows the Orient and understands the Oriental as no other American does. His aloofness, his smart military bearing, his air of finality which uninformed Americans have criticized, these traits captivated the Filipinos and other nationals who admire and respect a leader. His prose, which was ridiculed in the United States, was tailored to fit Oriental psychology. As to reports that he had large holdings in the Philippines, which motivated the nature of his strategy in the war, they were baseless canards. Of his integrity and courage there can be no question.

General MacArthur's knack for dealing with the Orientals was never better demonstrated than in his masterly administration of surrendered Japan. The soldier the Japanese feared in war became their hero in peace. He has in the flowery kingdom rescued the people from despotic medievalism. He has given them a constitution which outlines a democratic pattern for their country. He has built a new order in Japan and perhaps provided a new ally against a new enemy.

Not alone had General MacArthur returned to the Philippines to defeat the Japanese, but by so doing he made it possible for the Filipinos to press onward in orderly course toward an independence that had been rudely interrupted by the Japanese occupation; and in Japan he became the symbol of a democracy which in time should provide a friendly neighbor for the Philippines.

Statesman Osmena Becomes President [21]

At long last, Sergio Osmeña's self-sacrifice for the common good of the Filipino people was rewarded. At long last, the months of patient waiting were over and he could join his family in his native land. On the day of President Quezon's death, Vice President Osmeña succeeded to the Presidency. Side by side with General MacArthur, President Osmeña landed in Leyte.

Like the Supreme Commander of the Armed forces, the second President of the Commonwealth of the Philippines had returned. In his first proclamation on Philippine soil, he announced the reestablishment of the Commonwealth of the Philippines and an end to the "republic organized under enemy duress." However, a Civil Affairs

---

[21] Section originally read by Justice Manuel C. Briones. See seventh and final report of U. S. High Commissioner McNutt, pp. 4-6, 82-84.

Unit of the American Army continued to function until well along in the following year.

It was no easy task that confronted President Osmeña. In Washington, after taking over the Presidency, he was only able to set up a technical committee and to instigate hastily conceived measures. Once in the Philippines he had to wait on military expediency and the eventual surrender of the enemy. He came back to a land ravaged by war, blighted by disorder, and divided into domestic camps of alleged collaborationists and anti-collaborationists. In spite of all obstacles, progress toward rehabilitation and the reestablishment of a normal administration was made.

President Osmeña experienced difficulty in recruiting a workable organization. Naturally he named to the Cabinet and other offices men who had been conspicuous in the resistance movement and who were in his confidence. When the Legislature refused confirmation, the President composed differences as best he could and attempted appeasement of the opposing forces to obtain at least a semblance of national unity. Even when an exciting campaign was on to elect the first President of the Republic, he refused to leave his desk to make campaign speeches to advance his own candidacy.

There was nothing strange or unusual in Osmeña's behavior during the comparatively brief period he was to occupy the Presidential chair. He had always displayed poise; he retained that unhurried quality of dignity. He had always favored compromise to advance the country's interest even at the expense of personal ambition; he tried again the formula that in the past had proven so useful, but now there were new conditions and bitter rivalries that no formula could meet. He had stood unflinchingly for the independence of the Philippines and the maintenance of close relations with the United States; he continued to make these the basic tenets of his actions. Even in defeat, when the people indicated their wish to have the magnetic Roxas for President, Osmeña retained his composure, accepted the verdict without complaint, declined to cast any aspersions on his victorious rival, and retired quietly to his home in Cebu.

Sergio Osmeña was born in Cebu on September 9, 1878. His schooling was received in the Paulist College and Seminary of Cebu, the San Juan de Letran College, and the University of Santo Tomas; one of his classmates was Manuel Quezon. However, Osmeña's education is much broader in scope. Of a studious nature, he is widely read—particularly in the fields of law, history and politics—and widely travelled. The early environment of Osmeña made him a sincere adherent of the Roman Catholic faith and of a reverently religious bent.

The public career of Osmeña began as provincial *fiscal* of Cebu and Oriental Negros in 1904. Then elected Governor of Cebu, he gained additional prestige on being chosen President of the first Provincial Governor's Convention in 1906. Shortly thereafter, his province sent him as a delegate to the first Philippine Assembly. Delegate Osmeña was the logical candidate for Speaker, to which position he was elected by acclamation. He remained as Speaker until 1922, when he was elected Senator from Cebu. He remained a member of the Senate until he was elected Vice President of the Commonwealth of the Philippines. Reelected Vice President shortly before the Japanese occupation of the Philippines, Osmeña was forced into exile in the United States.

The war period found Osmeña living in Washington. They were not very profitable years for him. Whether by jealous design or merely scornful indifference, President Quezon relied increasingly less on the counsel of the Vice President. Far from revealing resentment, with the inscrutable calm for which Osmeña is famous, at the critical moment he voluntarily relinquished the right to the Presidency, which constitutionally was his in favor of Quezon. He took this stand because he was convinced it would not be for the best interests of the Philippines to change leaders during the war. Once more Osmeña had laid the offering of a supreme personal sacrifice on the altar of his country.

Osmeña was undisputed head of the *Nationalista* Party for fourteen years. When he decided to retain the Speakership of the House and in that position remain as head of the party, he lost out to President of the Senate Quezon. Thereafter Osmeña and Quezon were alternately rivals and cooperating chieftains. In the election to determine who should be the President of the Republic of the Philippines, Osmeña drew to his side many of his former supporters together with an incongruous group of radicals, while General Manuel Roxas fell heir to most of the support of the Quezon men. Even in death Quezon vanquished his rival Osmeña.

The foregoing biographical sketch of a well known public man needs embellishment to bring forth the sterling qualities of one of the outstanding leaders of the Filipino people. To begin with, let it be said that it fell to Sergio Osmeña's lot to organize and direct the scattered elements of nationalism during a critical epoch of Philippine history. Recall that the Filipino insurgents had been decisively overwhelmed on the field of battle. Osmeña had to accomplish by peaceful measures what warlike weapons had failed to accomplish. This he did by avoiding any hint of disloyalty to the American Government, cooperating with the sovereign power whenever he could, furnishing in himself an example of Filipino capaciy for self-government, and adroitly outmaneuvering American Governors General and thus gaining more rights for his people. No one can scan the career of this man without a gasp of astonishment at his success.

Consider the organization of the Philippine Assembly way back in 1907. Untried and unacquainted men made up its membership; and some of the older delegates were suspicious and envious of the young Speaker. Yet the Speaker was able to consolidate these divergent factions and to handle them efficiently. At the same time, favorable contacts with American Commissioners, an American Governor General, and critical visiting Secretary of War had to be maintained. Placidly the Speaker began by insisting, against opposition, that the Rules of the House of Representatives of the United States Congress be adopted. As placidly he began preparing himself for his job by studying parliamentary law and procedure. He gave evidence of his fairness by treating the minority with the maximum consideration. Within a short space of time no one doubted that Sergio Osmeña was as much Speaker of the Philippine Assembly as Joe Cannon had ever been in the zenith of his career as Speaker of the House of Representatives of the American Congress.

Subsequently as a member of the Philippine Senate, Osmeña continued to display his statesmanlike qualities. He was no longer Number One in authority, but that did not deter him from cooperating in the formulation of constructive legislation.

In the early days of the drive for Philippine independence, Osmeña was the directing head from Manila. The General in the field was Quezon. Later the roles were reversed. Osmeña was several times co-chairman of missions to the United States, including the one that brought home the Hare-Hawes-Cutting Act. It was in this field that he displayed his talents for diplomacy.

It is the man Osmeña that rouses particular interest. Many words have been scattered about in attempted analysis of his character. He has been called urbane in gaining his ends in negotiation, illimitably patient, serene, wise, astute, and cautious. All are in a way accurately analytical phrases. To them should be added the dominant rule of his life, courtesy. In his office he was the attentive listener. In his home he was the considerate host who with consummate tact entertained his guests.

Osmeña is happily married to Esperanza Limjap of the wealthy Manila family of that name. But the war years were not happy ones for Osmeña in far-off Washington, or for his wife in the Philippines who finally managed to escape to friendly areas to avoid Japanese retaliation for her husband's activities. One of Osmeña's sons lost his life as a guerrilla, and two other sons were allegedly tinged with collaboration. Typical of Osmeña was his refusal either by word or deed to intervene on behalf of the sons who were charged with helping the enemy. Osmeña is content to live modestly and sedately with his family in retirement in his home city of Cebu.

The breath of scandal has lashed prominent men of the Philippines for their fondness for clandestine affairs of the heart; it has never touched Osmeña. Some in public life are lax in their appointments; not Osmeña. He is one Filipino who keeps his engagements to the minute. Still others may say one thing and mean another; Osmeña with a reputation for complete integrity, fulfills his promises. One brief sentence sums up Sergio Osmeña's character: He is a gentleman, a Christian gentleman.

Osmeña has a sense of detachment which apparently nothing can penetrate. He much prefers negotiations to fighting. Yet when forced to do battle, he can do so courageously and determinedly. But with him, it is a battle of sportsmen. The exigencies of the situation brought him into opposition to Governor General Forbes, but the two remained personally good friends. Politics required that on two occasions he contest with Quezon at the polls, yet he and Quezon remained associates. A break in the ranks made Osmeña and Roxas rival candidates for the Presidency, but when the latter won, Osmeña was the first to congratulate the victor.

President Quezon once termed Sergio Osmeña "the best statesman that the Philippines has ever produced." That is a correct qualification of Osmeña. He is a statesman.

Sergio Osmeña personifies all that is best in Philippine history, politics and life. Former Speaker, former Vice President, former President Osmeña is a gentleman and a statesman.

CHAPTER IX

THE REPUBLIC OF THE PHILIPPINES INAUGURATED [1]

Pre-Independence Election

A national election was held in the Philippines on April 23, 1946. Behind that simple statement of fact were months of uncertainty and political maneuvering.

The presidential term should have ended on November 15, 1945 and should have been preceded by an election two months earlier. The holding of an election on the legally provided date was made impossible because of the presence of Japanese forces in certain sections of the Islands and the disruption of transportation and communications. Moreover, the Joint Resolution of the United States Congress passed in 1943 authorized the Commonwealth President to continue in office until "orderly democratic processes were restored" in the Philippines and until his successor elected by constitutional methods could qualify. Prodded into action by another proposed Joint Resolution which had passed the House of Representatives and was pending consideration in the Senate of the United States Congress, the Philippine Congress in special session approved a law effective on January 5, 1946 that provided for a national election on the above indicated date of April 23, for a new Congress to convene a month later, and for the incoming President to be inaugurated on May 28. [2]

A brief period of three months was available in which to conclude preparations for the holding of the election. Registration to make up a new list of voters was completed. Official ballots were printed and distributed. Polling places were found and set up. Obstacles which at first sight seemed insurmountable were overcome.

---

[1] The Blue Book, First Anniversary of the Republic of the Philippines contains source material. So likewise does the seventh and final report of Hon. Paul V. McNutt, U. S. High Commissioner to the Philippines, dated June 30, 1946, House Document No. 389. A series of well written articles by Edward W. Mill, at the time Assistant Chief of the Division of Philippine Affairs, Office of Far Eastern Affairs, Department of State, summarizes the problems of the Republic of the Philippines; see Department of State Bulletins of June 9, 1946, September 15, 1946, and June 29, 1947.

[2] Commonwealth Act No. 725.

Inauguration of the Republic of the Philippines on July 4, 1946, showing from left to right, U. S. High Commissioner Paul V. McNutt, President Manuel Roxas, Vice President Elpidio Quirino and General Douglas MacArthur.

The election conformed to the pattern of Philippine politics that had been in evidence for many years. The *Nacionalista* Party had been long dominant, with Quezon and Osmeña as leading figures. Now Quezon was dead, and his heir was Roxas. According to accepted practice, negotiations were in order to weld the two factions together, with either Osmeña or Roxas Number One and the other Number Two. Frenzied negotiations were, indeed, conducted according to ritual. But now Roxas balked and adamantly declined the proffer of the Vice Presidency on an Osmeña ticket, and of course Osmeña having been President could not decently accept the secondary office. An irrevocable split in the grand old party was inevitable.

In January, 1946 the two groups met in separate conventions. The "Loyalist" Osmeña wing of the *Nacionalista* Party nominated Sergio Osmeña for President and Senator Eulogio Rodriguez for Vice President. The Roxas faction of the *Nacionalista* Party, after adopting the name "*Nacionalista* Party (Liberal Wing)," nominated Manuel Roxas for President and Senator Elpidio Quirino for Vice President.

In addition to the two major parties, there were, as there had been, "splinter parties" traditionally leftist in political philosophy. The most important of these organizations were the Democratic Alliance—Hukbalahap—Peasants Union—CLO which supported Osmeña. The very fact of this backing, however, had the counter effect of losing Osmeña the votes of men and women of independent inclination who feared radical control.

The campaign followed the general course of previous elections in the Philippines. The platforms of the two parties were as alike as two peas in a pod. As was traditional, the sole issue was focused on the personal question: Should Osmeña or Roxas be chosen to lead? As befitted his temperament, Osmeña remained in Malacañan and contented himself with making one major speech in Manila three days before the election. Roxas, on the other hand, conducted an extensive campaign which took him all over the Islands, making hundreds of speeches.

The United States Government maintained a "hands off" attitude during the election. The United States High Commission was led to state that "The United States Government will carry out its pledge of aid to the Philippine people regardless of whom they choose as their next President." Inasmuch as it had been charged by an Osmeña adherent that if Roxas was elected the Philippines would receive not a cent of help, the statement of the High Commissioner was a comforting assurance to the Roxas people. American troops in the Islands were confined to their encampments to forestall any charge of intervention.

A fair election was held. Few disorders were reported. This was all the more praiseworthy considering the emotional crisis through which the people had so recently passed and the bitterness of the campaign. The exception to the general trend was terrorism in the disaffected areas in Central Luzon. A total of 2,601,218 votes were cast, a remarkable turnout in view of the difficulties encountered in voting.

In defiance of pre-election prognostications, Roxas won handily by a majority in excess of 200,000. The exact tabulation showed 1,333,392 votes for Roxas; 1,129,996 for Osmeña; and 8,538 for the candidate of the Modernist Party—the self-styled "Honorable Doctor H. C. Moncado, A.M., LL.M., D.C.L., Five-Star Supreme Commander in Chief."[3] Quirino won the Vice Presidency over Rodriguez by a reduced margin of 110,482 votes. The Roxas Liberal Party was also assured of control of the legislative body.

The result of the election cast not the slightest reflection on the name and fame of Sergio Osmeña. What the Phlippine electorate wanted was not an uneasy alliance of conservatives and radicals, but a middle-of-the-road policy of constructive liberalism under the dynamic leadership of the younger Manuel Roxas.

Tested from every angle, the Filipino people had taken the first step toward the restoration of normal civil processes of government in a Republic of their own making, with a sober sense of responsibility and with credit to themselves.

BIRTH OF A NATION[4]

July the fourth has become an historic date doubly significant. Not alone is it observed annually by the American people in celebration of their independence but as well by the Filipino people. For on July 4, 1946 a new nation taking the form of the Republic of the Philippines was born.

A sort of pre-inauguration rehearsal was held on May 28, 1946, when Manuel Roxas took his oath of office as the last President of the Commonwealth of the Philippines. The setting was not encouraging either in the physical or the psychological sense. The *papier-*

---

[3] For a characterization of "Five Star Moncado," see the Report to the Editors by John Lacerda, *Saturday Evening Post*, March 8, 1947.

[4] Blue Book, First Anniversary of the Republic of the Philippines contains inaugural addresses, copies of treaties, etc. Inauguration described in seventh and final report of U. S. High Commissioner McNutt, pp. 92-95, 125-138.

mâché resplendence of the reviewing stand was in sharp contrast to the shell-pocked husk of what had been Manila. Sensational stories that circulated about a possible assassination attempt upon the President and a Huk attack were symptomatic of the nervous tension that prevailed. The newly elected President had inherited problems involving a war-levelled land, the riddle of central Luzon of which the Huk rumors were evidence, and a bankrupt government.

The independence ceremony five weeks later evoked international interest. Twenty-three different nations were represented by high officials with colorful entourages. Fittingly, the United States had the largest delegation. High Commissioner Paul V. McNutt was the representative of the President of the United States. General of the Army Douglas MacArthur arrived from Japan to represent the armed forces of the United States. Postmaster General Robert E. Hannegan was the cabinet member in attendance. Senator Millard E. Tydings and Congressman C. Jasper Bell, chairmen respectively of the Senate and House Committees that had favorably reported Philippine legislation, headed the United States congressional delegation. Journalists from all over the world were present to publicize the historic occasion.

The Philippines also was present in force. Thousands upon thousands of Filipinos celebrated their independence with an orderly restraint that was particularly noticeable. And in the ceremonial stand a grey-haired and elderly man modestly took his place, good sportsman that he was, defeated candidate Sergio Osmeña. General Emilio Aguinaldo, President of the short-lived Republic of early American occupation days, also came up to pay his respects to the President of the real Republic.

The inaugural ceremonies had been so arranged that the United State occupied the first half of the program and the Philippines the second half. Following the invocation by Bishop Robert Wilmer came addresses by Senator Tydings, co-author of the Philippine Commonwealth and Independence Act of 1934, General MacArthur, liberator of the Philippines, and High Commissioner McNutt, who also read the proclamation of independence of the Republic of the Philippines. All speakers were well received, but General MacArthur was given the greatest ovation.

Next came a ceremony that deeply stirred the emotions. The American Flag, the stars of which had been sewed by Filipina ladies, was slowly lowered to the accompaniment of the American National Anthem, by the official representative of the President of the United States. The Philippine Flag was hoisted on the same flagstaff to the accompaniment of the Philippine National Anthem, by the incoming President of the Philippines. A twenty-one gun salute roared out the news that an independent state, the Republic of the Philippines had been proclaimed.

The oath of office was administered to Manuel Roxas, President of the Philippines, and Elpidio Quirino, Vice President of the Philippines, by Chief Justice Manuel Moran. President Roxas thereupon delivered his inaugural address. The closing prayer was given by Archbishop Gabriel M. Reyes. A military and civic parade, a commemorative tree planting, a state dinner at Malacañan Palace, and a reception and ball by the President and First Lady rounded out a busy day.

The Philippines had done very well by herself. If the independence day ceremonies lacked the pomp attendant on the inauguration of the Commonwealth of the Philippines ten years previously, the comparison merely underlined the more appropriate and dignified observance of the introduction of the Philippines into the family of nations. A background of war's horrors was hardly conducive to over-ostentatious display. The Philippines had extended hospitality in typical Philippine fashion, and in the democratic manner that befitted a people assuming the responsibilities of statehood.

If there was any flaw in the independence ceremonies it was American-induced. President Roosevelt in his lifetime, and President Truman subsequently, had promised to be present at the inauguration of the Republic of the Philippines. But the President of the United States was conspicuously absent. He was "too busy." Former Secretary Harold L. Ickes, in one of his newspaper columns, in typical waspish style condemned the President—and properly it would seem—for not honoring by his personal presence a people who had won their freedom.[5]

Transcendentally more important than any possible breach of etiquette was the fact that the American people had kept a promise. By this act of voluntary liberation, a force had been introduced into the Orient that influenced significantly the peoples in all the colonial-held areas of South-East Asia and the South Pacific.

President Roxas Charts His Course

In a series of notable addresses President Manuel Roxas outlined his program for the Republic of the Philippines, announced his concept of Philippine-American relations, and took a stand on contro-

---

[5] Harold L. Ickes, "Man to Man," *Washington Star*, July 1, 1946.

versial issues. These addresses, in their use of pure English, in their grasp of national and international problems, and in their keen analysis of paramount questions, displayed talent, industry and courage of a high order. Roxas, with responsibility thrust upon him, had evolved from a politician into a statesman who sought to lead the people of the newly recognized Philippine State out of the morass of war's devastation and internecine strife into the promised land of plenty and unity.

Previous to inauguration, following election to the Presidency, Roxas made a hurried trip to the United States. During his stay he delivered a series of major speeches. He took a definite stand in favor of the establishment of American military bases in the Philippines, and announced his support of the Trade Relations Act. As against those of his fellow countrymen who sought by every device to picture the Filipinos as Orientals whose future lay in the East, on one occasion he said: "We are not of the Orient, except by geography. We are part of the western world by reason of culture, religion, ideology, and economics. Although the color of our skin is brown, the temper of our minds and hearts is almost identical with yours. We expect to remain part of the west, possibly as the ideological bridge between the Occident and the Orient."

Returning to the Philippines, the President-elect prepared for induction as the last President of the Commonwealth. In an address delivered on this occasion, he stood before "the toppled columns of the legislative building . . . mute and weeping symbols of the land we have inherited from war," to make use of his words. He took cognizance of a situation that everyone could see and did his best to dispel the gloom of fear. In a message to the Philippine Congress, President Roxas laid down a comprehensive program to meet the chief problems of his country.

The inaugural address of the first President of the Republic of the Philippines on July 4, 1946 was, by reason of the setting and the occasion, history making in nature. In this address President Roxas recognized the fulfillment of the prediction made half a century before that the Filipinos would in truth "look back in gratitude to the day when God gave victory to American arms at Manila Bay, and placed this land under the sovereignty and protection of the United States." He then proceeded "to evaluate the significance of what had occurred." He went on to observe: "A new era has come to the Orient. The first democratic Republic has been established in this quarter of the globe." Next, turning his eyes to the dim and uncertain future, he emphasized that "From this day forward our international responsibility is absolute." He took note of the two "major poles of power in the world today, Russia and the United States," and he chose as the safest course, to follow "in the glistening wake of America." He admitted: "We are a troubled people. . . Against a background of destruction, we acquire our sovereignty, we receive our national heritage. We must perform near miracles to bring prosperity to this, our land." The memorable address concluded with the solemn assurance "that our people's happiness is our goal."

Time passed and other speeches were made by the frail President. But, as if by Providence directed, the last major output of a brain soon to be stilled by death was immeasurably the best in style, in clarity, and in content. On January 26, 1948, His Excellency Manuel Roxas, President of the Philippines, delivered a Message on the State of the Nation to the Congress that was to be his valedictory.

Ordeal of the Republic[6]

The Philippines started on its independent way a few scant months after the conclusion of the greatest war in all history, the worst bombed and the most destroyed country in the world. The only areas comparable to Manila in totality of destruction were Stalingrad in Soviet Russia and Warsaw in Poland. Even the havoc wrought by atom bombs in Japan did not account for as terrible a loss in lives and property as was suffered in the Philippines by reason of enemy occupation and the battles of liberation.

Turning from comparative tables but still speaking in cold statistics, over a million of the Philippine people were unaccounted for, and the number who lost their lives in the war undoubtedly reached to double that figure. The total damage in the Philippines resulting from World War II was estimated at two-thirds of the material wealth. Experts fixed the loss at approximately $6,000,000,000. Included in war's holocaust were entire *barrios* and cities, countless homes, and nearly half of the domestic and work animals upon which the people were so dependent.

Manila had once been a beauty spot. There the ancient and the modern had stood side by side—the old walled city, the old churches, the old residences reminiscent of Spain; the new office buildings, the new government structures, the new homes, the contribution of joint American-Filipino enterprise. With few exceptions all were gone. Manila, proud Pearl of the Orient, was eighty percent destroyed.

6 See Seventh and final report of U. S. High Commissioner McNutt, pp. 92 *et. seq.*; Clark Lee, *One Last Look Around*, ch. 21 (New York, 1947); and Harold H. Martin, "Manila Picks Up the Pieces," *Saturday Evening Post*, February 14, 1948.

The worst legacy of the war was the foulness the Japanese left behind them. Hostilities concomitants—death, torture, thievery, and inflation—had brought the morale of a fine people to the breaking point. War's end found them demoralized, weakened and divided.

It was on such a foundation of sand that President Manuel Roxas was expected to reconstruct a state and to rehabilitate a people. It was a Herculean task. The President faced it unflinchingly, even eagerly.

The newly inaugurated President had first to bring together a working team of cabinet officials. Political animosities precluded a coalition government. Recognition of out-and-out collaborationists was unwise if the Philippines was to get help from the United States. From the material left, the President chose a varied cabinet. It could be classed as a solid body of men who could be expected to cooperate with the Chief Executive. Brilliance of leadership would continue to be reflected by the President.

The President displayed political sagacity by naming the colorful guerrilla chieftain, Colonel Ruperto Kangleon as Secretary of National Defense. The President changed the status of Vice President Elpidio Quirino from that of an officer whose sole occupation under the Constitution was to await the death or disability of the President to a cabinet member with important duties by appointing him Secretary of Foreign Affairs. Joaquin M. Elizalde was properly returned to Washington to fill the post of first Ambassador to the United States. General Carlos P. Romulo was transferred from the national capitol to represent the Philippines in the United Nations, which he has done with credit to his country. The President finally revived and reconstituted the Council of State to fill the void of an advisory council of highest category.

An attempt was made to give attention to "first things first." But where there were so many matters needing immediate consideration—finances, public order, food, transportation, and relations with the United States—it was next to impossible to differentiate them as to importance. The new administration faced the problems and either temporized until definite solutions could be found or initiated studies of them.

The Philippines was near to bankruptcy; an American loan and increased revenues helped tide over the emergency. The Philippines could not afford to lose the support of the United States; a series of treaties, particularly an agreement reached on military bases, cemented Philippine-American relations. Reconstruction of public buildings, private homes and roads was an immediate necessity; combined American-Philippine efforts through means furnished by the U. S. Army, the War Damage payments, and the Philippine Rehabilitation Finance Corporation advanced progress. Action had to be taken against the collaborationists; the People's Court meted out slow but even-handed justice and the National War Crimes Office staff brought about a day of reckoning for the guilty. Trade had to be revived if exports were to approximate imports; gradually with copra and coconut oil taking the lead—for even the Japanese could not wipe out thousands of hectares of coconut trees—trade began to flow through regular channels. Agrarian unrest could not be bypassed; laws were enacted providing for a more equitable division between landlords and tenants, and when unrest developed into open defiance of the law, force was met with force.

The above constitutes but a fraction of the problems pressing in all at once on the newly established Republic. Further phases of the government's activities will be developed under appropriate subjects.

If there is any consolation in the adage that misery likes company, it can be added that other countries were, and are, worse off than the Philippines. Asia's billion people, for example, face deeper troubles than anything the Philippines can possibly suffer. As a matter of fact, the Philippines moved steadily forward on a definite course of recovery.

GRAFT, RACKETS, THIEVERY [7]

The Government of the Republic during the early years of its existence exhibited deficiencies of which the public was painfully aware. It was not conducive to happiness to read of scandals and more scandals, that were met by promises by officials to search out the guilty, but with only few punished. It was not comforting to surmise that the practice of easing relatives into jobs without regard to efficiency was being followed. The public was inclined to accept reasonable explanation for delay and for failures in prosecution; official smugness in tolerating graft, rackets and thievery was not so easily excused. And what was most galling was the Government's inaction in letting the people know the results of probes and investigations.

This weakness in the government must also have been evident to those in authority. One man no matter how high his reputation for personal integrity, could not handle all the minutiae of administration.

---

[7] The crusading articles appearing in the *Philippines Free Press* can be noted. Also see Blake Clark, "Are the Philippines Going the Way of China?", *Readers Digest*, June, 1950.

And when the faults of associates did claim attention, a kindly heart found it difficult to think ill of the malefactors.

The defect of administration apparent to all is a lack of basic honesty. It concerns a failure to stamp out with ruthless energy the grafters, the racketeers, and the thieves both high and low. Mammon seemed the God whom all too many worshipped. There were the misappropriations of relief goods immediately after liberation; the scandal in the disposition of surplus property; the Chinese immigration racket; the series of extravagant purchases of government supplies at exorbitant prices; the victimization of war damage claimants and Filipino veterans; the beer deals; the theft of government property by those to whom it was entrusted; a notorious estate transaction; anomalies in the Import Control Office; pilferage in the port area of Manila; and numerous other transgressions.

Law and order were at such a low ebb, one observant journalist told of a stroll through a crowded street in Manila that revealed approximately every fifth Filipino sporting a gun.[8] Public notices to deposit weapons and police check points were not conducive to allaying nervous tension.

Internal bickerings in the Liberal Party after the death of President Roxas brought about an exposé on the floor of the Senate of entrenched venality. The opposition *Nacionalistas*, holding high their own spotless hands for all to see, encouraged the washing of dirty linen in public. Of course many of the charges would not hold up in a court of law and were motivated by personal vengeance. But the time had arrived for distrust of officials to be effaced, for rottenness to be brought to light, and for the guilty to be punished.

In 1950 President Quirino at long last gave point to previous blasts against the evildoers by naming an "integrity board" to probe reports of graft and corruption in high government places. Action had been taken because of an unremitting campaign by Vice President Lopez for clean government.

The bleak picture here painted calls for a bit of lighter recoloring. In the first place, nepotism is flaunted in many lands. Graft is not limited to the Philippines. Just as lurid stories of black markets and abuse of position came out of Europe after the war. Nor was guilt confined to Filipinos exclusively; U. S. Army personnel connived in the nefarious looting of surplus property by which so many enriched

---

[8] Harold H. Martin, "Manila Picks Up the Pieces," in the *Saturday Evening Post*, February 14, 1948. On February 12, 1949 the *Philippines Free Press* in a slightly more conservative statement said that "almost one out of every ten men you meet in the street" in Manila sports a sidearm.

themselves. And lastly, conditions have considerably improved with precautions taken to prevent wrongdoing and with prosecution of some of those caught in the police net.

No housecleaning has taken place; possibly under conditions prevailing none could have succeeded. But there is a noticeable return to elemental decency.

The Collaboration Issue[9]

The special question of whether Jose P. Laurel was a quisling or a patriot—the larger question of what constituted collaboration with the Japanese and who were the collaborationists—divided public opinion in the Philippines during the war, continued to arouse sharp differences even after the proclamation of amnesty, and will never definitely be answered in the future. The best that can be done is to set down some of the generally accepted facts and to whittle down the confused issues to a narrower form.

What constituted collaboration? No one has given a satisfactory answer. As a matter of fact the phrase is not susceptible of precise definition—or application.

President Osmeña, whose unpleasant duty it was to face the problem even while the war was on, pertinently remarked in his famous Leyte broadcast that "We must not close our eyes to the realities of the occupation." Along the same line of thought was his official statement of policy on collaboration, which gained additional weight because it was approved by the Secretary of War, in which the President said: "Persons holding public office during enemy occupation, for the most part, fall within three categories: those prompted by a desire to protect the people, those actuated by fear of enemy reprisals, and those motivated by disloyalty to our government and cause. The motives which caused the retention of the office and conduct while in office, rather than the sole fact of its occupation, will be the criteria upon which such persons will be judged."

"Motives" and "Conduct" in office, rather than the sole fact of holding office, were to furnish the true criteria. This evolved into

---

[9] For one point of view see a courageous memorandum entitled "Collaborators of the Japanese," submitted by former Resident Commissioner Francisco Delgado to Secretary of the Interior Confesor on April 3, 1945, and Hernando J. Abaya, *Betrayal in the Philippines* (New York, 1946). Blunt-spoken Admiral Halsey termed the collaborators "a fine collection of quislings," *Admiral Halsey's Story*, p. 28. For an opposite point of view, see a book *The Saga of Jose P. Laurel*, by Teofilo del Castillo and Jose del Castillo (Manila, 1949). Collaboration impartially described in the seventh and final report of U. S. High Commissioner McNutt, pp. 6-9, 63-65.

the doctrine laid down by the Supreme Court of the Philippines that mere service in the occupation government did not in itself constitute indictable disloyalty. "Those who refused to co-operate, in the face of danger, were patriotic citizens," said the Supreme Court, but, added the court, "it does not follow that the faint-hearted, who gave in, were traitors." [10]

"Motives" and "Conduct"—these words serve to remind us of Sukarno, the first President of the Indonesian Republic. He was placed in power by the Japanese. He reciprocated in speeches praising the Fascist powers and damning the Allied Nations. Questioned about his apparent pro-Japanese leaning after their surrender, he is reported to have responded: "Yes, I said those things—but never in my heart." [11] One may be dubious about an alleged collaborator's sincerity in falling back on metaphysical reasons to explain his "motives" and to justify his "conduct." How can you prove him wrong!

The collaborationists were of several kinds and evidenced varying shades of "Motives" and "Conduct." There were the actively disloyal, like the sympathizers with Japan, the spies, the informers, and the members of the infamous *Makapilis*. There were the opportunists and profiteers whose defection to the enemy was prompted by a desire for position, favor, or wealth. There were the large group of inconspicuous officeholders and private citizens who were more or less forced to cooperate with the enemy. There were the pretenders who joined the Japanese-sponsored administration, but who remained loyal to the exiled government and to the United States. And there were those who, ordered to remain behind by the President of the Philippines, worked with the enemy to alleviate the suffering of the people. Each case has to be individually judged by facts and not by prejudice, rumor, or suspicion.

The Americans handled the collaboration mess about as gingerly as did the Filipinos. General MacArthur, in a proclamation dated December 9, 1944, declared it his purpose to hold in restraint for the duration of the war Philippine citizens who "voluntarily" gave aid to the enemy, whereafter they would be released to the Philippine Government. Some 5,000 persons were detained by the U. S. Army for investigation. They were eventually turned over to the Commonwealth Government for trial. The problem of what to do with the Filipino collaborators had been left on the Filipino doorstep. Wash-

---

[10] People of the Philippines *v.* Jose Luis Dodinez, decided by the Supreme Court of the Philippines on December 31, 1947.

[11] Quoted in Ralph Coniston, *The Future of Freedom in the Orient* (New York, 1947).

ington, however, continued to display an interest in the outcome.

Secretary of the Interior Harold L. Ickes, claiming jurisdiction over Philippine affairs because what was left of the High Commissioner's office was temporarily operating under his department, was most violent in urging relentless prosecution. In a radiogram to President Osmeña, he threatened that the Congress of the United States might hold up Philippine legislation unless action against the collaborationists was taken in the Philippines. The Congress, however, preferred to speak for itself and in due course approved legislation for the Philippines.

The President of the United States did indeed issue a directive on collaboration on October 26, 1945 to his Attorney General. The latter sent a special investigator to Manila. He returned with a voluminous report on which no action was taken. The final definite statement of policy announced by the President of the United States expressed confidence in the capacity of the Philippine people to make their own political decisions without intervention or direction by the United States. So having gone around in a circle, the American higher-ups had arrived back at the starting point.

President Quezon, as might be expected, retained faith in the loyalty of his compatriots who had accepted posts under the Japanese. In a letter to General MacArthur on January 28, 1942, the President said: "In reference to the men who had accepted positions in the commission established by the Japanese, every one of them wanted to come to Corregidor, but you told me that there was no room for them here. They are not quislings. . . They are not traitors. They are the victims of the adverse fortunes of war and I am sure they had no choice. Besides, it is most probable that they accepted their positions in order to safeguard the welfare of the civilian population in the occupied areas. I think, under the circumstances, America should look upon their situation sympathetically and understandingly." [12]

Months later in far away Florida, President Quezon's soul was torn with doubts about the loyalty of the Filipino collaborators. Nevertheless, in a conversation with his friend Roy W. Howard of the United Press in March, 1944, he was still able to affirm from his sickbed, that the men left behind were loyal and were acting under instructions from him.

President Osmeña in Manila pressured the Congress of the Philippines into authorizing a Peoples Court to try the numerous collaboration cases. Despite the efforts put forth by Solicitor General Lorenzo

---

[12] Quoted in Manuel Luis Quezon, *The Good Fight*, p. 260.

M. Tañada and Solicitor General Manuel Lim, the trials moved slowly. The tactics of defense counsel was to postpone and delay to await expected amnesty.

On January 28, 1948 President Roxas granted amnesty to political and economic collaborators with Japan "to heal the sores we might still carry in our hearts." Amnesty did not extend to spies or informers of the enemy, to persons accused of treason, or to crimes committed to help the enemy or suppress the resistance movement. The amnesty proclamation encountered scant opposition before meeting with approval in the legislative body. Among the cases dismissed was the one against Jose P. Laurel.

The most notorious of the collaborationist cases, for obvious reasons, was that of Laurel. Here was the Occupation President, seized in Japan by the United States Army, standing trial before a Filipino court on numerous counts. Here was one of the most brilliant of the Filipino leaders, democratically-trained at the University of the Philippines and at Yale, a professor of law and author of serious books, a former Senator, Cabinet Officer, and Supreme Court Justice, with a long record of public service, pleading not guilty to charges involving the gravest of all crimes and violently protesting that he was a patriot— a dramatic setting for a case that is no easier to elucidate than the broader problem of collaboration.

The Filipino Solicitor General had in his possession a mass of evidence which in his judgment would bring about the conviction of Laurel. The author has conferred with the chief prosecutors, both former law students, as was Laurel for that matter. He was afforded an opportunity to peruse a goodly portion of the allegedly incriminating documents. The effect produced was one of distaste. It was hard to understand how even duress, or collaboration "for the good of the people," necessitated expressions of "undying gratitude" for the "benevolence" and "magnanimity" of Japan, and the repetitious pledge cf cooperation in "this sacred war." But maybe this is biased Americanism asserting itself. And possibly the accused could have explained away his words or mitigated their significance. As in the case of Sukarno, who will ever know what was in Laurel's heart!

What is publicly available consists of fragmentary and circumstantial items as follows: 1. Laurel's action as a lawyer in accepting Japanese clients, including rendition of services as legal adviser of the Japanese Consulate; 2. his sending one son to a Japanese military school, and after his inauguration as President, sending another son to Japan as a *pensionado;* 3. his narrow escape from assassination while on a golf course, revealing the opinion of him held by a segment of his countrymen; 4. his alleged predilection for totalitarianism; 5. his speeches bitterly critical of the United States, in poor taste since made while under indictment and out on bail. None of the above factors, singly or jointly, merit more than suspicion, and suspicion is not equivalent to conviction.

In behalf of Laurel, it is argued that he did everything in his power to minimize Japanese atrocities, and that he successfully maneuvered to save the youth of the land from military conscription in the service of Japan.[13] To many people, including Americans who were on-the-scene observers, Laurel was a shock absorber for Japanese abuse. Had Laurel and equally prominent Filipinos refused positions offered them by the Japanese, other less experienced Filipinos—even rascals in the worst elements of the community—would have been installed in high government posts.

Two stories purporting to give the cause of Laurel's alleged anti-American feeling have circulated. One version is that social slights while a student at Yale University, together with the refusal of a hotel clerk to allow him to register because he was an Oriental, wounded Laurel's pride; this he flatly denies. The other story is to the effect that the law degree awarded Laurel by Yale was recalled. This has a basis of fact, but the actual fact is this: The incorrect designation of Doctor of Civil Law, inserted on the diplomas of the entire graduating class of the 1920 Laws at Yale, led to the recall of all diplomas, in order that correct ones could be issued for the *Juris Doctor* degree. No personal slight to Laurel was involved.[14]

Rising to his own defense, Laurel has time and again denied that he was or is unfriendly to the United States. He decries those critics who confuse his "love for my country first" with anti-Americanism.[15]

President Roxas was tolerant in judgment even of a prospective rival for Presidential honors. During the war he had expressed to an interviewer his belief that Laurel was honest in the conviction that what he [Laurel] was doing was for the best interests of the Filipino people. Laurel is not as charitable; during a call on the writer, he referred to the late President as "a moral coward."

---

[13] Laurel's exact words in September, 1944 were: "The Republic has but one course to pursue, and that is, to render every aid and assistance to the Imperial Japanese Government, short of conscription of Filipino manhood for active military service." Laurel explains that the Japanese had everything save men, anyway.

[14] The facts about the scholastic record of Jose P. Laurel while a student at Yale were obtained from Professor Wesley A. Sturgess, Dean of the School of Law, Yale University, in a letter dated May 10, 1948.

[15] Jose P. Laurel in a speech before the Manila Rotary Club, May 19, 1949; P. W. Reeves in a letter published in the *Congressional Record*, July 8, 1949, A 4578.

Finally, what might constitute collaboration with the enemy to Americans might convey an entirely different meaning to most Filipinos. The United States demanded loyalty from her citizens. The Philippines exacted the same loyalty from her citizens. But since willingness was lacking on the part of the Filipinos, there was no collaboration, and no disloyalty to the Philippines. So runs the Filipino argument aimed at elucidation of their position, that being compelled to abide by Japanese rule did not establish treason to the United States.

Chiseled down as the collaboration issue has been by official action and pronouncements, covered up as it has been by Executive- and Legislative-proclaimed amnesty, the outcome will please few persons. Laurel, *et al*, will still be classed by many with Quisling and Laval. Laurel, *et al*, will still be to others heroes and patriots.

AMERICA'S TARDY HELP [16]

The unparalleled record made by the United States during the half century of contact between Americans and Filipinos in the Philippines came near to being ruined in the months that brought World War II to an end.

It is true there had been American-Filipino misunderstandings before. In 1898, Aguinaldo's belief that a pledge of Philippine independence had been broken, aggravated by a denial to him of the fruits of victory, marked the beginning of jealousies between the Filipino General and the American Commander which culminated in hostilities. In 1907, an exhibition of over-exuberant patriotism following the Filipino's first popular election, brought about a patriotic American mass meeting in Manila and the exaltation of the flag. In 1913, American resentment against Governor General Harrison and his pro-Filipino policies was followed by the Governor General Wood-President of the Senate Quezon break of an opposite origin. There were other differences, too, between Americans and Filipinos. But the more serious of them have been erased by time, and the lesser were merely newsworthy for a day.

American post-war procrastination and rudeness lost many of the benefits of long years of good work. America's action, or more accurately speaking, America's lack of action in taking effective

---

[16] Note seventh and final report of U. S. High Commissioner McNutt, pp. 28-45. The Filipinos also felt that they had a grievance in the international field. As of June 1, 1946 the shattered Philippines had received a niggardly $3,375,000 allotment from the UNRRA. In contrast, approximately the same number of Jugoslavians, behind the iron curtain, were the recipients of more than $300,000,000.

measures to help the prostrate Philippines was most regrettable. Half-measures and delays blighted American-Philippine friendship, furnished a substitute of anti-American reaction for the once standard independence issue, and was an unpromising prelude to an American-sponsored Philippine independence.

During the war, promises—wonderful promises to bolster Filipino faith and courage in dark moments—were made. It matters not that some of these alleged promises had received no official sanction and have been disavowed. It matters not that statements passed on by word of mouth were misunderstood or exaggerated. The fact remains that it was no time to take a narrow attitude toward a new nation whose security and future destiny were so closely bound to the United States.

What happened was this: Liberation of the Philippines found a people pauperized and demoralized. The populace welcomed their American deliverers with ecstatic joy. The U. S. Army responded with sympathy and aid. Then friendly relations deteriorated. American soldiers on all too many occasions in the rebound of war gave ground for friction. Filipinos, with morale lowered by the war's excesses, looted and grafted. Manila and other cities became honky-tonk towns. Supreme headquarters moved on to encompass Japan's defeat, and on the surrender of the Nipponese to administer Japan.

The Philippines was left to civil administration. Neither the Filipino Commonwealth Government nor American officials were ready with means to meet the situation.

Paul V. McNutt, the last United States High Commissioner to the Philippines, returned at the war's end to the post he had held in happier days. In a voluminous and well-documented report, he charged his homeland with failing to fulfill its obligations to the Philippines. Mr. McNutt, by the exertion of his influence on a hesitant United States Congress, was able to soften the impact of his own accusations, with the eventual approval of constructive legislation. Yet the stubborn facts remained that the legislation was long delayed and to a sensitive Filipino people was inadequate payment for their manifold sacrifices.

President Roxas was the man mainly responsible for cementing Philippine-American relations. Especially was this true of his campaign to check anti-Americanism when the amendment to the Constitution granting Americans equal rights was before the people for ratification. The President had the good sense not to be lead into demagoguery popular for the moment. Instead he took the long view of realization that the Philippines needed American help and American capital, and above all the American market in which to sell Philippine products. As the President himself so well put it:

> We can, if we choose, reject special relations with the United States. We can orient our foreign relations as we determine best. We can become allied with China, with Siam, with England, or with France. We can become allied with Soviet Russia. We have full freedom of choice. That is implicit in the grant of sovereignty.
>
> But I assure you that as far as I am concerned, and I think I have some influence in the matter, we will do none of the things I have just mentioned. The magnetic pole of our foreign-policy gravitation will be the United States.[17]

Notwithstanding American-Filipino misunderstandings, Americans implemented promises with action, and Filipinos strengthened their voluntary ties with the United States. The mills of democracy in Washington ground slowly but the output eventually reflected American gratitude and permitted full-scale rehabilitation. The Filipino voters made their decision by the ratio of eight to one in favor of an amendment to their Constitution, which could be interpreted as a reiteration of their friendship for the United States.

The chief contribution of the United States to the stabilization of Philippine economy came with the enactment by the Congress of the United States of the Philippine Trade Act and the Philippine Rehabilitation Act. The approval date of the two measures, April 30, 1946, stands out like a reproving sign-post—twelve months delay following the liberation of Manila, with two scant months left before independence.

Both laws were basically sound. The Trade Act set up mutually advantageous trade relations between the Philippines and the United States for a twenty-eight year period beginning with the date of Philippine independence. The only objection to the Rehabilitation Act related to the amount authorized for compensation.

Senator Tyding's five day hurried stay in Manila in June, 1945 was sufficient for him to comprehend, to some extent, the devastation and the hardships borne by the Filipino people. He returned to the national capitol to paint a word picture of conditions in the stricken Philippines.[18] The representatives of the War Damage Corporation estimated the physical damage based on conservative pre-war values at $800,000,000. A technical commission appointed by the Com-

---

[17] Speech in Washington quoted in the *Christian Science Monitor*.
[18] Senator Tydings remarks appeared in the *Congressional Record* of June 7, 1945.

monwealth President, after an independent survey, estimated the damage incurred at $1,200,000,000. The Philippine Rehabilitation Act made available $520,000,000, and authorized the transfer of surplus property to the Philippine Government.

The Philippine War Damage Commission composed of Chairman Frank A. Waring and Commissioners Francisco A. Delgado and John A. O'Donnell went about its stupendous task in a workmanlike manner. An overall total of 1,250,000 private claims were received. Approximately 1,000,000 of these claims did not exceed $500, and on approval were paid in full. The larger claims were segregated and were liquidated on a $500 plus fifty-two percent basis.

It is undoubtedly true that a goodly portion of the smaller amounts received by claimants was quickly spent. On the other hand, the influence of this money flowing into trade channels was profoundly felt. It assisted rehabilitation in a major fashion.

Individual and corporate war damage claims were thus settled with money appropriated by the United States Congress, to reach a total of $400,000,000. The rehabilitation of public buildings and services was mostly completed by the mid-1950 deadline with possibly $120,000,000 expended. The U. S. war surplus material grant had a procurement cost of $1,000,000,000, with a realized recovery value of about $50,000,000. The activities of a dozen Federal agencies with Philippine training projects poured out thousands of American Treasury checks.

In other ways, officially and unofficially, directly and indirectly, the United States aided in the rehabilitation of the Philippines. For instance, the Reconstruction Finance Corporation granted the Philippines a loan of $60,000,000 to put the government on its feet. The U. S. Educational Foundation in the Philippines administers the exchange of persons program under the Fullbright Act.

The U. S. Army alone has paid to Filipino civilian employees from liberation in 1945 to 1950 approximately $250,000,000. The U. S. Army's distribution of supplies, mainly to Filipinos, has been estimated at half a billion dollars. The U. S. Veterans Administration in the Philippines distributes millions of pesos annually. Nearly $200,000,000 have gone to Filipino veterans for back pay.

The Philippine War Relief of the United States started its program of health and rehabilitation missions throughout the Philippines in April, 1946. Three years later the agency closed its program due to lack of operating funds. While missions were engaged in this worthy work, a million and a half pesos were spent and more than 8,000,000 persons were benefited. Various church groups, fraternal orders, and other organizations with headquarters in the United States have channeled aid from private donors totaling more than $10,000,000 into the Philippines.

Japanese reparations will not be nearly as much as originally forecast. Five million dollars worth of machine tools were actually received by the Philippines before the decision of the United States to end reparations from Japan was made. This action was based on the hard, practical consideration that any further drain on the economy of Japan would have to be subsidized by American taxpayers. Japanese properties of considerable value have been turned over to the Republic pursuant to the Alien Property Act.

If American aid to the Philippines had been tardy, it had eventually been substantial. In order to offset any wrong impression relative to American generosity to the Philippines, a table with a column of figures opposite each item was formulated.[19] It is not inserted because too many intangibles were present to permit of exactitude. But even with the elimination of questioned amounts, the total was astronomical.

The Joint Philippine-American Finance Commission estimated that the United States would make a total monetary contribution to the Philippines of $2,000,000,000 by 1950. Subsequently the American Ambassador to the Philippines pointed out that by the end of 1951 the United States will have routed to the Philippines $2,150,000,000 in one form or another—a sizable sum even in these days of inflated values. The writer's computation reaches even a higher amount. But after 1951—and this point is important—the billions of American dollars that have been pouring into the Islands may be reduced to a yearly rate of between fifty million and seventy-five million.

In 1949, American Ambassador Myron M. Cowen eased somewhat strained Philippine-American relations in addresses delivered in Manila.[20] Whatever the motive, whether to overcome bad publicity in an article about the failure of the American "Little Marshall Plan" for the Philippines which appeared in a financial journal, or whether to im-

---

[19] The Philippine Embassy in Washington offered helpful comment on December 7, 1948. Ambassador Myron M. Cowen cited figures on American aid in testimony before the U. S. Senate Foreign Relations Committee, April 18, 1950. Albino Z. SyCip, President of the China Banking Corporation of Manila writing on "American Economic Help To The Philippines" in 1950, expressed the view that it had been greatly exaggerated.

[20] Ambassador Cowen in addresses on May 26, 1949 and September 1, 1949. The article on the failure of the ECA — Type Plan in the Philippines was written by Ray Cromley for *The Wall Street Journal* of June 17, 1949.

plement the "unprecedented welcome" received by the President of the Philippines in the United States, attention was focused on the subject of American aid to the Philippines. Speaking of the period of reconstruction running from 1945 through 1951, figures were cited to demonstrate the substantial help afforded the Philippines by the people of the United States. Repeatedly laying emphasis on the necessity of a plan which provides for "maximum self-help" on the part of the Philippines, assurances were given that the United States Government will assist in finding ways of tapping the reservoirs of American private capital to supplement local capital and by furnishing technical knowledge and skill.

In 1950, an American Survey Mission recommended that the United States make available a quarter of a million dollars under a five year program provided urgent reforms were instituted, to help the Philippines avert an economic crisis.

THE ALMOST FORGOTTEN VETERAN

The most vulnerable point in the American program for the post-war Philippines was the shabby treatment of the Filipino veteran.

The Philippine Army was inducted into the American Army before the beginning of hostilities by the President of the United States. The Philippine Army was not released from military service until the eve of Philippine independence. There were 400,000 Filipinos who at one time or another, or in some capacity, served in the Philippine Army, became a part of the U. S. Army, or were recognized guerrillas, and there were countless numbers of Filipinos in the irregular guerrilla forces. In the words of President Truman: "The record of the Philippine soldier for bravery and loyalty is second to none. Their assignments were as bloody and difficult as any in which our American soldiers engaged." Under such conditions, one would naturally expect to find the Filipino veterans entitled to benefits bearing a reasonable relation to those received by the American veterans.[21]

The Congress of the United States in the First Rescission Act of February 18, 1946 denied the Filipino soldiers the benefits of the G. I. Bill of Rights, the mustering-out payment act, the terminal leave act, and the six months gratuity act. The Filipino veteran was held only entitled to insurance and pensions for death or disability.

---

21 President Truman in a communication to Congress on May 18, 1946. An on-the-spot report of the veteran issue was made on December 7, 1946 by David Sternberg for the *Christian Science Monitor*. His deduction was that this issue "is perhaps our weakest point."

Slowly but surely the callousness of the American attitude began to penetrate the legislative halls. It was all very well to go slow in recognition of Filipino guerrillas, most patriotic fighters, but, in some instances, sham patriots. It was all very well to expect the Philippines as an independent nation to assume the continuing burden of caring for injured veterans among their own people. There still remained unwarranted discrimination and a failure to fulfill lavish promises.

After a long wait, on July 25, 1947, the President of the United States signed a law authorizing the settlement of arrears in pay to Filipino veterans and recognized guerrillas. Of more than one million persons who claimed service with guerrilla units, some 260,000 were accepted as genuine. In the months after the enactment of the law, millions of pesos were paid out to officers and enlisted men. Regularly inducted Filipino soldiers whom the Japanese held as prisoners of war received in addition one dollar a day for each day of confinement. The cases which induced irritation were those where men received back pay checks for less than a peso or were found to be in arrears for accumulated insurance premiums.

After another year's delay, the United States Congress passed an act to assist the Philippine Republic in providing adequate medical care and treatment for veterans. Grants for the construction of hospitals and for expenses incidental to hospitalization were made. It was in nature an emergency measure for a period not to exceed five years.[22]

The U. S. Veterans Administration in the Philippines admits that there are unavoidable delays in processing claims. On the other hand, thousands of checks are distributed each month to Philippine veterans or their widows and orphans. The 1948 total was half a million checks totaling over $35,000,000.

As was proper, the Philippines supplemented American legislation with its own G. I. Bill of Rights.[23] The law authorized employment, educational and land settlement benefits and aid for veterans. The law also provided for the creation of a Philippine Veterans Board. The Board was charged with the important duty of compiling a permanent list of members of the Philippine Army and recognized or deserving guerrilla organizations. In the performance of this function the Board naturally received more brickbats than bouquets. In administering the benefits provided by the Act, the Board has received and approved or disapproved thousands of claims for death pensions.

[22] Public Law 865, 80th Congress, approved July 1, 1948.
[23] Republic Act No. 65.

The record when evaluated in its entirety is not too bad. It is susceptible of explanation, possibly of convincing justification. But America's piecemeal attempt at fulfillment of its debt to the Filipino veterans will never erase the hurt in many a Filipino heart.

It remained for a Filipino veteran by the name of Paulino Santos, now a humble classroom teacher, to put more grasping countrymen to shame. In a letter to the press he wrote: "I have not filed my application for back pay. Why? My purpose in participating in World War II was to serve my country and my people, so why should I ask for any compensation or reward?" In a money-mad world it is doubtful if this patriotic gesture will be emulated by many. Yet it is a viewpoint worthy of recognition.

Genuine parity, meaning a grant of full G. I. benefits to the Filipinos who fought for the United States, has not been met.

A Nation Mourns the Death of Manuel Roxas, First President of the Republic [24]

Stunned were the Filipino people when the startling news became known that Manuel Roxas, their President, was dead. At the last rites in Manila for a beloved son and leader, more than a million of his fellow countrymen—the high and the low—lined the funeral route with heads bowed, with eyes moist, and with souls wrenched. In other parts of the Philippines and in foreign lands, countless numbers of persons grieved at the passing of the great Malayan statesman.

To Manuel Roxas went the distinction of becoming the first President of the first Republic of the Philippines—in truth the first head of the first Malay democracy in all history. The honor was rightly his by birth as a Malay and by reason of outstanding ability and wide experience. With Manuel Quezon gone and Sergio Osmeña no longer his former vigorous self, it was generally recognized that Manuel Roxas was the one Filipino capable of uniting his people in the stupendous tasks of meeting the problems incident to war's devastation and the inauguration of an independent state, and of securing the indispensable help of the United States in solving those problems. The Filipino people had chosen as their leader one superbly equipped for high responsibility.

---

[24] See F. G. Bustos, *And Now Comes Roxas* (Manila, 1945). Erwin D. Canham, Editor of the *Christian Science Monitor*, in the July 9, 1947 issue reported his impressions of President Roxas in the following language: "President Roxas is one of the most impressive, convincing, and charming public men in the world. I have sat twice in his office during the last six months and watched him take a group of newspapermen completely and effortlessly into camp. He is simple, modest, factual. He seems to be — and undoubtedly is — a brilliant, conscientious public man."

Manuel Roxas was born in Capiz, Capiz on New Year's Day, 1892 of middle class parents. His early education was received in the public schools of the Philippines and in St. Joseph's College in Hongkong. His education in adult life was, however, wider in scope than any to be obtained in an educational institution, for he was a voracious reader of serious books and acquired an intimate knowledge of law, finance, and political and social sciences. These accomplishments were in time to make him a dynamic public speaker and a master of English prose.

Roxas began early to write "first" after his name. He was graduated in 1913 as the President of the first graduating class of the first law school in the Philippines to conduct its classes in English, the College of Law, University of the Philippines. He continued "first" when he passed the bar examination with the highest grade. That accomplishment caused Chief Justice Arellano of the Supreme Court to select Roxas to be his law clerk.

Roxas left his position in the Supreme Court in 1917 for a political career which was to fill the greater portion of his life. From Governor of Capiz at 27, he went to the House of Representatives which immediately elected him Speaker. His next position of importance was that of Secretary of Finance in the Commonwealth Cabinet of President Quezon. Following the interruption by the war of normal civil processes, Roxas joined MacArthur on Corregidor. The war over, he became President of the Philippine Senate. Elected President of the Republic of the Philippines, Roxas was again "first," and this time "first" in the land.

Fortunately for himself and, as a consequence, fortunately for the Philippines, Roxas grew in stature as he progressed. Practically everyone, even Presidents Quezon and Osmeña, recognized that Roxas was the coming man. In Quezon's incomplete autobiography "The Good Fight," the President of the Commonwealth of the Philippines mentions Roxas as an able and outstanding leader "needed by the Filipino people in the years to come."[25]

Outside the regular field of governmental administration, Roxas also distinguished himself. In the role of missioner to the United States, he was able through the favorable impression he made on members of Congress to become a powerful instrument in winning independence on favorable terms for the Philippines. In the constitutional convention, although Roxas was of the minority, his better preparation, his constant industry, and his quick intellect nevertheless

---

[25] See Manuel Luis Quezon, *The Good Fight*, pp. 192, 201, 280, 309.

brought recognition to him as the virtual floor leader of the convention and one of the principal draftsmen of the country's Constitution.

Manuel Roxas was the representative of the class of Filipinos commonly referred to as "the rising generation." These were the young Filipinos who were American-trained in the schools of the Philippines. Gradually they changed the whole outlook of their country: gave it a national language in English; gave it a knowledge of constitutional processes; gave it an outlook on the world which induced the vast majority of the Filipinos to resist the Japanese invader and to stand foursquare with the United States in defense of freedom. Manuel Roxas by reason of the acknowledged brilliancy of his leadership became the spokesman and idol of these groups of democratically thinking Filipinos.

While Roxas was the product of the American school system of the Philippines, he was nevertheless the true representative of the average Filipino in personal appearance and actions. In other words, he was more the Malay type than either of his confrères—than Quezon with Spanish *Conquistador* features and Spanish explosiveness; than Osmeña with the slant eyes of the Chinese and the serenity of the Oriental. In habits also, Roxas hit a balance between the other two leaders—not as irregular in engagements as Quezon; not as punctilious as Osmeña.

Roxas worked hard and diligently to solve the multifarious problems of his country. It was this unremitting devotion to official duties, along with the harassments and demands incident to high station, that exacted the penalty of his death. But from the cares of state he could readily turn to become the hospitable host. His weakness, if it could be so termed, was his consideration for everyone, a kindly compassion which would not permit him to take drastic action against the transgressor.

Roxas was inducted into office as the third and last President of the Commonwealth on May 28, 1946. Shortly thereafter, on July 4th of the same year, he became the first President of the Republic of the Philippines. Immediately and continuously he gave attention to the many and intricate problems pressing down on the lives of his fellow men. That he succeeded as well as he did is all the more remarkable considering the lack of a sufficient number of trusted lieutenants, the sad plight of the country, the human impossibility of rectifying conditions immediately, and the partisan, hostile attitude of those who either could not or would not understand.

It was perhaps inevitable that one as conspicuously successful as Roxas should become the target of those who were motivated by misdirected patriotism or by jealousy or hatred. The charge was repeated in various forms by critics, some of whom had no knowledge of the facts, that Roxas during the war was a collaborationist. It mattered not that General MacArthur vouched for Roxas' military record, later substantiated by High Commissioner McNutt. The venom of twisted mentalities was then directed at MacArthur and McNutt who in effect were called liars. One author even charged that General MacArthur deliberately shielded Roxas because of long-standing friendship.[26]

The facts are these: Shortly after Pearl Harbor, Roxas, as a member of the Philippine Army Reserve, offered his services to General MacArthur and was activated with the rank of Lieutenant Colonel. He was assigned as Liaison Officer between the Army Command and the Philippine Government. While on Corregidor, Roxas was particularly helpful in maintaining the morale of the Filipino soldiers and in securing much-needed food for the troops.

Roxas left Corregidor to join President Quezon in the southern islands, at the latter's request, but by his own choice remained behind when the President departed for the United States. Presidential powers, however, were delegated to Roxas. Captured and made a prisoner in Mindanao, Roxas was brought by the Japanese to Manila where every trick from brutality to kindness was used to get him to accept a high post in the puppet government. He was finally induced to help draft a new constitution and to act as food czar and Chairman of the Economic Planning Board, for the benefit of the people.

Under the noses of the Japanese, Roxas coordinated and systematized espionage operations. Connections were established with guerrillas, and MacArthur was provided with vital intelligence of enemy activities. Guerrilla leaders like Major Edwin F. Ramsey, Major Robert E. Lapham, Lieutenant Colonel Bernard L. Anderson, and Colonel Marcos V. Agustin ("Marking") speak in glowing terms of Roxas' guidance of the resistance movement.[27]

The situation became grave for Roxas when an incriminating message to him transmitted by Jose Ozamis was intercepted and when Juan Miguel Elizalde and Enrico Pirovano, two other trusted lieutenants, were arrested and liquidated. An order of execution was

---

[26] Robert Payne, *The Revolt of Asia*, p. 269 (New York, 1947).

[27] Quoted in Bustos, *And Now Comes Roxas*, pp. 247-253. Roxas' association with the underground movement is factually described by Marcial P. Lichauco, a friend in his confidence, in *Dear Mother Putnam*, a diary of the war in the Philippines (Manila, 1949). Major Ricardo C. Galang, *Secret Mission to the Philippines* (Manila, 1948) and Yay Marking, *The Crucible* (New York, 1950) can also be noted.

in fact issued by the Japanese high command, but was blocked by Occupation President Laurel. Subsequently the order was suppressed by General Takiji Wachi, Director General of the Japanese Military Administration in the Philippines.

Is it any wonder, then, that when the American forces picked up the Filipino officials near Baguio, by MacArthur's order Roxas was liberated, restored to military rank, and assigned to headquarters, while all the others were interned! On May 9, 1946, after the outcome of the presidential election in the Philippines was known, MacArthur's headquarters in Japan released an official statement, which in blunt words cleared Roxas of any taint of collaboration and acclaimed him one of the prime factors in the guerrilla movement.[28]

Typical of Roxas' life was his passing. He had suffered from a heart ailment for years, a condition which ill-treatment by the Japanese, and the shouldering of the vast responsibilities that bore down on him, did nothing to alleviate. He was stricken on April 15, 1948, shortly after making a strong speech at Clark Field, U. S. Air Base northwest of Manila, not far from the center of insurgent opposition to his administration. A friend of America and a foe of communism to the end, President Roxas declared "the liberty loving peoples of the world must stop, and if necessary fight any aggressor that may want to trample upon the liberties of other peoples or interfere in the free exercise of their sovereignty." He died that same night, with his wife and mother at his side.

An American publisher has remarked that President Roxas had gone up against conditions as trying as anything George Washington encountered in the early days of his Presidency. The same writer has added that when the final record is written, Roxas' accomplishments will compare favorably with those of Washington.[29]

What appears on a modest mausoleum in the Cemetery del Norte in Manila probably best expresses what is recorded in the judgment book of the Filipino people.

---

[28] Hernando J. Abaya, *Betrayal in the Philippines*, and David Bernstein, *The Philippine Story*, marshal the arguments of those who were convinced that Roxas was guilty of collaboration with the Japanese. For a view favorable to Roxas, see F. Mangahas, *The Story of Roxas, the War Years*, with Roxas confirming the facts. A neutral and balanced characterization of Roxas is that by H. Ford Wilkins, editor of the *Manila Daily Bulletin*, a Manila newspaperman who was a prisoner of the Japanese throughout the occupation and who had direct knowledge of the nature of Roxas' resistance to Japanese pressure and the extent of his alleged collaboration. The Wilkins article appeared in the *New York Sunday Times* and is recommended reading for those who want the facts on Roxas' war record.

[29] Roy W. Howard of the *United Press* on intimate terms with the Filipino leaders.

MANUEL ROXAS
Soldier, Statesman, Patriot
Friend of the Common Man
Champion of Democracy
Architect and Builder
of the Nation

His Excellency Elpidio Quirino, Second President of the Republic[30]

The unexpected and tragic death of President Manuel Roxas devolved the powers and duties of the President on Vice President Elpidio Quirino, as provided in the Constitution. He took the oath of office in a brief ceremony on April 17, 1948. President Quirino accordingly served out a term that was less than half completed. In January, 1950 he became President in his own right for a four year term.

The new President came to the helm of the Philippine ship of state no mere novice in practical politics and the science of government. Back of him was a rich experience in legislative and executive offices. He was respected for his integrity which no breath of scandal marred. He had a reputation for possessing an independent mind which no expedient of the moment could influence. President Quirino could be accepted as a Chief Executive who, to the best of his ability and to the limit of his physical strength, would endeavor to give the country a fruitful administration of public affairs.

Elpidio Quirino is an example of the opportunities which a democratic system offered to a poor but ambitious young Filipino. He was born in Vigan, Ilocos Sur on November 16, 1890. His father was the warden of the provincial jail and from his mother he received his first schooling. Young Elpidio's lowly lot made it necessary for him to obtain further education principally through his own efforts. By working as a barrio teacher at ₱12 a month and by walking five kilometers to the Vigan High School, he was able to begin his regular scholastic training. His education was continued in Manila where he earned his livelihood as a clerk while studying in the Manila High School and the University of the Philippines.

After graduation from the College of Law, University of the Philippines, Quirino soon attracted the attention of Senate President Quezon and became his secretary. Inspired by such a chief, it was natural for him to plunge into politics. He was elected to the House

---

[30] See the pamphlet, "Quirino the Leader, the Statesman."

of Representatives and later to the Senate. First Governor General Murphy and next President Quezon then named him Secretary of Finance and subsequently Secretary of the Interior. Elected a member of the constitutional convention, he contributed to the deliberations of that body. In 1941 Quirino was again elected to the Senate. The culmination of his career came with election as Vice President and subsequently as President of the Republic of the Philippines.

In a precedent-breaking move, President Roxas named the Vice President to the new and highly important cabinet post of Secretary of Foreign Affairs. Quirino was well equipped for the office, which in the beginning involved delicate negotiations with the United States, because of experience gained in previous contacts with American officials in the Philippines and as a trusted member of missions to the United States. He successfully concluded treaties with the United States without offending American representatives or losing their help, while standing firm in defense of his country's interests. At the same time he completed the organization of the Department of Foreign Affairs and of the Foreign Service and entered into treaties with many countries. Quirino gained additional respect for the young nation on a good will tour of the world.

President Quirino came to the Presidency under circumstances that would try any man's mettle. He had not been in good health. Not long before he had been forced to retire from participation in the food conference because of high blood pressure. On to his ailing shoulders fell responsibilities that would test the physically fit. He assumed the burdens of an office as nerve racking as any in the world with Christian fortitude and with an earnest determination to do right.

It is to be noted that Quirino's political record was spotted by victories and defeats. Invariably he accepted the bitter with the sweet in a sportsmanlike manner. That quality of poise and equanimity finds expression in his decisions on state matters.

President Quirino's character was molded by his ancestry. He is of Ilocano blood and comes from the people of Northern Luzon whose thrift, honesty and dependability are proverbial. These admirable qualities are reflected in the President's actions and policies.

President Quirino does not exemplify the sparkling or eloquent type of statesmanship. There is in him a lack of the fire and glamour of Quezon and Roxas. Nor does he possess their rare oratorical ability. His is a more direct, witty, and argumentative kind of speechmaking which gains points through geniality and persuasion. His is a slower-forming judgment.

The charge of collaboration did not plague President Quirino as it did his predecessor. At one time during the Japanese occupation he was imprisoned. During the enemy's fire and blood purge of Manila just before liberation, Quirino's wife and three of his five children were machine-gunned to death by the Japanese. These horrible pictures are indelibly stamped in his memory and have done much to undermine his health. The children who escaped, one a son and the other a daughter, are a comfort to their father. The vivacious daughter, Victoria, affectionately called "Vicky," became the official hostess of Malacañan.

Encouraging as the recovery strides toward normalcy in the Republic had been, there was plenty left for the President to do.

Quirino's major address as Vice President before his automatic elevation to the Presidency had been delivered in Washington in May, 1947.[31] It naturally and properly reflected the policies of the administration of which he was a part. A bid for survival, restrained nationalism, and friendship for the United States were the keynotes of the address. The President could not be expected to depart very much from that platform.

In mid-1949 President Quirino again visited the United States, and in so doing became the first chief executive of a sovereign Philippine Republic to set foot on American soil. The mission was well timed to coincide with a resurgence of American interest in the Far East. The gruelling trip enhanced the regard of the United States for the Philippines. In appearances before the Houses of Congress, the Filipino President, in forthright declarations that commanded respect, gave a glimpse of the sturdy, forward-looking attitude of his people toward their place in the world. He also rescued from oblivion specific matters of immense material benefit to the Filipino people that otherwise might have been lost through indifference and indecision.

The early actions of President Quirino indicated that "unity" would be the slogan, the goal of his administration. He would try to win back the Filipino peoples' confidence in their government, which meant getting rid of the rascals who had sabotaged a portion of the program of his predecessor. He would try to restore peace and order in the troubled areas of Central and Southern Luzon. In these efforts he only partly succeeded.

The President endeavored to bring the people and the Government closer together. This he did by making trips into the provinces.

---

[31] Address of Vice President Quirino on May 14, 1947 before the National Press Club of Washington, D. C. Reprinted in the *Congressional Record* of the same date.

This he did by delivering monthly "fireside chats" over the radio. The purpose was to present to the people in easily understood language an appraisal of the condition of the country and its problems.

As this policy unfolded, it evolved into a positive ideology based on the material development of all sources of wealth. The more immediate objectives were the restoration of peace and order and the institution of a social amelioration program. A determined house cleaning was pledged. The interests of the Nation were to be put ahead of all other interests.

Assuredly it was a man's size job President Quirino had chosen for himself. If he should fail in whole or in part, it would be understandable. If the President should succeed, his people could call him blessed.

Under two Presidents, the Republic of the Philippines had made substantial progress toward its supreme goal: the attainment of economic security under a regime of political freedom.

STATE OF THE NATION [32]

The true State of the Nation has, of course, varied from year to year. Speaking in the most general terms, conditions in the Philippines before the war could have been denominated as "Excellent," immediately after the conclusion of the war as "Bad," and through the 1946-50 reconstruction period as "Improving." From 1950 onward the times must be labeled as "Critical."

The two men best equipped to furnish a blueprint of the situation in their country were naturally Presidents Roxas and Quirino.

On January 26, 1948 President Roxas delivered before the First Congress of the Republic of the Philippines a message on the State of the Nation. He had addressed the elected representatives of the sovereign people on similar occasions. But as if by premonition that in a little over two months he was to be called before a higher power, he was moved to give an accounting of his stewardship to the Filipino people.

On January 24, 1949 President Quirino delivered before the last regular session of the First Congress another State of the Nation message. He had ascended to the Presidency on the death of President Roxas under distressing circumstances. But as visual proof that progress toward normalcy had been made, the President met the Congress in the historic hall of the reconstructed Legislative Building. President Quirino subsequently reiterated his views from his sickbed

---

[32] State of the Nation. The Messages of Presidents Roxas and Quirino are printed as public documents.

in Baltimore, Maryland, and from his desk in Malacañan Palace in Manila.

The Philippines had been a free and independent country for an appreciable period. It was time to take an inventory of successes and failures. It was time to strike a trial balance. President Roxas was ready with a last report that did him memorable honor. President Quirino was ready with longer messages that offered a wealth of information on the peoples' business.

In the 1948 message on the State of the Nation, President Roxas referred to his first message on the same topic, in which he had drawn a dark picture of the tragic conditions confronting the country. He informed the people that the crisis *had* passed; the program of rehabilitation was far advanced; there was relative prosperity in the land. The President next proceeded by an objective application of the Socratic method to present his case.

President Roxas concluded his message with an earnest plea for action. He asked one and all not to waste energies in partisan conflict, nor in any attempt to gain personal advantages, while they should be engaged in the all-consuming tasks of lifting the Republic from the ashes of war and insuring for the people all the blessings of peace and happiness. The President's last words were:

> What the future may have in store for you or for me is of no consequence. What will befall our people and the kind of heritage we leave to our children, and what we can do to make their lot a happy one, constitute the only problem that should absorb our thoughts and stir our hearts during these trying days which, I am sure, will also be days of triumph and glory for our Republic if we have the courage and the wisdom to meet the challenge of the times and to keep faith with the noble principles and traditions which have inspired and sustained us throughout the darkest period in our history. The stakes are too high and the risks are too great to allow ourselves to be swerved from our sworn duty to the nation. God help our people if we desert our trust!

President Quirino concluded his first message with a statement of policy. He said:

> When I assumed office, my only pledge was what I recited in my oath. I meant every word of it. My policy has been simple. I have only two main immediate objectives: the restoration of peace and order, and the strengthening of the

morale of the people and their faith and confidence in the government.

Limitations of space forbid itemization of the facts presented by the two Presidents and the quotations of the telling points made by them. Their frame of mind was one of confidence and hope. Not everyone will share their faith in the future.

A factual examination of the State of the Nation Messages shows them overly-optimistic in tone. But all will have to admit that the accomplishments of the five year reconstruction period have been phenomenal. Residents of the Philippines can realize this more fully than any casual observer from afar. Off to a perilous start, the comeback has been thoroughgoing and systematic.

The overall immediate targets are acceleration of further rehabilitation, achievement of a near balance in imports and exports, balancing of the budget, development of the national economy, elimination of governmental corruption, unification of the people, and adequate defenses against the spread of communism and its allied agencies of destruction.

Justice Claro M. Recto
President of the Philippine Constitutional Convention.

CHAPTER X

CONSTITUTION OF THE PHILIPPINES[1]

Philippine Constitutional History[2]

Two divergent civilizations, the Latin and the American, and two divergent systems of law, the Roman Civil Law and the Anglo-American Common Law, have met and blended in the Philippines. From these civilizations and laws have come the factors that have influenced the rise of popular government in the Philippines. Naturally the two countries whose institutions have most affected Philippine constitutional development have been Spain and the United States.

For over three centuries, the people of the Philippines were under the dominion of Spain. Of the various constitutions in force in Spain, only those with liberal ideas reached as far as the Philippines. During three periods in which the Spanish Constitution was effective in the Philippines, the latter had merely nominal representation in the Spanish Cortes. Nevertheless, although the Filipinos did not receive many direct benefits from a constitutional government, they did receive numerous indirect benefits from the Spanish administration. When the Spanish flag was hauled down for the last time in the Philippines and the American emblem was raised in its stead, the Filipino people, Filipinos in name and innate characteristics, were nevertheless thinking in many ways as Spaniards. The mental processes and culture of the Filipinos were partly those of the Latins.

For two score years, the American conception of good government was modified to meet Philippine conditions; American laws were bodily or partially transplanted to the Philippines; American educational methods were applied; and American thought was predominant. Accordingly, there could be no other result than that democratic institutions, as fostered under the Constitution of the United States, should become known in the Philippines and should there meet, and to a great extent overcome, the more conservative notions of Spanish times.

---

[1]Senator Lorenzo M. Tañada and Professor Enrique M. Fernando have authored a comprehensive work entitled *Constitution of the Philippines Annotated* (1949 edition, Manila).

[2] No acceptable Constitutional History of the Philippines has been written.

While the Constitution of the United States as a constitution was not in force in the Philippines, the influence of the document has nevertheless been felt. The Federal and state governments were taken as models for Philippine legislation. Any number of American constitutional ideas will be found embodied in the Constitution of the Philippines, while other ideas of a similiar tenor will continue to affect the lives of the people outside of the Constitution. It can be expected that even years after the proclamation of Philippine independence, certain of the American constitutional institutions will remain, while others will disappear or become blended with later innovations.

The basic Philippine constitutional document of American origin was the Instructions of the President to the Second Philippine Commission of April 7, 1900. The famous letter of Instructions has been aptly compared to the Magna Charta of ancient Britain, the Laws of the Indies of imperial Spain, and the Northwest Ordinance of the frontier days of the United States. The Instructions are entitled to a place in that select circle. This remarkable state paper formulated in an authoritative manner the fundamental principles upon which American policies toward the Philippines have rested. If any one document is to be selected as most evidencing the genesis of the Philippine Constitution, the letter of Instructions is entitled to such recognition.

The three organic laws between 1900 and 1935 were the Philippine Bill of 1902, the Jones Law of 1916, and the Philippine Commonwealth and Independence Act of 1934. The Philippine Bill, although it did not create a new government, was the basic law for fourteen years. The Jones Law was more nearly akin to an organic act. The Philippine Commonwealth and Independence Act was in nature an enabling act, the precepts of which were to be respected in framing a constitution.

The sad side to the history of these sun-kissed isles, as President Quirino has pointed out, is that every successive invader tried to fashion them after his own land.[3] Despite the odds against them, the Filipino people went through these processes with benefit to themselves. The Republic of the Philippines is the product of this evolutionary development.

Notwithstanding the long Spanish domination of the Islands, and notwithstanding the shorter although more potent American control, native traditions and customs in their essentials have remained unaffected. Outward form has changed, but inward thought has not

---

[3] Address in Washington, D. C. on May 14, 1947.

changed. The Filipino has neither been transmuted into a Spaniard nor an American. What we might call the Filipino soul has survived the centuries of contact with alien races. The Filipino has taken the gifts of foreigners sometimes because he had to and again because he wanted to, without, however, giving up his own national consciousness.

The revolts against Spain and the United States first permitted of a practical demonstration of Filipino aptitude for self-government. The most important constitutional document of this period was the Malolos Constitution of the Philippine Republic of 1899, the work principally of Felipe Calderon. Later, formal action thrice taken by the Philippine Assembly demonstrated the easily understood desire of the Filipino people to substitute a constitution of their own making for one imposed by a foreign sovereignty. That aspiration was properly satisfied by the right conceded by the Philippine Commonwealth and Independence Act to hold a constitutional convention and prepare a constitution.

Side by side with the organic law has marched Philippine constitutional development by judicial construction. The Supreme Court of the United States formerly and the Supreme Court of the Philippines of the past and the present have given the Islands all that was best in constitutional law. As in the United States, the courts have assumed the duty of interpreting the constitution. When necessary the Supreme Court will declare an act of the legislature, repugnant to the Constitution, invalid.

All this serves as a background. Henceforth it will be the Constitution of the Philippines which will be studied, construed and enforced to make Philippine Constitutional Law.

The Constitutional Convention [4]

The Constitution of the Philippines came into being as the result of the joint action of four different entities. They were: 1. the Congress of the United States; 2. the Constitutional Convention; 3. the President of the United States; and 4, the people of the Philippines. The Congressional Act, commonly referred to as the Philippine Commonwealth and Independence Act, authorized the calling of a Constitutional Convention to draft a constitution, subject to a series of mandatory conditions which could not be transcended.

Two hundred and two delegates to the Constitutional Convention

---

[4] Two excellent accounts written by delegates to the Convention are Jose M. Aruego, *The Framing of the Philippine Constitution* (Manila, 1936) and Miguel Cuaderno, *The Framing of the Constitution of the Philippines* (Manila, 1937).

were chosen at an election held on July 10, 1934. Barely one-half of the registered voters cast their ballots. A variety of reasons accounted for this apathy. Among them were the lack of partisan competition in most districts, the disinclination of candidates to spend money for food and transportation, and the feeling in some quarters that the convention would be a cut and dried affair.

The rival leaders of the two major parties, Senators Quezon and Osmeña, were not candidates for election as delegates. Other prominent figures similarly shunned election. Nevertheless, the delegates actually chosen constituted a representative group. They included many influential members of the Philippine Legislature. The Convention, however, was far from being a replica of the legislative body. Two delegates to the Convention, General Teodoro Sandiko and General Jose Alejandrino, had helped draft the Malolos Constitution of the short-lived Philippine Republic, thirty odd years before. Seven other delegates had served in the first Philippine Assembly of 1907. Resident Commissioners Guevera and Osias were members, as were future President Elpidio Quirino, former Supreme Court Justice Norberto Romualdez, former University President Rafael Palma, political scientists Reyes and Aruego, and leading lawyers like Vicente J. Francisco, Salvador Araneta, Godofredo Reyes, Paulino Gullas, and the two Sottos, Filemon and Vicente. A stabilizing influence on excitable partisanship was provided by a *bloc* led by Vicente Lopez of Iloilo, that included other businessmen animated by independence of judgment.

The Constitutional Convention assembled on the morning of July 30, 1934, in the hall of the House of Representatives, facing a large and interesting task—the establishment of an autonomous government, later to blend into an independent state. Few bodies designated to do this work have met under more favorable auspices.

The opening ceremonies were turned into a Batangas day. The temporary chairman, former Senator Jose P. Laurel; the permanent President, Senator Claro M. Recto; the Bishop, Mons. Alfredo Verzosa, who delivered the invocation; and the delegate, Attorney Eusebio Orense, who led the independent opposition from the floor— all were *Batangueños*. Even the busy sergeant-at-arms was from Batangas.

It was evident that the program had been carefully planned beforehand by the alliance between the majority and the minority parties. The leaders of the two factions worked in perfect harmony, and the machine was in excellent running order. The two stormy petrels, Tomas Confessor and Gregorio Perfecto, were overruled by strong-armed gavel wielding and the threat of removal by the sergeant-at-arms. Three chairs were on the rostrum, but one was hurriedly removed when it was apparent that Governor General Murphy was not to grace the occasion with his presence. Senate President Quezon opened the ceremonies, but the ripple of applause which he received was not in accord with the usual ovation given him, and among the independents especially there was a hint of objection to his presence in a convention to which he was not a delegate. However, as said, the plans perfected before the meeting were carried out without a hitch after a parliamentary tangle had threatened to prolong the session.

From day to day optimistic announcements were made that the Convention would conclude its task on such and such a date. The date, however, invariably had to be moved forward. In fact six full months were needed for the Convention to draft a constitution.

One reason for the slow progress in constitution-making was the unwieldiness of such a large body. This unwieldiness was further enhanced by the number of committees that were named, practically fifty in all. Some committees had as many as forty-five members, and the Sponsorship Committee numbered eighty-seven members. Eventually the folly of such a course became so apparent that a sub-committee of seven in the Sponsorship Committee was created to draft the Constitution. This Drafting Committee was composed of Delegates Filemon Sotto, Manuel Roxas, Manuel Briones, Vicente Singson Encarnacion, Norberto Romualdez, Miguel Cuaderno, and Conrado Benitez. The Committee, assisted by the Convention President, got down to work at once and succeeded in speeding up the deliberations of the Convention.

Another reason for delay was that freedom of discussion was allowed in committees and on the floor of the Convention. The delegates, naturally gifted public speakers, took frequent and long advantage of this privilege. Many of them in their dreams undoubtedly saw themselves wearing the mantle of James Madison or of Felipe Calderon, to be acclaimed in history as the author of the Philippine Constitution. The result was a miscellaneous and novel lot of constitutional projects and fruitless discussion, tempered by a sobering sense of responsibility which defeated most of the iconoclast amendments and provided intelligent and constructive debate.

Probably the longest debate, nearly three weeks in duration, on any one proposition was induced by the Osias Resolution to have the constitution in the making govern not only the Commonwealth but the Republic as well. The fundamental issue was ably discussed.

While the resolution met formal defeat, yet the idea prevailed. The Constitution of the Philippines has been accepted as the organic law of the Philippine Republic without question.

President Claro M. Recto presided over the Convention with judicial fairness. He provided the leadership essential to success. His tactful hand guided and pushed forward the constitutional document to completion. Practically all the delegates joined the President in helping to mold an acceptable constitution.

Aside from President Recto, the delegate whose transcendent ability was most generally recognized by his fellows was Manuel Roxas. This was a remarkable tribute to Roxas' standing, all the more startling because of the circumstances which surrounded it. When the Constitutional Convention opened, the *Antis* were in the majority and the *Pros* in the minority, and Roxas belonged to the minority. By mutual agreement partisanship was banned and the offices were divided, with Roxas contenting himself with modest membership on the Sponsorship Committee and later on the Drafting Committee. In these central committees and on the floor of the Convention, Manuel Roxas of the minority, by agreeing to cooperate and by taking a place in the ranks, emerged a leader and a draftsman of his country's Constitution.

The Constitution was approved lacking one vote of unanimity. The document was formally signed on February 19, 1935, amidst motion-picture scenes, with one delegate affixing his signature with blood freshly drawn from his veins. The Constitutional Convention could then adjourn with the assurance that it had patriotically and conscientiously tried to produce a good constitution.

Submission of the Constitution for Approval

The Constitution, having been formulated by the Convention, had next to be submitted to the President of the United States and following that to the Filipino people. A Commission made up of Senate President Quezon, Convention President Recto, and Minority Leader Roxas presented an official copy of the Constitution to the President in Washington for approval.

The task assigned the President of the United States was to determine whether or not the Constitution conformed to the provisions of the Congressional Enabling Act. In reaching a decision the President had the benefit of reports from executive departments of the National Government and of the advice of Governor General Murphy. The President was able to certify the acceptability of the Constitution.

On March 23, 1935, the Constitution was formally approved by the President in a brief but impressive ceremony in the presence of the Filipino Commission, the Secretary of War, the Governor General, and others. The Secretary of State was also in attendance, which was symbolic of the changed status of the Philippines.

With the signing of the Constitution of the Philippines, authorized by the Congressional Act which President Franklin D. Roosevelt had previously inspired, he placed himself among the three American Presidents—William McKinley and Woodrow Wilson being the other two—who had approved vitally important state documents which will do down in Philippine history. Another step in the orderly process leading to independence had been taken.

The Constitution of the Philippines was next submitted for the scrutiny of the Filipino electorate. Their vote had a twofold meaning. It meant acceptance or rejection of the Constitution and acceptance or rejection of independence.

Registered voters were afforded an opportunity to vote directly for or against the Constitution in an election held on May 14, 1935. Curiously enough, women, although practically disfranchised by the Constitution, were permitted to cast ballots on the ratification of this same Constitution. The question asked the electors was, "Do you vote for the ratification of the Constitution of the Philippines, with the Ordinance appended thereto?"

A campaign of publicity for the approval of the Constitution was supervised by government officials and convention delegates. A counter-campaign against the Constitution was carried on more insidiously by the radical group. When the votes were canvassed, it was found that the Constitution had been approved by an overwhelming majority.[5]

An analysis of the plebiscite figures discloses some interesting facts. In the first place, the vote even with the women participating was less than for a regular election. In the second place, the outcome represented a smashing victory for ratification of the Constitution and independence, to be exact, .965 percent for to .035 percent against. The region which cast the highest number of negative votes was the North, including Batanes, Mountain Province, Cagayan, and Isabela. Indeed, the Sub-Province of Benguet gave a majority against, as did three municipalities in Batanes. Also the Moro country, particularly Lanao, was not very enthusiastically for the Constitution and independence. The inferences to be drawn were, first, a fear of

[5] The votes were 1,213,046 for ratification of the Constitution and 44,963 against ratification.

Japan in the provinces situated nearest to that expanding empire, second, a predilection for American protection among the non-Christians, and third, an otherwise general desire to see the autonomous Commonwealth inaugurated and on its way to independence.

The Philippines was now ready to elect the officers provided for in the Constitution and, having done so, to inaugurate the Commonwealth Government.

AMENDMENTS TO THE CONSTITUTION

The Constitution has been amended in four major respects. Three amendments were ratified together within five years of the inauguration of the Philippine Commonwealth. The fourth amendment was adopted during the first year of the Republic. A change in the ordinance appended to the Constitution necessitated by an amendment of the Philippine Commonwealth and Independence Act in 1939 has become obsolete.

The Commonwealth approved amendments related to such vital matters as the composition of the legislative body and the terms of office of the President and Vice President. The Constitution had originally provided for a unicameral National Assembly. By the amendment there was substituted a bicameral Congress of the Philippines. The Constitution had originally provided that the President should hold office during a term of six years, with reelection for the following term prohibited. By the amendment, the system was changed to permit of a shortened tenure of office of two four year terms with an immediately succeeding third term prohibited.

A new feature was a provision for an independent Commission on Elections to have exclusive charge of the enforcement and administration of all laws relating to the conduct of elections. This amendment was induced by dissatisfaction relative to the conduct of elections.

The Ordinance now found appended to the Constitution was the outgrowth of provisions in the Philippine Trade Act of 1946 dealing with the rights of United States citizens and business enterprises. To make these parity rights effective necessitated approval of an amendment to the Philippine Constitution.

It must be confessed that there was no spontaneous demand on the part of the public for the adoption of any of these amendments. The people would have been satisfied with a one chamber legislature and a single six year term President and were not overly desirous of granting special rights to Americans. It was the Filipino administration in each instance that threw the weight of its all-prevailing influence in favor of the constitutional changes, except that President Quezon remained silent relative to the amendment that permitted him to hold office for eight instead of six years and would have allowed him to seek the Presidency of the Republic if he had lived. The parity amendment was approved mainly because of the vigorous campaign in its behalf conducted by President Roxas. The vote was about eight to one in favor of adoption of the amendment.[6]

The changes in the Constitution here outlined will be discussed further under appropriate subjects.

STRUCTURE OF THE GOVERNMENT[7]

The Constitutional Convention did what was expected of it when it molded a model of a constitution that fitted the frame prescribed by the Philippine Commonwealth and Independence Act. The required Bill of Rights was included. An ordinance of mandatory provisions was appended, but has become obsolete.

The Constitution authorized a plan that accomplished one of its main purposes. Continuity between the American-administered Government of the Philippine Islands and the autonomous Filipino Commonwealth was maintained. The Philippine Commonwealth evolved into the Philippine Republic without a hitch. In other words, it was to be a Constitution not alone for the present but for the future as well.

The Constitution adopted the system of checks and balances. The time-honored doctrine of separation of powers was accepted, with modifications to cope with Philippine actualities. The amended Constitution vests legislative power in the bicameral Congress of the Philippines, executive power in the President of the Philippines, and judicial power in the Supreme Court and inferior courts. The Congress of the Philippines is granted general authority subject to specific prohibitions. The President is made a strong executive, but with dictatorship avoided. The Supreme Court is expected to be independent in every sense of the word. Actually the one, two, three order maintained in the Constitution conveys little significance, for everyone realizes that executive power in the person of the President outranks the other two powers.

Except that there will be a Filipino President instead of an American Governor General, and a completely *Filipinized* Supreme Court

---

[6] Votes for the parity amendment, 1,744,899. Votes against, 226,257. Information furnished by the Commission on Elections.

[7] See Jose P. Laurel, *The Three Powers Under the Philippine Constitution* (Manila, 1936).

instead of a partly American-controlled body, the general setup remained pretty much the same, at least in theory, under the Republic of the Philippines. The observer will experience little difficulty in recognizing the parts of the governmental machine.

New Features [8]

While the Constitution contained the provisions expected to be found in a fundamental law, it also included a number of novel features. The document was built solidly on experience. It copied the time tested principles of the American constitutional system. At the same time the Constitution departed from precedent to reflect faithfully Filipino sentiment.

Two innovations sanctioned by the original Constitution have already gone by the boards. The unicameral National Assembly was discarded for the more usual bicameral Congress of the Philippines. With more regret must be written down the action that did away with a six year term for the President with election for the following term prohibited. The Constitution in its original form had in that respect taken a step well in advance of the American system. The amendment was introduced because of the feeling that one man was indispensable, whereas the Constitution was intended to avoid that very contingency by not making it possible for anyone to entrench himself in power.[9]

Following a preamble and a formal section descriptive of the national territory, the Constitution starts off with a "Declaration of Principles," five in all. The first Principle, declaring the Philippines to be a republican state with sovereignty residing in the people, will be discussed in the succeeding section.

The second and third Principles concern the defense of the State. When it was declared therein that "The defense of the State is a prime duty of government, and in the fulfillment of this duty all citizens may be required to render personal military . . . service," the Constitution merely confirmed a power which all governments possess. But the Philippine Constitution went further by including where the asterisks appear in the quoted Principle the words "or civil." Requiring all citizens to render personal civil service can mean nothing less than authority for the conscription of labor in time of peace as well as of war. The working models for this drastic provision, according to General Alejandrino who sponsored it, were

---

[8] For an American appraisal of the novel features of the Philippine Constitution, see Grayson L. Kirk, *Philippine Independence*, Ch. VII.

[9] Discussed under the section dealing with the tenure of office of the President.

the totalitarian states of Germany, Bulgaria, and Soviet Russia. The General gloated over the fact that by virtue of this provision in the Constitution "there shall not be and cannot be any question as to the right or power of the State to compel its citizens to render whatever service may be required of them." The impact of a clause which reduced individualism to a minimum is attempted to be softened by a succeeding pious renunciation of war by the Philippines "as an instrument of national policy."

Principles four and five promise support in the rearing of the youth "for civic efficiency" and in the promotion of social justice "to insure the well being and economic security of all the people." The humane theories here expressed are implemented in a practical manner in other portions of the Constitution. The conservation and utilization of natural resources are strictly regulated. The government is authorized to enter the field of business "in the interest of the national welfare and defense." The State affords "protection to labor."

Passing on to consideration of the Bill of Rights, it will first be noted that the constitution makers did not take advantage of the opportunity afforded them to supply three rights previously denied them under American-inspired organic law. For instance, there was no insistent demand then, and little public agitation since the Constitution was approved, for the implantation of trial by jury. Nevertheless, the Philippine Bill of Rights goes beyond any previous Philippine Organic Act and beyond the Constitution of the United States to guarantee liberty of abode and movement; a qualified privacy of communication and correspondence; and the right to form associations or societies. In obedience to the current concept of social justice, it is provided that "Free access to the courts shall not be denied to any person by reason of poverty."

The Philippine Constitution rejected three familiar provisions of the Constitution of the United States. Citizenship by blood instead of citizenship by birth is recognized in the Philippines. The cumbersome American-sanctioned electoral system, which repeatedly has permitted Presidents to be elected with a minority of popular votes, was not duplicated; instead the Philippine electorate vote directly for President and Vice President. The Vice President of the Philippines was rescued from the obscurity which has made the Vice President of the United States the butt of stale jokes, to be made eligible to become a real administrative associate of the President.

The Philippine Constitution, as amended, contained other provisions, novel or original according to the viewpoint, but at least new for the Philippines. One such was authorization of a non-partisan Electoral Tribunal for each legislative Chamber, including three Justices of the Supreme Court. In another departure from American precedents, power to approve or disapprove appointments was vested in a Commission on Appointments consisting of twelve Senators and twelve Congressmen elected by each House on the basis of proportional representation of the political parties therein. Avoidance of a one vote margin on constitutional questions was met by the requirement that no treaty or law may be declared unconstitutional without the concurrence of two-thirds of all the members of the Supreme Court.

A REPUBLICAN STATE

The Philippine Constitution purports to set up a republican state. But the test of a constitution comes not in words but in how it functions in practice. What kind or sort of a government does the Philippines actually have?

Before the adoption of the Philippine Constitution, it had been generally accepted that a republican form of government existed in the Philippines. The model had naturally been the Federal and state governments of the United States. Has anything occurred to transform that pattern into some other sort of political ideology?

In the Philippines, as in the United States, sovereignty resides in the people. In the Philippines, as in the United States, there is a government by representatives chosen by the people. The powers entrusted to the government of the Philippine Republic, as in the United States, are distributed among three supposedly independent and coordinate departments, the legislative, the executive and the judicial. It cannot logically be said that at this point the analogy ceases, for that would involve an intensive study of the activities of the American Government. It can be added with more reason that democratic processes in the Philippines do not exactly reflect American precedents; nor need they conform to any set pattern. No Canute can stay progress.

The authors of the Philippine Constitution were confronted with the basic question of whether to provide for the presidential or parliamentary type of government. Previously there had been evident a decided drift toward a responsible government. With the recognition of a premier *de facto* in the person of the Filipino President of the Senate, the inauguration of a Council of State with executive and legislative membership, and with members of the legislature coincidentally holding executive and legislative offices, the Philippine system stood midway between the American presidential system and the English parliamentary system. Nevertheless, with full liberty of choice, the Constitutional Convention deliberately chose the presidential form of government. The Constitution specifically inhibits a member of the legislature from holding a cabinet post without resigning his legislative office.

Having thus decided the question of a form of government in favor of the presidential type, the Constitution proceeded to give the Executive a predominant position. Commonwealth President Quezon on assumption of office quickly disabused one and all of any notion that he would not be a strong executive by imposing his will on the legislative body. In President Roxas was evidenced the same kind of dynamic leadership and the consolidation of power in his own hands.

The philosophy of government underlying the Philippine Constitutional System subordinates the individual to the good of the State. President Quezon termed it "the philosophy of government intervention whenever the needs of the country required it." President Roxas in his inaugural address described the favored system as embracing "free but guided enterprise" to be defended "against the deceptive allures of communism, of militarism, and of fascism." The ever-increasing number of government corporations shows that theory has been put into practice.

The foregoing need not convey frightening implications. The Philippines is not communistic. It is not fascist. The most that can be said is that there are socialistic tendencies. The same sort of paternalism that places the hand of government in business, more and yet more, is discernible in countries like Great Britain, France, and the United States, and they are accepted as democratic nations.

The Philippines is truly a Republic.

A COMMENTARY

The Constitution of the Philippines is a good Constitution. It is more. It is a good Filipino Constitution.

The Constitution exemplifies the quality of brevity. Less than 10,000 words are required to mark the permanent outlines and to designate its objects. The language used meets the essential requisite of definiteness.

The Constitution is Filipino in words, spirit and concept. Wisely it reflected Spanish and American antecedents. Wisely the authors of the Constitution resisted the urge to insert bizarre proposals into the fundamental framework. With less justification can the delegates defend the ideas lifted from totalitarian sources. Withal, the Constitution remains an instrument drafted by Filipinos for Filipinos.

A readily understandable nationalism pervades the Constitution. The preamble begins with mention of "The Filipino people" not "The people of the Philippines," as originally intended. The first section of the first article describes "The Philippines," not "The Philippine Islands"; the latter term conveyed too many unpleasant memories of a former colonial status. And so the basic law is the "Constitution of the Philippines"; the Legislature, the "Congress of the Philippines"; the President, the "President of the Philippines"; the Supreme Court, the "Supreme Court of the Philippines"; and the Republic, the "Republic of the Philippines."

The same thought carried one step further makes only a natural born citizen eligible to become President, Vice President, a Senator, or a Member of the House of Representatives. The nationalistic spirit is reflected even more intensely in the constitutional provision that all natural resources, including minerals, belong to the State. Private agricultural land cannot be transferred to unqualified persons, that is, to aliens. Legislation enacted on such subjects as immigration and naturalization have certainly not softened the impact of nationalistic feeling. Decisions of the Supreme Court of the Philippines have had no other recourse than to confirm the law as it is.

The Constitution represents a concerted effort to produce a workmanlike document. It can be placed side by side with other constitutions and need not suffer by comparison. The Constitution of the Philippines is a fundamental law which observed the requirements of the Enabling Act; which discreetly avoided degenerating into a code; which just as wisely refused to be led into the expression of dangerous doctrines; and which is suited to conditions in the Philippines. Balancing the defects against the merits, the latter far outweigh the former.

A final word. Place yourself in the position of a Filipino delegate drafting the first Constitution for the first republican state of the Orient, and it is doubtful if you would have acted differently than the Filipino delegate. The authors of the Constitution of the Philippines displayed a high degree of political capacity.

The foregoing does not mean that constitutional history will remain static in the Philippines. Already the question has been posed of whether the Constitution of the 1935-40 Commonwealth embodies the ideals and satisfies the necessities of the 1950-55 Republic. And the one who leads in the discussion is none other than Justice Recto, the President of the Convention that drafted the Constitution.[10] He favors the calling of a new Constitutional Convention. Senate President Cuenco, on the other hand, advocates the adoption of vital amendments to the Constitution.

That a Constitutional Convention will be held in the near future no one can doubt. Let us hope that in its deliberations the body will not be swept too far away from safe mooring, that change simply for the sake of change will not be endorsed, and that what is truly a good Filipino Constitution will not be made into a Constitution still Filipino but yet not quite as good. If the delegates act as wisely in their deliberations as the fathers of the 1935 Constitution did, the outcome will be a credit to the Filipino people. It is predicted that the representatives of the sovereign people will act cautiously.

---

[10] Claro M. Recto in a series of articles under the title "Our Constitution" in the *Manila Times* beginning on February 6, 1949.

CHAPTER XI

THE PRESIDENCY

A Strong Executive

The Republic of the Philippines has a strong executive. This is as it should be.

The Filipino people have become accustomed to centralized leadership. The local chieftains in ancient times, the Spanish Viceroys in past centuries, the Commanding Generals during the Philippine Revolutions, and the American Governors General in more recent days, each represented the focus of power, the one man to be obeyed and to look to for redress of grievances. By reason of such experience, the psychology of the masses reacts more favorably to a government dominated by one person than to more democratic direction.

The Philippine Constitution entrusts executive power to a single official, the President, and confers on him vast and unusual powers. The electorate chose for President of the Commonwealth a strong man in the person of Manuel Quezon. The people in the first election for President of the Republic next turned to the dynamic Manuel Roxas for guidance. President Quezon and President Roxas each made vigorous use of his authority to make the Constitution a living force.

On the advent of the Philippine Commonwealth, the extra-legal position of national leadership was merged with the constitutional office of President. To the President was delegated virtually all the powers that had been granted to the Governor General. By giving effect to the Hamiltonian postulate of the necessity of an energetic executive to attain good government, and by the process of accretion to already conceded powers, the President arrived at a predominant position in the land. A strong executive on paper evolved into a strong executive in practice. And along with what was termed "unity of authority" went correspondingly heavy responsibility.

In outer form, there is a resemblance between the office of President of the Philippines and the office of President of the United States. But there the analogy ceases. The President of the Philippines possesses specific authority that the United States President would like to exercise but cannot because it is not granted him.

To an unprejudiced observer, it would appear that the repre-

Hon. Elpidio Quirino
Second President of the Republic of the Philippines.

sentatives of the Filipino people acted wisely in establishing a well fortified presidency. The people acted advisedly when they called to the office fellow countrymen qualified to lead.

A firm hand is needed to suppress possible regional, mass or national discontent. A firm hand is also needed to guide a new Republic, with a Latin and an American background, but located in the Orient in close contact with *Chinafied*, *Japanized*, and *Sovietized* countries.

Every consideration calls for a strong Chief Executive, but not for a dictatorship.

PRESIDENTIAL POWERS AND PERQUISITES [1]

What has been stated in the last preceding section relative to the Philippines having a strong executive will be better understood as we proceed to an enumeration of the powers granted the President.

What first attracts attention is that "the executive power" as distinguished from "the supreme executive power"—the latter expression operating as a limitation—is vested in the President. Moreover, this executive power is concentrated in one man, the President, and is not dispersed among a number of officials as is done in some of the state constitutions. The all-pervading authority of the President is bulwarked by a grant of extensive powers. [2]

The President exercises the executive power of control and supervision of the entire executive department, national and local. Presidential control extends to the departments, bureaus and offices in the integrated executive organization. Presidential supervision over all local governments amounts in practice to nothing less than control.

In his relations with the Congress of the Philippines, the President of the Philippines has prerogatives not conferred on the President of the United States. The President of the Philippines in the capacity of "determining body" annually submits a budget of receipts and expenditures for consideration by the legislature; the Congress may not increase the appropriations recommended by the President, except those for the legislative and judicial departments. The veto power of the President extends not only to bills in their entireties, but to separate items in an appropriation bill or a revenue or tariff bill. "Riders" attached to appropriation bills are prohibited. Special sessions of the

---

[1] Article VII of the Constitution of the Philippines, as amended, concerns the Executive Department and the President of the Philippines.

[2] Mathews, *Principles of State Administration*, pp. 79, 80 distinguishes "the executive power" from "the supreme executive power." The scope of the executive power was underscored by the Supreme Court of the Philippines in Planas *v.* Gil, 37 Off. Gaz. 1228 and Villena *v.* Secretary of the Interior, 38 Off. Gaz. 527.

Congress when called by the President may be limited to the consideration of subjects designated by him.[3]

The Constitution imposes on the President the obligation to "take care that the laws be faithfully executed." The President's duty as executor of the law has been reenforced with even greater authority than has been vested in the President of the United States. The President of the Philippines is not alone made the commander in chief of all armed forces of the Philippines, but he is empowered to call them out "to prevent or suppress lawless violence, invasion, insurrection, or rebellion." In such cases he may suspend the writ of *habeas corpus* or place the Philippines or any part thereof under martial law.

The President may also, by delegation by the Congress, exercise additional powers, extraordinary in scope.[4] When thus authorized he can fix tariff rates, import or export quotas, and tonnage and wharfage dues. In times of war or other national emergency, he can govern through rules and regulations. President Quezon, it will be recalled, was granted emergency power by the Congress just prior to the Japanese invasion of the Philippines. He conducted the Government-in-Exile under the aegis of suspended constitutionalism throughout the war. This emergency authority was used by the successor Presidents of the Republic even after peace came to the land.

Still the enumeration of the powers of the President are far from complete. We will mention the most important of them.

The President appoints, "with the consent" (not "advice and consent") of the Commission on Appointments of the Congress, the heads of the executive departments and bureaus; high ranking officers of the Army, Navy and Air Forces; Ambassadors, other public ministers, and consuls; members of the Supreme Court and Court of Appeals, and judges of inferior courts; Members of the Commission on Elections, and the Auditor General. He can grant reprieves, commutations of sentences and pardons, and, with the consent of the Congress, amnesty. He controls foreign affairs, and with the concurrence of two-thirds of all the members of the Senate, enters into treaties with other countries.

For performing all the foregoing duties and many others that custom dictates the President shall assume, he receives an annual salary of ₱30,000 ($15,000) and is allowed an official residence, Malacañan Palace. He may also enjoy the cool breezes of Baguio while sojourning in the well appointed summer home assigned him there, and he may find surcease from official cares while sailing over tropic seas on the

---

[3] Constitution of the Philippines, Article VI, as amended, secs. 19, 20, 9.

[4] Constitution of the Philippines, Article VI, as amended, secs. 22 (2) 26.

presidential yacht *Apo*. The compensation and perquisites of the President, however, are less than what the Governor General and the High Commissioner formerly received, and are less than that allotted the heads of other states. Nevertheless, there are any number of patriots who would cheerfully make the sacrifice to ascend the Olympic heights to the office of President.

To underline again the thought, in the President of the Philippines is centralized, with a minimum of safeguards, national authority. He determines general policies. He dominates the administration. He controls foreign relations. He guides legislation. Except through the power of appointment, he does not come in contact with the judiciary and can thus defend its independence.

Indubitably that is the kind of government that the Filipino people wanted. Indubitably that is the kind of government that the Philippines needed. Indubitably that is the kind of government that the country will have.

THE VICE PRESIDENT [5]

The executive official next in rank to the President is the Vice President.

The Vice President does not, as in the United States, preside over the Senate. Whether the Vice President in the Philippines will be a figurehead or a full partner in the administration of the national government depends on the wishes of the President. The Constitution authorizes the President to appoint the Vice President a member of the Cabinet and also head of an executive department.[6]

Presidents Quezon, Roxas, and Quirino took advantage of the constitutional provision to rescue the Vice President from obscurity. President Quezon made Vice President Osmeña Secretary of Public Instruction for a time. President Roxas called Vice President Quirino to the Cabinet to organize the Department of Foreign Affairs. President Quirino, following his election to the office, designated Vice President Lopez Chairman of the Government Enterprises Council which supervised government corporations, and subsequently when the Cabinet was reorganized appointed him Secretary of Agriculture and Natural Resources.

The Vice President is elected along with the President by direct vote of the people for a term of four years. He must possess the same

[5] Article VII of the Constitution of the Philippines, as amended, concerns the Vice President. The Vice Presidency was discussed by Claro M. Recto in an article appearing in the *Manila Times*, February 9, 1949.

[6] Constitution of the Philippines, Article VII, sec. 11 (3).

qualifications required of the President. The Vice President becomes President permanently in case the President-elect dies before the beginning of the term. The powers and duties of the President automatically devolve upon the Vice President in the event of the removal of the President from office, or his death, resignation, or inability to serve. The President of the Senate and the Speaker of the House of Representatives are, in that order, next in line of presidential succession.[7]

As long as the President and the Vice President come from the same party or from a coalition of parties all will be well. The Vice President will then be called to the Cabinet and will be a close adviser of the President. But if the President belongs to one party and the Vice President to another party, and there is no alliance of the two parties, the Vice President will have to be content with an empty honor and with drawing his salary. Under such conditions, the Vice President can only expend his surplus energies at dinner parties and official receptions, whilst as heir apparent he keeps a death watch on the President.

Justice Recto, the President of the Convention which drafted the Constitution, considers the Vice Presidency of the Philippines "an empty honor." He adds that "neither the Republic nor the Constitution would . . . lose by its abolition." It is doubtful if this iconoclastic view will gain ready acceptance.

THE COUNCIL OF STATE[8]

The governmental body with the high sounding name of "Council of State" was brought into being by an executive order of Governor General Harrison, on the suggestion of Sergio Osmeña, Speaker of the House of Representatives. The Council then served the double purpose of assuring executive-legislative and American-Filipino cooperation. It also provided unified and responsible leadership by confirming the titular position of the Speaker as next in rank to the Governor General.

Governor General Stimson, after some hesitation, rehabilitated the Council of State but with diminished powers. Under succeeding Governors General its importance decreased. For instance, Governor

---

[7] Republic Act No. 181, approved June 21, 1947.

[8] The Council of State was created by Ex. Or. No. 37, October 16, 1918 (Harrison); reconstituted by Ex. Or. No. 130, August 30, 1928 (Stimson); abolished and revised by Ex. Or. No. 144, March 17, 1938 (Quezon), and enlarged by Roxas and Quirino. See Francis Burton Harrison, *The Cornerstone of Philippine Independence*, pp. 210-215.

General Murphy called only three or four formal meetings of the Council.

Commonwealth President Quezon, by means of an executive order, created a new and enlarged Council of State. President Roxas continued it under the Republic. In addition to such members as the heads of the executive departments, the President of the Senate, the Speaker of the House, the Senate President *Pro tempore*, the Speaker *Pro tempore*, and the Majority Floor Leaders, the Council of State has had from three to five additional appointive members of distinction.

More than any of his predecessors in the executive office, President Quirino relied on the Council of State for advice. From an innocuous and ornamental body, the Council of State has become a useful component of the government organism.

PRESIDENTIAL TENURE [9]

It has heretofore been mentioned that in accordance with the Philippine Constitution in its original form, the President was elected by direct vote to serve for a term of six years, with reelection for the following term prohibited. The Philippines had improved on the American system. The Philippines had set a constitutional pattern for other lands to copy.

All the plaudits showered on the fathers of the Constitution for statesmanlike draftsmanship came to naught when, in response to unconvincing opportunism, the provisions that concerned the tenure of the President went into the discard. The constitutional amendment that was approved reduced the presidential term to four years and made the incumbent of the office eligible for reelection, with the proviso that no person may serve as President for more than eight consecutive years. The amendment was tailored to fit the personal cases of two men, Manuel Quezon and Sergio Osmeña. It permitted of President Quezon's reelection, contemplated that he would step aside at the end of two years of the second term in favor of Vice President Osmeña, and had in view President Quezon becoming a candidate for President of the Philippine Republic. Only the hand of death intervened to disrupt the fine political scheme.

It is submitted that every logical consideration speaks for the constitutional provision regarding the term of office of the President in its original form. Little of convincing weight can be said in favor of the politically inspired amendment.

[9] Presidential tenure determined in the Constitution of the Philippines, as amended, by Article VII, secs. 2, 3, 4, 5.

The six year tenure of office insured permanence of policy and vigor of action. The President was given sufficient time to carry through a well defined program of administration. On the other hand, the prohibition against reelection on the expiration of the six year term minimized the dangers of dictatorship and freed the President from the baneful influence of partisan convenience. The temptation to devote his energies to a campaign for reelection and to mold his policies to curry popular favor and support was removed.

President Quezon was the recipient of the benefits accruing from adoption of the amendments to the Constitution. Yet, no one better than he sensed the dangers that lurked in acceding to constitutional changes induced by considerations of a personal character. In addressing the Constitutional Convention at the conclusion of its labors, he said:

> There is, however, one great danger in having a strong executive department, and that is the danger of dictatorship. And here again this Convention has shown its vision and wisdom when it provided that there shall be no reelection for the position of chief executive. This clause in the constitution guarantees for the Filipino people the impossibility, or at least the improbability, of ever having here a chief executive that will try to perpetuate himself in power. We are familiar with the history of the Central and South American Republics. We know that to a large extent the revolutions which continually rocked such republics has been due to the fact that their chief executives were permitted to present themselves as candidates for reelection.[10]

President Quezon finally convinced himself, as so often have other public men, that he could not run away from duty. He was reelected to the Presidency in the face of the reasons which he had so well stated for not being a candidate. As for President Roxas, it is no secret that from the first day of his term he gave attention to building his fences for reelection.

The Republic could appropriately give thought to a return to the single six year term of office for the President. Face would not be lost in so doing. The best interests of the country would be served.

DEFENSES AGAINST DICTATORSHIP

What the authors of the Philippine Constitution strove to establish was an executive power which will actually govern, with a firm and

---

[10] Address of President Quezon to the Constitutional Convention February 5, 1935. To the same effect, Address of President Quezon to the National Assembly, August 16, 1939.

steady hand, unembarrassed by vexatious interference by other departments.[11] What the critics of the Constitution feared was a self-perpetuating presidential autocracy. Was a happy balance struck of a strong executive with defenses set up against the possibility of dictatorship?

The theory underlying the original Constitution was well defined. True, there was to be an extraordinarily strong presidency to last for six years, but any tendency of an executive to center on building up a political machine to perpetuate himself in office instead of serving the best interests of the people was blocked by prohibiting reelection. With the amendments to the Constitution approved, that safeguard was eliminated. What have we left?

The exercise of executive power, vast as it is, is not limitless. It is the sworn duty of the President to preserve and defend the Constitution, execute the laws, do justice to every man, and consecrate himself to the service of the Nation. It is to be presumed that no man would so stultify himself as to take an oath only to violate it. If the President should so bemean himself, he might make himself liable to impeachment by the legislative branch. And the Congress and the Supreme Court in their respective spheres are expected to be brakes on presidential excesses.

In its last analysis, the safety of democratic processes will depend on two contingencies. The first will be the extent to which a vigilant electorate acts as a check on any executive whose ego becomes intoxicated with the panoply of power; an effective opposition party can become the vehicle for the expression of grievances. The second safeguard can be realized by a return to a single six year presidential system. Both defenses against the inroads of dictatorship demand that the forces of public opinion man the ramparts of democracy.

THE CABINET

The administration in the Republic of the Philippines is carried on, under the "control" of the President, by executive departments. At the moment there are twelve of these departments, namely: the Department of Foreign Affairs, the Department of the Interior, the Department of Finance, the Department of Justice, the Department of Agriculture and Natural Resources, the Department of Public Works and Communications, the Department of Education, the Department of Labor, the Department of National Defense, the Department of Health, the Department of Commerce and Industry, and the

---

[11] Closing address of Claro M. Recto, President of the Constitutional Convention on February 8, 1935.

Department of Economic Coordination. To these should be added the Executive Secretary, who daily becomes the mouthpiece of the President in a variety of important matters. The Secretaries of the above listed Departments, with the Budget Commissioner and the Commissioner of Social Welfare, together constitute the Cabinet that acts in an advisory capacity to the President.

Executive departments were organized coincident with the implantation of civil authority after the Spanish-American War. Over a span of years four departments were thought sufficient. Gradually the pressure of expansion and division of authority became too great to be resisted, and twelve or more central offices are now deemed necessary where a lesser number once functioned. Likewise, while a Cabinet official was formerly able to supervise the offices under him, later this was changed, and each department was given an undersecretary to help his chief, and some departments even claimed to need two or three under-secretaries as assistants.

The nature of the Cabinet was also gradually transformed. The Jones Law required that all executive functions of the government must be under the direct control of the Governor General. Nevertheless, the Cabinet came to be responsible in part to the Philippine Legislature. The members of the Cabinet were appointed by the Governor General only after consultation with the Filipino leaders, who restricted their recommendations to persons affiliated with the dominant party. Included among the members of the Cabinet were legislators.

The development of such practices made it difficult to classify the government. In theory it was patterned after the American Government and so was of the Presidential type. In practice the government approached nearer to the parliamentary system of government. First Osmeña, and later Quezon, was the titular head of the party in power and the responsible leader of the Filipino participation in the government. This brought realization to the Governor General of the necessity of maintaining harmonious relations with the Filipino leaders to insure a successful administration. Osmeña and Quezon although not in the Cabinet were of the Cabinet, in fact if not in name were Premiers.

The administrative structure of the government under the Republic remains just about the same as under the American-controlled Philippine Government. Except that the executive branch has expanded in size, little difficulty is experienced in identifying the various offices. In only two respects have functional changes taken place. The heads of departments upon their own initiative, or upon the request of either House, may be heard by such House on any matter pertaining to their departments. However, the government is brought back to the presidential type by the constitutional prohibition against any Senator or Member of the House holding any other office or employment in the government without forfeiting his seat.

The Secretary of a department supervises the activities of his department under the general direction of the President. However, since his time is taken up with attendance at cabinet and other meetings, seemingly never ending conferences, and the fulfillment of social obligations, administrative details must be passed on to someone else to be looked after. The "someone" whose training permits him to handle administrative matters of all kinds is a permanent official found in each department called the under-secretary.

The under-secretaries, whose talents are usually hidden in anonymity, constitute the professional administrators of a bureaucracy that might otherwise lose itself amidst the details of buck-passing endorsements that hamper the output of the government. As was proved when the Secretaries of Departments in a body presented their resignations to Governor General Wood and had them accepted, the government machinery not only did not stop, but continued to function efficiently with the under-secretaries at the throttle.

Big men have filled Cabinet posts in the Philippine Government. Among them were capable Americans like W. Morgan Shuster, Charles E. Yeater, Eugene A. Gilmore, and Joseph Ralston Hayden in Public Instruction (Education). Among them were also capable Filipinos like Gregorio Araneta, the first Filipino to become secretary of an executive department, that of Finance and Justice; Rafael Palma, the first official to occupy concurrently legislative and executive positions, namely, member of the Philippine Senate and Secretary of the Interior; and Victorino Mapa and Jose Abad Santos, each of whom stepped aside as a member of the Supreme Court to become Secretary of Justice. These men set a high standard of excellence for the present heads of the executive departments in the Philippine Republic to meet.

Executive Bureaus and Offices [12]

Under the executive departments are grouped the various bureaus, divisions, boards, commissions, and offices. Each department includes a varying number of these entities. The organizational setup is never static but constantly is changed through creation or elimination,

---

[12] Executive bureaus and offices were reorganized after the war by Executive Order No. 94 of October 4, 1947. Reorganized again in 1950. The Official Directory in more extensive form is obtainable.

through transfer or combination. For this reason it would serve no purpose to present an organization outline of these governmental units under their respective departments.

The Civil Service [13]

Both the American administration of the Philippines and the successor Filipino regime evinced a sincere desire to establish an advanced type of civil service system.

President McKinley in his Instructions to the Second Philippine Commission assigned priority to the institution of an efficient system for the selection of government employees. The fifth act approved by the Philippine Commission on September 19, 1900 was the Civil Service Law entitled "An Act for the establishment and maintenance of an efficient and honest civil service in the Philippine Islands." The Philippine Civil Service thus created, while naturally pretty much a replica of an American model, nevertheless, since the Commission was free to do so, improved on the model.

Under the Commonwealth of the Philippines the merit and fitness system was not only continued but received express guarantee in its Constitution which also served as the Constitution of the Republic. [14] It did more. It broadened the scope of the classified service, pushing the frontiers of the merit system far into the smallest units of local government which had hitherto been beyond the pale of the Civil Service Law. The fundamental law recognizes only three exceptions to the competitive examination principle, namely, appointments to positions which are policy-determining, primarily confidential, or highly technical in nature. To strengthen the system, officers and employees in the Civil Service are prohibited from engaging in partisan political activities and from receiving additional or double compensation unless authorized by law. Under the Constitution they may not also be removed except for cause as provided by law.

As now existing, the Bureau of Civil Service is a first class bureau headed by a Commissioner of Civil Service. Decisions of the Commissioner on administrative investigations may be appealed to the Civil Service Board of Appeals. A heavy burden is thrown on the Bureau of Civil Service in the conduct of examinations, in establishing registers of eligibles for all branches and subdivisions of the service, in certifying appointments and promotions, and in deciding administra-

---

[13] J. R. Hayden, *The Philippines, A Study in National Development*, Chs. IV, V, contains a sympathetic account of the civil service. Jose Gil, Commissioner of Civil Service, aided with facts and suggestions.

[14] Constitution of the Philippines, as amended, Article XII.

tive cases. A peculiar function entrusted in this jurisdiction to the public personnel agency is the supervision of the conduct of the examinations given for the private practice of the various professions, except the bar examination. The Bureau of Civil Service now exercises the power of removal formerly vested in the heads of Departments.

A recent Executive Order[15] introduced an innovation that may properly be called a new deal for the small employee. So-called Councils of Personnel Administration were organized in all bureaus and offices of the Government. Each such Council was authorized "to examine the records of efficiency and fitness of all employees in its respective office with a view to making appropriate recommendations, in accordance with the Civil Service Law and Rules, concerning officials and employees who may be found inefficient, inept, incompetent, or otherwise unfit for further efficient service." Thus, in democratic fashion, the small employee's voice will be heard on matters relating to his welfare and advancement in the service.

Civil service employees work seven hours a day, except on Saturdays, throughout the year, and not including the hot season from April 1 to June 1 when five or six hour a day periods are kept. They are allowed vacation and sick leave. Accrued leave, originally provided to attract Americans to the service, was abolished by the Filipino administration as altogether too reminiscent of a colonial status. A Government Insurance System was established in the early days of the Commonwealth.

In 1934, before the establishment of the Commonwealth, an Act providing for the retirement of citizens of the United States in the Philippine Civil Service and appropriating funds therefor was passed. About the same time, the teachers, health service, and Constabulary pension systems, in imminent danger of going bankrupt, were abolished. Particularly for American teachers, whose average age was over sixty and with some of them wholly dependent on their pensions for livelihood, this would have been a catastrophe of the worst order. Energetic representations by the United States High Commissioner caused the restoration of the pensions.

In this matter of a life pension as a necessary complement of the merit system as well as a remedy for the problem of superannuation, the Filipino employees themselves face no bright prospect. Act 2589, otherwise known as the Osmeña Retirement Law, has been found to be sadly inadequate and to offer no sufficient inducement to employees who have spent the best years of their lives in the government service

---

[15] Executive Order No. 94, of October 1, 1947.

to retire on a modest gratuity during their old age. But it seems the government, while realizing the need for a good pension law, is not prepared financially to push through such a project. The obligation to provide civil service employees with a reasonable retirement gratuity, based on a workable system, stems from the same impulse that has influenced modern governments in recent years to enact legislation on social security. The establishment of an adequate retirement system will pay good dividends in the form of increased efficiency and greater loyalty on the part of civil service employees.

From the beginning of American occupation, the policy was to favor Filipinos for government positions. The result was a steady *Filipinization* of the service. In 1935, when the Commonwealth of the Philippines was inaugurated, there was a total of 21,000 regular employees in the civil service, all Filipinos except for 300 Americans, mostly teachers. As of 1950, approximately 70,000 Filipinos were employed in the National Service and in the City of Manila alone, without including the number of employees in the provincial and municipal governments which in round figures is approximately 100,000. The few Americans associated with the Republic of the Philippines are mostly advisers. On the other hand, the Government of the United States has staffed its agencies in the Philippines with literally hundreds of employees.

It is axiomatic that just as the taste of the pudding is in the eating, so is the success of the Civil Service Law measured not by ideas and principles, no matter how progressive in intent they may be, but by how the law works. Practically from the day of the enactment of the first Civil Service Law down to the immediate present, charges of favoritism, nepotism and politicalism have been aired. The administration of the Civil Service Law under the Philippine Republic has not escaped attack. It has repeatedly been charged that there has been a serious deterioration in the observance of the merit system.

This is hardly the forum in which to canonize or castigate officials who shoulder responsibility for the enforcement of the Civil Service Law. Dr. William S. Washburn, the first Director of Civil Service, and following Directors were high type men who were completely sold on the desirability of a strict observance of Civil Service regulations. Jose Gil, Director and Commissioner of Civil Service since 1923, their worthy successor, is an experienced administrator of spotless integrity. He would not wittingly weaken the system he is expected to enforce and defend.

A few deductions relative to the merits of the Philippine Civil Service System may properly be made. In the first place, the promotional process appears to have been generally observed. It is gratifying to note that the great majority of the chiefs of bureaus and at least four or five heads of Departments are career men who have earned gradual promotion from the lower ranks in the classified service. Department and Bureau Chiefs seem not to have given preference to persons from their own region, but have only been interested in recognition of fitness for office based on merit. On the other hand, the evil genie of family and political ties has reared its ugly head to claim and to receive special and unmerited recognition for favorites. The demands of patronage by the spoilsmen will ever infiltrate to undermine the best and noblest plan.

Speaking from the vantage point of a former civil service examinee and confirming experience with observation, the author expresses admiration for the many fine men and women, both Americans and Filipinos, who made up the Philippine Civil Service. As a lot they labored faithfully, and more often than not on pitifully small salaries some as low as three hundred sixty pesos ($180.00) per annum.[16] The author also expresses the opinion that the defects of the Civil Service System, while admittedly present, do not anywhere near balance the merits of a system that played a vital part in advancing good government in the Philippines. It should be the set aim to maintain a civil service based on merit and completely disassociated from partisan politics.

MALACAÑAN PALACE [17]

The official residence of the President of the Philippines is Malacañan Palace in Manila. The occupancy of historic Malacañan by the President means more to the Filipinos than just a graceful gesture; it typifies emancipation from alien rule. Where once dwelt Spanish and American Viceroys now lives a Filipino chosen by Filipinos to administer their government.

Malacañan Palace was originally a country house for the Spanish Governors General, but when the earthquake of 1863 destroyed the official palace in the Walled City in Manila, the representatives of the Spanish Crown took up their abode in Malacañan. As a matter of course, thereafter it became the residence of American Governors General.

Malacañan Palace is situated in the San Miguel District, in fact its next-door neighbor is the San Miguel Brewery. The structure looms

---

[16] The Congress of the Philippines has approved a law fixing the minimum salary for teachers and national employees.

[17] See a description by an occupant for seven years, Francis Burton Harrison, *The Cornerstone of Philippine Independence*, pp. 61-63.

behind a well kept lawn and big trees. Malacañan's balcony projects over the swiftly flowing Pasig River, the same river on which Governor and Mrs. Taft celebrated a Venetian Carnival, with the corpulent Taft resplendent in the flowing robes of a Doge of Venice. The gardens around the Palace and across the river in Malacañan Park become a fairyland when illuminated for an evening's entertainment. The typically Filipino *Bahay Kubo* is available for informal gatherings.

Malacañan has been thoroughly modernized since American occupation. Each occupant was led to add his personal touch in changes, but fortunately under expert direction. Governor General Harrison, a Democrat, thoughtfully superintended the erection of an Executive Building next door to the Palace for the use of Republican successors. Governor General Davis, after having to seek repose in his office so that official visitors could be accommodated, saw to it that Malacañan was enlarged. Commonwealth President Quezon, in keeping with his taste for finer things, had the structure entirely remodeled and refurbished. After the conclusion of World War II, although Malacañan had been spared the fate that destroyed so many other buildings, repairs had to be made. President Quirino sought to brighten the drab aspect with colorful rugs and furnishings.

Fortunately none of these many alterations of Malacañan have departed substantially from the original lines. It still is reminiscent of Spanish architecture, although possibly not at its best. As now existing, the Palace serves as a delightful home for the President, has sufficient guest rooms, and has a huge floor space admirably fitted for large receptions.

As you pass up the grand stairway you sense the magnificence that was Spain's, the power that was America's, and the right that is the Philippines. At the head of the stairway, to the left as you enter, is to be seen the famous painting by Juan Luna depicting Legaspi's blood compact with Sikatuna, Chieftain of Bohol. To the right is the immense reception room with glistening chandeliers, where stands the President to extend cordial welcome to his guests. Later, after cocktails have been imbibed, dinner will be served in the paneled and artistic banquet hall.

Here in Malacañan the President receives with impressive dignity the social-loving people of the Islands. Malacañan assumes gala beauty with these functions. An official ball is a sight never to be forgotten. Myriads of electric lights. The military bands playing popular airs. A never-ending stream of the favored four hundred grown into two thousand or more. Smartly dressed women. Army, Navy and Air officers proudly displaying their decorations. And then after a smiling but weary Chief Executive has left the receiving line, the stately *rigodon de honor*, a legacy from Spanish pomp, opens the ball.

Malacañan Palace is a distinguished piece of architecture. But it symbolizes even more than the fine arts. It is tragedy, comedy, drama —all rolled into a stage setting of history in the making.

CHAPTER XII

THE CONGRESS OF THE PHILIPPINES

LEGISLATIVE BODIES OF THE FORMER GOVERNMENT OF
THE PHILIPPINE ISLANDS[1]

The immediate predecessors of the Congress of the Republic of
the Philippines were the Philippine Commission, the Philippine Assembly, and the Philippine Legislature of the Government of the
Philippine Islands, and the National Assembly of the Commonwealth
of the Philippines. They formed a splendid background of legislative
experience for the law-making body of the Republic.

The Philippine Commission came on the scene of its future activities with no guide of any sort, except the McKinley-Root Instructions, which were of a general character, and with but one
Commissioner acquainted with local conditions. That under such
handicaps the Philippine Commission was able to perform so well the
legislative part of its program, in conjunction with the executive duties
of its members, was a credit to American adaptability, initiative and
industry.

The Philippine Commission was organized as an appointive body
with exclusive legislative authority over the entire Archipelago. It
thus remained until the establishment of the Philippine Assembly,
with which it divided authority in the so-called Christian region. In
the early days, not only was the Philippine Commission a unicameral
body, but it was a commission in fact as well as in name. With the
exception of three Filipino Commissioners without portfolios, the
remaining Commissioners were the American heads of executive departments. The Commission disappeared entirely with the creation
of the Philippine Senate in 1916.

A legislative body of the nature of the Philippine Commission
could be expected to pass bills rapidly. The small membership, the
lack of an applauding audience, and the immense amount of work
which the Commissioners were called upon to perform were not
conducive to oratory. Not that all the laws enacted by the Commission were the product of this swift process. Many laws, and these

[1] See D. R. Williams, *The Odyssey of the Philippine Commission* (Chicago, 1913).

Hon. Sergio Osmeña
First Speaker of the Philippine Assembly and Second President
of the Commonwealth of the Philippines.

the main pieces of legislation, were the result of months of study and deliberation.

The Philippine Commission with amazing dispatch, energy and thoroughness laid the basis of Philippine statutory law.

The trouble with the Philippine Commission was that the people had no direct voice in the making of their laws. To remedy this situation, Civil Governor Taft insisted that provision be made in the Philippine Bill of 1902 for the setting up of a representative legislative chamber. In the face of opposition from the standpatters and of forebodings from those pessimistically inclined, this unparalleled act in the history of colonization was sanctioned. Mr. Taft, now become Secretary of War, made a special trip to the Philippines to inaugurate the Philippine Assembly on October 16, 1907.

The Philippine Assembly organized with Sergio Osmeña as Speaker and Manuel Quezon as Floor Leader. Neither of them yet thirty, both had the gift of leadership which was to make themselves and the Assembly successes. Additional prestige was gained when Secretary of War Taft announced that the Speaker of the Philippine Assembly was to be considered the second personage in rank in the Philippines. Gradually the Speaker drew power closer to himself and consolidated his position as the leader of the Filipino element in the government.

Bring to mind here that when the Philippine Assembly began to function it was the first representative body of its kind in the Islands' history. No traditions were behind it. No precedents could be cited to steer its course. A few members had belonged to the Malolos Congress, but the great majority of them were entirely without legislative experience. How readily under such conditions a gathering could have degenerated into a leaderless mob. How disappointing could have been the record of an untried body of men. How pleased chronic croakers would have been at the failure of the Philippine Assembly. In spite of all drawbacks, the Philippine Assembly fulfilled its purposes.

The Philippine Assembly in association with the Philippine Commission carried on the work of legislation. But now bills could not go through the legislative mill so rapidly as when there was no check on the Philippine Commission. Disputes between the two bodies were inevitable. Some differences could be compromised, but others could not. In the case of appropriations came a stalemate, and the Governor General assumed the right to allocate the budget items. But more important than anything, valuable lessons in law-making were learned by the accredited representatives of the Filipino people.

It was not difficult for the Philippine Senate to supplant the Philippine Commission. The Filipinos already had been given in 1913 a majority on the Philippine Commission, and so the change simply amounted to the substitution of an elective process for an appointive process. Manuel Quezon was elected President of the Philippine Senate, and with him went the prestige of having secured increased autonomy and the Congressional promise of ultimate independence for his people. Later he was to be joined in the Senate by Sergio Osmeña, former Speaker of the House, and the Speakership was to go to the brilliant young Governor of Capiz, just elected to the House, Manuel Roxas.

Before the establishment of the Commonwealth of the Philippines, legislative power in the Philippines was vested in the Philippine Legislature composed of a small Senate of twenty-four members and a large House of Representatives of nearly a hundred members. With the exception of men to represent the non-Christian Provinces, who were appointed by the Governor General, they were elected by districts. In organization and procedure, the Legislature followed the general scheme of American law-making bodies.

The Philippine Commission, the Philippine Assembly, and the Philippine Legislature all made excellent legislative records.

THE UNICAMERAL NATIONAL ASSEMBLY OF THE FORMER COMMONWEALTH[2]

The Philippines and the State of Nebraska ran a close race for the distinction of being the first jurisdiction under the American flag, in modern times, to initiate the experiment of a one-house legislature. Nebraska took action first, but the Philippines got her unicameral National Assembly into operation first. In both instances the arguments that carried most weight were that the system would simplify the legislative process, effect economy, and determine responsibility.[3]

While these points in support of unicameralism were made, and while pride in keeping one step ahead of progressive nations was understandable, the plain truth is that establishment of the Unicameral National Assembly came about by accident. The delegates to the Constitutional Convention could not agree regarding the composition of the upper House of the proposed legislature. As in the

[2] See J. R. Hayden, *The Philippines, A Study in National Development*, Ch. IX.

[3] Valedictory Address of Claro M. Recto, President of the Constitutional Convention. Also radio speech in Washington, D. C., on March 26, 1935.

convention that drafted the Constitution of the United States, the advocates of the smaller entities were jealous of their bigger neighbors. But unlike the situation in the American Constitutional Convention, no plan that placated the defenders of provincial rights could gain a majority vote. Hence legislative power was vested in a National Assembly composed of ninety-eight members elected triennially from single-member districts (except that other methods were provided for three provinces).

Hardly was the ink dry on the Constitution, than agitation was started to abandon theoretical unicameralism in favor of classic bicameralism. The change was not difficult to effectuate. Probably on a clear cut unicameral issue, a majority of the delegates to the Constitutional Convention would have voted for a two chamber legislative body. Then, too, Commonwealth President Quezon had not been sold on the unicameral idea and his slightest word never went unheeded. More important still, members of the National Assembly were constantly being made to feel that they were mere "rubber stamps" of executive demands; they saw a better chance to assert their independence in a larger, slower moving two-house Legislature. Hence scarcely five years after the Philippines had embarked on the experiment of unicameralism, it was cast overboard.

It cannot be said that the National Assembly, operating without the restraint imposed by a coordinate legislative chamber, had in any sense been a failure. In fact this charge was hardly ever hurled against it. The Assembly had busied itself with the enactment of important legislation. That it had acted in response to executive pressure could not be denied. Nevertheless it was the same Filipino leadership as before, with the only difference that now leadership came not from a fellow legislator but from the executive mansion.

The pendulum had swung back to normalcy in government. In effect, by amending the Constitution to provide for a bicameral legislature, the country had sanctioned a conservative policy, for a small Senate of elder statesmen could be expected to act to restrain a larger and more radically inclined House.

THE BICAMERAL CONGRESS OF THE REPUBLIC [4]

Just prior to the Japanese invasion in 1941, the National Assembly was replaced by the Congress of the Philippines consisting of the Senate and the House of Representatives. That is the system existing in the Philippine Republic.

[4] Article VI of the Constitution of the Philippines, as amended, concerns the Legislative Department and the Congress of the Philippines.

The Senate is composed of twenty-four Senators elected at large for terms of six years. The Constitution imposes a limit of one hundred and twenty Members on the House, with an apportionment authorized within three years after the return of every enumeration. The House has had ninety-eight Members distributed among the several provinces according to population, with each province having at least one Member.

Following the tabulation of the 1948 Census, an earnest effort was made to effectuate constitutional authority. But as nearly always happens in such cases, population rivalries kept a reapportionment bill from gaining legislative approval. Only Manila was able to secure an increase in the number of representative districts from two to four—and this by special legislation in possible contravention of the Constitution. However, it can be expected that eventually the number of Congressmen will be raised near to the one hundred and twenty maximum.

Comparing the present system with what had gone before and with American practice, it will be observed that six year terms for Senators are retained. New ground was plowed in fixing on the longer period of four years in place of the briefer period of two years for Members of the House. American Congressmen and State Legislators elected to hold office, only immediately thereafter finding themselves compelled to begin a campaign for reelection, would undoubtedly applaud this innovation. More debatable is the "block" method of selecting Senators, permitting of boss rule and the influence of money.

To become a Senator a person must be a natural born citizen of the Philippines, at least thirty-five years of age, a qualified voter, and a resident of the Philippines for not less than two years immediately prior to his election. A Member of the House must also be a natural born citizen of the Philippines, and in addition at least twenty-five years of age, a qualified voter, and a resident of the province for which chosen for not less than one year immediately prior to his election. Laying these provisions side by side with the provisions of the original Constitution relating to the National Assembly which they superseded, it will be noticed that no longer will a naturalized citizen be eligible to election in either House of Congress. The age requirement, formerly thirty for Members of the National Assembly, was raised to thirty-five for Senators and lowered to twenty-five for Members of the House. The residence qualification for Senators was increased from one year to two years and was left as it was for Members of the House.

The Congress convenes annually in regular session on the fourth Monday of January. Special sessions may be called by the President. Regular sessions are limited to one hundred days and special sessions to thirty days, exclusive of Sundays.

After the war the Congress was compelled to meet in makeshift quarters, the Senate in a wing of the City Hall and the House in a revamped school building. It was found, however, that the central portion of the former magnificent Legislative Building could be rebuilt without entailing too heavy an expense. So there the Congress will function until some date in the indefinite future when the Capitol project in Quezon City takes form.

The principal officer in the Senate is the President, and in the House is the Speaker. Each House also chooses a Secretary and a Sergeant-at-Arms, determines its rules, and keeps a Journal of its proceedings. The committee system is utilized for the conduct of hearings and the formulation of legislation.

Last, but certainly not least, viewed from the standpoint of financially hard-pressed legislators, Senators and Representatives each receives an annual compensation of ₱7,200 ($3,600). This is an increase from the ₱5,000 ($2,500) paid them before the Constitution was amended. The President of the Senate and the Speaker of the House each is allotted ₱16,000 ($8,000) per annum. The perquisites allowed the legislators are not exorbitant when measured against their living and campaign expenses and political obligations.

The organizational features of the Congress of the Philippines are seen to reflect, in the main, American practice.

The second Philippine Congress that began to function in 1950 contributed to the restoration of faith in the administration. Independence of judgment on the part of solons affiliated with the majority party, in contrast to former subservience to executive pressure, was displayed. At the same time the minority fiscalized legislation without descending to puerile opposition. A strong tendency toward economy appealed favorably to the public. Shocking irregularities involving high government officials and private citizens were fearlessly investigated. All in all the public interest was protected.

LEGISLATIVE POWER

Legislative power is vested in the Congress in general terms subject to specific prohibitions. That was the rule under the Government of the Philippine Islands. That is the rule under the Republic of the Philippines. It means that the Congress is empowered to legislate on every matter concerning the Philippines, subject only to such limitations as are expressly or impliedly provided for in the Constitution. The Congress has a wider range in the legislative field than the Congress of the United States or any State Legislature.[5]

Certain powers are explicitly granted the Congress. For instance, in the Congress (with the concurrence of two-thirds of all the Members of each House) is lodged the sole power to declare war. Within certain limitations the legislative body may prescribe the jurisdiction of the various courts. The Constitution enjoins the Congress to take steps towards the development and adoption of a common national language based on one of the existing native languages; to promote scientific research and invention; to provide for a complete and adequate system of education including free primary instruction and citizen training for adult citizens; to afford protection for labor, and to regulate the relations between landowner and tenant and between labor and capital in industry and agriculture.

The field of legislative power is delimited by various restrictive provisions found in the Constitution. These include the familiar limitations on legislation of the Bill of Rights. Also there are regulations regarding the raising and appropriation of money, the utilization of natural resources, and the granting of franchises.

The traditional provision that money bills shall originate in the lower House has been greatly expanded by the 1940 Amendment to the Constitution. It is specifically provided that all appropriation, revenue or tariff bills, bills authorizing an increase of the public debt, bills of local application, and private bills shall originate exclusively in the House of Representatives. The Senate may, however, propose or concur with amendments.

Bills passed by the Congress are presented to the President for approval. The President has the right to veto a bill or any separate item in an appropriation, revenue or tariff bill. Thereafter the Congress has the right by a two-thirds vote of all the Members of each House to reconsider and pass the bill or item over the President's veto. In the latter case the bill becomes a law notwithstanding the disapproval of the President.

It is impracticable to enumerate the measures approved by the Congress of the Philippines. Suffice it to say that the laws placed on the statute books include Acts of transcendental importance to the future of the country.

---

[5] Ocampo v. Cabangis (1910) 15 Phil. 620, 631; *In re* Arnault (1950).

CONGRESSIONAL COMMISSIONS

Having sanctioned the principle of unicameralism, the Philippine Constitutional Convention was confronted with a number of embarrassing questions. It solved them in an ingenious manner. Associated with the National Assembly were to be three commissions, the Electoral Commission, the Commission on Appointments, and the Commission on Impeachment. With a reversion to bicameralism, the Electoral Commission, changed in name to Electoral Tribunal, and the Commission on Appointments were continued in a modified form. The Commission on Impeachment was discarded as unnecessary.

The Electoral Commission was established because of dissatisfaction with the manner in which election contests had been handled by the former Philippine Legislature. The Philippine Electoral Commission found its counterpart in the constitutions of European countries and in the special commission that was provided to settle the Tilden-Hayes contested election for President of the United States. The mixed commission which was provided for was a compromise between the English system of assigning election contests to the courts and the prevailing American system of making the houses of the legislative branch the sole judges of the election of their members.

Both the Senate and the House of Representatives now have an Electoral Tribunal. Three Justices of the Supreme Court, together with six members equally divided between the majority party and the minority party of each legislative chamber, compose the two tribunals. The Electoral Tribunals are made the sole judges of contests involving the seats of the members of the respective houses.[6]

The Justices of the Supreme Court having been given the balance of power and the minority having been granted equal rights with the majority, non-partisan adjudication of election contests is pretty well assured. The complaints that have been aired against the mixed judicial-legislative body have centered on the fear that the Supreme Court might be drawn into politics and that the Court might be over-burdened with work. The Court has held that the Electoral Tribunals are constitutional entities independent of and distinct from the legislature.[7]

---

[6] Electoral Tribunals are authorized by the Constitution of the Philippines, as amended, Article VI, secs. 11, 13.

[7] Suanes v. Chief Accountant of the Senate, October 26, 1948.

The Commission on Appointments in effect took the place of the Philippine Senate during the time the National Assembly constituted the sole organ to enact legislation. With bicameralism resumed and the Senate restored, nevertheless the Commission on Appointments was not thrown overboard. Instead it was transformed into a Commission on Appointments of the Congress with power to approve or disapprove nominations made by the President of the Philippines.[8] This Commission consists of twelve Senators and twelve Representatives, elected by each House, respectively, upon the basis of the proportional representation of the political parties therein. A drastic prohibition of the Constitution that no member of the Commission on Appointments shall appear as counsel before any court inferior to the Supreme Court and the Court of Appeals has caused some of the ablest lawyers of the Congress to decline to serve on the Commission. The President of the Senate acts as Chairman *ex officio* of the Commission, but without vote, except in case of a tie.

While the provisions in the Philippine Constitution for Electoral Tribunals with Justices of the Supreme Court sitting alongside the members of the legislature to judge contests involving elections to the Congress may look strange, it is believed that a stabilizing influence in politics has resulted. A Commission on Appointments representing both legislative houses with the power to act on nominations to office by the Chief Executive may also look strange to the constitutional lawyer. But is there any good reason why the members of the upper house should not share with their brethren of the lower house the power to scrutinize appointments? The Philippines has taken two forward steps in constitutional government.

IMPEACHMENT [9]

The abolition of the Commission on Impeachment by the 1940 amendments to the Constitution did not carry with it nullification of the impeachment process. Only the procedure for the trial of cases of this nature was changed. Philippine practice in this respect reflects the influence of American precedents.

The House of Representatives, by a vote of two-thirds of all its Members, has the sole power to impeach. Impeachments are then tried by the Senate. When the President is on trial, the Chief Justice of the Supreme Court presides. The officers made liable to removal from

---

[8] Commission on Appointments authorized by the Constitution of the Philippines, as amended, Article VI, secs. 12, 13.

[9] The subject of impeachment is governed by the Constitution of the Philippines, as amended, Article IX. Note *In re* Sotto, January 21, 1949.

office on impeachment are the President, the Vice President, the Justices of the Supreme Court and the Court of Appeals, the Members of the Commission on Elections, and the Auditor General. The grounds for action are conviction of culpable violation of the Constitution, treason, bribery, or other high crimes. The concurrence of three-fourths of all the Members of the Senate is necessary for conviction.

Twice in 1948-49 impeachment proceedings were seriously threatened. Justice Gregorio Perfecto of the Supreme Court and President Elpidio Quirino were made the objects of actions to remove them from office. In each instance the proposed impeachment was carelessly begun. In each instance proof of culpable violation of the Constitution was lacking. The net loser was the Filipino people whose government was sullied before mankind.

The Supreme Court of the Philippines had found a reporter in contempt of court for failure to reveal the source of information of a newspaper story telling of a leak in the bar examination. Senator Vicente Sotto, the author of the statute interpreted by the Court, rushed to the defense of the reporter with an attack on the Court. He was likewise held in contempt of court. Mr. Justice Perfecto felt called upon to add a concurring opinion, which tended not to restore the dignity of the court. In lurid phrases Mr. Justice Perfecto wrote of Senator Sotto that the latter was "an individual who has lowered himself to unfathomable depths of moral depravity—a despicable habitual liar, unscrupulous vilifier and slanderer, unrepentant blackguard and blackmailer, shameful and shameless libeler, unmindful of the principles of decency as all hardened criminals. He is a disgrace to the human species. He is a shame to the Senate. . . His contemptible conduct . . . seemed compatible only with the complete irresponsibility of schizophrenics, idiots, or those suffering from doddery. . . Respondent belongs to that gang of unprincipled politicians headed by a Senate President. . ."

Various charges against Mr. Justice Perfecto, including use of the above quoted language, were aired in the lower House. They were halfheartedly pressed. It was the general feeling that while the bitter epithets utilized were unbecoming of a member of the highest court in the land, they did not constitute a ground for impeachment. The death of the respondent closed the proceedings.

President Quirino's impeachment was sought on five counts. It was plainly a political maneuver by means of which the Avelino faction in the Liberal Party could wreck vengeance on the man who had put their leader on the hot spot. It was a move in which the opposition *Nacionalistas* could joyfully join in order to injure the presidential aspirations of their most formidable rival. The President offered suitable explanation of the charges laid at his door. The most that could be said against him was that he had tolerated extravagance when economy in official and semi-official expenditures should have been the rule. The House sustained the President by a large majority.

THE SPEAKER OF THE HOUSE

The Constitution provides that the House of Representatives shall elect its Speaker. Taking that simple statement as a text, there could be woven about it practically the entire history of the modern development of democratic institutions in the Philippines. It is also a human interest story of contrasting personalities of strength and weakness.

When you mention the word "Speaker" you automatically add "Osmeña." It was Speaker Osmeña who set the pattern for the office and who now furnishes the traditions. He was a Czar—a benevolent Czar to be sure, but still a Czar—of the Philippine Assembly. Osmeña occupied that pinnacle of power because he combined in himself the party presidency and the Filipino leadership in the government. Even after the leadership passed to the President of the Senate, the Speaker remained the dominant figure in the lower House. Speakers Manuel Roxas and Quintin Paredes carried on capably in this manner.

With the inauguration of the Philippine Commonwealth, leadership accompanied President Quezon to the executive office. There could not be two founts of power. Hence Paredes, a strong Speaker, went out and Gil Montilla, an amiable Speaker, came in. The Speaker was made "merely a presiding officer." Legislative initiative, such as it was, emanated from Floor Leader Jose E. Romero, who was made chairman of the Committee on Committees as well as the Committee on Rules.

A system of this nature could not long continue. The legislators became tired of being termed, and in reality being, rubber stamps of executive-inspired legislation. They had lost their self-esteem and with it their independence. Also, too heavy responsibility was cast on one man, President Quezon, who personified executive power and legislative power.

A remedy was found in the drafting of talented Secretary of Justice Jose Yulo for the political job of Speaker, and joining with him as Floor Leader the experienced former Speaker Quintin Paredes. It was a happy choice. By the adoption of new rules and the skillful use of the same, the team of Yulo and Paredes brought back the legislative body to the place it was expected to occupy in a democracy of checks and balances. The President remained the virile national leader to be sure, but he was relieved of the trivia of legislation. The Speaker assumed practically all of his traditional powers. The Floor Leader became a floor leader in every sense of the term. The legislative and executive powers once more operated separately and not as one.

With Manuel Roxas as President of the Republic, he assumed the mantle of responsibile leadership. He felt free to call members of the legislature for conferences to express his views and compose differences. The most important pieces of legislation were executive-backed. Yet Speaker Eugenio Perez, if not the militant personality that some of his predecessors were, nevertheless in a quiet and astute manner guided legislation through the House; eventually he became the political-wise President of the Liberal Party.

It is incontestably true that none of the Speakers after Osmeña could have been elected to the office without the nod of the party leader. Roxas, Paredes, Montilla, and Yulo were chosen because their names were agreeable to President Quezon; and Perez became Speaker because of the approval of President Roxas. In making a choice the two Presidents felt themselves in no way bound to respect seniority.

The Philippine Government may in theory be one of laws, but in practice the Government is pretty much one of men. And this is said in no disparaging tone. The Philippines needs leaders as much as she does principles.

THE PRESIDENT OF THE SENATE

Just as the Speakership of the House has back of it traditions set by the first Speaker, so does the Presidency of the Senate bear the imprint of Manuel Quezon, the first President of the Senate in the pre-Commonwealth Philippine Legislature. Not that the President of the Senate now wears the badge of authority of his illustrious predecessor; he does not. National leadership in the Republic properly abides with the President of the Philippines in Malacañan. Nevertheless the President of the Senate is much more than the presiding officer of the upper chamber of the Congress.

The legislative act making the President of the Senate next in succession after the Vice President to the Presidency of the Nation just about determines the rank of the Senate President in the government hierarchy. If you take into account the power that the President of the Senate can exercise over proposed legislation and nominations to office, the aura of authority emanating from the office cannot be lightly disregarded. Then if to titular rank and actual power there be added any extra-curricular influence of party leadership, the important position of the occupant of the office is better understood.

The President of the Senate from the inauguration of the Philippine Republic to early 1949 was Senator Jose Avelino. Coincidentally he was the directing head of the majority Liberal Party. He was recognized, even by the opposition, as a skillful and resourceful politician. His was the job of dispensing patronage to the faithful, which he did with smiling assurance, although he must have carried home with him many a headache after a day spent in meeting the never ending horde of office seekers.

The opposition *Nacionalistas* were well led by Senator Camilo Osias. Senator Osias climaxed a public career that included high educational posts and Resident Commissioner to the United States by battling the well entrenched majority in the 1947 election, to win popular favor by a large vote.

After the death of President Roxas, Liberal unity in the Senate gradually disintegrated. The Liberal majority eventually gravitated into two bands, one in support of President Avelino and the other antagonistic to him. The latter group, with the aid of the *Nacionalistas*, ousted Senator Avelino as President and substituted for him veteran Senator Mariano J. Cuenco.

This action coupled with the suspension of Senator Avelino shook the country from end to end. It was the prelude to a new alignment in parties and constituted the opening volley in the approaching presidential election.

Legislative Practices

The Congress of the Philippines and its predecessors in the legislative branch were modeled in name and procedure after the Congress of the United States. The form and customs of legislative bodies in European and Latin American countries were not copied. Nonetheless the Philippine legislative structure was in no sense a literal imitation of American precedents. As in practically everything else, legislative practices were adapted to Philippine needs and methods.

The rules of the United States Congress were substantially adopted by the first Philippine Assembly. Instead, however, of the Speaker exercising control over the affairs of the House through occupancy of the chairmanship of the Committee on Rules, as was the practice at the time in the American Congress, the conduct of business was delegated to a committee under the chairmanship of another member.

Instead of various committees which dealt with appropriations, the Assembly made provision for one appropriation committee. In course of time, the Philippine Legislature further modified American practice, but in the wrong way, by providing for an unconscionable number of committees with unwieldy membership. For instance the lower House in the 1946-49 Congress, with ninety-eight members, had fifty-two standing committees including an Appropriation Committee with thirty-seven members.

A favorite device to insure harmony in the Legislature was the frequent calling of caucuses of members of the majority party. Speaker Osmeña was particularly fond of this means of maintaining party discipline and of whipping recalcitrant members into line. Legislation thus emanated not from committees but from a party, and over this party stood its chief, who could virtually dictate or veto legislation. The redeeming features of rule by caucus were that it served to reunite divergent blocs in an over large majority and to provide a forum for the airing of grievances against the officers in power.

Mention has been made of the speed with which the Philippine Commission could make and unmake laws. An idea would come to the Governor General or the Secretary of a department. A stenographer is called. A bill is dictated. In the next to the last section of the bill is automatically inserted the provision that the public good requiring the speedy enactment of this bill, passage of the same is hereby expedited. The bill is introduced in the Commission, is passed, and is on the statute books. All possibly in the same day.

The Beekman Winthrop episode is a classic example of the ease with which a law was made to fit the case. Mr. Winthrop was the Executive Secretary of the Commission. It was desired to give him a position on the Philippine Bench. The organic law for the judiciary provided as qualifications for a Judge that he should: 1. be more than thirty years of age, and 2. have practised law at least five years before appointment. Unhappily for all concerned, young Mr. Winthrop was not thirty and had not practiced law for five years. Forthwith a special law was passed. The age requirement was reduced to twenty-five and the legal practice requirement was made alternative, with a clause providing that the appointee should have been a graduate for three years of a law school of recognized standing. Executive Secretary Winthrop became Judge Winthrop and decided a famous case.

The Philippine Legislature gravitated to the other extreme of putting off the work of today until *mañana*, until in fact *mañana* had become the last night of the last day when there could be no more *mañanas.* This practice, so easily susceptible to slipshod legislation, was railed against by the Chief Executives, for it threw a heavy burden on them when they had to winnow the wheat from the chaff, the wise bills from the unwise bills. The practice also resulted in the rail-roading of bills of which the average legislator knew nothing. It remained for President of the Senate Cuenco to declare adjourned the last session of the Senate of the First Congress of the Republic at twelve o'clock midnight—possibly a minute before—to the consterna-tion of Senators plotting to depose him. The surprise move left the House of Representatives with no other recourse but to follow suit, which it did in utter confusion. Left without legislative action were the appropriation act, the public works bill, the electoral code, and a long list of measures.

It is current rumor that because so many bills have been rushed through the legislative mill on the last day of the session, some of them were doctored subsequent to the *sine die* adjournment of the Legis-lature. The finger of guilt pointed most often to the public works bill and the "pork barrel" items in it. Oft denied by legislative leaders, veteran reporters vouch for the truthfulness of the charge that bills were rewritten after the Legislature had adjourned or, to touch on the point more lightly, that "mistakes" were found and "corrected." What is certain is that days intervened before a bill reached the Bureau of Printing and before even those most vitally concerned were able to secure copies of it.

Attempts to prevent the passage of bills wholesale during the much condemned "*sine die* session" of the Legislature have come from two directions. The Constitution requires the printing and distribution of copies of a bill at least three days prior to final passage by the Congress "except when the President shall have certified to the neces-sity of its immediate enactment."[10] Procedural changes in the Rules approved by the Legislature in 1939 provided that except by a two-thirds *aye* and *nay* vote, no bill shall be considered on second reading in any regular session that had not been reported by the proper com-mittee fifteen days in advance of adjournment.

Even calmly approved constitutional and procedural provisions can be hastily cast aside when last minute "railroading" of bills is de-manded. The second regular session of the Congress adjourned at half past eight Friday morning (May 21, 1948), the official clock having stopped at midnight. This amount of legislative overtime just about balanced the average record of State Legislatures; but the Legislature

---

[10] Constitution of the Philippines, as amended, Article VI, sec. 21 (2).

of Puerto Rico has been known to remain in session for a week after the organically provided adjournment hour.

"Pork barrel" continued to be the major concern of many solons. If the lawmaker looked forward to reelection—and who among them did not—generous public works outlays for his district would constitute the clinching assurance of victory. So the amount to which each Senator and Congressman was extra-legally entitled—₱200,000 in the 1948 Public Works Act—was eagerly sought. What was sarcastically referred to as "a mendicant attitude among Congressmen" was developed. The control over disbursement of "pork barrel" became a powerful weapon in the hands of the Chief Executive.

CHAPTER XIII

THE JUDICIARY

Philippine Justice

No jurisdiction exhibits more unique—and generally praiseworthy —legal features than the Philippines. To mention a few: 1. the appointment of judges to serve practically for life; 2. the absence of the jury system, placing on the trial judge the burden of deciding the facts as well as applying the law; 3. the sanction of two official court languages—English and Spanish—and the constant necessity to interpret from the vernacular to one of these languages; 4. a Supreme Court of eleven members, with wide constitutional powers; 5. the interpretation and enforcement of an amalgamated civil law-common law; and 6. the use of the Torrens and Cadastral systems of trying titles to land. With reference to these six topics, no person of standing has advocated seriously the election of judges in the Philippines, or the implantation of the jury system. The dual use of English and Spanish in the courts is an inconvenience and a necessary evil, made so because of the lack of determination to insist on English exclusively. The last three topics above enumerated will be discussed in succeeding sections of this chapter.

The judicial system of the Republic of the Philippines has been kept fairly simple and flexible. The Constitution vests the judicial power in the Supreme Court and in such inferior courts as may be established by law. The Supreme Court is granted specified jurisdiction of which it may not be deprived.[1] It thus stands at the apex of the independent Judicial Department, endowed with substantial power to enforce the Constitution and to protect the rights of the people. Wisely the kinds of inferior courts, their jurisdiction, and the qualifications of the judges have been left for determination by the Congress.

The independence of the Judicial Department, co-equal in power and influence with the other two departments and free from the unwelcome intrusion of either the President, the Congress, or any

[1] Constitution of the Philippines, Article VIII.

Hon. Cayetano Arellano
First Chief Justice in time and rank of the Supreme Court of the
Philippines, in the gown of a Doctor of Laws of Yale University.

outside source, has been sincerely desired by all right thinking citizens. This objective was partially attained through the appointment of judges for what amounted to life tenures of office, and through permitting of removal only by impeachment of Justices of the Supreme Court and of the Court of Appeals, and by an orderly procedure for other judges. Nevertheless the judiciary has had to be constantly on the alert to thwart encroachments by the other departments. Fortunately the Supreme Court has proved a zealous defender of judicial independence.

Twice under the Government of the Philippine Islands laws were enacted which placed judges below the Supreme Court at the mercy of the Governor General and which caused the removal of many judges. Presumably there were proven charges against these judges of which the public knew nothing, but if so the investigations were star-chamber conducted. The same unsatisfactory procedure was followed by President Quezon during the first year of the Commonwealth. Among others, Judge of First Instance Delfin Jaranilla was summarily dismissed from the service, possibly by way of reprisal for his action in joining counsel for Governor General Wood in the Wood-Quezon Board of Control Cases. Judge Jaranilla later served with distinction on the International Military Tribunal for the Far East, which tried the war criminals in Japan.

At one time it was the practice to assign a judge of first instance to try a particular case. The intimation that a certain kind of verdict was wanted was not lost on the judge. It remained for at least three Filipino jurists to furnish inspiring examples of judicial rectitude. Manuel Araullo, a judge of first instance at the time, disproved the belief that the courts of justice could be influenced, by boldly rendering a decision contrary to American-indicated wishes. Judges Andres Borromeo and Pedro Concepcion made their names famous in two celebrated cases. The author had the honor of writing the majority opinions in both instances.

Andres Borromeo had been duly appointed and commissioned judge of first instance of the twenty-fourth judicial district comprising the Provinces of Surigao and Misamis. For six years he acted as judge in those provinces, but through his unbending character offended the local politicians. Accordingly, he was appointed to another district, an appointment which he declined to accept. The Supreme Court, to the amazement of everyone, sustained the "fighting judge," as Judge Borromeo had come to be called, on the ground that a judge of first instance can be made a judge of another district only with his consent. In its broader aspects the decision rested on the fundamental conception of an independent and incorruptible judiciary.[2]

The ruling in the Borromeo case did not sit well with the Philippine Legislature. So a law was passed which provided for a lottery of judicial positions every five years. Again another fearless judge, Hon. Pedro Concepcion, was found to test the constitutionality of the law. The Supreme Court held the law invalid.[3]

The Constitution of the Philippines wrote *finis* to the practice of executive assignment of judges, by sensibly providing that no judge appointed for a particular district shall be designated or transferred to another district without the approval of the Supreme Court.[4]

The prompt administration of justice is another ideal which in the Philippines as elsewhere has been aimed at with varying degrees of success. Spanish procedure seemed skillfully adapted to attaining interminable delays. American-inspired laws tended to hasten legal processes. Nevertheless, cases still proceed through months and years of trials, postponements and appeals, to the dismay of the litigants.[5]

The Cu Unjieng case is believed to constitute some kind of a record for judicial prolixity. The accused, Mariano Cu Unjieng, was a rich Chinese merchant of Manila. He was charged with the crimes of swindling and falsification to the grave financial prejudice of a foreign bank. The trial lasted over two years. One hundred and forty-four witnesses were examined. One witness was the subject of cross examination for three months. The transcript of the evidence was composed of 23,000 typewritten pages. Nearly 50,000 exhibits were introduced. Apellant's "brief" on appeal contained 2,000 printed pages; the Government's "brief" was not much shorter. A member of the appellate court, Mr. Justice Diaz, spent the better part of a year studying the case. The opinions of the Supreme Court covered one hundred and sixty-nine printed pages. Finally after all of this Herculean effort, the accused was placed behind prison bars where he belonged.[6]

Possibly altogether too much prominence has been given to the unusual in Philippine legal history. As a matter of fact, the Philippine courts of the Republic of the Philippines are well planned and function in a normal manner. Philippine justice is probably in no

[2] Borromeo *v.* Mariano, 41 Phil. 322.

[3] Concepcion *v.* Paredes, 42 Phil. 599.

[4] Constitution of the Philippines, Article VIII, sec. 7.

[5] See Conde *v.* Rivera, 45 Phil. 650; People *v.* Manguiat, 51 Phil. 406; and Mercado *v.* Judge, 37 Off. Gaz. 904.

[6] People *v.* Cu Unjieng, 61 Phil. 236, 906.

better and no worse a condition than that in the United States and other countries.

THE SUPREME COURT OF THE PHILIPPINES

The Supreme Court is the keystone of the judicial arch of the Republic. For more than three centuries and a half, and under three banners, it has enjoyed that distinction. Possibly we should include a fourth flag, that of the rising sun during Japanese occupation, but those are days we would like to forget.

In 1598 the *Audiencia de Manila,* as reformed by Spain, began to function and continued to do so without interruption for exactly three hundred years. As an incident of the Spanish-American War, the court was reorganized under an English name after the American occupation of Manila. In 1936 the Supreme Court passed completely into Filipino hands. It now occupies an important place in the Republic of the Philippines.

The membership of the Supreme Court has varied from seven to eleven. On one occasion the Philippine Legislature enacted a law which provided for an unwieldy court of fifteen; the law never went into operation because the United States Senate wisely refused to confirm the Presidential nominations. Under the Republic the court consists of eleven members, a Chief Justice and ten Associate Justices. It functions only *in banc.*

At this point it may be remarked that the above indicated arrangement does not make for efficiency. The Court is overburdened with work. Eleven Justices meeting together invite lengthy deliberation. A reduction in membership from eleven to nine, with a lesser number of cases assigned for consideration, would better permit the Court to fulfill its responsibilities.

The Constitution provides that no person may be appointed a member of the Supreme Court unless he has been five years a citizen of the Philippines, is at least forty years of age, and has for ten years or more been a judge of a court of record or engaged in the practice of law in the Philippines. The retirement age is fixed at seventy years. These are qualifications intended to limit membership on the Court to middle aged judges or lawyers well seasoned by experience. The wisdom and conservatism of maturity had been desired more than the energy and progressiveness of youth. The author wryly observes that this constitutional provision would have barred his appointment to the Court, made when he was thirty-five years of age.

The Supreme Court of the Philippines has been granted jurisdiction equivalent to that of the highest court of a state which also includes an intermediate court of appeals in its judicial system. It has been, and is, a tribunal of great power and dignity. Most of its practices conform to those of other appellate courts. In certain respects the Constitution has introduced fundamental changes in customary procedure. In other respects the Court has harrowed new ground.

The Constitution requires that the conclusions in any case submitted to it shall be reached in consultation before the case is assigned to a Justice for the writing of an opinion; the purport of this provision is to make impossible one-judge decisions. The Constitution further makes it mandatory on any dissenting Justice to state the reasons for his dissent; if a member wishes to disagree with his colleagues let him take the time to explain his stand. Finally the Constitution provides that no treaty or law may be declared unconstitutional without the concurrence of two-thirds of all the members of the court. This last mentioned Philippine innovation has been advanced by clear thinkers as a worthwhile change in procedure for the Supreme Court of the United States, when the judiciary must in effect veto action taken by the other two departments, because repugnant to the Constitution.

The Supreme Court has ever been a hard working tribunal. Before the relief afforded by the Constitution in restricting its jurisdiction to important matters and before the institution of the Court of Appeals, the Court was required to decide 2,000 cases annually to keep its docket clear. (In 1934, the last complete year before the establishment of the Philippine Commonwealth, the Supreme Court disposed of 2,316 cases.) Nor were these all routine matters. Many cases resulted in the announcement of legal doctrines of paramount importance either by the Supreme Court of the Philippines or by the Supreme Court of the United States when the latter Court assumed jurisdiction. Particularly in the field of constitutional law and comparative law were leading cases to be found. The doctrine of "judicial supremacy," and its proper exercise in the determination of conflicting claims of authority in the executive and legislative branches, has engaged the Supreme Court of the Republic in notable cases.

The policy of the United States when it was in control of the Philippines was to maintain an American majority of one on the Court. During the administration of President Wilson an attempt was made to shift the balance to the Filipino side, but this plan was defeated when the United States Senate turned down the nominations. A few months before the inauguration of the Philippine Commonwealth, President Roosevelt, coincidentally with the approval of the

Philippine Constitution, named Hon. Claro M. Recto, the President of the Convention which drafted the Constitution, a member of the Court, thus giving the Filipinos a majority. Shortly after the inauguration of the Philippine Commonwealth the American Justices retired.

The policy of the United States during the same period of time was to have a Filipino Chief Justice. The jurists who filled the position commanded the respect of their colleagues and the confidence of the public.

The most revealing comment on an arrangement whereby the Americans had a majority on the Court but the Chief Justice was a Filipino is that the records of the Court can be searched in vain for a case decided on racial lines. It is dangerous to make sweeping deductions, but this writer's observation was that the Filipino Justices excelled in knowledge of Philippine law and invariably in conference conducted themselves with decorum, while the American Justices, occasionally brusque in manner, constituted the impelling force that got things done. The condition of the Court under the Republic would seem to indicate that the same relative situation still prevails. The Filipino magistrates hand down well written opinions—but the docket of the Court is far from clear.

The Supreme Court of the Philippines has had distinguished members. Some of the Filipino Justices will be mentioned in the following section. The standing of the Court was evidenced by the calibre of the Americans who left responsible positions to accept appointments to the Court. Justice E. Finley Johnson, a former law Professor of the University of Michigan, had the longest service, twenty-nine years. Justices Willard, Elliott, Johns and Ostrand, among others, transferred from judicial offices in the States and Santo Domingo to the Court. Justice Thomas A. Street had been a law Professor and learned text writer; Justice F. C. Fisher, the leader of the Philippine Bar; Justice John A. Hull, Judge Advocate General of the United States Army; and Justice George C. Butte, Vice Governor. Justice Sherman Moreland, former Speaker of the House in the New York Legislature, made the dissenting opinion the vehicle for the display of a brilliant mind. Others came to the Court by way of promotion.

The Supreme Court of the Republic of the Philippines has back of it a great history and notable traditions. Secretary of War Dern in his address on the inauguration of the Commonwealth of the Philippines paid tribute to the Court by characterizing it "as an everlasting credit to both the American and the Filipino peoples."

The Republic of the Philippines is blessed with a High Court which, in quality of membership and of output, will bear comparison with any appellate tribunal of any nation. Like its predecessors in pre-Republic days, the Supreme Court is presided over by a respected Chief Justice and counts with respected Associate Justices. Like its predecessors, it promulgates learned opinions of transcendental significance.

A Galaxy Of Filipino Jurists[7]

Many Filipinos have displayed unusual aptitude for the legal profession. In Spanish times it was one of the few careers open to ambitious young men. More recently the lure of politics and position has been the magnet that has drawn the scions of the leading families to the law. A combined biographical sketch of the lawyers of the Philippines would be equivalent to a constitutional history of the Islands.

Eight jurisconsults representative of the best in Philippine culture were Cayetano S. Arellano, first Chief Justice under the American administration; Florentino Torres, senior Associate Justice; Victorino Mapa, second Chief Justice; Manuel Araullo, third Chief Justice; Ignacio Villamor, Associate Justice; Ramon Avanceña, fourth Chief Justice; Jose Abad Santos, fifth Chief Justice; and Manuel Moran, Chief Justice in the Republic of the Philippines. The author served on the Court with all of them except Mr. Chief Justice Moran, whom he has known many years. Avanceña, Villamor, and Abad Santos had also been associates in the Attorney General's office and the last two again in the University of the Philippines. The author treasures deeply his close association with these fine *compañeros*.

When the Supreme Court was organized in the early days of American occupation, a splendid choice was made when Cayetano S. Arellano, Florentino Torres, and Victorino Mapa were named to the Court. All had acquired valuable legal experience under the Spanish regime. Arellano was already recognized as the Islands' most eminent jurist. Torres and Mapa, the first in Manila and the second in Iloilo, did not enjoy quite the same prestige as Arellano, but nevertheless were highly esteemed. The elevation of Araullo, Avanceña, Villamor, Abad Santos, and Moran to the Court was a logical sequence

---

[7] See memorial addresses delivered on the occasion of the deaths of Chief Justice Cayetano S. Arellano, Chief Justice Manuel Araullo, Chief Justice Victorino Mapa, Justice Florentino Torres, Justice Ignacio Villamor, and Chief Justice Jose Abad Santos, which evidence the universal esteem in which they were held, found in Vol. 41 Phil. (Arellano); 46 Phil. (Araullo); 49 Phil. (Mapa and Torres); 56 Phil. (Villamor); and in pamphlet form (Abad Santos).

to the records that they had made in other responsible positions. All eight, it may be observed, were devout Christians, all were men of spotless integrity, and all were lawyers of national renown.

Cayetano S. Arellano was the first Chief Justice in time and rank in the Philippines. He helped greatly in establishing the American administration in the Islands. Thereafter for nearly twenty years, during the formative period of Philippine jurisprudence, he presided over the Supreme Court. The Chief Justice was particularly strong in canon law and civil law. His decisions were so luminous and convincing that it is still customary for lawyers, in citing one of his opinions, to stress the point that it was written by Chief Justice Arellano. In addition, the Chief Justice was an erudite scholar, a cultured gentleman, and a charming conversationalist. Chief Justice Arellano's place is secure in Philippine jurisprudence and history.

Florentino Torres was of a different mold than his *confrère* Arellano. Torres was a fine figure of a man, robust and active. It did one good to see him walking with vigorous stride through the court corridors. In disposing of court work he was similarly industrious, and in conference was scornful of hypocrisy in all its forms. Yet always he was a gentleman. Then in the sunset of his life came disappointment when another was preferred for the Chief Justiceship made vacant by the resignation of Chief Justice Arellano. Again that same display of self-respect when Florentino Torres resigned in silent protest—independent to the last.

Victorino Mapa, the third of the original triumvirate of Filipino jurists, was in turn of a different character from the other two. He had not the vigorous health of Torres, and, handicapped by a weak body, was physically unable to turn out many decisions. His opinions in form and substance also contrasted sharply with those of Chief Justice Arellano. Where the opinions of Arellano reflected Spanish breadth, Mapa's were more American in trend and were conspicuous for their brevity and logic. It is generally considered that Mapa had the finest legal mind on the Court. Invariably his views also reflected intense patriotism. This characteristic Justice Mapa displayed when he withdrew from congenial duties on the Supreme Court to become Secretary of Justice. Reward came to him when he was returned to the Supreme Court as its Chief Justice.

Manuel Araullo was educated in Spain and as a result reflected the best Spanish traditions. He was Judge of First Instance and Chairman of the Code Committee before coming to the Supreme Court. There he labored diligently and efficiently. Keenly sensitive to attempts at influence, he repeatedly gave evidence of his scorn of such ill-advised moves. Keenly jealous of judicial prestige, he defended the courts valiantly against all intrusion. When the Mayor of Manila flouted the order of the Supreme Court, Araullo it was who stood for drastic action. When the Legislature passed the judiciary lottery law, Araullo it was who took an uncompromising stand in favor of holding the law invalid. Yet again he could be as tender as a child and was especially tolerant of the escapades of youth. Chief Justice Araullo was a just judge.

Ignacio Villamor's versatility was displayed in many fields. Successively he was a Judge of First Instance, the Attorney General, the first Filipino Executive Secretary, the first Filipino President of the University of the Philippines, the first Filipino head of the Census, and an Associate Justice of the Supreme Court. Always he found time for scholastic research and was able to contribute greatly to Philippine Literature. Justice Villamor's two predominant qualities were his industry and his kind-heartedness. His Ilocano ancestry seemed to give him the desire for work. His inability to say "no" handicapped him for the performance of executive duties, but endeared him to countless persons who were the recipients of his benefactions.

Ramon Avanceña's experience as Judge of First Instance, Attorney General, and Associate Justice well equipped him for the office of Chief Justice. Withal, he remained a modest, unassuming man. It is told of him that when offered the position of Attorney General he wished to decline, doubting his ability, and was only convinced when it was shown that it was his duty to accept. As a judge he displayed the characteristics of Mapa, being small in stature, and in method being concise and logical in expression. Chief Justice Avenceña held the confidence of the public, at a time when it was most needed, when the Court became a completely *Filipinized* agency under an autonomous Commonwealth.

The heroic mold of Chief Justice Jose Abad Santos and his tragic death at the hands of the Japanese are described in a previous chapter. Justices Antonio Villa-Real and Anacleto Diaz were retired members of the Court, who were similarly barbarously liquidated by the invaders. Former Justice James C. Vickers was unable to survive the privations of internment. All were judges of lofty character and wide experience.

The tradition of the honorable lives of these jurists is being carried on by Manuel Moran, the Chief Justice of the Supreme Court in the Republic of the Philippines. He is their worthy successor, the trustee of their bequests of good names and good records. But in addition,

Mr. Chief Justice Moran, in the vigor of his years, possesses one quality partially lacking in his predecessors. He is able not exactly to dominate the Court, in the sense that Marshall dominated the Supreme Court of the United States, but rather tactfully to lead the Court. And this is providential because out of his past judicial experience and legal learning, the Chief Justice has to find the wisdom to reconstruct, amidst the wreckage of war, a new Court capable of serving a new Republic.

Cayetano S. Arellano, the jurist; Florentino Torras, the independent; Victorino Mapa, the logician; Manuel Araullo, the just; Ignacio Villamor, the industrious; Ramon Avanceña, the modest; Jose Abad Santos, the hero; Manuel Moran, the builder—any country is fortunate which can count with such illustrious sons.

INFERIOR COURTS

The non-constitutional courts of the Philippines consist of the Court of Appeals, Courts of First Instance, and city and justice of the peace courts.

The Court of Appeals was established to relieve the Supreme Court of most cases involving questions of fact and to decide cases not falling within the exclusive jurisdiction of the high court.[8] The Court of Appeals consists of fifteen Justices, one of whom is the Presiding Justice, and works in five divisions of three Justices each. It has accomplished the purposes set for it in a satisfactory manner. Concise judgments in quantity are what are expected of this Court.

The Courts of First Instance are the trial courts of record and major importance which come closest to the people. They are grouped in districts, with one or more judges named to each district. Sessions are held not only in the provincial capitols but also in other municipalities. The actuations of these judges, along with those of the *fiscals* who represent the government in their courts, determine to a marked extent the reputation of the judiciary.

The city and justice of the peace courts are important legal arms in view of their accessibility to the masses. Unfortunately these offices, all too often filled with political protégés and poorly equipped men, fail to maintain the respect of litigants. In an endeavor to improve the service, salaries were raised and circuit courts were formed wherever feasible.

Judges of all the courts are appointed by the President with the consent of the Commission on Appointments. It is to the fount of

[8] The Court of Appeals was recreated by Republic Act No. 52, approved October 4, 1946.

power that the public must, therefore, look for care in selection, for courage in disregarding partisan recommendations, and for unflagging support of the judges of the lower courts.

Administering Justice

The Department of Justice combines the functions of a Cabinet Member and an Attorney General. The Attorney General was the principal law officer of the Government until 1932 when the position was abolished. The reputation of the Department has been enhanced by the fact that a number of distinguished jurists left congenial life positions on the Supreme Bench to accept appointment to the less secure and more nerve racking office of Secretary of Justice.

The Solicitor General is an important law officer of the Government. He represents the Government before the Supreme Court and other courts. No position in the Republic is more vitally demanding in knowledge, courage and integrity. These qualities were particularly needed in the prosecution of collaboration and treason charges. Fortunately the Solicitor General proved equal to the occasion.

The Secretary of Justice supervises a wide variety of executive and *quasi* judicial agencies. Among the matters thus handled are prisons, paroles, criminal investigations, immigration, legal aid, tenancy law enforcement, usury, and land registration. The Securities and Exchange Commission registers stock corporations; acting in a negative manner it prevents the issuance and circulation of watered stocks. The Public Service Commission supervises the activities of utilities and disposes of applications for certificates of public convenience. The Court of Industrial Relations attempts to settle strikes brought within its jurisdiction.

The key men in the Department of Justice are the provincial and city *fiscals*. Appointed by the President with the consent of the Commission on Appointments, the *fiscal* may need political support to secure the position. At the same time, he has to cast aside all influence if he is to be a successful law officer of the province or city. The *fiscal's* display of competency or lack of responsibility will decide, in great measure, the degree of public confidence in the administration of justice. The Supreme Court of the Republic threw its weight behind *fiscals* when, in the Lacson case, it found the office included in the unclassified civil service, thus leaving the President without power to transfer a *fiscal* to another province without his consent or to remove him without cause.[9]

---

[9] Lacson *v.* Romero, G. R. No. L-3081, October 14, 1949.

To balance the power lodged in the prosecuting office, the rights of accused persons are defended by privately employed counsel or public defenders. The merits of the public defender system, a recent innovation in the Philippines, are well known. Theoretically the idea is sound. In practical operation the record made by a few public defenders leaves much to be desired.

THE N. B. I.[10]

The Philippines possesses a modest counterpart of the F. B. I. (Federal Bureau of Investigation) in the N. B. I. (National Bureau of Investigation). Upon the N. B. I. of the Department of Justice are devolved important functions and equally important authority. Among other things this arm of the law undertakes investigations of crimes, gives technical aid to prosecuting officers, maintains a scientific crime laboratory, and trains city and municipal police officers. No taint of scandal has marred the record of the agency.

The J. Edgar Hoover of the Philippines is the highly competent N. B. I. Chief, Joaquin Pardo de Tavera. He inherited the strength of character of the Tavera family.

PHILIPPINE LAW[11]

The Philippines is unique in that Philippine law is an amalgamation of practically all types of juridical thought. No less than four of the legal systems of the world, the Roman civil law, the Anglo-American common law, the Mohammedan law, and the Malay customary law, have met in the Philippines and there blended.

Roman law as precisely developed by Justinian spread to Spain and by Spain was transplanted to the Philippines in codified form. The common law of the Englishmen went with them to the United States, was in that country expanded, and followed the flag to the Philippines. The Koran, the sacred law book of Mohammedanism, was taken by the followers of Islam to Mindanao and Sulu in the Philippine group, and to this day is observed. And the native customs of the Filipinos more and more became law to be respected.

The statutory law as now existing in the Philippines consists of the following main elements: the Civil Code, the Code of Commerce, the Revised Penal Code, the Revised Administrative Code, the Rules of Court on pleading, practice and procedure, and laws

---

10 The N. B. I. was created by Republic Act No. 157 of June 19, 1947.

11 See Eugene A. Gilmore (former Vice Governor of the Philippines), "The Development of Law in the Philippines," XVI Iowa Law Journal (June 1, 1931) 465, and *In re* Shoop, 41 Phil. 213 for an exposition of the status of Philippine law.

enacted by the legislative body. The Civil Code, the Code of Commerce, and the Revised Penal Code are of Spanish origin, but all have been amended, and largely superseded, by more modern Filipino-generated statutes. The Rules of Court and the Revised Administrative Code are American-inspired.

The Constitution repealed the Code of Criminal Procedure, being General Orders No. 58 of the American Military Governor, and the Code of Civil Procedure enacted by the Philippine Commission and based on the laws of the States from which the various Commissioners came. To fill the void, the Constitution authorized the Supreme Court to promulgate rules concerning pleading, practice and procedure. This power the Court proceeded to use, after first creating a Committee of judges and lawyers of which Justice Recto was the Chairman.

Recognition of the principle for the Philippines that the rule-making power is essentially a judicial function reflected the modern trend of advanced thought in the United States. It was in accord with action taken by the Congress of the United States in granting such power to the Supreme Court and other Federal courts. Unfortunately, the Philippine Constitution only went half way, because it empowered the Congress of the Philippines to repeal, alter or supplement rules promulgated by the Supreme Court. To give the Court its due, it should be added that the rule-making power has been used "to strip procedure of unnecessary forms, technicalities, and distinctions and permit the advance of causes to the decision of their merits with a minimum of procedural encumbrances." [12]

The Philippine Commission, the Philippine Legislature, the National Assembly, and the Congress of the Philippines—each of the successive legislative bodies—have not erred on the side of paucity of legislation. The result was an output of literally thousands of acts. With prolixity there went hand in hand uncertainty as to what was the law on any subject. The remedy called for repeal, elimination and codification. A compilation of Philippine statutory law, made necessary by war's destruction, was well accomplished for the Military Commander by Attorney Julian N. Wolfson of the Philippine Bar.

Plans looking to the codification of Philippine law have repeatedly been authorized but have proved only partially successful. One Code Committee labored long only to be able to produce the Revised Administrative Code in completed form. Another Committee eventually presented the Revised Penal Code which was approved. During

---

[12] Chief Justice Hughes in an address delivered before the American Law Institute, May 9, 1935.

the Japanese occupation, a Commission of some twenty members was organized but accomplished nothing. The latest effort in this direction saw a Code Commission created to revise the old Codes and to draft new ones, strengthened by contributions from the laws of other countries and more in harmony with Filipino customs. The Code Commission composed of five well qualified members, headed by the learned Dr. Jorge Bocobo, laboring diligently, finished work on codes of advanced type—of altogether too advanced type some would add. The Civil Code adopted by the Congress in 1949 seeks to implement concepts of democracy and social justice.

Efforts have also been made to bring to public knowledge the scattered customary laws of the Islands. The most recent attempt along this line resulted in something worthwhile. Backed by the American Council of Learned Societies, a committee on Indonesian customary law was formed to conduct researches. The services of Dr. F. D. Holleman, a Dutch scholar of Java, were secured, and he, after making use of the abundant material collected by Dr. H. Otley Beyer of the University of the Philippines, made a report.

Legal treatises are particularly abundant in the Philippines. A few of these books denote scholarship, but most of them consist of compilations or annotations of the Codes or of school outlines. Spanish commentators are invoked, but to a much greater extent are American textbooks and cases cited and used. The net result is a Philippine Common Law based on jurisprudence essentially American in spirit.

At this writing (1950) 7,000 men and women are admitted to the Philippine Bar. On the basis of a population of 20,000,000 this is one lawyer to about every 3,000 inhabitants. Ordinarily this would not be considered a high percentage, but it is for the economically poor Philippines. Except for a few well established American law firms, the lawyers are Filipinos.

Philippine law is a fascinating subject for research in the laboratory of actual experience. Not even Louisiana or Puerto Rico, with their civil law backgrounds, have as much to offer the student of comparative law as has the Republic of the Philippines.

LAND TITLES

The Torrens system of confirming land titles, as introduced in South Australia and as developed in the State of Massachusetts, has been reproduced in the Philippines. In addition, the Philippines has gone a step further by approving a cadastral law, which is a compulsory means of establishing titles.

What with the old Spanish grants and vague possessory rights, the determination of the ownership of land was in a bad way. A bold effort to grapple with the problem of simplification of titles to land was needed—hence, the implantation of the Torrens system.

The purpose of the Torrens system law was to encourage and assist owners of real estate in procuring the registry of property. It was intended to decree land titles that shall be final and indisputable. The advantages of increased land values and increased security would then follow as a matter of course.

Still not entirely satisfied, the Insular authorities devised a broader scheme which would literally make alleged owners of land prove their titles. What is known as the Cadastral Law was enacted by the Philippine Legislature.

The term *cadastre*, from which the word "cadastral" is derived, is of French origin, and is used to indicate both a survey of land and a judicial hearing. The purpose of the cadastral system is the same as the Torrens system—incontestability of title. Only where the Torrens system is permissive, the cadastral system is compulsory. The Government denominates a particular tract of land as a "cadastre" and it is surveyed. Notice is given that anyone claiming to own land within the boundaries of the designated tract must come in and prove title. The judge conducts hearings and adjudicates titles.

The trouble with this Utopian-conceived system was that the Government did not have the resources and personnel available to survey and settle land titles for the entire Archipelago—not even in normal times. Pile on to these difficulties, the havoc brought about by the loss or destruction of titles during the war, and the ensuing need to reconstruct almost a million records, and the burden thrown on the Bureau of Lands, the Land Registration Office, and the Courts, will be better appreciated.

Thus handicapped, at the rate the Government is proceeding, centuries will be needed to finish the job. Nevertheless the work must go on. Incontestable titles to land are essential for the maintenance of public order and for the economic development of the Philippines.

Hon. Carlos P. Romulo
Ambassador and Chief of the Philippine Mission to the
United Nations; Secretary of Foreign Affairs.

CHAPTER XIV

INTERNATIONAL RELATIONS

The Foreign Service[1]

When the Republic of the Philippines was inaugurated, civil servants of the people had received training, and had gained experience, in practically every branch of governmental endeavor except the international field. Until the day before that fateful July the fourth in 1946, the United States had exercised direct control over the foreign relations of the Philippines. As a consequence, an entirely new Department of Foreign Affairs had to be built around a few months old Office of Foreign Relations, and the personnel for a diplomatic and consular service had to be recruited. It speaks well for the competency of Vice President Quirino as the head of the Department of Foreign Affairs, and of Under Secretary Bernabe Africa and his successor Felino Neri, that the Department was so quickly and efficiently organized.

The United States assigned officials from the Department of State to advise in the development of a foreign service for the Philippine Republic. Prospective Filipino foreign affairs officers received instruction in the United States Department of State Foreign Service Officers Training School.

Embassies and Legations were provided for the principal countries where Filipino interests are found. Obviously the most important was the United States. Six-goal polo playing Joaquin M. ("Mike") Elizalde made an easy transition from Resident Commissioner from the Philippines to the United States, a post which he had capably filled, to become the first Philippine Ambassador in Washington. Well known Filipinos headed Philippine Missions to the United Nations and to Japan, China, and Indonesia. Qualified men were sent abroad

---

[1] The Foreign Service. Under Secretary of Foreign Affairs Felino Neri furnished the author with materials. See the pamphlet "Quirino, the Leader, the Statesman" and the Department of Foreign Affairs, Treaty Series. The Office of Foreign Relations was created in September, 1945 by Commonwealth Act No. 683. The Department of Foreign Affairs was created by Commonwealth Act No. 792, effective July 4, 1946. President Roxas organized the Department and the Foreign Service by Executive Order No. 18, dated September 16, 1946.

to Legations in the United Kingdom of Great Britain, Italy, France, Spain, Thailand (Siam), Australia, and Argentina.

No legitimate cause for complaint can be registered against the calibre of the men drafted to become Ambassadors and Ministers to foreign lands. Nor can one criticize their actuations as diplomats. But obviously—and necessarily—their duties had to be performed out of the Philippines, and not in the Philippines. Yet they came back frequently to "report on the situation of the countries" to which they were assigned—and these reports were made most leisurely, with weeks running into months.

Philippine Consulates General were opened in New York, San Francisco, and Honolulu, and in a few important cities outside the United States. Consulates are functioning at other commercial and population centers. Geographical propinquity ultimately caused the Philippines to exchange consular representatives with Indonesia, India, Pakistan, and Korea.

The Consulates were generally staffed with high class men and women who, with glaring exceptions, appear to have been selected without special regard to political considerations. They have performed their diverse duties with signal success.[2] Trade and travel between the Philippines and foreign countries have been facilitated. Fees have been collected that make a number of the Consulates more than self-supporting. Filipino affairs and rights, both personal and communal, have been looked after.

Besides perfecting an organization, the Philippine Department of Foreign Affairs has been kept busy negotiating numerous treaties, agreements and conventions. With the United States treaties and agreements were concluded involving general relations, trade relations, conciliation, air navigation, fisheries, a consular convention, a postal convention, military bases, military assistance, meteorological facilities, the coast and geodetic survey, surplus property, alien property, etc. Various other agreements and conventions and treaties of amity with foreign countries were entered into.

The Philippines accepted membership in ten international organizations. This resulted in participation in important conferences. The young Republic acted with circumspection and dignity in its relations with all nations.

The foregoing description of organizational and functional activities fails to do justice to the accomplishments of the Department of Foreign Affairs. Back of each appointment to a diplomatic or con-

---

[2] The view of Filipino economist and columnist Vicente Villamin of Los Angeles, California, writing in the *Manila Daily Bulletin*.

sular post were investigations and conferences. Back of each treaty were long hours of study and patient but firm negotiations. The record made was remarkable indeed. Where the Department of Foreign Affairs was most vulnerable to criticism was in non-acceptance of the unanswerable fact that Filipino prestige abroad was not enhanced by lavish expenditures, while supported by inadequate income at home.

PHILIPPINE AFFAIRS IN WASHINGTON [3]

Because of the special relations existing between the Philippines and the United States, the Washington end of the diplomatic line is particularly important. Fortunately the Philippines is represented at the national capital by an Ambassador and staff who understand their country's economic problems and who are received in the best circles. Fortunately the Division of Philippine Affairs in the Office of Far Eastern Affairs of the Department of State has had as its Chief likable and experienced Richard R. Ely, recently become Deputy Director of Philippine and Southeast Asia Affairs.

The nearest approach to an American colonial office was formerly the Bureau of Insular Affairs in the War Department, originally organized in December, 1898. This bureau acted as an intermediary in matters of administration between the civil government of the United States and the Government of the Philippine Islands. Its work was performed by specially designated army officers in a manner to draw forth words of praise from Americans and Filipinos alike.

As a result of a peculiarly worded order promulgated under the Reorganization Act of 1939, the functions of the Bureau of Insular Affairs were consolidated with the Division of Territories and Island Possessions in the Department of the Interior. A Philippine Section was established in the Division. The Chief of the Division of Territories and Island Possessions exercised little real authority.

With the advent of Philippine independence, a Philippine Section in a Division of the Department of the Interior was an anachronism. The Division of Philippine Affairs in the Office of Far Eastern Affairs of the Department of the State became the central agency and clearing house for Philippine questions. The Division has relationship with the Philippine Embassy on all matters affecting Philippine-American interests and problems. Liaison with this main contact point of the Philippines with the United States has been maintained with benefit to both parties.

---

[3] The functions of the Division of Philippine Affairs, Department of State, are set forth in the State Department Manual.

Membership in the United Nations

A self-governing Philippines achieved recognition just in time to sign the Charter of the United Nations. The Philippines, as befits a small country that finds its best hope for peace in an agency like the United Nations Organization, has given it loyal support. In turn the Philippines has filled an important role in the international body out of all proportion to its size.

The Philippine delegation has contributed profoundly to the deliberations of the United Nations at Lake Success and Paris. On any fundamental issue between democracy and totalitarianism the Philippines has lined up with the United States. Occasionally, however, there have been Philippine defections from the orthodox Washington line. The Philippines has been consistent in the application of democratic principles, by taking the side of exploited peoples as against their colonial masters. Because of championship of the dependent peoples' right to freedom, the Philippines was assigned to the Trusteeship Council.

Representative Filipinos have been honored by selection for membership in auxiliary agencies of the United Nations. Ambassador Carlos P. Romulo headed the U. N. Freedom of Information Conference at Geneva, Switzerland. Senator Melecio Arranz and Dr. Rufino Luna represented the Philippines on the U. N. Commission to supervise elections in Korea, and Senator Vicente J. Francisco competently filled a similar touchy job on the Palestine Commission. Not only was the Philippines represented on the Economic Commission for Asia and the Far East, but it played host to that body at the abortive meeting at the summer capitol in Baguio.

The Philippines has been the recipient of appropriate help from the United Nations. The U. N. Economic and Social Council was created to make the four freedoms of the Atlantic Charter a living reality. Social welfare and economic advisers were offered to whatever member nation might ask for them. The Philippines was provided with advisers and paid its share of their salaries and expenses. The Philippines was also authorized to send *pensionados* abroad to study social work. The Philippines similarly became a beneficiary of the United Nations International Childrens Emergency Fund.

One prime reason for the Philippines high rating in international circles was the effective work done by Brigadier General Carlos P. Romulo, the Chief of the Philippine Mission to the United Nations with the rank of Ambassador. General Romulo brought to his high diplomatic post a full life of experience as a journalist, soldier and author, and has made good use of that experience to enhance his reputation and in so doing add to the prestige of his country. He has been universally acclaimed the most eloquent speaker to appear on the rostrum of the United Nations meetings. He passed from representation of the Philippines to become the spokesman for all colonial peoples. Frederick S. ("Fritz") Marquardt, a newspaperman well known in the Philippines, after covering the deliberations of the United Nations for a number of weeks, commented: "Romulo does a top job here. He is, I believe, the most popular delegate at U. N."[4] Confirmation of the statement came with the election in 1949 of General Romulo as President of the Fourth General Assembly of the United Nations. The following year he was elevated to Philippine Secretary of Foreign Affairs.

In brief, the Philippines has alike contributed to the success of the United Nations and benefited from association with the world organization.

SOUTHEAST ASIA OR PACIFIC UNION[5]

Is there a need for some sort of confederation of free states in a Southeast Asia or Pacific Union? Should the Republic of the Philippines join a league of this nature?

It is believed that events are moving toward an affirmative answer to both questions. The Americas have had their Pan-American Union and have their actual functioning Organization of American States. The Western European Nations have united to protect their common interests. The Arab States have their League. The South Pacific Commission is a consultative body consisting of representatives of the United States, the United Kingdom, the Netherlands, France, Australia, and New Zealand. Why not a similar Asiatic or Pacific organization to include the Republic of the Philippines? It is not merely a dream. The logic of events fully justifies the formation of a regional association of Asiatic Nations.

Already delegates have met in 1946 at New Delhi, India in the first Inter-Asian Relations Conference. The continent's thirty repub-

---

[4] From a letter of Mr. Marquardt, foreign news editor of the *Chicago Sun-Times*, in the *Philippines Free Press* of November 29, 1947. In a broadcast over the N.B.C. network on October 30, 1946, H. V. Kaltenborn said, "Romulo is the best orator of the General Assembly. He was the best in San Francisco, he still is."

[5] Some of the material was obtained from on-the-spot observers of the two Delhi and the Baguio Conferences. Report of the Proceedings and Documentation of the First Asian Relations Conference was distributed by the Institute of Pacific Relations. Note Lennox A. Mills, *The New World of Southeast Asia*, pp. 13-17, 329-334.

lics, colonies and kingdoms were represented. Included was a Philippine delegation.

The second 1949 Conference at the same city had even greater significance. Brought together were delegates from far Africa, the Middle East, the Near East, the South East, and the Southeast Pacific, representing nineteen nations in all and including the Republic of the Philippines. The delegates wisely confined their immediate purpose to advancing the cause of Indonesia's freedom. But individual delegates spoke out in no uncertain terms. India's Prime Minister Pandit Jawaharlal Nehru warned the Western World that it must stop treating Asia like a poor relation. The Philippines' Carlos P. Romulo called for a more permanent and compact body confined to countries of Southeast Asia.

The peoples concerned in the Inter-Asian Conferences numbered more than half the world's population and one-third of the membership of the United Natinos. Potentially they represented the majority of the world in manpower and resources. A Pan-Malayan or Southeast Asia Federation would not be so sprawling and imbued with conflicting interests. It could assist in the settlement of disputes in this part of the world. It could create a bulwark against onrushing communism. It could even evolve into an alliance for mutual protection.

These or other considerations induced President Quirino to initiate a Pacific Union, the counterpart of the Western European Union. The announcement was dramatized in a meeting between Generalissimo Chiang Kai-shek of Nationalist China and the Filipino Chief Executive in July, 1949 in the summer capitol of the Philippines. Immediately there appeared sharp differences relative to the composition and objectives of the contemplated organization.

The concept of the union, as eventually announced in the Philippines, was to bring the free countries of Southeast Asia into closer association with one another and to promote the political, economic and cultural development of the participating states. Such narrowed objectives in effect abrogated the Quirino-Chiang Kai-shek joint statement which sounded a call to all the nations of the Far East to form a union for the purpose of achieving solidarity to contain and counteract the communistic menace. Nationalist China and with it Korea, which had enthusiastically supported the original idea, would not be interested in a non-military movement. Japan, Indo-China and other regions would be barred because they were not "free."

Even delimited geographically to countries within a wide belt extending east to west from New Zealand to Pakistan, and restricted in purpose to exclude military commitments and the mention of communism, the proposed Southeast Asia Union had practical obstacles to overcome. As pointed out by Dr. Brooks Emery, President of the Foreign Policy Association, the Philippines was in no position to back its ideological leadership with the material power that is the concomitant of leadership. It seemed preferable for the Philippines to put its own house in order before spending money on a grandiose international conference of doubtful practicability.

The third regional conference convened in May, 1950, with the Philippines the host and with Secretary Romulo the presiding officer. Seven nations—Australia, Ceylon, India, Indonesia, Pakistan, Philippines, and Thailand—participated. An omnibus resolution was unanimously approved. Therein areas of agreement in the political, economic, social and cultural fields were confirmed.

Divergence of opinion as to the actual accomplishments of the meeting was evident. On the negative side, it could not escape notice that the two Asian countries with the most weight, China and Japan, were not represented. Nor were there concrete results. No full-fledged Asiatic Union was formed. Self-imposed limitations narrowed the results, and as a consequence there was no realistic facing up to the threat of communism.

As against criticism of this nature, it could be said with reason that the movement was initiated in Asia and conformed to a world-wide trend toward regional cooperation, with due regard for the charter of the United Nations. Spiritual unity and a feeling of oneness were attained. The ground was laid for closer integration of policy among the participating states on matters of common interest. The voice of Asia had been heard proclaiming that in the future it would speak for itself.

An Oriental Renaissance is in progress that will take centuries to complete. A Pacific Charter of human relations is being written as the counterpart of the Atlantic Charter. The decision of the United States to grant independence to the Philippines had repercussions in the Far East. The peoples in this part of the world are demanding, and are in a great part getting, freedom from external control. They have been preoccupied with a single objective, that of throwing off the alien yoke. Within each area lie frictions and jealousies that will provide tinder for internal strife for years to come.

While the white man's prestige has fallen to a low ebb and while the nationalist spirit has arisen to the same extent, that does not signify that peace and happiness have come to Asiatic peoples. All too many of them, through no fault of their own, have received inadequate preparation for self-government. It may well be that they have succeeded in ridding themselves of the outlanders, only to replace them with home governments that will benefit not the mass of the people but the chosen few who rule.

The Asiatics are now not well acquainted with one another. The Filipinos have closer associations with the United States than with the neighboring Indonesians. The Filipinos have enjoyed few contacts with the Siamese, the Burmese, or the Indians. Nevertheless the Philippines forms part of Malaysia and cannot be dissociated from it. It would be well, therefore, for the members of the great family to be introduced to one another, to get to understand mutual problems, and to unite in at least a loose confederation for mutual aid. Geographical propinquity, racial affinity, and common interests add up to a Southeast Asia Union. In such a movement, the Republic of the Philippines could appropriately continue to display an interest.

The Diplomatic and Consular Offices in Manila

With the Republic of the Philippines counting with the recognition of practically every nation, it was natural for those with important interests to establish diplomatic and consular missions in Manila. In all, about thirty such nations have thus acted. The United States is represented by an Ambassador, as are Nationalist China and the Republic of Indonesia. The United Kingdom of Great Britain, Australia, Thailand, Spain, France, Italy, Netherlands, Norway, Sweden, and Argentina have Legations with Ministers. These countries and various other foreign lands maintain consulates in Manila. The diplomats and consuls accredited to the Philippines constitute a distinguished body of men.

It was properly decided that the American diplomatic establishment in the Philippines after independence would be an Embassy. Relations between the United States and the Philippines differ from those with any other country. The duties of the United States Ambassador to the Philippines are more varied than those of any other representative abroad.

The Philippines is independent politically, completely and unreservedly. But the Philippines economy is closely tied to that of the United States. American military bases, by mutual agreement, are found at strategic points throughout the Islands. Various United States Government agencies operate in the Philippines. In a word, American responsibility did not end when the Philippines became a Republic.

It is mandatory that the United States give attention to the Philippines. This means, as someone has pointed out, that the task of the United States Ambassador to the Philippines is not alone one of explaining the United States to the Philippines, but of explaining the Philippines to Washington.

The Chancery of the American Embassy occupies the establishment on Dewey Boulevard in Manila that was originally erected for the United States High Commissioner. The building has been entirely renovated and shows no trace of war damage. The Embassy proper is located not far away. The residence erected in Baguio for the High Commissioner became the summer home of the Ambassador.

Necessary changes in personnel were made when the High Commissioner's office became the Embassy of the United States. But some of the original officials remained. Evett D. Hester, Counselor for Economic Affairs, had filled equivalent positions on the staff of the Governor General and the High Commissioner.

The United States had maintained a Consulate General in Manila before Philippine independence to handle passports and visas. The Consulate now performs all the functions regularly assigned to such an office.

Privileges and Disabilities of Resident Aliens

Since the Philippines is a sovereign state, it has the inherent and absolute right to refuse admission to aliens, to admit them upon such conditions as it may see fit to prescribe, or to deport them. On the other hand, when aliens are permitted to enter the Philippines for purposes of travel, trade or sojourn, they have access to the courts, are entitled to the equal protection of the laws, and cannot be deprived of life, liberty or property without due process of law. They are, however, excluded from privileges such as the rights to vote, to hold office, to participate in public works, and to engage in certain occupations. Every alien must pay an initial fifty pesos registration fee.

In 1939-40, the Philippine Legislature, with the assistance of American experts, adopted an Immigration Act that received the approval of the President of the United States.[6] The Act regulated the admission of aliens by setting a flat annual quota of five hundred on the entrance of nationals from any one country. The law was designed to serve three purposes: to stop the uncontrolled flow of the Japanese

---

[6] Commonwealth Act No. 613, approved by President Roosevelt on August 26, 1940, amended by Republic Act No. 503 of June 13, 1950.

into the Islands; to discard the obnoxious and discriminating features of the Chinese Exclusion Law; and to protect the Philippines from mass immigration.

As was to be expected, the Chinese were the ones to take full advantage of the authorized quota. But in the enforcement of the law, there emerged quotas within the quota. Members of the Philippine Congress, unabashed, accomplished certificates for lucky Chinese at considerable amounts for the quota assigned the legislator. A revealing public admission by the immigration chief brought about an official investigation and blew the lid off the profitable racket. In 1950 the Philippine Congress enacted legislation embodying stringent rules relative to the admission of aliens into the Islands and reducing the quota of immigrants from five hundred to fifty.

The Philippines likewise approved complemental legislation on naturalization.[7] The new law followed the lines of the citizenship provisions of the Philippine Constitution, which, unlike the United States Constitution, rests upon the principle of citizenship by blood. The law simply reflected the nationalistic exclusiveness of the Philippine Constitution. The bar against the naturalization of other Orientals was removed, to be sure, but in so doing other bars were erected that effectively limit the acquisition of citizenship.

To be eligible for naturalization, the applicant must possess the following qualifications: ten years continuous residence in the Philippines; good moral character and irreproachable conduct; ownership of reality in the Philippines worth not less than ₱5,000 ($2,500) or some known lucrative trade, profession or lawful occupation; ability to speak and write English or Spanish "and any one of the principal Philippine languages"; and enrollment of his children of school age in a public school or a recognized private school where Philippine history, government and civics are taught. Persons are disqualified for citizenship who, "during the period of their residence in the Philippines, have not mingled socially with the Filipinos, or who have not evinced a sincere desire to learn and embrace the customs, traditions, and ideals of the Filipinos." A court decision granting an application does not become executory until after two years from its promulgation.

Enforced to the letter, these requirements would make it impossible for a person in the laborer class to become a Philippine citizen. Even a foreigner with a substantial economic stake in the country might find it difficult to establish that he has "conducted himself in a

---

[7] Commonwealth Act No. 473, of June 17, 1939; Republic Act No. 530 of June 16, 1950.

proper and irreproachable manner during the entire period of his residence in the Philippines," that he is able to speak and write "one of the principal Philippine languages," and that he has "mingled socially with the Filipinos."

Under the Constitution of the Philippines all natural resources belong to the state. As a consequence resident aliens may not dispose of, exploit, develop, or utilize the national resources of the country, or hold any franchise for the operation of a public utility.[8] In a leading case,[9] the Supreme Court of the Philippines, speaking through the Chief Justice, held that aliens may not acquire private or public agricultural lands, including residential lands. It was admitted that the effect of the decision was to preclude aliens from owning sites where they might build their homes, but not from acquiring lease contracts.

With the advent of Philippine independence, Americans passed to the category of aliens. However, they constitute a special class insofar as their rights in the Philippines are concerned.

The much debated Parity Amendment to the Philippine Constitution acknowledged that United States citizens and business enterprises had the same rights as Philippine citizens in the natural resources and the operation of public utilities of the Philippines. Pursuant to the provisions of the Philippine Trade Act of 1946, United States citizens and their wives and unmarried children under eighteen years of age, who actually resided in the Philippines continuously during the period of forty-two months ending November 30, 1941, if entering the Philippines between July 4, 1946 and July 3, 1951, for the purpose of resuming residence in the Philippines, are given a non-quota status; they are considered lawfully admitted for permanent residence. Twelve hundred American citizens are permitted to enter the Philippines annually, in each of the calendar years 1946 to 1951, to remain for a maximum period of five years.[10]

It may be that in striving for a unified nation, the Filipino leaders have only succeeded in storing up trouble when stronger neighbors are ready to exert pressure against stringent immigration and naturalization laws. It may be that concessions made to the United States, to gain access to the American market, may furnish a basis for a campaign for economic self-sufficiency that could degenerate into unreasoned anti-Americanism.

---

[8] Constitution of the Philippines, as amended, Article XIII.

[9] Alexander A. Krivenko v. Register of Deeds, City of Manila, (November 15, 1947).

[10] Philippine Trade Act of 1946, secs. 331, 332, and 402 (e) and the Agreement entered into by the Philippines and the United States.

FOREIGN COMMUNITIES IN THE PHILIPPINES [11]

Aliens residing in the Philippines constitute approximately two percent of the population. As would be expected, the largest contingent of them is found in the metropolitan area of Manila. More specifically stated, according to the latest available estimate, the foreign population of the Philippines totals at least 200,000.

The figures fail to tell the whole story. Chinese and Spanish blood streams are found in 2,000,000 of the Philippine population, 1,800,000 being descendants of Chinese ancestors, and 200,000 being Spanish *mestizos*. To a lesser extent Americans and Filipinos have intermarried. Happily for all concerned the Japanese, though they occupied the Islands for three years, left few racial reminders behind.

The foreign communities exert an influence in excess of their numerical ratio. Formerly the Spaniards dominated the life of the country. At present the Americans exert the most influence on Philippine policies. And in the future it is possible that the Chinese will intrude into the inner circle of power. It would appear that the Filipinos in their desire to govern themselves will continue to count on attempted alien interference.

In the hands of the foreign groups are found a large proportion of the business of the Archipelago. Americans handle more than a third of the total volume of foreign trade. The Chinese are not far behind, and in addition are actively engaged in the Island's retail trade. The Spaniards and other nationals have large investments. In the close community of Philippine merchants are several long established and prosperous British, French, Swiss, and Indian firms of high standing.

There seems to be a *camaraderie* among men in the Far East not found in those who have lived the narrower home life.[12] The American becomes less American, less impetuous; the Briton less British, less formal; the Spaniard less Spanish, less tempestuous; and the Chinese

[11] Dr. Leon Ma. Gonzales, Director of the Bureau of Census and Statistics, in response to a questionnaire supplied the following data: "Approximate numbers of (a) Americans 21,856; (b) Spaniards 2,834; (c) Chinese 295,149; (d) Russians 109; (e) Japanese 97; Total 320,045. (Based on partial reports of City and Municipal Treasurers)"

Tables Nos. 93, 94, *Journal of Philippine Statistics*, January-June, 1949 list a much smaller number of aliens in the Philippines. The Bureau of Immigration gives the number of registered aliens as follows: Americans 14,226; Chinese 161,158; Spaniards 3,062. With others a total of 161,158. Around 15,000 Americans and 1,750 Spaniards are registered in their respective consulates. The Chinese Consul General's estimate of the Chinese is 160,000.

[12] For a spicy account of a Briton's life in the Philippines see Walter Young, *A Merry Banker in the Far East.*

less Chinese, less mysterious. In their clubs and over their drinks men become men and not signposts of national idiosyncrasies.

AMERICAN PIONEERS

William H. Taft, the first Civil Governor of the Philippines, in an Iloilo speech, made pointed mention of "corroded Americans in business who if they did not like what was going on in the Islands were free to take the first boat for the United States." The usually jolly and affable Taft had been goaded to such caustic reference to Americans residing in the Philippines by their bitter and, what appeared to him, unfair opposition to his policy of "the Philippines for the Filipinos." That constituted a difference of approach to a basic issue and has long since been forgotten.

Manila Americans, however, continued to be the targets of the shafts of fellow countrymen. A distinguished member of the United States Senate who gave his name to a Philippine independence act, only later as counsel for the sugar interests to oppose separation, in referring to Manila's business community wrote: "Their sense of importance and responsibility as the mentors of Uncle Sam is amazing. . . . They have cultivated strutting till it has arrived at the dignity of a fine art." A researcher and writer not long before the outbreak of World War II described the Philippine oldtimers as "garrulous incompetents" who constituted, she added, "a sacrosanct aristocracy." More recently a famed war correspondent termed Manila's merchants "second and third raters."[13]

It would appear but just to view the American businessmen of the Philippines more objectively and understandingly. It may well be that some of the slanderous words, descriptive of their sins of omission and commission, were induced by a sojourn in tropical surroundings that caused an astigmatic vision or jaundiced resentment.

The American community is not large. Slightly more than 15,000 Americans, outside of the Armed Forces, reside in the Philippines. The reason for such a paucity of numbers has been that the Philippine policy of the United States was not conducive to security. The average American preferred to rent a house or apartment when he might have built a home; to invest his capital cautiously when he might have plunged heavily; to exist in the Philippines when he might have lived in the Philippines. This condition of affairs is all the more evident under the Philippine Republic because a large proportion of the

---

[13] Note Florence Horn, *Orphans of the Pacific* and Clarke Lee, *One Last Look Around*, ch. 21.

Americans found in the Islands are stationed there on account of employment with Federal agencies.

Americans were drawn to the Philippines in divers ways, as soldiers, as teachers, and as contracted employees. Many of those who came out with the expeditionary troops at the time of the Spanish-American War were discharged in the Philippines and remained. So have other representatives of the armed forces of World War II who chose to throw in their lot with the Philippine Republic. These men are invaluable assets in their communities. They have worked hard and by merit hold key jobs or own their own businesses. To them the Philippines is, and will ever be, home. The American pioneers constitute the backbone of Philippine business.

Americans in the Philippines stood up against the impact of the Japanese conquest. True, some of them have had to seek havens of rest in the United States because of ruined health. But many of the American business and professional men are right back on the job; in fact certain ones have never left the Islands for even brief vacations. The same old names on commercial firms and store fronts still greet the eyes.

It has been said with reason that all too many Americans built for themselves a barricaded life and insulated themselves against the rest of the Philippines. In post-Spanish-American War days, Clark's Restaurant at Number 2, Escolta, Manila was a popular rendezvous for Americans; there, colorful Tom Pritchard, who later opened up "Tom's Dixie Kitchen" and its successor "Tom's Club Cafe," presided in the culinary department. Even more noted was "the round table" in Manila, where daily in the environs of the American Chamber of Commerce, about a huge oval table, Manila's leading businessmen met for luncheon, there to grouse about petty inconveniences, to berate Governor General Harrison and Filipino *politicos*, and to air their views on problems great and small. Captain H. L. Heath and Senator George H. Fairchild were long the presiding geniuses of the Knights of the Round Table.

Most Americans have a genuine liking for the Filipinos and have known how to express that liking without either becoming effusive or offensive. The Filipinos have reciprocated. Nevertheless, without conscious effort and certainly without desire, American habits have run counter to Filipino habits. Differences in language brought embarrassing moments to both nationalities. Unavoidably all too often the big-hearted, good-natured, well-intentioned, curio-collecting American was an enigma to the Filipino and gave the impression of racial snobbery without meaning to do so.

With every fair ground of criticism of the Insular Americans conceded, yet it remains indisputable that no finer groups were ever gathered together than were forced by circumstances to form associations in the Philippines.

It was American capital that opened up the Philippines to trade, leaving other capital to follow. With the coming of Philippine independence, it still is the American dollar that is wanted. The relatively few Americans residing in the Philippines have aided immeasurably in the development of their adopted country. The $200,000,-000 of American capital invested in the Philippines, the estimate of the United States Tariff Commission in 1935, when compared to the millions in other foreign lands, was relatively small, but at least represented a fair percentage of the total foreign investments of the United States. Moreover, but a small part of the American investments in the Islands is mobile and susceptible to easy withdrawal. The future of numerous Americans is tied up with the destiny of the Philippine Republic.

In the matter of public service, it was the Americans who initiated and managed all sorts of civic enterprises. This was true of such worthwhile organizations as the Red Cross and the Boy Scouts, to name two examples. The American Philippine Guardian Association was founded by General Leonard Wood to guide and care for children wholly or partly of American blood who are without proper protectors. The acute problem laid on the doorstep of the Association is help for the 5,000 or more destitute babies abandoned by their servicemen fathers of the U. S. Army of Occupation of the Philippines of World War II.

Of Americans in public life who got their start in the Philippines we have heard. They include Governors General, High Commissioners, Generals of the Army, and Admirals of the Navy. In civil life were to be found men as useful, but more out of the range of notice. No one could call the roll of honor of these Americans who made good. Pages would not suffice to tell their stories.

The contributions of Americans to Philippine progress are mentioned elsewhere in this volume—of Carson Taylor and F. Theo. Rogers to journalism, of John W. Hausserman to mining, and of Dr. H. Otley Beyer to science, to cite a few names. Dr. Beyer, leading authority on archeology and ethnology, Miss Mary E. Polley, pioneer educator, and Irving Hart, a one-man philanthropic organization, together with a French Sister and a Belgian Priest, were fittingly honored by the Womens International League in 1949 in a simple ceremony.

Other fine Americans have departed the Philippine scene. Colonel J. E. H. Stevenot, Vice President of the Telephone Company and prominent in Boy Scout circles, lost his life while on a mission in the South Pacific during the war. Sam Gaches, the directing head of large business interests, succumbed soon after liberation. Horace Pond, former President of an important import and export corporation, lives in retirement in the United States, as do other well known Manilians. The list is only well begun.

These men and other Americans like them amassed passable fortunes. They were good citizens who helped better the Islands. The oldtimers are a band diminishing in number who more and more find rest in some cemetery in their adopted country or in the homeland.

Three organizations in the Philippines are exclusively for Americans. The American Chamber of Commerce continued to function under the tactful guidance of Frederic H. Stevens and successor Presidents. The American Association of the Philippines was organized with Attorney Ewald E. Selph as President. The Elks Club, rebuilt on the former site in Manila, was inaugurated in 1949.

Americans with business interests in the Philippines have had legitimate grounds for complaint. They had assumed that they were not required to pay income taxes to both the United States and the Philippine Governments. Until sometime after the inauguration of President Franklin D. Roosevelt, the Federal government had no internal revenue representative in the Philippines. Then Washington ruled that the Income Tax Law had been evaded for more than a decade, and a collector was sent out to open an office in Manila. Almost every taxable American was classed as a violator of the law. With taxes to be collected since 1918 with interest and penalties added, American investments, vital to the Philippine economy, were burdened with a tremendous handicap.

American businessmen favor a tax incentive to private investment and trade. This would result, it is said, if American companies operating in the Philippines were exempted from the corporate income taxes imposed by the United States Government. The exemption right of an individual citizen of the United States, who is a resident of the Philippines during the entire taxable year, is already protected by provisions of the U. S. Internal Revenue Code.[14]

Back in "God's Country" are returned Americans who served in the Philippines. They have their clubs in Los Angeles, San Francisco,

---

[14] Sec. 16, U.S. Internal Revenue Code concerns: "(a) Earned income from sources without the United States.—(1)Foreign resident for entire taxable year."

and New York. There they foregather from time to time to live over Philippine experiences. They are men and women who gave full value during their service in the Philippines. In each is a longing to go back to the scenes of his yesterdays. Of course, they would not find the Islands as they picture them. But it is to their life in the Philippines that memory clings.

> For the church-bells are a callin'
> And it's there that we would be—
> By Manila's old Luneta,
> Lookin' lazy at the sea.

CULTURAL CONNECTIONS WITH SPAIN

Already five decades have elapsed since Spain withdrew from the Philippines. Yet despite the long separation, the Philippines remains traditionally linked with Spain. Daily, Filipinos converse in the language of Castile; worship in the churches which Spain's influence erected; observe the laws which Spain granted them; and exhibit Spanish mannerisms.

Wherefore such preference for things Spanish?

The answer is obvious. The long Spanish domination of the Islands firmly embedded Latin ideas. Spanish officials and missionaries mixed with the people and, through precept and example, changed the mode of life of the Filipinos.

Spain once controlled Philippine commerce, but that is past history. Today Spain retains but a trifling portion of Philippine trade. One tangible bond is still maintained by the long established *Compañia General de Tabacos de Filipinas*. Not only does *Tabacalera* mean tobacco as its name declares, but the company has branched out into sugar, hemp and copra.

The Spanish group in the Philippines is not large. Altogether only 1,750 Spaniards are officially registered at the Spanish Consulates, but there must be at least another 1,000 residing in the Islands who consider themselves Spaniards. The Spanish population of the Philippines is less than in pre-war days.[15]

One intriguing development in the Spanish communities was their sharp and bitter cleavage into Franco supporters and Franco haters. Of a different nature has been the tendency of well known Spaniards to seek Philippine or American citizenship. Joaquin M. Elizalde, head of the vast Elizalde interests and Ambassador from the Philippines to

---

[15] Letter from the Spanish Consul of Manila.

the United States, is an example of one who acquired Philippine citizenship. Colonel Andres Soriano, financial wizard, followed the second course to become an American citizen.

The Spanish communities everywhere constitute interesting groups. Their rendezvous, social and otherwise, is *El Casino Español*, customarily a Club, a Consulate, and a Chamber of Commerce all in one. The Spanish *Casino* of Manila, while not as artistic in design and as conveniently located as the club house which was destroyed during the war, nevertheless furnishes a fit setting for the little Spanish world.

The Spanish language, and with it Spanish culture, is fighting a losing battle with English-speaking and partly Americanized Filipino youths. Yet love and respect for the former mother country should and will persist in the Philippines for ages to come. *Viva España!*

THE CHINESE CONQUEST OF THE PHILIPPINES [16]

The ubiquitous Chinese are found in practically every country on the globe and in most remote places. The Philippines is no exception. Indeed, despite an ungracious reception, the Chinese have exhibited a marked predilection for residence in the Philippines. In the Chinese quarter of Manila alone, there are ninety thousand celestials. Numbering nearly one percent of the total population, the Philippine Chinese are responsible for another eight percent of Filipinos through whose veins course the mixed blood which has given vigor—mental and physical—to the Philippine race. It was in this wise that the Chinese penetrated, settled, and became a vital factor in the Philippines.

The influence of the Chinese on the Philippines has been marked for centuries. As far back as the third millenium B.C., traders from Cathay came to barter with the natives of the Islands. With the arrival of the Spaniards, Chinese merchants continued to come to the Philippines. Under Spanish and American regimes, much of the retail and a considerable portion of the wholesale trade passed into the hands of the Chinese. Varying estimates of the percent of the Philippine nation's trade which is controlled by the Chinese have been made—forty to eighty percent—but whatever the exact amount, it is high.

The Spaniards bore down heavily on the Chinese settlers. Yet

---

[16] See Berthold Laufer, *The Relations of the Chinese to the Philippine Islands* (Washington, 1908) and Dr. H. Otley Beyer, *Early History and Philippine Relations with Foreign Countries, Especially China* (Manila, 1948).

taxed heavily, exploited by government officials, even persecuted, the Chinese continued to thrive. Their success was a credit to their pertinacity. Then with American occupation came Chinese Exclusion Laws. The legal barrier kept the Islands from being flooded with cheap labor. Still it was curious how many Chinese managed to enter the Islands in diverse ways.

The Chinese problem was one that the autonomous Philippine Commonwealth and the independent Philippine Republic could not side-step. The census of 1939 showed 117,487 alien Chinese in the Philippines; ten years later another estimate of their number came close to 200,000. Wily immigrants had found means mainly by smuggling to enter the Philippine haven. Much of the trade which before the war was divided between the Chinese and Japanese, with the war's conclusion passed into the control of the former. The pressure of an overflow population from China and the dominance of the sons of China of the economic life of the Philippines were factors that the Philippines was compelled to take into consideration.

The Commonwealth of the Philippines acting upon American advice and with American approval, without which the measure could not have become a law, fixed an annual quota of five hundred immigrants for any one nationality, including the Chinese. The Republic of the Philippines reduced the immigration quota to fifty. Nationalism of trade has resulted in the Chinese being ousted from the public markets.

The industry of the Chinese is proverbial. While the Filipino, the Spaniard, or the American is engaged in dancing and spending, the Chinese is working and saving. As their standard of living is low, as long hours of hard work count, and as frugality tells, even under adverse conditions the Chinese prosper. The Chinese coolie carrying heavy loads across his shoulders becomes the *tienda*-keeper on the corner, with sales for a *centavo* here and *centavo* there; and the *tienda*-keeper becomes the corpulent and wealthy merchant who is baptized a Christian and who marries a daughter of the country. In a generation the Chinese merchant's children are accepted as Filipinos. The Yangcos, the Cojuangos, the Tambuntings, the Limjaps, are merely surnames adapted from ideographs to Roman letters; and the Rizals, the Aguinaldos, the Osmeñas, to mention a few well-known names, have Chinese forbears in their families.

Do not get the impression that the Chinaman is miserly, for he is not. On occasion he is a "good sport." What celebrations were held on Chinese New Year! What beautiful gifts were made to Filipinos, Americans, and foreigners—always in the right quarter—and the highest officials accepted them as a matter of course! What wonderful banquets the rich merchants gave—twenty to thirty courses, liquor aplenty, hospitality so bountiful as to make the occasion an ordeal, but still an ordeal to be anticipated by the numerous guests!

Chiefly because of their dominant economic position and partly out of envy, the local Chinese are disliked by the Filipino masses. In the past terrible massacres of the Chinese have occurred, and in recent times anti-Chinese riots have not been unknown. Following liberation a new wave of resentment against the Chinese swept the Islands.

There is no reason to believe that this expression of nationalistic sentiment, even though based on the illogical ground of cupidity, will lessen. The Chinese as in the past will be attacked and despoiled but, as also in the past, will return to rule over the commerce of the easy-going Philippines. The individual Chinese will suffer unless a sufficiently aroused and powerful home government should intervene in his behalf.

The high standard of honesty of the Chinese in the Philippines in his business dealings has received favorable comment. The merchant who could not liquidate his obligations on Chinese New Year was the exception. But that standard of ethics and that practice, generally speaking, are gone. It is too bad for there was no more picturesque figure than the shrewd, jolly, rotund Chinese merchant who dearly loved to get the better of his adversary in a deal, but whose word was his bond. Of course there remain many Chinese merchants of high standing who have adapted themselves to modern business methods while retaining their inborn enterprise. The Sy Cip brothers, Alfonso and Albino, the former the President Emeritus of the Chinese General Chamber of Commerce and the latter the University-trained President of the China Banking Corporation, are examples of respected Chinese businessmen.

The Chinese of the Philippines have been known as a peaceful race, not interested in the politics of the country, who only resent and resist discriminatory laws. Their business and social life centers in an extra-governmental community organization, the Chinese General Chamber of Commerce. It supports a wide list of activities both business and civic in nature. It also maintains close relations with the homeland.

The Chinese conquered the Philippines peaceably by becoming part of the country and by reason of persistent thrift and unyielding endurance. They are a community large in number, and even more important commercially, that must be reckoned with and treated fairly by an independent Philippines if trouble is to be averted. The fortunes of the Republic of the Philippines, whether the people like it or not, are inextricably linked with those of China.

SAYONARA JAPAN

Sayonara—"Goodby"—to the Japan of yesterday with her Fascist regime of truculent military dictators, with her grandiose plans for conquest, and with her evilly designed Greater East Asia Co-Prosperity Sphere. Lost to Japan are Korea, Manchukuo, the Kuriles, Formosa, her Pacific island holdings, and her occupied lands—all of which has special meaning for the Philippines. Out of business are a formerly active Philippine Society of Japan, the Filipino pro-Japanese propagandists, and the Japanese fifth column of the war. For the time being the Filipinos need have no fear of a Japanese bogie man.

Japan's association with the Philippines began early. That country had had considerable commerce with the Philippines before the Spaniards came to Luzon, and several settlements are attributed to them. Neither so numerous nor so persistent as the Chinese in ancient and medieval times, it was only in the years immediately preceding World War II that the Japanese asserted themselves. In the trade of Manila and the Islands, the Japanese became interested to the dismay of the Chinese. To the growth of Baguio the Japanese contributed. And to Davao on the southeastern end of the island of Mindanao the Japanese drifted, to make of it literally a New Japan.

In pre-war days, 30,000 Japanese resided in the Philippines. Over one-half of them were concentrated in Davao. The Japanese came to Manila because it was the trade center, to Baguio because of a salubrious climate quite similar to that found in Japan's Hakone region, and to Davao attracted by the rich natural resources. In the Davao region the Japanese took over the arable lands of the pagan Mandayas and Bagobos and of easily-persuaded Filipino owners by devious means, legal or otherwise. To give the Japanese due credit, it must be conceded that they were chiefly instrumental in turning a wilderness into the most important hemp-producing center in the world and in developing the copra, lumber and fishing industries. Likewise the truth compels the statement that the Japanese community in Davao was thrifty, orderly and peaceable.

The Japanese pretty well dominated the fishing industry of the Islands before the war. Most of the fishing crafts were operated by the Japanese. They made use of modern methods of deep sea fishing in Philippine waters. A steady supply of fish, one of the staple foods of the Filipinos, depended on the Japanese, and the latter were able to meet the demands of the market because of their thorough preparedness.[17]

It was always Japan for the Japanese. They brought Japanese women with them to the Islands, retained their own customs and habits, and remained Japanese. In trade, imports of Japanese goods to the Philippines were double the exports of Philippine products to Japan. Fully eighty percent of the business of Davao was in the hands of the Japanese and was conducted for their sole benefit.

During the war many of these "thrifty, orderly and peaceable" Japanese natives suddenly turned up in military uniforms and occupied relatively important posts. The fortunes of war either eliminated them, brought them to trial for violation of the laws of war and of humanity, or sent them scurrying to Japan. Years after the cessation of hostilities finds hardly a Japanese left in the Islands, not even the few who claimed Philippine citizenship. They dare not show their faces, for the dislike of the Filipinos for them merges into cold hate that would bode ill for the right to live if Japanese were found in their midst.

The Filipinos have remained cool to any rapprochement with Japan. Anti-Japanese feeling has not waned among the Filipinos. Memories still rankle. But limited and supervised trade between Japan and the Philippines has begun.

In course of time the democratic Philippines will resume normal relations with a Japan in which democracy is in the making. But for the nonce it is not *Banzai* Japan but *Sayonara*.

THE YELLOW PERIL [18]

It is easy to become mawkishly emotional or deliberately sensational in dealing with a subject comprehended within the popularly coined phrase "The Yellow Peril." There is no desire to be either. But fact finding harms no one.

The first fact to which attention should be directed is one of geography. Turn to your map of the world and locate the Philippine Islands in the western Pacific. You will note China bordering on the coastline of the Pacific side of Asia. With or without Manchuria, it is a sizable country one and one half times as large as the United

---

[17] Suisan Shubo, "A Survey of Japanese Fishing Enterprises in the South Seas," *Contemporary Opinions on Current Topics*, May 1, 1940, estimated the number of Japanese fishermen in the Philippines at 1,250.

[18] See J. Ralston Hayden, "China, Japan, and the Philippines," *Foreign Affairs*, July, 1933, p. 711, and Carlos P. Romulo and others, *Changing Tides in the Far East* (1934).

States. Lying to the west of the Philippines, China is less than a couple of days sailing distance away and but a few hours by air. Turn again to the map and you will observe a string of islands, all Japanese, paralleling the eastern coast of Asia from the Kurile Islands in the north (lost to Soviet Russia) to Formosa (lost to China) in the south. But a step separates Formosa and islands to the east from the Philippine Archipelago.

Other considerations force out of the picture the nearby political entities of British Hongkong, Portuguese Macao, French Indo China, the Dutch propelled Indonesia, and the United States, holder of the trusteeship over the former Japanese mandate of the Marianas, Carolines, and Marshalls. The Philippines is within easy reach of China and Japan.

The second fact to which attention should be directed is one of population. Twenty million Filipinos spread out over more than one hundred thousand square miles leave room for millions more of settlers. China's teeming millions, on the other hand, crowd its borders to the bursting and starvation point. Japan in the "target" year of 1953, chosen for planning purposes by the Overseas Consultants, will have a population of 85,000,000 jammed into an area not much bigger than the Philippines. These yellow races are breeding faster than the white race, and as fast as the brown race. Japan, for example, has a birthrate of three million annually. The pressure of excess populations constitutes perplexing problems for China and Japan, and to the same extent become problems for the Philippines.

The deduction is inescapable that China and Japan need the unutilized lands of the Philippines for the overflow of their increasingly large populations.

The next fact to which attention should be directed is one of current history. China is no longer the remote land of romantic mystery, queer customs, and pigtailed men and bound-feet women. Even harassed as she is by civil war, by communist-fomented victories, and by sky-high inflation, China is accepted as one of the big powers. Likewise Japan is no longer the medieval Shogun State living under the pall of truculent dictatorship, of Emperor worship, and of insincere politeness. China, in the brief span of recorded history, has threatened, and may again endeavor, to draw the Philippines within the orbit of her influence. Japan's occupation of the Philippines is so recent as to require no comment to point a moral.

China's and Japan's potential strength regenerates a fear among the Filipinos that once again they may be the victims of aggression and dominated by powerful foreigners. Developments in these neighboring countries cannot fail to exert a tremendous and decisive influence on the Philippines.

"Pinoys" Abroad [19]

In the year 982 A.D., a band of Philippine Islanders visited Canton, China, for trade. This was the earliest authentic account of Filipinos abroad. But it was not to be the last.

The Filipinos became great wanderers. Adventurous "Manila men" sailed the seas. Two hundred of them in 1860 constituted the bodyguard of the American General Ward in the service of China. Long before the present era, Filipino sailors had reached New Orleans in the State of Louisiana and formed a settlement that exists to this day. Other Filipino youths in Spanish times gravitated to Europe for study. In recent years Filipinos have faced toward the United States and its territories for adventure and education, with Hawaii and California claiming the largest numbers.

Considerable groups of Filipinos are found in foreign countries. In Spain the Filipinos and Spaniards interested in continuing cultural relations with the former Spanish colony have formed a Philippine-Spanish society. Filipino musicians have been much sought after and pursue their vocations in practically every land. Possibly 5,000 would be a fair estimate of Filipinos living abroad outside of the United States.

The Filipinos residing in the United States are colloquially called "Pinoys." An estimate of the number of "Pinoys" residing in the continental United States, based on the best available sources, arrives at 50,000.[20] Nine-tenths are males, which offers a problem. As we know that over 50,000 Filipinos call Hawaii home, and others are found in Guam, there must be at least 100,000 of them living under

[19] Note the following: Bruno Lasker, *Filipino Immigration to Continental United States and to Hawaii* (University of Chicago Press, 1931). This is a report made for the American Council, Institute of Pacific Relations. Carlos Bulosan, *America Is In The Heart* (New York, 1943). A finely written book by a well known Filipino author. Manuel Buaken, *I Have Lived With the American People*, (Caxton, Caldwell, Idaho, 1948). The revelation of life in the United States as it affected one intelligent Filipino youth. Carey McWilliams, *Brothers Under the Skin*, Ch. VII (Boston, 1948).

[20] Estimates of number of Filipinos in the United States: 45,208 (U. S. 1930 Census); 45,563 (U. S. 1940 Census, Special Report of June 10, 1943); 60,000 one-fourth American citizens (Philippine Consulate of Los Angeles); 50,000 one-fourth American citizens (Vicente Villamin, well informed Filipino columnist); 85,000, one-half American citizens (Publisher Gregorio C. Aquino of the *Philippine Star Press*). Between 1943 and 1948 some 27,000 Filipinos were naturalized (General Hilario Camino Moncado in the winter 1949 *Moncadian*, p. 3).

the American flag, of whom approximately one-third are American citizens. Not at all a bad numerical showing for the venturesome "Pinoys."

With the coming of independence to the Philippines, Filipinos passed from being classed as American nationals to become exclusively Philippine citizens. Immigration of Filipinos was properly placed on a reciprocal basis with the approval of legislation by the United States Congress establishing a quota for Filipinos similar to that for Chinese. At the same time a source of discontent was removed by permitting the naturalization of Filipinos as American citizens. Applications by Filipinos to emigrate to the United States are far in excess of the basic quota. Thousands of Filipinos have availed themselves of the right to become American citizens. Hilario Camino Moncado, the ubiquitous and much titled President of the Filipino Federation of America, set an example for his followers to emulate by applying for United States citizenship.

In the halcyon years of American prosperity, many sons of Juan de la Cruz were contracted by the Hawaiian Sugar Planters Association. Recruiting of laborers was last in evidence in 1945 when some 7,000 men, women and children were sent over. Other Filipinos found employment in Guam and Okinawa. Such artificial stimuli to immigration will likely soon stop. The Filipino communities in the United States must be considered as permanent in nature, with merely the normal increase provided by the birthrate.

The Filipinos who adventured into a new land had experiences both bad and good—in the early days mostly bad. They found employment where they could; on the farms of California, in the fish canneries of Alaska, and at menial tasks of any sort. Inevitably the immigrants were exploited by Americans and victimized by fellow Filipinos. They crowded gambling houses, were ensnared by blonde sirens, and were euchred out of hard earned wages. A normal life was lacking. Intelligent leadership was needed but was not provided.

Racial prejudice against Orientals resulted in laws that discriminated against Filipinos, particularly in California. A disparaging opinion of Filipinos became prevalent, and all too often individual Filipinos did nothing to better their reputations. A blot on the good name of the United States was the persecution of Filipinos that culminated in acute conflicts in 1928-30 in Yakima Valley, Washington and in Santa Cruz County, California.

This is one side of a picture where racial antagonism fanned by irresponsible elements in California caused injustice to be done Filipinos. In other regions and under different circumstances Filipinos received fair and considerate treatment. They were welcomed into American homes, were treated as equals, and were the recipients of courtesies by Americans who leaned over backwards to be helpful.

Even before the war, conditions affecting the life of Filipinos in the United States had begun to stabilize. Class resentment against Filipino labor had quieted with the passage of the Philippine Commonwealth and Independence Act. Filipinos had sought out places for themselves in the American economy. Most were employed in work which would otherwise not have been done at all. Discipline and leadership had been found.

With the coming of war there could be no question of where the Filipino stood. Thousands had served in World War I. Thousands more gave a repeat performance in World War II by volunteering to form Filipino regiments.[21]

Peace found the Filipinos residing in the United States enjoying a satisfactory status. Americans, generally and individually, recognized the true worth of Filipino comrades. The Filipinos by their own efforts had bettered themselves. The bums, the panderers, the gamblers are almost extinct. Many Filipinos are happily married, own their own homes, and are respected members of the community.

One prime cause of friction was removed when the Supreme Court of California, in a tight 4-3 decision, handed down in 1948, ruled out race as a barrier to marriage.[22] The seventy-six year miscegenation statute had been amended in 1933 to prohibit marriages between members of the Caucasian race and those of the Malay race. The codal ban on racial intermarriage was declared unconstitutional. No longer will a Filipino man and an American woman have to go beyond the boundaries of California to enter into the bonds of matrimony.

The Philippines best ambassadors of good will are the many fine young Filipinos who are studying in the United States. Some are doing so on their own means; others through comity arrangements financed by the United States Government; and still others are *pensionados* of the Philippine Republic. Practically all have made good.

An unofficial representative of Philippine interests is the Filipino

---

[21] See Major Ricardo C. Galang, *Secret Mission to the Philippines.*

[22] Perez *v.* Lippold finding sections 60 and 69 of the Civil Code of California as amended, violated both the Federal and State Constitutions guaranteeing equal rights to citizens. Reported in the *Los Angeles Daily Journal* of October 4, 1948.

economist and columnist Vicente Villamin.[23] At one time he may not have been overly popular with Filipino politicians because of his opposition to an early grant of Philippine independence. With that debatable question settled, Villamin accepted the accomplished fact in a sportsmanlike manner, and busied himself with matters of vital interest to his country. He was especially concerned about the lack of parity of aid granted the Filipino veterans. Villamin knows his way around Washington and in his presentation of cases deals in facts. Vicente Villamin and his accomplished wife are highly respected by countless numbers of Americans.

The Filipinos in the United States retain ties with the homeland. In any one year the money orders issued in the continental United States and Hawaii for payment in the Philippines total millions of dollars. Jasons among them occasionally drift back to the old home town in the Philippines, without the golden fleece to be sure, but wearing with an air of assurance dark woolen suits. Gradually the suit and the assurance fade away together, and soon there is little to distinguish them from their less traveled brothers.

The weaknesses of the Filipino character reflect what has been assigned to him by his detractors. He is prone to show off in dress and entertainment that he can ill afford. He joins a bewildering variety of lodges and social clubs, but finds it difficult to unify them. Chicago, for instance, not long since sadly reported three celebrations of Rizal Day, instead of the one commemoration of the death of the great Filipino that would have been befitting. The Filipino Inter-Community Organization of America has been more notable for what it has not, than for what it has, accomplished.[24]

The "Pinoys" are pretty well Americanized. They should be assimilated into the body politic on a plane of equality and friendship. They, in turn, should not alone insist on rights, but should fulfill their obligations in the same willing spirit that innately is theirs.

---

[23] Vicente Villamin's well written articles appear in the *Manila Daily Bulletin*.

[24] Note the challenging editorial in the *Manila Post Herald*, official organ of Manila Post 464, American Legion, of February, 1947, in which a plea for Filipino unity was made by a Filipino editor.

CHAPTER XV

LOCAL GOVERNMENT

Manila, the Metropolis [1]

Manila is the metropolis, commercial, cultural and social center, and most important city of the Philippine group. It is also the capital of the Republic of the Philippines, and for practical reasons will likely thus remain for years, notwithstanding grandiose plans that call for the development of nearby Quezon City as the nation's official capital.

Manila is situated on the shore of Manila Bay on the Island of Luzon. It faces to the west and looks out on the Cavite Naval Station and the former island fortress of Corregidor; the Mariveles Mountains in the background frame the world's most varied and beautiful sunsets. To the east are rolling hills, blue and hazy in the distance. The city proper lies on a flat plain which straddles the Pasig River. The suburbs crowd out into the foothills and into other municipalities to provide homes for the city residents.

Manila, it was said, is the capital of the Republic. Ever since government was established in Manila in 1571 by the Spanish Commander, it has been the seat of the central administration of the Philippines. World War II's misfortunes forced government offices to seek any kind of makeshift shelter. But a magnificent capital site is slowly taking form in Quezon City.

Manila is the largest city in the Islands. Its population has steadily increased. In the metropolitan area live one and a half million people.[2] In all likelihood the city will continue to grow in numbers. Within the urban limits is found a cosmopolitan community in which many races are represented.

---

[1] The historical continuity of a municipality embracing the inhabitants of the territory now occupied by the City of Manila was sketched by the Supreme Court of the United States in Vilas v. Manila, 220 U. S. 345. Note Percy A. Hill, *Romance and Adventure in Old Manila* (Manila, 1928).

[2] According to the 1939 Census, Manila had a population of 623,492. The 1948 Census places the population of Manila excluding students at 983,906. The Public Service Commission's estimate for Manila and its environs is 1,337,956. Manila police state that Manila including the floating population has a population of one and a half million and may soon reach two million.

It was further stated that Manila is the commercial center of the Archipelago. The city lying athwart the shipping and air lanes occupies a strategic position. The chief port of entry of the Philippines, to its customs house come the products of foreign nations and from its piers are sent out the varied exports of the Islands. Transportation in the city is furnished by a miscellaneous lot of busses, taxis and horse-drawn vehicles. Starting from the city on land are various bus lines and the Manila Railroad, running north and south. Radiating from Manila are the great interocean steamship companies and airways, and the coastwise trade. In the city itself are found banks, importing and exporting firms, manufacturing establishments, and wholesale and retail merchants.

Manila is bound to continue to be a great business mart. It cannot help but be so, situated as it is at the crossroads of the ocean steamship and air lines and close as it is to the Orient's storehouse of wealth. No longer is Manila a straggling, sleepy town with a general air of *mañana* about its streets. On the contrary, it is a city full of stir and bustle of money-grubbing enterprises.

In addition to its political and commercial aspects, Manila has a cultural and social side. Within the city limits are located colleges, universities, hospitals and clubs. At night Manila is a city of bright lights and equally bright gayety. As lively as Shanghai Manila offers suitable consolation for jaded nerves. The movie houses show the current films. The restaurants welcome guests at stiff prices. Cabarets and night clubs are omnipresent.

Manila's government operates under a charter originally modeled upon the congressional act providing for the administration of the District of Columbia. Manila is governed by a Mayor and a Municipal Board. The Mayor has been appointed heretofore by the President of the Republic. The Members of the Municipal Board are elected at large by the sovereign people, who have taken a perverse delight in voting against whatever party is in power in the Nation. Such a system, whereby the Mayor represents national authority and the Municipal Board responds to local pressure, is an invitation to friction. His Honor's ideas of efficiency and the Municipal Board's conception of what should be done seldom concur. Manila's populace is constantly being entertained by these family quarrels.

The Manila of the 1945-50 post-war era is as different from the city residents knew before the war as that modern city was from the old Spanish town which Americans entered in 1898.

Once aptly called "The Pearl of the Orient," Manila could indeed claim to be a beautiful city. Since 1905 it had in the main adhered to the Burnham plan for development. The booster could point to the imposing Pier 7, to the magnificent Jones Bridge—a monument to that sympathetic friend of the Filipinos—to the Walled City reputed the best example in the world of medieval construction, to fine old churches, and to modern clubs, hotels, and office buildings. Most of these landmarks were bloody sacrifices laid on the altar of war.

Five years after liberation, Manila is a ghost of its former self. True the great city no longer is a shambles. Cleanup and reconstruction have made admirable progress. City-wide paving projects are slowly restoring main thoroughfares to a condition comparable to that prior to the war. Weak replicas of former landmarks rather apologetically raise their heads. But hastily built shacks and temporary structures are a common sight. The tourist will take away with him memories of a Manila malodorous and dirty and of a snarled traffic of honking horns.

The one vitally lacking element in the proper rehabilitation and maintenance of Manila is money. The city administration must rely on a rickety financial system inadequately supported by taxes and dependent upon a national government stipend, which has never been fixed by law. The immediate problems which beset the city concerning misfeasance and malfeasance in office, tax evasions, sidewalk vendors, and squatters on public property—even traffic complications—could be met and partially solved by stern measures. But improvement of peace and order and sanitation conditions, fire prevention, and expansion of public works required appropriations, and sufficient appropriations were not forthcoming.

A returned Rip Van Winkle may yet find his way about patched post-war Manila. The approach by sea to the waterfront will be as satisfying. The Luneta, long famous as a park and promenade, borders Manila Bay to the piers and is being expanded to include the former Wallace Field. Dewey Boulevard winds along the bay front from the direction of Cavite to the south until it debouches into the Luneta; but now the former fashionable esplanade is the habitat of the night clubs. Set back a little from the bay and overlooking the Luneta is the Manila Hotel, very little changed. In the same setting are the Army and Navy Club, the newly erected Elks Club and Majestic Hotel (the former University Club), and the Chancery of the American Embassy.

The Escolta, that short and crooked street paralleling the Pasig River on its north bank, remains the main shopping section. Similarly you may find the Chinese quarter in the district of Binondo and the

Tondo slum with its teeming population. Out Pasay way is Rizal Memorial Field with its fine athletic plant. The Polo Club, however, has sold its bay front property to move to San Pedro Makati.

Even attired in faded raiment, Manila cannot well be disregarded. To the metropolis will continue to come the politician, the businessman, the student, the adventurer, and the tourist. They may meet disappointment in the restored Manila. They will nevertheless find that though changed in aspect and outlook Manila, more than any other great city, presents a scene of vivid contrasts—the old of historic interest, the new of urgent utility. Here East meets West, and West becomes East.

The old Manila is gone, but the new Manila has its compensations.

Quezon, the Official Capital

On July 17, 1948 Quezon City, namesake of the late President, replaced Manila as the official capital of the Republic of the Philippines. "From now on Manila will be our show window and Quezon City our workshop insofar as our government is concerned," declared President Quirino as he signed the law authorizing the move.

The "dream city" will slowly take form as a dream realized. Originally conceived by President Quezon as an outlet for Manila's expanding population and called "New Manila," in 1939 the Commonwealth Legislature changed it to "Quezon City" and granted the community a special charter.[3] Shortly after the inauguration of the Republic, President Roxas created a Committee to select the most suitable site on which to build the new capital city of the Philippines.

The choice of the Ipo-Novaliches area in Quezon City was logical—in truth inevitable. Manila is low, hot, and overcrowded. Baguio is located too far from the center of business and political life. Tagaytay has disadvantages including close proximity to Taal Volcano. In contrast Quezon City offers a sufficient area of high ground, easily accessible and already partially developed.

All this does not signify that with the waving of a wand a beautiful capital sprang forth. The sum of $25,000,000 was made available by the United States War Damage Commission to construct new buildings. But before cash can be transformed into concrete, the planning commission must complete its work, the blueprints must be studied and approved, and months of construction must precede the government's actual move to the fashionable and fast growing city northeast of Manila.

[3] Commonwealth Act No. 502, as amended by Republic Act No. 333, approved July 17, 1948.

A goodly number of straggler offices will have to content themselves with conditions in busy and stuffy old Manila for a long time to come. Government offices closely related to business and commerce will remain in Manila. Among these entities are the Bureau of Customs, the Bureau of Internal Revenue, and the Bureau of Posts. And already the grand plan for the capitol in Quezon City has been modified to meet official necessity. The Legislative Building and the war-shattered shells of the University of the Philippines have been reconstructed for government occupancy.

Baguio, the Summer Capital [4]

The author may be pardoned if he takes a paternal pride in Baguio, variously termed the Summer Capital, the Pines City, the City in the Sky, and the Simla of the Philippines. In 1909 as a young attorney, he prepared the Baguio Charter for the consideration of the Philippine Commission. On approval, a new city, the City of Baguio, was on the map.[5] Exactly twenty-five years later, the author—now a dignified Justice of the Supreme Court—came again to Baguio to codify and revise the city ordinances. And what a change had taken place in the mountain resort during the intervening quarter of a century! Baguio had more than fulfilled a dream of a city of distances and of homes, a health Mecca for the Orient, a second capital of the Philippines.

On American occupation of the Philippines, Baguio was little more than a name. Two influential members of the Philippine Commission, Dean C. Worcester and William H. Taft, became its champions. The anecdote is classic of how Taft, in search of health, gave heed to Worcester's suggestion, and having arrived in Baguio and having found Baguio to be all that was claimed for it, cabled Secretary of War Root at Washington: "Stood trip well, rode horseback to 5,000 feet altitude." Root, having a picture of Taft's three hundred pounds, replied, "How is horse?" To Governor General Forbes also goes credit for insisting on the improvement of Baguio and for furnishing the inspiration for its incorporation as a city.

While in the beginning Baguio was not overly popular with the Filipinos, their attitude gradually changed. Leaders like Presidents Quezon, Roxas and Quirino sought relaxation from official duties amidst the pine-laden air of the mountain city.

---

[4] See Dean C. Worcester, *The Philippines, Past and Present*, Hayden edition of 1930, Ch. XVII, and Charles G. Reade, *Town Planning in the Philippines* (1928), being a survey of Baguio by the expert on town planning of the Federated Malay States.

[5] Act No. 1963, effective September 1, 1909, since amended.

When it was thought to open Baguio to traffic, an Army engineer was consulted who reported that a road could be built within six months at a cost of ₱150,000 ($75,000). But when finished, the Benguet Road, now known as Kennon Road, had taken three years to complete and had cost ₱6,000,000 ($3,000,000). Aside from the criticism involved because of its appalling cost, Kennon Road is admitted to be a triumph of engineering skill and highway maintenance. Winding from the rice- and sugar-central plain of Luzon through narrow canyons, and requiring horseshoe curves to make the grades, it is considered one of the finest mountain roads in the world. Two additional means of access to Baguio, also scenically worthwhile, were later provided with the completion of the Naguilian Trail and the road from Bontoc.

The City of Baguio is in the center of a wide, rolling plateau surrounded by towering peaks covered with virgin pine forests. The marvel of it all is that such a place with all the advantages of the temperate zone is found in the tropics. In Baguio is located Camp John Hay, which is a post of the United States Armed Forces and a wonderful piece of landscape gardening.

Being over 5,000 feet above sea level, the climate of Baguio is cool and the air invigorating. What a godsend Baguio is during the hot season when the lowlands wilt with the heat! Not so pleasant are the torrential rains which, during the rainy season, flood the hills. It is then a Baguio true to its name. Baguio holds a world record for rainfall.

Baguio has been and is a well-known mining center. Two profitable mines, Benguet Consolidated and Balatoc, are located nearby. Other mining properties are being developed and are in the producing stage. Baguio has enjoyed a mildly exciting gold boom.

Baguio, like her sister City of Manila, was horribly defaced by the ruthlessness of war. In the wake of the numerous bombings ninety percent of the buildings were left in ruins. Even Mansion House, summer residence of the President of the Philippines and in a manner of speaking the last seat of Japanese power in the Islands, was not spared. But plans for the reconstruction of Baguio, by Presidential direction, were given priority.

Baguio is slowly rising from its ashes to retrieve some of its lost splendor. The Catholic Cathedral, an unmistakable landmark, stands proudly atop a hill ready to welcome the worshipers. Session Road, the shopping center hurriedly repaired, is once more jammed with lowlanders during the summer months. The Country Club, hardly touched by war, rings again with gay laughter. The scenic spots continue to attract the sightseers.

Baguio has a modified city manager form of government. From the standpoint of efficiency and financial stability, it has been the best governed municipality in the Philippines. Good roads and improvements of various kinds have been obtained by making use of special assessments. Speculation in land values has been avoided by requiring that lots sold by the government have houses erected upon them within stipulated periods of time. The city's proud boast has been that it has no unsightly monuments or billboards, and that it tolerates no cockpits, dance halls, or red light districts.

Baguio has been as fortunate in the men who have unwaveringly supported the development of the mountain city as in the excellence of its form of government. The commanding officers of Camp John Hay have been enthusiastic supporters of all movements looking to the betterment of Baguio. The Mayors of Baguio have combined the technical training of the engineer with the skill of the efficiency expert. Mayor E. J. Halsema, a casualty of the war, was not content to be a routine desk-sitter, and the results of his initiative and energy were embodied in many public improvements. Dr. Jose Cariño, University of Chicago-trained physician, was a scion of a well known Igorot family who brought to the Mayor's chair the viewpoint of a native son.

Baguio has much to offer the permanent resident and the casual visitor: splendidly situated; well served by air, train or bus; possessed of intramural miles of metalled and asphalted roads; blessed with a soil bountifully ladened with nature's gifts; boasting a cosmopolitan population—high ranking officials, cadets and soldiers, miners, picturesque Igorots, Chinese merchants, Filipino teachers, American tourists —all attracted by the climate of clean, bracing, lifegiving air flowing over the verdant forests.

The Chartered Cities, including Cebu [6]

Like the childish jingle, there was one chartered city, Manila. Then there were two, Baguio, and three, Quezon, so organized for obvious reasons. But other municipalities lined up and obtained entrance into the select circle. Not to be outdone, Basilan—an Island south of Zamboanga—claimed and obtained recognition, and now there are twenty-six chartered cities. It is to be doubted, however, if membership in the close fraternity of cities will stop here.

---

[6] Data furnished by the Department of the Interior.

It may be that the gift from the national government of a special charter adds to the prestige of the favored city. The honoree is lifted above *hoi polloi*—above the common herd of municipalities. The accolade, however, carries with it a citation openly announcing that the Mayor and the chief administrative officers will henceforth be appointed by the President of the Republic. Municipal autonomy, consisting of the right of election, had been traded for a more or less empty honor. Fortunately the persons appointed Mayors of the chartered cities have in the main been men of outstanding ability. Fortunately, also, the Congress set a pattern for Bacolod City in consonance with the principles of popular government when, in 1949, legislation was approved which made the Mayor, Vice Mayor, and all the Councilors of that city elective.

The chartered cities include Cebu, the second largest city of the Islands, claiming to have 200,000 inhabitants,[7] and Iloilo, which is Cebu's principal rival for commercial supremacy in the Southern Islands. From the historical standpoint, Cebu is one of the most interesting places in the Archipelago.

It will be recalled that it was at Cebu that Magellan landed on his epochal voyage in 1521. It was at Cebu, according to Chevalier Pigafetta, the worthy chronicler of Magellan's expedition, that the latter presented an image of the Holy Child Jesus to the Cebuano queen and erected the *Cruz Milagrosa*. It was at Cebu that Legaspi set up the first government of Spain in 1569. It was at Cebu that San Carlos College, the first convent and school in the Philippines, was founded. Cebu was the first Christian settlement in the Orient.

Cebu's traditions and ancient relics did not save it from destruction during World War II. At war's end, the Cebuanos took up the weary task of rebuilding their city. They have made commendable progress. Nowhere else in the Philippines has a ruined city been so speedily and efficiently reconstructed.

Zamboanga, the Beautiful[8]

The very name Zamboanga carries a lilt in its easy flowing syllables. The Spaniards caught perfectly the charm of the place. They had a song of Zamboanga which began like this:

No te vayas, no te vayas de Zamboanga,
Que me puedes, que me puedes olvidar;
No te vayas, no te vayas, si me dejas
Que yo sin ti no puedo estar.

---

[7] The 1948 Census places the population of the City of Cebu at 167,508.
[8] See John R. White, *Bullets and Bolos*, pp. 192, 193.

Do not leave, oh, do not leave fair Zamboanga,
Forget me not, forget me not, my dear;
Do not leave, oh, do not leave, for if you leave me
E'en Zamboanga will be sad and drear.

The visitor who finds Manila tropically disappointing cannot help but be enchanted with Zamboanga.

Across the opalescent waters slip the Moro vintas with painted sails like giant butterflies. The shore as far as you can see is lined with coconut palms among which nestle little Moro villages propped up over the water. A wharf pokes its nose impudently out from an old Spanish town. Lies before you Zamboanga, quaint and picturesque, gleaming beneath its palm and almond trees—the Zamboanga which an American journalist called "an orchid blossom on the edge of a star-splashed, tropic sea." A stage setting for a light opera. The kind of tropical town you see in the movies.

More prosaically described, Zamboanga is a sleepy city of the southern group, beautifully situated on the southwestern tip of the Island of Mindanao. Although only four degrees above the equator, Zamboanga is blessed with cooling breezes and, owing to an equable rainfall and freedom from typhoons, is one of the garden spots of the Philippines. In no other town in the Archipelago can a greater or more interesting mixture of races be seen. The Moro element is noticeable, and among the Moros are seen the sea gypsies and the long haired and fancifully dressed Yacans.

Besides beauty, Zamboanga registers another claim to fame. Zamboanga asserts that it is "the largest city in the world in point of area (1,059 square miles)." Just how Los Angeles will react to a statement emanating from the faraway equatorial seas which trespasses on its own bid for bigness, one cannot say. At least Zamboanga is a beautiful—and in one sense a large—city.

No city came closer to complete destruction during World War II than Zamboanga. Yet, even the God of War could not obliterate the picturesque features of the city. The tropical setting remains. The cosmopolitan residents have returned. Today, as of yore, it is hard to leave beautiful Zamboanga.

PAGSANJAN, THE PROGRESSIVE[9]

Manila is not the Philippines. Nor is Manila plus Quezon, plus Baguio, plus Cebu, plus Iloilo the Philippines. Scattered over the Islands are nearly a thousand municipalities. In these smaller com-

---

[9] Data furnished by Pagsanjan residents.

munities live the masses of the people who make up the backbone of the country.

The town proper contains an old church facing an open *plaza*, the municipal building, the stores, and the more substantial houses. The town itself covers many miles, with *barrios* jutting into one another.

These municipalities are of five classes, determined by average annual income. The chief municipal officers are the Mayor (formerly the President), the Vice Mayor, the Councilors who are elected by direct vote, and the Treasurer and the Secretary who are appointed. The officer lowest in rank but possessing considerable authority because he comes in direct contact with the people is the lieutenant of *barrio*. He is commonly referred to as the "teniente."

A typical Filipino community is Pagsanjan, a scenic spot in Laguna Province and a symbol of progress.

Pagsanjan is about two hours from Manila by good automobile road. For much of the distance the car passes along sugar-cane and coconut-palm-lined roads. Arrived at Pagsanjan, one finds a little city in which the residents take pardonable pride. The hurt was consequently felt all the more when the Japanese deliberately, and for no reason, destroyed the beautiful homes, even the large and ancient church. Many of the disheartened residents have taken up their abode in Manila.

Whether due to unusual Oriental ancestry or other cause, Pagsanjan has long stood for progress in every line. Particularly are the people extraordinarily devoted to education. Many of Pagsanjan's ambitious sons and daughters have gone forth to acquire educations in Philippine and American schools and to become worthwhile citizens.

Pagsanjan is a tourist center. People come from afar to get the thrill of a lifetime as they gaze at the natural beauty of Pagsanjan Falls. This they do as the paddlers in their narrow and unstable *bancas* (canoes) thread the rocks and churning rapids perilously but safely.

The Pagsanjan Falls are enchanting. They find their proper setting in the surrounding hills. Nature's gifts have been well handed out to a people who appreciate them and who with true Filipino hospitality make them available for strangers.

Here is to Pagsanjan, worthy to be chosen as evidencing all that is best in a Filipino community!

Occidental Negros, the Sugar Province

The provinces in the Philippines correspond to counties in the

United States. There are some fifty provinces in all. The elective officers in the regular provinces are the Provincial Governor and the two members of the Provincial Board, the three constituting the Provincial Board. The first person in importance and power is the Governor. Commonly he is a man of substance and the political leader of his region.

The provinces vary in population and size from Batanes, with some 10,000 inhabitants living on seventy-four square miles of the Northernmost islands to Cebu in the South, with a dense population reaching to well over the million mark. The provinces are classified according to income.

Presumably every province has some claim to fame. Cavite, for instance, can ask for recognition on account of fathering the Philippine Revolution. However, for a brief description of a particularly appealing province, no mistake would be made by the choice of Occidental Negros.

The people of Occidental Negros are anything but commonplace. In insurrectionary days they did not wait for the revolution proper to prosper, but daringly set up an independent government of their own. Came the sugar boom, and they took full advantage of it to grow half of the sugar produced in the Philippines. Even the womenfolk are not ordinary, for they have won names for themselves as being particularly *simpatica*. (The Spanish word does not translate fully into English as "congenial" or "winsome.")

Possibly the trait most characteristic of the people of Negros is their inexhaustible hospitality. The land is owned by ten percent of the families. The *haciendas* run for miles. On these *haciendas* the wealthy owners live in state. The luxuries are demanded as necessities. A real Philippine welcome in its most bountiful form awaits one and all in Occidental Negros.

The province has erected a palatial capitol building at Bacolod commensurate with its wealth. Not content with this, the province has provided a sumptuous mansion for its Governor. From the capitol good roads radiate out to the sugar plantations. The homes of the people are generally well constructed.

Whether in the future we shall celebrate with Occidental Negros in its prosperity, or whether we shall condole with the province when—as happened during the Japanese occupation—the sugar bubble shall have burst, remains for someone wiser to say. But of the future the wealthy *hacendados* rarely take account. They are content to live lavishly in the present.

Dr. Jose P. Laurel
President of the Occupation
"Republic of the Philippines."

CHAPTER XVI

POLITICS

Suffrage and Elections [1]

The Philippine electoral system is ultra-conservative in nature and difficult to execute.

Suffrage is restricted to citizens of the Philippines who are able to read and write.[2] Since only about one-half of the population over ten years of age is literate, the onerous extent of the restriction on the right of suffrage is evident.

In addition to the literacy requirement, the Constitution provides that suffrage may be exercised by citizens not otherwise disqualified by law, who are twenty-one years of age, and who shall have resided in the Philippines for one year and in the municipality where they propose to vote for at least six months. In effect the law bars the illiterate, the insane, minors, foreigners, and persons convicted of certain offenses. Members of the armed forces of the Philippines, once disfranchised, can now vote.

Under the controlling provisions of the Philippine Constitution, it was anticipated at one time that suffrage would be exercised only by male citizens. Women were to be denied the privilege, unless not less than 300,000 of them who possessed the necessary qualifications should vote affirmatively on the question of women suffrage in a plebiscite to be held within two years after the adoption of the Constitution. The plebiscite was held on April 30, 1937. The feminine contingent gave the lie to the scoffers who loudly proclaimed that the women themselves did not desire the franchise by casting nearly 500,000 votes at the ratio of ten in the affirmative to one in the negative. A wrong had been righted through the efforts of the aggrieved party, the women, who had demonstrated that they were just as much interested in the welfare of the country as were their men-folk.

The original election law enacted by the Philippine Commission was an adaptation of the Australian ballot system to Philippine

---

[1] See Senator Vicente J. Francisco, *The Revised Election Law*, Republic Act No. 180 (Manila, 1947).

[2] Constitution of the Philippines, Article V.

conditions. The first election under this law was held on July 30, 1907, and included the choice of delegates to the newly provided Philippine Assembly. Repeatedly, thereafter, the election law was amended and revamped in an earnest endeavor to permit of no perversion of the popular will. The portions of the law that gave rise to most disputes were the provisions regulating the appointment of election inspectors for each precinct, to represent the contesting parties.

The method provided for the ascertainment of election results is difficult of fulfillment. Instead of being provided with voting machines or printed ballots containing the names of political parties and of candidates, the elector merely having to make a mark to indicate his choice, in the Philippines the voter must prepare his ballot by writing in the name of a political party or the names of the candidates he desires to vote for. The perplexities attendant on sleuthing out the voter's intention, complicated by nearly indecipherable writing and wrong spelling, can easily be imagined.

The Revised Election Code fixes a limit on the expenditures that may be incurred by or on behalf of a candidate. This requirement constitutes but a slight barrier to the use of large campaign chests which have often had the effect of bankrupting aspirants for office. A candidate has been known to spend as much as ₱100,000 in a single campaign. When two sugar barons collide head-on for popular favor, their campaigns are likely to shake the district from end to end.

The burden on the aspirants for public office is made even heavier by election contests. The prime cause of all this is the well known Philippine trait amour propre (amor proprio, self love), which leads candidates to make use of methods, legitimate and illegitimate, to win, and which does not permit the defeated contestants gracefully to congratulate their successful opponents. "To save face" is indispensable.

The number of persons who qualify as voters has steadily increased. The number of qualified electors who have exercised the right of suffrage has varied, depending on the degree of interest in the campaign. In the first Commonwealth election of 1935, approximately 1,600,000 males were registered, and of these slightly over a million voted. In the first election for the Republic in 1946, the total number of registered voters (male and female) was 2,897,-993, of whom 2,601,218 cast their votes. For the 1947 election of the Republic for Congressional and other offices, registration of voters went beyond the 4,200,000 mark; of this total 3,257,001 exercised the franchise.[3]

The press reported that in the 1948 presidential election in the United States only fifty-one percent of the total eligibles actually voted. By way of comparison, it will be noted that eighty-eight percent of the registered voters went to the polls in the 1946 presidential election in the Philippines.

The Philippines seems content with its conservative electoral system. Neither the recall, the initiative, nor the referendum are in force. None of the advanced ideas designed to equalize the powers of the voters has been adopted. Direct primaries are not advocated, and instead conventions are held for the purpose of agreement on platforms and party candidates.

A fair deduction is that Filipino voters have taken sufficient interest in elections. A further conclusion is that the system in the main has proved successful.

THE COMMISSION ON ELECTIONS

What amounted to the establishment of a fourth department of the government came about in 1940, with the approval of an amendment to the Constitution under a separate Article, providing for an independent Commission on Elections.[4] This revolutionary step was taken because of dissatisfaction with the manner in which elections were conducted.

The Commission on Elections is composed of a Chairman and two other Members appointed by the President with the consent of the Commission of Appointments. The Members hold office for nine years, with staggered terms. They may not be reappointed and may be removed from office only by impeachment. They are prohibited during their continuance in office from engaging in the practice of any profession.

The Commission is given exclusive charge of the enforcement and administration of the laws relating to the conduct of elections. These matters include the determination of the number and location of polling places and the appointment of election inspectors and other election officials. All law enforcement agencies may be required to act as its deputies. No pardon, parole or suspension of sentence for

[3] Figures for the 1946 and 1947 elections were furnished by the Commission on Elections.

[4] Constitution of the Philippines, as amended, Article X.

the violation of any election law may be granted without the favorable recommendation of the Commission.

The experience of the Philippines during a forty year period has revealed clean and well conducted elections and also elections not so clean and well conducted.

Every major Philippine election has given rise to heated protestations of fraud. Occasionally the charges have been substantiated and the guilty punished. More often than not, the cries of anguish have come from poor losers who were unable to accept defeat gracefully. What can be expected is that fraud will not be limited to any one party, but that the derelictions of whatever party is in power will exceed those of the opposition.

The aftermath of two transcendentally important Philippine elections furnished contrasting examples of sportsmanship.

General Aguinaldo repeatedly charged during and after the first Commonwealth election of 1935 that he was the victim of intimidation and official pressure. The events following the election were fraught with danger, for even the life of President-elect Quezon was threatened. An unbiased view of the election leads to the conclusion that it was free from serious disorders, and that the result reflected a nation-wide endorsement of the leadership of President Quezon.

The first election to choose national officers for the Republic was in direct contrast to the Commonwealth election last described. The 1946 battle was hard-fought to be sure. When the returns were in, President Osmeña, in defeat, discouraged all efforts of his followers to discredit the victory of President-elect Roxas.

President Osmeña conceded his opponent's victory in the following message:

April 29, 1946.

The people have spoken and we must abide by the decision. That is democracy.

I wish to express my deep appreciation of the loyal support of the many hundreds of thousands of our people, and also my gratitude to the men and women in the Government service who worked so hard and so faithfully with me during the past trying year.

A two-party system is a tried and tested division of the electorate in a democracy, but once the Chief Executive is chosen, he should have the whole country behind him in the rightful exercise of his duties. To prolong the passions of election time could lead only to tragic civil strife.

I wish my successor well and pray that he will be given the wisdom and strength for the great task which he will shortly assume as the first Chief Executive of the Philippine Republic. He will carry very heavy responsibilities for us all, and we must support him in everything that is right.

The above quoted words of President Osmeña set a classic example for all who strive for public office and lose to emulate. To Osmeña the statesman, national unity meant more than personal glory. He had indeed lost an election, but in so doing he retained the respect of his countrymen.

With the approval of the Constitutional amendment that established the Commission on Elections, it was the expectation that the Commission could insure free, orderly and honest elections. It is more than doubtful if the Commission has met this test.

An examination of the novel Constitutional provision reveals that the President of the Republic, in conjunction with a pliable Commission on Appointments, can name to the Commission on Elections men subservient to executive will. The supposition will be that the President will not thus act, but on the contrary will search out men of character who will indeed make the Commission "independent" of all influence. The President also has it within his power to refuse to aid the Commission in the enforcement of the election laws. Again the supposition will be that even against the interests of his party, the President will throw the weight of the administration behind the Commission. Unfortunately human nature cannot be changed. The loopholes in the Constitutional provision cannot easily be closed.

The 1949 election revealed a void in the Constitution. Loud complaints of irregularities and illegalities were aired. But to no avail. The Constitution had made no provision for action in connection with presidential elections.

The implications arising from the foregoing brief comments on the worthwhile innovation are that the public should not expect the Commission on Elections to accomplish miracles. Already murmurs of adverse criticism on the lack of more courageous action on the part of the Commission have been heard. Such talk may be expected to rise in volume. It would be greatly to be deplored if popular discontent should nullify efforts to safeguard elections. The Commission on Elections is one instrument for the attainment of good government, but only one instrument.

THE FEDERAL PARTY [5]

The first political party to be formed in the Philippines was the Federal Party. It came into being with the encouragement of representatives of the American Government in 1900, just as Filipino resistance to the expeditionary forces of the U. S. Army was disintegrating. The party's immediate purpose was peace.

The organizers of the Federal Party gave invaluable assistance to the American authorities in pacifying the Islands. With the insurrection put down, the Filipino leaders who advocated acceptance of American sovereignty helped in the establishment of civil government.

Dr. Trinidad H. Pardo de Tavera, brilliant scholar and publicist, was the most potent single figure in the party. He was appointed to the Philippine Commission. Other important leaders of the party were Benito Legarda and Jose R. de Luzuriaga. They, too, were named members of the Philippine Commission.

In the unsettled years prior to the election for the first Philippine Assembly in 1907, legislation made it a criminal offense to advocate Philippine independence. Under those conditions the Federal Party was led to make ultimate statehood in the American Union its goal for the Philippines. It was soon proved to be an unpopular issue. The Federal Party was decisively defeated by the newly formed groups which favored immediate independence.

Although the Federal Party disappeared from the political scene, it could nevertheless be said of the short-lived party that it had served the country well by stabilizing chaotic conditions. The lineal descendants of the Federalists were the *Progresista* and the *Democrata* opposition parties.

THE NACIONALISTA MAJORITY [6]

The dominant political party in the Philippines has been one with the word *Nacionalista* in its title. For well over thirty years the *Nacionalista* Party had complete control of the elective part of the national government and nearly absolute control of the provincial

---

[5] J. R. Hayden, *The Philippines, A Study in National Development*, Part two, contains valuable material on political parties and national leadership. Maximo M. Kalaw, *The Development of Philippine Politics*, 1872-1920 (Manila, 1926) is another scholarly account of political parties. Note particularly T. H. Pardo de Tavera, *A History of the Federal Party*, Report, Philippine Commission 1901, Vol. I, appendix A.

[6] See Maximo M. Kalaw, *The Development of Philippine Politics*, 1872-1920.

and municipal governments. In 1935 and again in 1941 it united the circle of power by winning the offices of President and Vice President.

During this long period of time, the party recognized only two leaders, Sergio Osmeña and Manuel Quezon. Osmeña was the President of the party from 1907 to 1922. Quezon occupied this position from 1922 to 1937. Thereafter the two leaders graciously yielded the front position of party President to Speaker Jose Yulo, without, however, relinquishing the reins of authority.

The organization of the *Nacionalista* Party was brought about in 1907 through the fusion of a number of groups all favoring independence. The party remained in this form until 1922 when the inevitable happened. The rivalry of the two ambitious leaders, Osmeña and Quezon, caused a break, Quezon to denounce Osmeña's dictatorship and to form a party of his own known as the *Colectivistas*, and Osmeña to remain with the old guard known as the *Unipersonalistas*. The election returns showed that neither possessed a majority in the House of Representatives; so in preference to joining the *Democratas*, they entered into a working alliance. A reunion was formalized in 1924. Only now the positions were reversed. Where before Osmeña was Number One, he was Number Two, and where before Quezon was Number Two, he was Number One.

There was harmony in *Nacionalista* ranks until 1934 when Osmeña brought back from Washington an independence law, to the discomfiture of Quezon. The latter, not to be outgeneraled, promptly maneuvered the defeat of Osmeña's law. That accomplished, Quezon proceeded to court approval for his own measure. The *Nacionalistas* split wide open into the *Partido Nacionalista-Democrata*, called the *Antis*, and the *Partido Nacionalista-Democrata Pro Independencia*, called the *Pros*. The *Antis* triumphed in bitterly fought elections. Quezon was once more in the saddle.

For a second time it was realized that fratricidal strife might be political suicide. The time tested formula of compromise was brought forth and dusted off. A coalition was agreed upon, with Quezon the candidate for President of the Commonwealth, and Osmeña the candidate for Vice President. There followed as a matter of course another merger of the two factions into the *Nacionalista* Party.

The singular history of the *Nacionalista* Party was apparently brought to an end in 1946, when presumably the party divided once and for all into Roxas Liberals and Osmeña Loyalists. Use of adjectives "apparently" and "presumably" in the last sentence is a precautionary measure. Who knows but that again the wayward political children will return to the fold of the mother party, will make up, and will join in peans of joy and thanksgiving.

The question may now be pertinently asked: Why did the *Nacionalista* Party so completely and uninterruptedly dominate the political life of the Philippines for practically four decades? Why?

The answer is fourfold. First, Principles. The *Nacionalistas* were the determined advocates of immediate independence for the Philippines, and this was an issue that never failed to win popular support. Second, Leadership. Originally under Osmeña, and next under Quezon's virile and skillful generalship, the party advanced to victories. Third, Organization. Power rested in the hands of one man aided by a few other men in his confidence, and that power was used adroitly to build up a great political machine of office holders and would-be office holders. Fourth, Patronage. The spoils of public office were at the disposal of party leaders and were distributed where they could be used to best advantage.

The Democrata Minority

For practically thirty years—from the day in 1907 when suffrage was first made the instrument of popular government down to the autonomous period of 1935-40—valiant and repeated efforts were made to provide effective opposition to the all-powerful *Nacionalista* Party. Opposition of a sort was indeed furnished. The different parties and varying alliances never came near to unseating the cocky *Nacionalistas*.

The *Partido Democrata Nacional* was organized in 1917. It was made up of the *Progresistas*, who had inherited the *Federalista* stigma of being heralded as *Americanistas*, and the newly formed *Terceristas* of General Teodoro Sandiko. Thenceforth until its inglorious demise the *Democrata* Party was doomed to play the minor role of younger brother in the Filipino drama.

When the split occurred in the ranks of the *Nacionalista* Party in 1922, the *Democratas* were afforded a golden opportunity to ride into power on a popular tide of dissatisfaction. The party was merely able to take advantage partially of the situation. After the directorate of the *Democrata* Party was inveigled by the reunited *Nacionalista Consolidado* Party into forming a National Supreme Council, the *Democrata* Party abdicated its position as an effective political organization.

In 1933-34 the *Democrata* Party, moribund for some time, was dissolved as a national organization; one branch joined the Quezon *Antis* and the other branch the Osmeña *Pros*. Then a curious phenomenon occurred: the *Democratas* who, united, met defeat, divided were victorious. The *Democrata Antis* swept the Bicol region to the marked advantage of their newly acquired *Nacionalista Anti* brethren, and the *Democrata Pros* helped in carrying Manila, Cebu, and Iloilo for their *Nacionalista Pro* cronies. To cap it all, three former *Democratas* were handed the principal positions in the Constitutional Convention, those of President, First Vice President, and Second Vice President.

The Philippines "loyal opposition" was led by statesmen imbued with the highest ideals. Possibly that is the reason these men did not better succeed; their primary concern was more regard for the public welfare than partisan advantage. Juan Sumulong, the party President, reflected this type of thought. His was the well balanced mind that won universal respect but could not grasp the complexities of politics. Claro M. Recto was a leader of similar mold. Talented, brilliant, versatile, Recto went forward to become President of the Constitutional Convention, a Justice of the Supreme Court, and a Senator elected by the largest nation-wide vote. And there were others like Gregorio Perfecto, ever the fighter, who became a member of the Supreme Court.

The record made by the *Democratas* was not one for which apologies need be offered. They had at least scrutinized the actions of a powerful majority which otherwise might have been tempted to sanction arbitrary measures.

ONE PARTY GOVERNMENT UNDER THE COMMONWEALTH [7]

Throughout the Commonwealth period, from the day of its inception in 1935 until the election that was held just prior to ringing down the curtain on this period of Philippine history, the Philippines had a one party government.

The political party that was born on September 20, 1937 of the fusion of the two major parties known as the *Antis* and the *Pros*, and christened the *Nacionalista* Party, was the most formidable political group ever formed in the Philippines. It was backed by at least three-fourths of the electorate. It included among its adherents practically all the experienced politicians—Quezon, Osmeña, Roxas, Yulo, Paredes, Recto—most emphatically Quezon, who ruled the party and the government.

This one party government monopolized elective and appointive offices. In the election of 1938 *Nacionalistas* triumphed in every one of the National Assembly's constituencies. Succeeding local and na-

[7] See J. R. Hayden, *The Philippines, A Study in National Development*, Ch. XVII.

tional elections were hardly less unanimously favorable for the government forces.

Opposition to the *Nacionalista* Party and the *Nacionalista*-controlled administration was pitifully weak. The National Socialist and Republican Parties were synthetically constituted organizations formed to advance the presidential candidacies of General Aguinaldo and Bishop Aglipay, respectively; after their disheartening defeat at the polls the two parties expired from inanition. The opposition was loosely grouped in the Popular Front, later termed the Allied Minorities, to which minor parties owed more or less allegiance. The Commonwealth Government was only harassed by guerrilla sniping from small groups of discontented and dissatisfied "outs," "has beens," and radicals, aided and abetted by a few skilled politicians.

The veteran leader Juan Sumulong did his best to provide the Philippines with an effective opposition. All his efforts were futile. The anti-administration elements lacked a constructive program, a campaign chest, and patriotic cohesiveness in purpose. The result was dismal failure for the Sumulong-Javier ticket's attempt to unseat the Quezon-Osmeña combination in 1941, when the latter offered themselves for reelection as President and Vice President of the Commonwealth.

After the Commonwealth of the Philippines had been in operation about a year and a half, and its ground work had been laid, the author, at the time on the staff of the United States High Commissioner, was asked to answer the question: Is there a dictatorship in the Philippines? In the resulting memorandum, attention was directed to the domination of the Government by one political party, and the domination of the party by the President of the Philippines; to provisions in the Philippine Constitution adroitly drafted to permit of a strong executive who might evolve into a legalized dictator; and to an executive-controlled legislature that had weakly abdicated authority at the behest of the President. Looking at the other side of the picture, consideration was given to the natural inclination of the Filipino masses to give allegiance to whomever was ready to assume leadership, legal or non-legal. For an independent government in the Philippines to have a fair chance of survival amidst increasing local discontent, it was conceded that centralization of power in one strong man was essential. The conclusion was that no urgent justification existed for the President of the United States to exercise his right of intervention. [8]

The Philippines had to wait for jealous elements in an unwieldy

[8] Memorandum for the United States High Commissioner, dated July 7, 1937.

majority to make themselves felt, in other words for another split in the *Nacionalista* Party, to have what is desirable in a democratic government—the two party system.

THE TWO PARTY SYSTEM FOR THE REPUBLIC

Unlike the Government of the Philippine Islands and the Commonwealth of the Philippines, the successor Republic of the Philippines throughout the first Presidential term counted with a real party of opposition. This was for the good of the country. It is generally recognized that the role of the minority party in representative government is as important as that of the majority party.

It was perhaps inevitable that until the third split in the *Nacionalista* Party in 1946, the Philippines should have but one real party. The goal was independence. In contrast, any other objective seemed out of place. Hence the *Nacionalista* Party was able to secure wide support, because the party more than any other organization symbolized the national aspiration for freedom.

With the break in *Nacionalista* ranks in the pre-Republic election, conditions in the Philippines were ripe for the inauguration of the two party system. The perennial independence issue was dead, except that a few demagogues might attempt to invoke nationalistic resentment against American economic penetration. The Liberals under Roxas, having won the election, had to carry the burden of governmental responsibility. Having initiated policies to meet pressing problems, the majority was forced to defend those policies. The minority was furnished with ammunition with which to blast the Government.

The Liberal majority party and the *Nacionalista* Loyalist minority party were not far apart in standing and power. The electoral vote divided between them in the pre-Republic election did not swing overwhelmingly in either direction. In the first election following the inauguration of the Republic, while the Liberals continued to win, it was not a clean sweep by any means.

In quality of leadership there was a fairly even division of talent between the two parties. The Liberals had as chieftain first President Roxas and then President Quirino, with a vast bureaucracy back of them; also the party had Senate President Jose Avelino, Speaker Eugenio Perez, former Speaker Jose Yulo, and former Speaker and Resident Commissioner Quintin Paredes. The opposition *Nacionalistas* could counter with experienced leaders including former Senator Eulogio Rodriguez, President of the party, battling Senators Camilo Osias and Tomas Confesor, Minority Floor Leader in the House Cipriano P. Primicias, and former Senator Jose O. Vera, campaign manager in 1946. Somewhat in the nature of question marks were Secretary Jose C. Zulueta, catalogued a Liberal, and Jose P. Laurel, claimed by the *Nacionalistas*. Secretary Zulueta wielded influence in the Island of Panay but did not always see eye to eye with the Liberal leaders. Dr. Laurel, able and ambitious, was making a comeback. He represented a political element not to be taken lightly.[9]

The opposition *Nacionalistas* who at one time seemed on the verge of dissolution found new courage. The demise of President Roxas removed at once a friend and a foe. He believed sincerely in the two party system and encouraged the minority to fiscalize his actions. On his initiative, the minority leaders in the Congress were provided with secretaries and clerical assistance in the 1947 Appropriation Act. At the same time, it is doubtful if Roxas could have been defeated for a second term if he had lived. The death of the President thus made it a more even contest between the two parties.

In uneasy alliance with the *Nacionalistas* was the Democratic Alliance. It was not altogether a happy partnership. Among the *Nacionalistas* were conservatives like President Osmeña and his running mate former Senator Rodriguez, who must welcome Judge Jesus Barrera and his communist-tainted Democratic Alliance into the fold. In the *Nacionalista* ranks were bitter anti-collaborationists like Cabili and Confesor who must accept alleged collaborators as brothers. The one common denominator for all these divergent elements was an all-consuming desire to kick the Liberals out of office and take their places. The opposition had it within its power to dwell on alleged government ineptitude, government-tolerated graft, and government-inspired election frauds.

The Republic of the Philippines needs two parties, a majority to govern, and a minority to lead the opposition. The ideal to be sought is that the majority govern, without abuse of power, and that the minority resist stoutly, without resort to fomenting disorder or insurrection.

REALIGNMENTS FOR THE 1949 ELECTION [10]

The frail thread which had tied the Liberal Party together snapped less than a year after the death of President Roxas. His name and that of the Liberal Party were synonymous. It was his party. And Roxas was the party's strong man.

Vice President Quirino assumed the Presidency of the Republic

[9] David Bernstein in "America and Dr. Laurel," in the October, 1948 issue of *Harpers Magazine*, appraised Dr. Laurel as the spearhead of Asian resistance to the United States.

[10] Facts based on current Manila newspaper and news magazine accounts.

by right of succession. He naturally desired to occupy it by mandate of the people. But there was Senate President Jose Avelino to be taken into account, and he was a seasoned tactician who controlled the party machinery.

Rumors connecting the Senate head with scandals had been current for months. On February 18, 1949, President Avelino dramatically descended from the rostrum to defend himself and to castigate his enemies. He won the first round and a vote of confidence.

When the Senate next convened, the opposition *Nacionalistas* had ceased being bewildered and were ready to take a definite stand in favor of clean government. Although the Senate President abruptly declared the session adjourned, the opposition and the pro-Quirino Liberal Senators, numbering twelve out of twenty-two available, remained, named an Acting President, and paved the way for the presentation of formal charges against Senator Avelino. With the Avelino Senators boycotting the Senate but with the remainder continuing to function, the case of the two Senate Presidents was handed the Supreme Court for decision. The Court first refused to assume jurisdiction, and then abruptly about-faced and sustained the rump Senate's actuations.

Following an investigation and hearings, the Senate found Senator Avelino guilty of: 1. defrauding the Government in a beer deal; 2. advocating the toleration of graft and corruption; 3. evading payment of income taxes; and 4. justifying the perpetration of election frauds. He was suspended for one year.

The developments in the Senate blew the lid off the most sensational political mess in the short history of the Republic. Following the exposé in the Senate the disgruntled Avelino supporters countered with charges against President Quirino and Senators Cuenco and Arranz. The Tea Pot Dome scandal of the United States sank into insignificance in comparison with muck-raking in the Philippines, part villification and part proven corruption. Plenty of debris from political sewers was available for the approaching election.

The two party system was succeeded by a tripartite system at least temporarily. Three conventions proceeded with anticipated outcomes, except that the largely attended but confused gathering of the Quirino faction of the Liberal Party was unable to agree on a nominee for Vice President, and left the choice of a running mate to President Quirino. The Liberal Party nominated President Elpidio Quirino for President and Senator Fernando Lopez for Vice President; the Liberal Party (Avelino Wing), former Senate President Jose Avelino for President and Senator Vicente Francisco for Vice President; the

Nacionalista Party, former Occupation President Jose P. Laurel for President and Justice Manuel Briones for Vice President.

Each of the presidential nominees was out to secure vindication by the electorate: Quirino for his acts during an inherited term; Avelino to disprove charges leveled against him; and Laurel to live down collaboration slurs. The nominees for Vice President were all qualified for high offices; Lopez, a level headed business executive; Francisco, the country's leading lawyer; and Briones, a respected Judge.

As the campaign progressed, groups and individuals coalesced. The splinter groups—the Young Philippines, Popular Front, *Democrata Nacional*, and Philippine Youth Party—fused with the *Nacionalista* Party. On the other hand, Senators Tomas Cabili and Tomas Confesor bolted the *Nacionalistas* to support the Quirino-Lopez ticket. In turn the Quirino Liberals lost former Secretary Jose C. Zulueta and Senator Lorenzo M. Tañada. Zulueta formed his own *Colectivista* Party with Laurel its candidate for President. Senator Tañada, the Filipino with enough intestinal fortitude to prosecute Occupation President Laurel and others before amnesty cleared them, to lead in the ouster of Senate President Avelino, and to express disgust at the "indefensible" inaction of the administration in the immigration cases, formed the Citizens Party. It was an organization with high ideals but no money.

The national election of 1949 did not center on who had the better program for the Nation. In its final analysis, it was a three-cornered fight, with no holds barred, of personalities. The Quirino Liberals blandly conceded that collaboration was not an issue, only to show Japanese films of Laurel's activities and to spotlight the unproved allegation that his election would alienate the United States. The Laurel *Nacionalistas* blasted venality and extravagance in the government, with a ₱5,000 Quirino bed the prize exhibit, heedless of their own delinquencies. Candidate Avelino sniped at his rivals from the hustings. The man, not principles, was again the determining desideratum.

The campaign was the dirtiest and bloodiest in all Philippine history. Election incidents reached a climax in open revolt by disgusted political dissidents in Laurel's home Province of Batangas, following announcement of the outcome and revelations of the chicanery, fraud and terrorism utilized to attain it. There was even an intimation from unbiased sources that mature democracy, Philippine brand, was a snare and a delusion. More charitably evaluated, the political convulsions may be considered merely manifestations of the "growing pains" of the young Republic.

When the furor was over, Elpidio Quirino had been elected President and Fernando Lopez Vice President by comfortable pluralities. The Liberal Party had likewise gained clear-cut control of both houses of the Philippine Congress.

And then the "unbelievable" happened, or perhaps the right word would be "believable," for anything is possible in Philippine politics. The two estranged wings of the Liberal Party agreed to bury their hatchets. Senator Avelino was momentarily reinstated as President of the Senate. President Quirino was proclaimed President with 1,803,-808 votes, as against 1,318,330 for Laurel and 419,890 for Avelino. Senator Lopez was proclaimed Vice President by an even larger plurality.

PRACTICAL POLITICS

The Filipino is a born politician. It is said of him that he could give Tammany the aces in the pack and still win the game. The politician of politicians was President Quezon, who repeatedly proved his right to the title as he outmaneuvered local adversaries and American Governors General, who found themselves mere tyros in playing their hands, and bested American representatives in Congress. The odds were never so great that he could not squeeze through to victory.

Just why the Filipinos should be good politicians no one has ever offered to explain. Certainly they possess natural talent which has been perfected by constant practice. Possibly this native aptitude for politics comes from the Oriental's predilection for intrigue, to which has been added an acquired blend of Spanish fire and audacity.

There are a variety of reasons why politics has come to have such a large part—some would add an unnecessarily large part—in the life of the people. In the first place, Philippine democracy is in its younger years. At such times the best brains are attracted to public office. Those whose activities in more normal years would be directed to agriculture and commerce are inevitably drawn into the maelstrom of politics. This phenomenon has been observed in the early history of other countries. It was particularly evident in the development of self-government in the Philippines.

In the second place, the Philippine Government is in nature paternalistic. It is customary for the people to look to the Government not only for redress of grievances but for material assistance. Government positions are deemed most desirable, especially by white-collar-trained young men. Some of them may be requisitioned for the civil service, but others have to use pull or influence to land jobs. Add to these two classes, the candidates, successful and unsuccessful, for public office, and their leaders, and a respectable percentage of the population is included.

In the third place, the people look upon law as the noblest and highest of professions. This sentiment influences the scions of the best families to seek the title of *abogado* (lawyer). When these young men have concluded their legal studies and passed the bar examination, they find the securing of cases and fees hard, and all too often impossible, problems. The result is a tendency to devote their attention to politics. Even those Filipino lawyers who have acquired tolerable practices are unable to resist the temptation to go into politics. Hardly a Filipino member of the bar can be named who either has not been or is not a politician.

What has been said about Philippine politics acting as a magnet to draw to itself the best brains of the country will be better understood by mention of the names of some of the men who have proved the truth of the phenomenon. Teodoro R. Yangco was the businessman-philanthropist; yet he became Resident Commissioner to the United States. Vicente Madrigal was another millionaire executive; yet he ran for and was elected to the Senate. Norberto Romualdez retired from the Supreme Court; yet he became a member of the National Assembly. Jose Yulo was the leading corporation lawyer; yet he gave up his lucrative practice to accept appointment as Secretary of Justice and later election as Speaker and party President. To name a prominent Filipino who at one time or another has not entered the political arena would be difficult.

The methods used by Filipino politicians combine all the technique of America and add thereto local trimmings. The radio and airplane have been brought into play for campaign purposes. The more generally accepted style calls for public meetings with many long speeches. As orators the Filipino politicians have no superiors and few peers. The voters have acquired a system of their own, and unabashed call upon the local politician for free legal advice, for financial handouts, and for the payment of taxes, and on election days expect and get free transportation. The candidate who speaks the language of the people, who is one of them, and who is a free spender is the successful politician.

Practical politics has thus far dictated that if the candidate for President comes from Luzon, the Vice President shall hail from the Visayas, or *vice versa*. Hence the first ticket was Quezon from Tayabas on Luzon and Osmeña from the Visayan Island of Cebu. Then the order was reversed with Roxas representing Capiz in the Visayas and Quirino, Ilocos Sur on Luzon. The practice, modified to meet differing conditions, was followed in the choice of candidates in the national election of 1949.

Observers have often commented on the absence of any "clear-cut normal insular issues between the two principal parties."[11] This lack of election contests centered on principles is readily understandable, if it is recalled that until independence came to the Philippines, the one goal was the obtaining of independence. Under those conditions the questions debated simply reflected personalities. With more settled conditions prevailing in the Republic of the Philippines, differences of opinion on matters of national interest can reasonably be expected to be settled by majority vote. The *Ins* will try to stay in and the *Outs* will try to get in. But in addition one party can reflect conservatism and the other liberalism, while the radicals will inevitably be present.

It has been popular, especially for Americans, to lambast the Filipino politician unmercifully. Some of these critics, it has been observed, have failed to note the mote in their own eye in their desire to see the beam in their brother's eye, for among them have been American office holders. Viewed more objectively, no just cause can be adduced to blame the Filipino for being ambitious and for taking an interest in the welfare of his country. All in all, the Filipino *politico* is a lovable individual, who in his own way is a patriot, and who is more often than not seeking to do the right thing.

---

[11] Governor General Henry L. Stimson in Annual Report of 1928, p. 5. Quoted in Stimson and Bundy, *On Active Service in Peace and War*, p. 134.

CHAPTER XVII

FINANCE[1]

MONETARY SYSTEM[2]

Legislation approved by the Republic of the Philippines in 1948 amounted to a virtual declaration of financial emancipation to match the political freedom won two years previously. From a dollar exchange standard backed one hundred percent by United States dollars deposited either in the United States Treasury or in American banks, the Philippine monetary system passed to local control, with authority resting in a coincidentally established Central Bank and Monetary Board.

During the early days of American occupation, nondescript coins of fluctuating values circulated to the harassment of everyone. These were displaced in 1903 by a well planned monetary system established by American experts in public finance. The currency of the Philippines was linked with the currency of the United States. For better or worse the fate of the dollar became the fate of the peso.

The unit of value in the Philippines is the Philippine peso, with a value equal to one-half of the American dollar. The circulating medium is mainly silver and paper. The coins in use are the peso, half peso, twenty-centavo piece, and ten-centavo piece, all of silver; the five-centavo piece, of nickel; and the one-centavo piece, of copper.

Philippine currency is small in size and of artistic design. The convenience of the paper money of the Philippines is conspicuous when placed side by side with the bills of other countries, as for instance with those of bed-blanket dimensions which Hongkong formerly inflicted on its residents. American paper money is now exactly the same size as the Philippine paper medium.

---

[1] The report of the Joint Philippine-American Finance Commission of June 7, 1947 contains valuable source material. Printed as House Document No. 390. Special acknowledgments are due the authors of this report for facts on finance and related subjects. Miguel Cuaderno, Chairman of the Philippine Section of the Commission now become Governor of the Central Bank, read and checked portions of this chapter.

[2] Monetary system. As formerly existing, described in W. Cameron Forbes, *The Philippine Islands*, Vol. 1, Ch. VI. As now functioning, described in the joint Philippine-American Finance Commission Report, pp. 46-53, and by David L. Grove and John Exter, "The Philippine Central Bank Act," August, 1948 Federal Reserve Bulletin. The Central Bank was created by Republic Act No. 265.

In 1928 when the United States Treasury Department was contemplating the adoption for the United States of a paper currency of the same size as that of the Philippines, the Secretary of the Treasury asked the Philippine Government to change the designs and colors of the Philippine currency in order that the latter might not be mistaken for the new small-sized paper currency of the United States. This request amused Governor General Stimson, because Secretary of Finance Miguel Unson, broaching the matter to him, jokingly remarked that the United States Government, not content with imitating the Philippine paper currency, in order to suit its purpose had the audacity to ask the Philippine Government to change the designs and colors of its paper currency.

The Philippine peso has been maintained at the authorized rate with the American dollar, except during the years 1919-21 when the peso depreciated as much as sixteen percent. Again beginning in 1949, black market operations made ready convertibility of pesos into dollars difficult.

When the American dollar was devaluated in 1934, the Philippine Government had its gold standard and treasury certificate funds on deposit in member banks of the Federal Reserve System. The American Government made a large profit out of this transaction. The interesting question was if the Philippine Government would be allowed a gain at the same ratio. The answer came in an Act initiated by United States Treasury officials and approved by the Congress which credited the Philippines with the profits resulting from the increased gold value of her deposits. In cold figures the Philippine Currency Refund Act credited the Philippine Government with $23,862,750.78. But no appropriation has been set aside to fulfill the commitment, although representations have been made repeatedly.

Legal certificates (treasury certificates and coins) are issued exclusively by the Central Bank. The faces of America's famous men will disappear from the paper money, to be replaced by Filipino heroes. The Philippine Mint is not operating due to destruction during the war.

Military peso notes, facetiously called "Mickey Mouse" currency by the Filipinos, were placed in circulation by the Japanese during their temporary occupation of the Philippines. Between two and three billion of this paper, it has been estimated, was dumped into the Islands. At the same time the foreign banks in Manila were ordered liquidated, with the Bank of Taiwan acting as liquidator. The value of the Japanese peso steadily dropped until it became virtually worthless. With the Japanese defeat, the legal effect which should be given to payment of pre-war credits made with "Mickey Mouse" paper became a ticklish problem. Generally speaking, such transactions have been sustained.[3]

Equally critical problems concerned guerrilla and emergency notes which were distributed in various parts of the Philippines during the Japanese occupation. Philippine and American officials have provided funds for the redemption of this script, amounting to around ₱120,-000,000.

Unlike other enemy-occupied countries the Philippines has had a stable currency. Back of it are adequate dollar balances in the United States. The effective money supply in the Philippines in 1950 amounted to over ₱600,000,000. This was much more than the pre-war monetary circulation, but was less than in the 1946-48 period of the Republic.[4] Measured by the peso's capacity to procure the prime necessities of life, it was worth less than one-third of its pre-war value.

In the latter part of 1949, an urgent situation arose which demanded immediate correction. The monetary reserves dived to ₱450,000,000. The flight of American dollars from the Philippines, if not arrested, would undermine economic stability. The drastic remedy applied was to subject all transactions in gold and foreign exchange to licensing by the Central Bank. Action had been taken with the sanction of all parties concerned including the President of the United States.

Under the terms of an executive agreement entered into between the United States and the Philippines pursuant to the Philippine Trade Act of 1946, the Philippine Republic has agreed that "the value of Philippine currency in relation to the United States dollar shall not be changed, the convertibility of pesos into dollars shall not be suspended, and no restrictions shall be imposed on the transfer of funds from the Philippines to the United States except by agreement with the President of the United States." Under the articles of agreement of the International Monetary Fund, of which the Philippines is a charter member, the par value of the peso has been set at one-half of the United States dollar. In establishing a Central Bank and in revising the currency system, it is believed that the Republic of the Philippines

---

[3] See Francisco Ortigas Jr., "Aftermath of Japanese Currency in the Philippines," *Commercial and Financial Chronicle*, March 13, 1947, and the decision of the Supreme Court of the Philippines in Haw Pia *v*. China Banking Corporation, April 9, 1948.

[4] Average monetary circulation in 1948, according to the Bureau of Census and Statistics was ₱815,593,671. The Central Bank issued the following statement of currency issue, as of November 29, 1950. Total notes and coins ₱688,137,549. Central Bank Circular No. 20 on Exchange Control was issued on December 9, 1949.

observed the spirit of the above agreements. No alteration in the par value of the peso is contemplated.

The basic change in the Philippine financial system effectuated by the Republic had been under consideration for more than a decade. It was felt that the automatic gold exchange standard system was unsuitable for an independent Philippines. An excessive portion of the national wealth was tied up in the United States, when it might better be utilized for development in the critical years of the young Republic. A managed currency system, it was argued, will set up greater flexibility and will to some degree insulate the domestic economy against temporary unbalance.

The Central Bank was authorized to make extraordinary advances not exceeding ₱200,000,000, up to 1951, to the Philippine Government for income-producing projects. Releases depend on the country's international reserve position, the prevailing level of prices, the amount of money in circulation, and other equally important economic factors. Priority was given to agricultural development.

The Central Bank is a banker's bank, acting as a depository for commercial institutions. It will not deal directly with the public except through its open market operations. The Bank's Monetary Board of seven members is granted wide powers to administer the Nation's monetary and banking system. It is generally agreed that upon these men is cast a tremendous responsibility. Upon the soundness of the judgment they exercise will depend the success of the modern monetary system. An encouraging note is that the Governor of the Central Bank is experienced, independent and competent Miguel Cuaderno.

The flexible monetary system of the Philippine Republic efficiently administered can profoundly influence for the better the course of the country's economic development, but if recklessly managed it can, to the same extent, bring about economic chaos.

BANKING[5]

Banking and credit facilities are provided by a number of well organized banks. These financial institutions are more and more making their resources available to promote the growth of the national economy. They operate under the general supervision of the Central Bank.

Of the commercial banks operating in Manila, two are branches

---

[5] See Report of the Joint Philippine-American Finance Commission, pp. 54-62. A list of Philippine Banks with appended information was furnished by E. Byron Ford of the Philippine Trust Company.

of world-wide American financial institutions, and a third is a local bank American-owned; two are branches of British banks; two are Chinese-owned; two are controlled by the Catholic Archdiocese of Manila; two have Filipino backing; and three are government-financed. Branches and agencies are found in the principal cities. The Japanese, who during the occupation took over the Philippine banks, now have no bank of their own.

The Government is represented by the Central Bank, the Rehabilitation Finance Corporation, better known as the RFC, and the Philippine National Bank. The Central Bank is roughly analogous to the Federal Reserve System of the United States. The RFC absorbed the Agricultural and Industrial Bank; it was established to aid in agricultural, industrial and residential reconstruction.[6] The Philippine National Bank through its branches, agencies and sub-agencies provides nation-wide banking facilities.

The Philippine Government's excursion into the banking field has passed through three phases. The first is a sordid tale of nearly unbelievable mismanagement, graft, and the violation of every rule that good banking practice dictates. The second is a factual report of prudent management, honesty, and conformity to accepted business principles. The third is a partial fulfillment of a program of adjustment and expansion to meet the economic demands of an independent nation.

The Philippine National Bank was created in 1916. Dr. H. Parker Willis, Secretary of the United States Federal Reserve Board, came out to see the Bank started. Then Samuel Ferguson, an employee of the Government who had seen service in the Supreme Court and in the office of the Governor General, but without previous banking experience, was put in charge. He was succeeded in the presidential office by General Venancio Concepcion, also without banking experience. General Concepcion later served a prison term.

In 1919 the affairs of the Bank were examined by F. Coates, Jr., clearing-house examiner of Cleveland, Ohio, and in 1921 by Haskins and Sells, certified public accountants of New York City. These reports brought to light the astonishing state of the Bank's finances. Among other things, there was disclosed the following: slight surveillance was exercised over the main office and practically no control over the branches and agencies; funds were loaned on slight investigation and without adequate security; the Government reserves to protect its currency were transferred to insecure investments; an ex-

<hr>

[6] Rehabilitation Finance Corporation, Republic Act No. 85, approved October 29, 1946.

change speculation with Shanghai involved a loss of ₱14,000,000; a large portion of the investment made by the Government in the capital stock and the government deposit were forfeited; the principal losses totalled over ₱60,000,000. During a brief period of six years the Bank had been wrecked. It was insolvent.

Now for a more pleasing picture. E. W. Wilson, an experienced banker from San Francisco, was made President of the Philippine National Bank. The Rehabilitation Act of 1924, passed by the Philippine Legislature, put the Bank in a legal position to operate and was supported by the greater borrowing power of the Philippine Government. The process of liquidating the frozen assets, mostly in sugar centrals, was begun. The Bank began to make money. Year by year it steadily improved its position.

The Philippine National Bank, now in the constructive third phase of its variegated history, is plagued by irregularities and swindles by its employees.

The Public Debt[7]

The Republic of the Philippines set out on its independent course in a fairly strong financial position. The entire debt of the Government, national and local, is relatively small. The net obligations of the Republic are a mere trifle in comparison with the enormous debt loads which other peoples must carry.

Legislation approved by the United States Congress formerly restricted the borrowing power of the Philippine Government. The result of this carefully conceived policy was that when the Philippine Commonwealth was inaugurated, the public debt of the Philippines only amounted to ₱154,364,700. Deducting the sinking fund reserve of approximately ₱59,000,000, the net debt was about ₱95,000,000. Before the war interrupted normal transactions, the fiscal program of the Philippine Commonwealth had further reduced government indebtedness.

As of the date of July 4, 1946 when the Republic of the Philippines was proclaimed, outstanding government obligations, less accumulated sinking funds, amounted to ₱69,354,062. Of this total, a goodly portion represented dollar bonds, largely owned in the United States and carrying the implicit guarantee of the United States Government. The remainder were guaranteed peso obligations mostly held by Philippine banks, insurance companies, and trust funds. In 1947, cer-

---

[7] M. Guevara, Treasurer of the Philippines, furnished data concerning bonded indebtedness.

tain bonds issued prior to May 1, 1934 and amounting to ₱26,201,000 were destroyed as provided by law.

The Philippine Republic was compelled to negotiate a net loan of ₱120,000,000 ($60,000,000) from the United States Reconstruction Finance Corporation to cover budgetary deficits for the first fiscal year. Credits to aid in reconstruction have been sought from time to time. Important action with far reaching implications was taken in 1948 and again in 1949, when the Congress of the Philippines granted the President authority to borrow sizable sums from the United States Export-Import Bank and the World Bank to finance power development.

It needs to be repeated that the entire debt, direct and guaranteed, of the Philippine Republic, is relatively small. On a *per capita* basis, it is not over ten pesos. Considered in relation to the value of the taxable property and the taxing capacity of the Government, the external debt is low. Philippine bonds have invariably been sold advantageously at good figures in the American market. The internal debt can be expanded locally to good advantage. In fact domestic borrowing may be imperatively needed to meet obligations maturing in the early 1950s.

THE BUDGET [8]

Profiting from past experience, the budget system was established in the Philippines four years before the enactment by the Congress of the United States of the Budget and Accounting Law of 1921. Thirty years later it can be affirmed that the Philippine budgetary system is sound in theory.

In compliance with provisions in the Constitution, the President of the Philippines submits within fifteen days of the opening of each regular session of the Congress a budget of receipts and expenditures. The financial plan is prepared by the Budget Commission, of which the Commissioner of the Budget is the expert director. This agency is the nerve center of the Government. The authority of the Budget Commission is enhanced by the Constitutional prohibition which estops the Congress from increasing the appropriations recommended by the President for the operation of the Government, except the appropriations for the Congress and the Judicial Department.[8]

[8] See report of the Joint Philippine-American Finance Commission, pp. 18-24, 76-80 and Appendix VI. Quirino E. Austria described and analyzed the budgeting system of the Philippine Commonwealth in *Philippine Social Service Review* (July, 1935). He discussed the subject "Is the Philippines Budgetary System Sound?" in the *Manila Chronicle* of November 28, 1948.

[9] Constitution of the Philippines, as amended, Article VI, sec. 19 (1).

The statement has often been made that up to the date of the advent of the Philippine Republic, the budget had always been balanced. This was not technically true in 1930, 1931, and 1932. But even in those years surpluses accumulated from previous years were sufficient to make up the deficits.

The total annual appropriations of the Insular Government amounted to ₱26,000,000 in 1908. For each of the years in the decade preceding the inauguration of the Commonwealth Government in 1935, the figures had averaged ₱84,000,000. The budget for 1940, the last normal year of the Commonwealth, excluding expenditures from the Coconut Oil Excise Tax Fund, exceeded ₱100,000,000. If these sums seem large, let it be added that the Government of the Philippine Republic finds it difficult to meet all proper demands with annual appropriations of ₱400,000,000, and even more difficult to find the money to meet expenditures.

After liberation, it was inevitable for Philippine finances to be in the red. What was not intended was that the Government should fall into a "morass of deficits," to make use of the language of the President of the Republic in his 1951 budget message to the Congress. Conceded officially were recurring deficits for the 1946-49 fiscal years, deficiency spending far beyond the authorized appropriations for 1950, and a Central Bank overdraft. The Chairman of the Senate Finance Committee warned that the Philippines faced a deficit of about ₱421,000,000 by the end of the 1951 fiscal year if new tax measures were not approved. Clever accounting devices failed to becloud the precarious, although far from hopeless, fiscal position of the Government.

The President repeatedly urged an "austerity" program of public expenditures. The hard facts revealed little or no adherence to such a sensible plan. The 1951 budget as presented to the Congress by the President called for the staggering outlay of ₱344,109,350, the highest in the country's history. If to this sum there be added ₱20,000,000 appropriated for the integrated Armed Forces, and other millions of pesos to provide for the schools, public works projects, and supplementary outlays, the grand total would be something more than ₱400,000,000. The Congress made an earnest effort to clip the stupendous figures, in preference to imposing new burdens on a people whose taxpaying capacity was growing less. Headway was made to the extent that the 1951 budget was pruned down to ₱260,822,554.

The announcement was officially made that the 1950 budget had been balanced. This statement was proved patently untrue. An equally incorrect deduction that the 1951 budget would show a net surplus in excess of ₱40,000,000 emanated from Malacañan. Discounting this sort of mystic optimism, if five years after the conclusion of the war the budget comes even close to a balance, it is no mean feat. It would stand as no small accomplishment in a land that suffered more physical war damage than any other country in the Far East.

At this point a little moralizing might be in order. Examples of thrift should properly be set by high officials who preach austerity. Instead the public is regaled with lavish display, with the President seeking a higher level of spending for his own office, and with the economy-minded House and Senate sanctioning increased appropriations for their respective chambers. Small matters, comparatively speaking to be sure, but the Philippines in the trying years ahead could well take heed to practice real frugality and austerity.

An analysis of income and expenditures will tend to clarify the fiscal situation.

INCOME [10]

The income of the National Government of the Philippine Republic is mainly derived from import duties, internal revenue taxes, and the earnings of certain government corporations. The import duties are primarily for revenue and only incidentally for protection of local industries. The principal sources of government income derived from internal revenue are: the license, business and occupation taxes including the sales tax; the excise taxes on alcoholic beverages, cigarettes, and gasoline and oil; the income tax; estate, inheritance and gift taxes; the documentary tax; the immigration tax; the residence tax; forest charges; mining royalties and an *ad valorem* tax upon the output of privately owned mines; and the war profits tax.

A source of easy and large income provided by the vagaries of U. S. Congressional legislation was the Coconut Oil Excise Tax. Between 1934 and 1942 the revenue accruing to the Commonwealth Government from the levy of three cents per pound on coconut oil shipped to the United States amounted to well over ₱200,000,000. The fund accounted for approximately one-third of the operating costs of the government for that period. The accumulated windfalls served a good purpose, when during the first year of the Philippine Republic ₱110,400,000 were transferred from the Coconut Oil

---

[10] See Report of the Joint Philippine-American Finance Commission, pp. 25-40, and the National Internal Revenue Code. Supervising Examiner Florentino Amansec served as a consultant.

Excise Fund to constitute a considerable portion of extraordinary income.

During the ten years the Government of the Commonwealth was in operation, approximately ₱335,000,000 were remitted to it by the United States Government from coconut oil excise taxes and sugar processing taxes. This huge sum stood out vividly in comparison with revenues from all Philippine sources for the same period of ₱600,000,000. This was an unhealthy condition of public finances. It is just as well that it disappeared from the Philippine scene.

A somewhat similar situation came about during the early years of the Philippine Republic because of the heavy volume of United States Government payments. These proved a prime help in time of need. As income from this source diminishes, it will have to be made up elsewhere.

The Tax Commission of the Philippines of 1939 and the Joint Philippine-American Finance Commission of 1947 agreed that an equitable tax system should distribute "the tax burden more nearly on the basis of ability to pay." In application, this principle has meant less emphasis on consumption taxes and more emphasis on income and inheritance taxes and excise and percentage taxes on the so-called luxuries. The sales tax—a consumption tax—was continued. Excise taxes; license, business and occupation taxes; the income tax; and the documentary stamp tax were increased by varying percentages. The war profits tax provided for a progressive tax on increases in net worth per annum between December 8, 1941 and February 26, 1945.

A tax peculiar to the Philippines and long in use was the cedula tax. This token tax of two pesos a year was paid by all male inhabitants of the Philippines, with a few exceptions, between the ages of eighteen and sixty. Aside from constituting a tax measure, cedulas served as certificates of identification. The Commonwealth Government abolished the cedula tax, presumably because it savored overly much of colonial rule. To take its place a residence tax was imposed. Every regularly employed inhabitant is expected to pay it. The annual tax for individuals is fifty centavos and for corporations is five pesos, and the tax increases in accordance with a fixed schedule on the basis of property and income.

The sales tax has been in force in the Philippines since the Internal Revenue Law was first enacted in 1904. Originally fixed at one-third of one percent, subsequently it was raised to one percent, and still later, successively, to one and one-half percent, to three percent, to five percent, to as high as fifty percent on certain luxuries. Giving head to merchants' protests, the cumulative sales tax was stopped in

1939. More recently a procedure vigorously scored was the collection of a "compensating tax" at the time of importation of merchandise. Evasion of the sales tax on a petty scale is widespread.

In fact enforcement of all the tax laws has been difficult. During the Japanese occupation, evasion of taxes became a symbol of resistance. As a result, the efficiency of the agencies responsible for the collection of taxes declined. Experienced personnel left the Government to accept better-paying jobs. Criminal prosecutions of tax evaders were infrequent. The existence of all these factors has had a demoralizing effect on taxpayers who under more normal conditions would step up and pay their taxes.

The Finance Secretary has admitted that not more than twenty-five percent of the taxes was being collected. An interesting commentary on such tax evasion is, according to the Collector of Internal Revenue, that the worst slackers are in order, Chinese, East Indians, and Filipinos. For being the most honest taxpayers, the Collector hands it to Americans and Europeans.

The Department of Finance favors the strengthening of the revenue collecting services, the intensifying of the collection of taxes, and rigorous enforcement of the tax laws. The cost of collection is modest. It could appropriately be increased with a view to putting a stop to evasion of the tax laws.

The rich in the Philippines are few. In 1947, for instance, 165,000 individual income tax returns were filed, and only 50,000 of these individuals had to pay. Moreover, business is pretty well monopolized by foreigners. The temptation will ever be present to soak the alien elite to benefit the Filipino masses.

The *per capita* tax burden of the Philippines even under the postwar increases is low—₱11.00 for 1947. If you deduct the high percent of the taxes which foreigners pay, the showing in comparison with other countries is even more remarkable. The consolidated tax collections for all branches of the Philippine Republic for 1947, constituted about four percent of the national income.

REAL PROPERTY TAX[11]

The largest single source of municipal revenue is the real property tax.

The rate levied by the City of Manila is one and one-half percent and is lower for the other local units. Assessments, however, have trebled. Manila alone collected nearly ₱7,000,000 from this tax in 1948.

---

[11] Annual 1948 Report of Mayor Manuel de la Fuente of Manila was used.

Direct in application, the real property tax shoe pinches most the masses. Complaints against it have been many and vociferous. Petitions for remission of the tax swamp the government. In 1946 only fifty-eight percent of the taxes assessed were collected. But the government plans to continue the real property tax and to make it the mainstay of local government revenues.

EXPENDITURES

The Republic of the Philippines is self-sustaining. The entire cost of administration is borne by local taxpayers. This has been true since the beginning of American occupation. Even the salary of the American Governor General was paid out of revenues collected in the Philippines.

From another angle it can be said with some degree of accuracy that the Islands have been a financial burden on the United States. If mathematically and meticulously inclined, an addition of all American-originated appropriations for Philippine expenditures, from 1898 to 1941, would make a grand total of ₱2,000,000,000 ($1,000,000,-000). The sum shrinks from its superficial bigness, when it is recalled that the estimated billion dollars was for a period of over forty years, that a considerable portion of the expenditures was Army and Navy appropriations of primary interest to the United States, and that commercial advantages were obtained through relations with the Philippines.[12]

American aid to the Philippine Republic requires no justification. All factors considered, it has not erred on the side of liberality. The payment of war damage claims, emergency loans to the hard-pressed Republic, and the opening of the American market to Philippine products were all so essential that argument centered on means and not on policies.

An examination of the budgets of the Republic discloses that Education continues to claim a large allotment—thirty percent—of public funds. Expenditures not formerly made by the Philippine Government are those for the Department of Foreign Affairs and an expanded Department of National Defense. To meet the appropriations for national defense and maintenance of law and order requires the setting up of another forty percent of the general fund of the National Treasury.

In a democracy of the character of the Philippines, the tendency

---

[12] U. S. contribution to cost of civil government in the Philippines was negligible. Catherine Porter, *Crisis in the Philippines*, Ch. II.

has been, and presumably will be, to perpetuate a bureaucracy. This will mean large and constantly increasing expenditures for salaries and wages; in the 1950 budget, forty-three percent of the total was allocated for this purpose. To the same degree will money be lacking for public improvements. It constitutes a fiscal trend that should not be encouraged.

Under the conditions in which the Philippine Republic finds itself, it has done about as well as the remainder of the restless world in giving value received for taxes.

The Government in Business [13]

The Republic of the Philippines has pushed deeply into business. The hand of an insatiable Government reaches into everything.

The number of Government-owned or -controlled corporations is impressive. The Blue Book of the Republic and the Official Directory list twenty-four. The Chairmen of the Board of Directors of a number of these Government entities are cabinet officers. But this industrial empire became so vast that it was necessary to coordinate activities first by means of the Government Enterprises Council, and subsequently by placing most of these corporations in a Department of Economic Coordination. [14]

The above statements can be best elucidated by mention of the enterprises in which the Government is involved. It is in banking; transportation; insurance; warehousing; smelting; fisheries; real estate; the hotel business; the shipping business; the electric light business; cement production; power production; petroleum discovery and production; coal mining; textile manufacture; paper manufacture; water distribution; rice, corn, sugar, coconut, hemp, and tobacco planting and marketing; and wholesale and retail trade. It is even in gambling. Nor is this all. New and varied projects continue to claim and to receive governmental recognition. One of the latest undertakings is the purchase of three ocean-going vessels in line with the

---

[13] The article by Professor Claude A. Buss of Stanford University appearing in an early 1949 issue of *Fortune* can be noted. Teodoro M. Locsin, staff member in the *Philippines Free Press* of April 10, 1948, lists the government enterprises and discusses the subject, "The Hand of Government." The Government Enterprises Council and the National Development Company made progress reports in 1949. As of June 30, 1949, the National Development Company reported investments, stock in subsidiaries and private corporations, and current projects totaling nearly ₱40,000,000.

[14] Late in 1950 the President of the Philippines reduced the number of Government corporations from twenty-four to sixteen. At the same time the Department of Economic Coordination was abolished and the Office of Economic Administrator was created.

Government's program to expand the overseas merchant marine. Other basic industries suggested for promotion include a great shipyard, a steel mill, a fertilizer plant, and a national machinery corporation.

Looked at from another angle this represents a telling force in the economy of the Nation. The Government Enterprises Council reports aggregate assets amounting to over one billion pesos. Of the total, fifty-nine percent belongs to financing and credit firms; thirteen percent to public utilities and services; six percent to industrial development firms; and seven percent to fund raising. The National Development Company alone has a paid up capital of ₱26,410,300 and investments in excess of that amount. A tight control over this nationalized business will have to be exercised if private enterprise be not squelched.

The overall profits of the government corporations have annually exceeded the losses, and the latter are accepted in some instances as subordinate to the advancement of the public interest. A net gain of ₱13,700,000 was reported for the fiscal year 1948. The steadiest income producer has been the Cebu Portland Cement Company. The Philippine National Bank regularly reports profits. On the other hand, the Manila Railroad Company and the National Coconut Corporation, among others, lose money.

From the bureaucratic standpoint, everyone of these government-sponsored enterprises can be justified. That is obvious, for otherwise they would not have been fostered in the first place. Some of them like the Government Service Insurance System, the Metropolitan Water District, and the Land Settlement and Development Corporation are so plainly needed as to require no defense. Other enterprises are excused because of the timidity of private capital to enter competitive commercial fields.

The Republic of the Philippines, by embracing what its first President termed "guided enterprise," is in good company. The oldest English-speaking community, Great Britain, has openly and formally nationalized vital industries. Puerto Rico, with a history quite similar to that of the Philippines, has perhaps gone farther in sanctioning governmental intrusion into private enterprise than has the Philippine Republic. Even the United States, where over eighty government-conceived corporations are in existence with assets exceeding $20,000,-000,000, is no timid explorer.

Objections to the implantation of planned economy systems apply to all, and specifically to the Philippines.

Fundamentally it cannot too often be stated that the Philippine form of government was conceived as a representative Republic. There is no fit place in a government of checks and balances for a fourth power, consisting of corporations, to which authority is delegated to a staggering degree. These government corporations represent a kind of creeping state socialism. They go into business saying that they will pioneer the way for private investment, but they forget to go out of business. They build up a costly bureaucracy, in which politics intrudes to lower efficiency, and in which records are replete with instances of maladministration of public property and funds.

President Quirino in an unprecedented policy decision in 1949 invited private enterprise to take over the industrial projects of the Government. Government corporations dealing in prime commodities were excepted from the offer. Leaders of Philippine business hailed the announcement as timely and significant. It may provide the incentive to draw more Filipino capital into enterprises in which the Government has pioneered. The nail manufacturing plant was the first Government entity to pass to private ownership.

It is to be hoped that the Quirino plan will continue to meet with a favorable response from the investing public. It is likewise to be hoped that the remaining government corporations will be managed with reasonable efficiency. There is a place in the Philippine economy for governmental financing of new ventures. There is also a place for private enterprise, hard work and thrift.

INDUSTRIALIZATION[15]

The Republic of the Philippines envisions a long range, billion dollar plan calculated eventually to make it independent economically as well as politically and financially. This means breaking away from its sugar economy. This means diversification of business and intensified industrialization.

Heretofore Philippine economy has centered around sugar. No great effort was made to promote diversification to produce a well balanced trade. The products of the Islands were left mostly in the raw or unfinished state. Yet this was not an absolutely inclusive statement. The Philippines manufactured coconut oil and dessicated coconut, cigars and cigarettes, distilled spirits and fermented liquors,

---

[15] See Report of the American Agricultural Mission to the Philippines, *International Agricultural Collaboration Series*, No. 3, June 1947, pp. 26, 27. Also see Memorandum on Philippine Economic Development by Thomas Hibben, pp. 13-30, listing the possibilities for increased production of non-foodstuffs for consumption and export, attached to the Report of the Joint Philippine-American Finance Commission.

cordage, buttons, shoes, shell fixtures, and cement. Finished lumber came from the mills. Hand-made fine hats and embroideries were produced in the homes.

The critical years ahead are 1950-54. War damage payments and other American monetary aid, in most part, will have terminated. The Philippines will have to adjust itself to the progressive application of the tariffs of the United States after 1954. A plan had to be developed to attract American capital assistance and to give the fledgling Republic an outlet into new markets, both local and foreign. Industrialization, it was argued, would integrate these purposes.

At the instance of the Philippine Republic, the H. E. Beyster Corporation of Detroit organized a technical commission to survey the Philippine economy and recommend means to exploit industrial possibilities, in a broad program of rehabilitation and expansion. The commission proceeded to screen Philippine resources and potentials. After two years of labor and considerable fanfare, a long report was produced. A revised version was later made public. The Beyster Commission recommended expenditures over a fifteen to twenty year period for establishing new industries and effecting what was called an agro-industrial economy.

The Beyster Plan was damned with faint praise. Representatives of the International Bank for Reconstruction and Development, otherwise known as the World Bank, were quoted by the press as declaring that the plan was ninety percent unworkable, but that twenty-five percent of the projects might prove worthy of consideration if worked out in detail with more supporting data.

The Philippines has enjoyed "temporary but fictitious prosperity," to quote the words of the Governor of the Central Bank. Based on this premise and anticipating a depression in the critical years ahead, the Philippine Government initiated curative action. An ambitious five year economic, rehabilitation, and development program was worked out. The careful World Bank considered an application but did not advance the requested ₱30,000,000 to finance two hydro-electric projects. Other loans to make possible the realization of full-scale power development will be sought.

In justice to all concerned it should be added that implementation of the industrialization program has already resulted in practical projects. The installation of a paper mill would appear to be a worth-while venture, since abundant fibers adaptable to paper making are available in the Philippines. The establishment of a plastic industry by private interests, aided by Government exemption from the payment of internal revenue taxes, is still another instance of a new enterprise deemed essential to rehabilitation. A costly plan involving electrification, based on the development of power, and aimed at the revolutionizing of industry and the substitution of mechanization for hand labor, will have to await future decision relative to its success.

The part of the program which aimed to induce a satisfactory flow of American investment dollars into the Islands has proved disappointing. Realistically considered, that failure is not surprising. Capital seeks security and certainty, and there is altogether too much insecurity in the Far East and too much uncertainty in trade in the Philippines to suit the hardheaded investor. Likewise the agitation for nationalistic protectionism serves to frighten, rather than to attract, foreign investments. Import and currency control, while basically sound from the Filipino viewpoint, certainly did not allay fear abroad. The Philippines can expect venture capital from outside to aid in economic development in a modest degree, but would be making a costly mistake in placing overly much reliance on it.

A possible hindrance to Philippine industrialization is seen in the United States policy of allowing the revival of commercial life in Japan to help in its reconstruction.[16] Hence the reluctance of the Philippines to send Japan the raw products of the Islands, receiving in return finished products "made in Japan," thus destroying infant Philippine industries. Yet business is business. The war has not changed the laws of economics. These axioms apply today just as much as yesterday. They rest on cold facts and not on understandable sentiment. The Philippines must seek outlets in trade other than in the United States market—and there is Japan.

It will be a long and hard road for the Filipino people from the old agrarianism to the new industrialization and balanced economy. But what hated Japan could do in developing a mercantile empire, the more favored Philippines can do—or at least that is the hope.

General Auditing Office[17]

One of the oldest government institutions in the Philippines is the General Auditing Office. This office in the Republic of the Philippines is the lineal descendent of the Bureau of Audits, the head of which was the Insular Auditor of the American-administered Government of the Philippine Islands.

---

[16] Laurence K. Rosinger is a report published jointly by the Foreign Policy Association and the American Institute of Pacific Relations in 1948.

[17] See Quirino Austria, "The General Auditing Office of the Philippine Commonwealth," *Philippine Social Service Review*, April, 1935, p. 124. Auditor General Manuel Agregado furnished valuable information and an outline of the Auditor's powers and duties.

Under the American administration, the Insular Auditor was one of the most important officials in the Philippine service. In power and influence the Insular Auditor did not suffer by comparison with the Comptroller General of the United States. Under the vigorous propulsion of an independent auditor, the inclination was for the office never to shirk responsibility, but rather to meet trouble more than half way, even if by so doing the office passed beyond the uttermost limits of its legal powers.

The Constitution of the Philippines deemed the General Auditing Office of such transcendental importance that one complete article was set aside to delineate its powers and duties.[18] The office is placed under the direction and control of the Auditor General. This official is appointed by the President of the Philippines with the consent of the Commission on Appointments for a term of ten years, and may not be reappointed. His compensation cannot be diminished during his continuance in office; actually he receives an annual salary of ₱15,000. The decisions of the Auditor General may be appealed to the President, whose action shall be final; but when the aggrieved party is a private person or entity, an appeal may be taken directly to a court of record.

The powers and duties of the Auditor General are markedly similar to those of the Insular Auditor whom he succeeded. As far as could Constitutionally be done, the office was made independent and protected from interference by any of the three departments of government. The office has thus become the central agency for the checking, auditing and settlement of collections and expenditures.

A succession of sterling Americans who occupied the post of Insular Auditor transformed what could have been an innocuous examiner of accounts into an office that demanded honesty and regularity in administration. The office was most in the limelight during the incumbency of Ben F. Wright. He ruled that the use of public funds to defray the expenses of commissions of independence was illegal and was sustained. When, however, the zealous Auditor wandered over into the domains of other officials who naturally resented the intrusion, he had to be sternly set right by the Supreme Courts of the United States and the Philippines.[19]

The last Insular Auditor under the American regime was J. Weldon Jones. Drafted from the faculty of Ohio State University,

---

[18] Constitution of the Philippines, Article XI. Jose M. Aruego, *The Framing of the Philippine Constitution*, Vol. II, Ch. XXXVII, discusses this Article of the amended Constitution, as he does in *Know Your Constitution*, p. 138.

[19] Wright *v.* Ynchausti, 272 U. S. 640; Tan C. Tee & Co., *v.* Wright, 53 Phil. 172.

he gave professionally competent service in the performance of manifold duties. On the inauguration of the Philippine Commonwealth, Mr. Jones became financial adviser to the American High Commissioner, and later Acting High Commissioner, in which capacity his pleasing personality made him popular with all classes of the community. He now capably fills an important post in the Bureau of the Budget in Washington.

For several years before the disappearance of the American administration, the Bureau of Audits had been *Filipinized* except for the top position. With the emergence of the Filipino-controlled Commonwealth, it was thus logical for Deputy Insular Auditor Jaime Hernandez to become the first Auditor General. In Manila, and later as an important cog in the Government-in-Exile, he performed his functions in accordance with a fine sense of responsibility. He was later succeeded by Paciano Dizon, Comptroller of the Manila Railroad. When illness compelled the latter to retire, the appointment as Auditor General went to Manuel Agregado, an experienced official.

The position of the General Auditing Office under the abnormal conditions existing in the young Philippine Republic is extremely important. The confusion incident to war was an invitation to graft. The breakdown in individual morality and the difficulty of supervision of minor employees brought on scandals of major proportions. The prying eyes of expert accountants and the probes of trained investigators, acting under the direction of the Auditor General, have constituted the means to reenforce the dictum that a public office is a public trust. Numerous irregularities and shortages have been discovered. Investigations of abnormalities have been initiated and concluded, with beneficial results. But a beginning has only been made.

CHAPTER XVIII

TRADE[1]

PHILIPPINE COMMERCE

Philippine commerce has passed through three stages to arrive at the modern post-war phase under the Republic of the Philippines. In pre-Spanish days trade of an irregular nature was carried on with neighboring countries, among them China. The Spaniards imposed a detrimental policy of trade limitations, which was not abolished until the early part of the nineteenth century. The Americans directed the channels of commerce to the United States, and in so doing gave an impetus to the production of the basic export products of the Philippines.

In the years before the outbreak of World War II, the Philippines sold her products in the protected American market and in other foreign markets, and made purchases in these countries. The trade of the Philippines totaled as much as half a billion pesos annually. The bulk of the trade was with the United States. Generally speaking, the exports consisted of raw materials and the imports of finished products.

The Philippines during this pre-war period transacted business mostly with six countries. The relative national positions based on average trade with the Philippines in order were: the United States, Japan, Great Britain, China, Germany, and Spain. After the war, for obvious reasons, trade was not immediately resumed with Japan and Germany. The unstable nature of China's finances, and the post-war troubles of European countries, offered meager lucrative induce-

---

[1] This chapter was originally read by Cornelio Balmaceda, at the time Director of Commerce. Later as Secretary of Commerce and Industry, Mr. Balmaceda again aided with information, as did S. R. Mendinueto, Director of Commerce, and Dr. Leon Ma. Gonzales, Director of the Bureau of the Census and Statistics. Data on the subject of trade will be found in the following reports: Report of the American Agricultural Mission to the Philippines, *International Agricultural Collaboration Series*, No. 3, June, 1947; Report of the Joint Philippine-American Finance Commission, House Document No. 390, and particularly Memorandum on Philippine Economic Development by Thomas Hibben, attached to the Report; and seventh and final report of the U. S. High Commissioner to the Philippines, House Document No. 389, pp. 28-41, 116-124. The Chamber of Commerce of the Philippines has published "Philippines '49 Business Guidebook." Note Vicente Villamin, "Fifty Years of Philippine-American Trade," *Manila Daily Bulletin*, Fiftieth Anniversary Edition, 1950.

ments. The world situation made the Philippines almost wholly dependent on the American market for the sale of products and the purchase of much needed supplies. Surprisingly, in the face of opposition to the resumption of normal relations with a former enemy, the year 1949 found Japan in the Number Two position in Philippine trade. A Philippine-Japan barter agreement in the amount of ₱50,000,000 was negotiated in 1950.

Over the years the hard facts have shown an unbalanced Philippine trade. In 1934, for instance, Philippine exports to the United States were valued at more than one and a half times Philippine imports from the United States. In the same year, the Philippines bought twice as much from Japan, Germany, and China as was sold those countries. However, by 1940 a near balance between exports to the United States and imports from that country had been struck.

The total foreign trade under the Philippine Republic approximates ₱1,800,000,000 ($900,000,000) annually.[2] This represents a steady rise from VJ Day. It is three times pre-war value. The increase is accounted for by a voracious demand on the part of the Philippines for consumer and hard goods to make up for wartime scarcity, and by mounting exports headed by coconut products. Three-fourths of this trade is with the United States.

The post-war years have shown an unfavorable trade balance for the Philippines. In 1949 it amounted to over ₱600,000,000 ($300,-000,000). This is a situation fraught with peril. The constant aim must be to narrow the gap between incoming and outgoing trade.

The signposts of Philippine commerce are there for all to see. The vital importance of the foreign trade to the Philippine economy is self-evident. The Philippines is dependent upon an export market in one country, the United States. Exports must be increased or imports decreased to reach a balance assuring monetary stability.

PHILIPPINE-AMERICAN TRADE RELATIONS[3]

Behind the present trade relations of the Philippines with the United State is a background of a century and a half of commercial intercourse. American merchants were among the first to enter the Islands when the Port of Manila was opened to commerce by the Spanish Government. In 1859 it was reported that "of the foreign

[2] In 1948 the total foreign trade of the Philippines amounted to ₱1,774,819,524, of which imports totaled ₱1,136,409,068 and exports ₱638,410,456.

[3] See Cornelio Balmaceda, *Background of Philippine-American Trade* (Manila, 1934); Miguel Cuaderno, *Tariff History Traced, Evaluated* (Manila, 1949); and Pedro E. Abelarde, *American Tariff Policy Toward the Philippines* (New York, 1947).

merchants in Manila, the United States occupies the first place with more than a third of the total value of exports." However, during the last decades of Spanish rule, American commercial supremacy in the Philippines was eclipsed by the aggressiveness of British competitors.

The United States in the Treaty of Paris confirmed equality of treatment to Spanish merchandise for a period of ten years, expiring in 1909. In that year the Paine Tariff Act inaugurated reciprocal free trade, subject to minor restrictions, with the Islands. It was superseded by the Underwood Act of 1913 which established un-restricted free trade between the United States and the Philippines.

The agitation against unlimited importation of Philippine products into the United States took concrete form in the enactment of the Philippine Commonwealth and Independence Act and acceptance of the Act by the Philippines Legislature in 1934. The Act provided for a gradual transition of Philippine-American trade relations from the then existing free-trade basis to full tariff status. Quotas were set up for sugar, coconut oil and cordage. Beginning with the sixth year and continuing through the tenth year after the inauguration of the Commonwealth of the Philippines, a graduated export tax was to be levied on all products of the Islands imported into the United States. Coincident with the proclamation of Philippine independence, products of Philippine origin were to be subject to the same rate of duty levied upon like articles imported from other foreign countries.

Even while the Independence Act combining politico-economic features was in process of enactment, there came a realization to sober-minded friends of the Philippines that political freedom without economic strength to support it would be a ghastly illusion. President Roosevelt expressed the hope that "imperfections or inequalities in the law could be corrected." The Philippine Legislature in accepting the law requested an investigation of conditions in the Islands in the light of economic necessities.

First a Joint Congressional Committee, next an Inter-departmental Committee on Philippine Affairs, and finally a Joint Preparatory Committee composed of American and Filipino experts were set up to consider the problem posed by a readjustment of American-Philippine trade relations. The report of the last named Committee furnished the basis in part of the Economic Adjustment Act of August 7, 1939. Gradually declining duty-free quotas were substituted during the remaining Commonwealth period for gradually increasing export taxes upon shipments to the United States of merchandise, which the export taxes would have completely excluded from the

American market soon after their imposition in 1941. However, this amendatory legislation, while easing the strain, did not go beyond 1946 and consequently fell short of meeting the most important recommendations of the Joint Preparatory Committee.

The 1939 Congressional Act had scarcely gone into effect when the economic plight of the Philippines again claimed attention. The deteriorating world situation began more and more to be felt in the Philippines. Philippine economy was in a precarious state due to the European war, unsettled conditions in the Far East and at home, and an acute shortage of shipping. The Congress of the United States acted to suspend for one year the progressive reduction of quotas and the collection of export taxes. Final approval of this emergency legislation was delayed until shortly after Pearl Harbor when promised relief was no longer usable.

It may have been for the best that what Senator Vandenberg termed "the progressive disintegration" of the Independence Act stopped here. Hastily given economic injections were no panacea. What was indicated was a thorough checkup and long range treatment. The Philippine Trade Act of 1946 was the eventual answer.

PHILIPPINE TRADE ACT OF 1946[4]

The Philippine Trade Act of 1946, sometimes called the Bell Act in recognition of Judge C. Jasper Bell, chairman of the House Committee on Insular Affairs who sponsored the measure, was designed to put Philippine-American trade relations on a reasonably permanent basis. The law's objectives were threefold, namely, to afford the economy of the Islands time to adjust itself to the realities of economic independence geared to political independence, to effect a gradual change from reliance on the United States market to normal competitive trade, and to secure for the United States important trade advantages.

The Philippine Commonwealth and Independence Act, as amended in 1939, contemplated the calling of an American-Philippine trade conference, for the purpose of formulating recommendations as to future trade relations between the United States and the Philippines. The time element of the war never permitted the implementation of this safety valve provision.

---

[4] Genesis of the 1946 Trade Act described and an analysis of its provisions made, in seventh and final report of the U. S. High Commissioner to the Philippines, pp. 30-41. High Commissioner McNutt's able marshaling of the facts was largely responsible for favorable Congressional action on the Trade Act. Further see Pedro E. Abelarde, *American Tariff Policy Towards the Philippines*, pp. 190-200.

In an endeavor to provide a means by which to plan a post-war program, the United States Congress approved a joint resolution in 1943 which provided for a Filipino Rehabilitation Commission consisting of nine American and nine Filipino members. The Commission met in joint session a few times. The Filipino members advanced a formula based on perpetual free trade. The American members rejected this proposition as impossible of fulfillment. No progress was made. Neither could the various departments represented on the Interdepartmental Committee on Philippine Affairs reach agreement on an acceptable formula.

In the meantime the agreed date of July 4, 1946 when Philippine independence would be proclaimed drew steadily nearer. Each passing day worked to the disadvantage of the Philippines. The complex problem was how to keep a promise and how to make that promise real by making adequate provision for the restoration of the Philippine economy. It was no easy task to reconcile conflicting interests and to establish a policy fair to the Philippines and not too burdensome on the United States.

As so often happens in the drafting and enactment of statutes, in this instance divergent bills were introduced in the House and the Senate; hearings before the informed House Insular Affairs Committee and the uninformed Ways and Means Committee were held and included a convincing statement by High Commissioner McNutt; the administration exerted pressure for action; conferences were called; and finally a compromise was effected. President Osmeña went on record with a strong endorsement in principle of the broad purposes and objectives of the bill and with an appeal for the expedition of its passage. Both parties in the Congress joined in unqualified support. What came out of the legislative mill represented unremitting effort on the part of many men and their best thought, in an earnest endeavor to fulfill commitments, legal and moral, to do justice to a war tested ally and ward, and to validate unprecedented action to make Philippine independence possible.

The Trade Act and the Executive Trade Agreement, subsequently executed by the President of the United States and the President of the Philippines, prescribed the respective obligations of the parties. Economic relations between the two countries were determined for a period of twenty-eight years after Philippine independence, that is until July 3, 1974. Free trade on a reciprocal basis would be in effect for eight years. It was the feeling that the Philippines needed this allotted time to put its war-shattered house in order.

Beginning at the expiration of the calendar year 1955, during the succeeding years, a graduated duty starting at ten percent and increasing annually by five percent will be imposed on dutiable Philippine products entering the United States and on American products entering the Philippines, with the exception of coconut oil, cigars, tobacco and pearl or shell buttons. Quotas for these four articles imported into the United States were fixed, but beginning in 1955 will be reduced annually; the amount of the quotas will be duty-free. Absolute quotas were provided for sugar, cordage and rice for the entire twenty-eight year period. These commodities will be subject to the increasing five percent annual tariff duties after 1954. The quotas fixed in the Trade Act did not vary substantially from those provided in previous legislation.

Certain of the obligations assumed by the Republic of the Philippines, in order to benefit from what amounted to an American subsidy of Philippine trade, were not difficult of fulfillment. The commercial life of the Islands needed American business and technical men; a promise to admit into the Philippines 1,200 non-quota Americans of this class annually to 1951 fitted into the purposes of the Trade Act. The Philippine peso had been pegged to the American dollar for years; it would benefit the Islands to have an assurance of a stable currency.

On the other hand, an obligation to guarantee non-discriminatory taxation against Americans was getting close to the tender ground of Philippine nationalism. The necessity of amending the Philippine Constitution to provide equal rights for American citizens in the development of natural resources and the ownership and operation of public utilities provided a forum for violent attacks. A sobering sense of what defeat of the Constitutional amendment would mean to the economic life of the young Republic—for with defeat the Trade Act would go, with no assurance that approval of any better substitute could be hoped for—resulted in overwhelming approval of the amendment.

The real test of the soundness of the Trade Act and of Filipino economic capacity will come in 1954 when adjustments to meet the gradual loss of the favored position in the American market must be made.

A Trade Critique

A distinguished list of critics have spoken disparagingly of the nature of American-Philippine trade relations.

The incompatibility of reciprocal free trade between the United States and the Philippines established in 1909, and amplified four years later, and a definite promise by the United States of ultimate independence for the Philippines made in 1916, has been frequently stressed. High Commissioner McNutt condensed this line of thought with the pungent observation: "On one hand, we [the Americans] sought to sever the ties, on the other we chained them [the Filipinos] ever closer to us."[5] It remained for the Filipino economist, Dr. Pedro B. Abelarde to give a different slant to the matter. Wrote Dr. Abelarde: "In dealing with the Insular Tariff, Congress acted in the main, in the interest of American producers while the American officials in the Philippines were insistent throughout on the interest of the Islands."[6]

Free trade with the United States was not sought originally by the Filipinos. Instead, the Philippine Assembly passed a resolution deploring free trade, and this sentiment was echoed in Washington by Resident Commissioner Ocampo. It is probably the only instance in history of prosperity being forced on to a dependent people against their will.

The crass materialism displayed by the economic provisions of the Philippine Commonwealth and Independence Act, which had in view first limitation and second extinction of free trade, is difficult to defend. Yet the Filipino leaders were in no position to complain. They had stepped down from their former high moral stand against free trade to barter economic advantage for lobbyist help. They were content to take a chance on political emancipation without an assurance of economic aid to make their liberty secure.

The last phase in American-Philippine economic history directs attention to the Philippine Trade Act of 1946 and its mandatory provision guaranteeing parity rights for American citizens in the Philippines. Faulty Congressional phrasing, which made use of the word "exploitation" with unfortunate connotations, can be excused as inadvertent usage. More difficult to argue away was insistence on a policy which savored of discrimination, which forced an amendment of the Philippine Constitution, and which provided a focal point for political demagoguery, heated nationalist feeling, and even anti-Americanism.

Here again the Filipino leaders could not very well register an official complaint. President Osmeña was estopped to attack a law which he had endorsed. President Roxas, while free to condemn a

---

[5] Statement of High Commissioner McNutt made on July 7, 1939. Mr. McNutt dwelt on the same idea in an address at a World Week luncheon in New York City on May 4, 1947. To the same effect were the observations of former Governor General Theodore Roosevelt in *Colonial Policies of the United States*, pp. 152, 153.

[6] Pedro E. Abelarde, *American Tariff Policy Towards the Philippines*, p. 202.

law to which he had not been a party, nevertheless needed American help if his administration was to succeed. With the vision of the states-man, he espoused what could have been an unpopular cause, and threw the weight of his influence behind the forces working for the ratifica-tion of the Constitutional amendment.

The tempest thus started has not subsided. The Government of the Philippine Republic has gone as far as it dared to attain financial and economic independence without actually breaching the trade compact. A proposal to reserve thirty to fifty percent of the total import quota for any article in favor of new Filipino importers re-ceived Congressional approval. The Chamber of Commerce of the Philippines is formally on record as favoring the amendment of the Philippine Trade Act of 1946 to permit of selective free trade between the Philippines and the United States. Ever so often individual Filipinos summarize alleged discriminatory provisions in the Trade Act and ask for their repeal. Agitation of this sort to obtain modifica-tion of the trade agreement can be expected to continue.

It is not proposed to present a brief in support of the measures which have defined American-Philippine trade relations. Yet it is only fair to observe that at the time each of these Acts was adopted, it can be assumed that its authors had in view the best interests of the two countries. That they succeeded in the approximate attainment of their objectives cannot be doubted. Of all the countries in the world, only two, Cuba and the Philippines, had received grants of preferential con-cessions from the United States.

Free trade with the United States has been the most potent factor in the commercial development of the Islands. It had the effect of encouraging the growth of Philippine exports to the United States and of American exports to the Philippines. On the free market in the United States the Filipinos built their prosperiy. As reciprocity worked out, it was not exactly reciprocity, for it was the Philippines which made more money out of the United States than the United States made out of the Philippines. Governor General Forbes, the businessman called to public service, has written: "No one can study the economic growth of the Islands . . . without reaching the conclu-sion that the advantages from the trade relations accruing to the Philip-pine people have exceeded those accruing to the people of the United States."[7]

The Philippines benefitted. American official systematically en-couraged economic development. American businessmen made avail-

---

[7] W. Cameron Forbes, *The Philippine Islands,* revised edition of 1945, p. 70.

able adventure capital to make development real. True, the exports of the Islands were sold mainly in the United States. But has anyone risen to point out where any other comparable market was available or what capital other than American in appreciable amounts could have been lured to the Philippines? Without this economic program there would have been no rise in the standard of living, and there would have been less money available for schools, hospitals and roads. It is doubtful that without assurance of such a stable economic base political independence could have been effectuated.

The United States was also a gainer. Why deny it, as some would appear to wish to do? What was wrong in the United States looking after her own interests while extending a helping hand to the Philippines? Between the conclusion of the Spanish-American War in 1899 and the beginning of World War II in 1941, the United States sold to the Philippines goods valued at two billion dollars. The share of the United States in the Philippine trade rose from ten to twenty-five percent in the initial period, to seventy-five percent in the Commonwealth 1935-40 era, to an even higher percentage in 1946-50 under the Republic of the Philippines.

The Philippines needs American trade. The United States needs Philippine trade. On that factual principle can be based mutually beneficial commercial relations between the two countries.

EXPORTS[8]

The economic life of the Philippines stems from the production and exportation of agricultural commodities. As a corollary to this statement, account should be taken of the sale of lumber and of the increasing shipments of Philippine minerals. The output of the manufacturing establishments and of the fisheries is hardly sufficient to satisfy local requirements.

The order of importance of the different Philippine exports has varied with changing conditions. Hemp, once first, has had to take a back seat. Sugar went ahead to become the predominant product. In 1941 gold moved forward to challenge sugar for the premier place, and in conjunction with other minerals may be expected again to race agricultural rivals for honors. The post-war years saw coconut products take over the lead.

---

[8] See Memorandum on Philippine Economic Development by Thomas Hibben, attached to the Report of the Joint Philippine-American Finance Commission, and S. R. Mendinueto, Director of Commerce, "Philippine Export Trade," a speech delivered before the Convention of Filipino Businessmen on July 7, 1946. Facts were gathered from reports of the Bureau of Census and Statistics.

Philippine exports before the war were sufficient to offset imports and leave a favorable balance of trade. Immediately after the war the trend was the other way. As industries revived, the export of coconut products boomed, with sugar, hemp, tobacco, mining, and lumbering recovering more slowly. It is the expectation that the gap between the money going out of the Philippines in payment for foreign goods and the money coming in as payment for Philippine products will be finally bridged.

The overseas export trade of the Philippines has been directed toward the American market. Before the war eighty percent of the annual exports of the Islands were shipped to the United States; in the case of sugar ninety-nine and nine-tenths percent showed even more exclusive dependence on the American market. After the war the export advantage in favor of the United States was maintained. The tremendous volume of business with the United States was accounted for by free trade between the two countries and the ability of American manufacturers to produce goods for sale in the Philippines.

The year 1948 registered the biggest export trade in the history of the Philippines. Exports advanced to over ₱600,000,000 ($300,-000,000), which was ₱100,000,000 ($50,000,000) more than the previous year. Post-war exports were more than double the highest record reached in any pre-war year. Nevertheless the Philippines fell far short of filling the United States quotas of their seven principal exports. And exports still had to make a considerable climb to balance imports.

The volume of Philippine exports is relatively satisfactory. Yet that conclusion does not signify that efforts should not be made to increase the production of export items. The slack in the tapering off of United States payments has to be eased. The people will literally have to earn the higher standard of living to which they have become accustomed.

The weakness of the Philippines' export position is the great reliance placed on access to the American market. But what European and Oriental trade has developed has resulted in a favorable trade balance for the Philippines. It would appear to be a sensible policy to continue to take full advantage of sales to the United States, but to combine therewith the development of markets in other lands and the satisfaction of domestic needs by domestic-fomented industries.

IMPORTS

During the course of lengthy debates on the floor of the Congress of the United States on the Philippine question, in which arguments were marshalled for and against the imposition of restrictions on imports to the United States, one plain fact was entirely lost to view: The Philippines had ranked as high as the fifth best customer of the United States. A long list of items manufactured in the United States had found their first or second largest export market in the Philippines.

It is true that there was not a reciprocally-balanced trade between the two countries. Yet the statistics showed that the Philippines obtained over sixty percent of its total annual imports from the United States. In 1940 the proportional American share had risen to eighty percent. (In that pre-war year Philippine purchases in the United States amounted to $210,630,854 out of total foreign imports of $269,462,542.) The volume of Philippine commerce had been an important inducement to American shipping to engage in the Far Eastern trade.

An analysis of the principal Philippine imports from the United States before the outbreak of World War II discloses some intriguing facts. Food and food products constituted a major item, and included were dairy products by the interests which objected to unrestricted entry of Philippine-produced coconut oil. Flour and vegetables, also proceeding from the objecting American farmers, were other products in this classification. Cotton manufacturers entered the Philippines in large quantities, with low priced Japanese merchandise eventually underselling American articles. Manufactures of iron and steel were imported from the United States in appreciable amounts. The Philippines leads all countries in the Far East in the number of automobiles *per capita* of population, and these cars came from the United States.

The coming of peace to the Philippines following the horrible war interlude mirrored emergency conditions. The insatiable demand was for food and textiles. The result was an avalanche of imports more than twice as high in value as in any pre-war year. In 1946 Philippine imports amounted to about ₱600,000,000 ($300,000,000). Except for unavailability of goods and shipping bottlenecks, the volume of imports would have been even greater. In 1948 and 1949 they reached and passed the one billion peso mark.

With a return to normal conditions, wartime deficiencies of consumer goods have been pretty well satisfied. The domestic production of goods and textiles had helped ease the strain. Durable and capital goods, imported to assist in rehabilitation were more and more in demand. Automobiles, trucks and machinery were becoming available and were being sold on debarkation.

An Import Control Law [9] was enacted by the Congress of the Philippines in 1948, and again in 1950. The President by executive order tightened import percentages and the Central Bank clamped on credit and exchange control. The purposes in view were to decrease expenditures for luxury and non-essential imports, to save the available supply of dollar exchange for the purchase of essential equipment and materials for the reconstruction and development of the national economy, and to promote local production and the use of local products. Resulting savings in foreign exchange for one year were estimated at ₱150,000,000. But the Government stood to lose heavily in taxation revenues, the prices of essential commodities began to skyrocket, and the Import Control Office became the headache of frustrated businessmen.

THE TARIFF

The formulation of a Philippine tariff policy up to 1946 had never been a domestic responsibility. The Jones Law and the Philippine Commonwealth and Independence Act merely authorized the Philippine Legislature to enact laws affecting imports and exports with reference to countries other than the United States, with the approval of the President of the United States. Advantage was not often taken of this restricted authority. Philippine economy throughout the years remained geared to a policy formulated way back in 1909 in Washington.

It is high time for the Republic of the Philippines to have a tariff of its own, within the limitation of commitments under the provisions of the Philippine Trade Act of 1946. Tariff schedules which have not been revised since they were set up two-score years ago should be examined and made responsive to present-day needs.

In the past, Philippine tariff laws were intended primarily to raise revenue. Indeed, this purpose was baldly so stated in the title of the Act of Congress of 1909. In the future, the trend will be toward protection of home industries.

The Philippine Trade Act prohibits the collection of an internal tax on articles which are the products of the United States coming into the Philippines, or on articles manufactured wholly or in part from such articles, in an amount in excess of that paid on like articles which are the product of the Philippines or of any foreign country.

---

[9] The original Import Control Law, Republic Act No. 330, was superseded by Republic Act No. 426 of May 19, 1950. An article in the *London Times* of March 11, 1950 accurately reviewed the "Crisis in the Philippines."

No tax may be imposed on American products if none is levied on like Philippine articles. With these provisions in the forefront, it is the contention of Filipino businessmen that it is impossible to industrialize the Philippines within the framework of the Trade Act. The claim is made that the Philippines lacks freedom to protect new industries against powerful American competition.

The problem boils down to not losing the privileged position for Philippine agricultural exports in the American market, while at the same time protecting infant manufacturing in the Philippines against foreign competition. Prices which will not be beyond the purchasing power of the people constitute another factor to be taken into consideration.

DOMESTIC TRADE

So much emphasis has been laid on trade with foreign countries that little attention has been paid to trade within the Philippines. The Filipino may export his sugar, coconut oil, hemp, and tobacco to other lands and import alien commodities, yet the fact remains that right at home he sells, barters and buys to the extent of financial capacity. Rice and corn, for example, are grown, sold and bought in the Islands. So likewise are most of the fish, vegetables, and fruits that are consumed. Pottery products find their way into many homes. In the matter of dress, shoes and slippers, textiles and cloth from native materials, and hats both for the elite and laborers are manufactured locally.

The volume of domestic trade is sizable. Yet the fact is that the country must depend on its foreign trade in order to survive.

The lamentable truth is also that not much more than half of the domestic trade is in the hands of the Filipinos. Yet even this proportion is an improvement on the fifteen percent at the time of the inauguration of the Commonwealth and the thirty-seven percent reported for 1939. In this connection it is believed that while figures may not lie, they may also not speak the whole truth. The Chinese at one time controlled eighty percent of the retail trade. The indefatigable Chinese do not give up a profitable market except under great pressure. The Japanese who in a brief period of time raised their participation in Philippine business to twenty-five percent have been driven out of the Philippines; not so the Chinese who seem to thrive alike in prosperity and adversity.

The Government of the Republic, with the cooperation of the Philippine Chamber of Commerce, is showing a determination to increase Filipino self-sufficiency in the domestic trade. A Philippine protectionist policy is advocated. The development of local manufacturing, for instance of cigarettes, to minimize tremendous importations of American cigarettes is being underscored by the Government. NEPA is revived to promote patronage of home industries and business enterprises. A measure to limit the issuance of licenses for retail trade to aliens is favored.

This nationalist policy is readily understandable. Fulfillment is not so easy. In the first place the peculiar distrust of the people for homegrown and manufactured articles, as inferior to foreign importations, has to be eradicated and overcome. In the second place the displacement of American entrepreneurs runs counter to the spirit of a trade agreement Constitutionally confirmed, and of Chinese retailers, into international complications. Nevertheless native industries are being fostered. Preachments to "buy Philippine" are heeded and are getting results.

TRANSPORTATION [10]

The statement has often been made that the Philippines was the most completely dislocated battleground of World War II. The nearly one hundred percent damage done to most modes of transportation in the Islands established the truth of the allegation beyond question.

The High Commissioner to the Philippines in his final report portrayed a dismal picture of destruction. Bridges, piers and roads were in shambles; mile after mile of concrete highways had been taken up for use on Japanese airports. Interisland shipping was nonexistent; practically all vessels engaged in this trade were lost. The railroads were unusable; rolling stock had been carried away to Japan.

Viewed in the light of economic facts, the progressive betterment of the transportation situation in the Philippines approached the miraculous. The United States Armed Forces had a vital stake in the maintenance of communications and made available emergency help. So likewise did the United States Maritime Commission and other Federal agencies. The contribution of United States funds to the road and bridge rehabilitation program amounted to ₱76,000,000. The Bureau of Public Works of the Philippine Republic added another ₱24,000,000, cooperated in the preparation of plans, and furnished technical assistance.

---

[10] There can be noted seventh and final Report of the U. S. High Commissioner, pp. 19-23, 122-124; Memorandum by Thomas Hibben on Philippine Economic Development, pp. 46-49, attached to Report of the Joint Philippine-American Finance Commission, and W. Cameron Forbes, *The Philippine Islands*, revised edition of 1945, Ch. VIII.

With these introductory matters elucidated, we are in a position to take a long view of transportation in the Philippines.

The construction of good roads was one of the major accomplishments of the American administration of the Philippines. The antiquated Spanish road system boasted less than 1,000 kilometers of right of way, and this was available for travel only during the dry season and then but to a limited extent. Year by year old roads were improved and new roads were added by the Bureau of Public Works. Under the Philippine Commonwealth there were approximately 25,000 kilometers of roads, of which one-half were first class. The roads and bridges estimated to have been seventy-eight percent damaged by the war have been rehabilitated. In excess of 1,000 kilometers of new roads have been added to the highway system.[11]

Philippine highways have been put to good use by all manner of vehicles. Registration of passenger cars was reduced over one-half by the war, but post-war importations rapidly filled the void. Various classes of utilities operate under the watchful eyes of the Public Service Commission. Some of these bus and truck lines are well established and equipped, while others are fly-by-night affairs which operate converted jeeps and command cars acquired from surplus army equipment. Manila alone is said to have over a hundred operators of taxicabs, while thousands of jitney busses cruise the streets with reckless abandon.

Philippine shipping has likewise experienced its ups and downs. In bygone days travel on an interisland vessel was a trying ordeal. To make the trip bearable the passenger had to arrange to sleep on deck on a cot, and copious draughts of red wine were needed to wash down the unpalatable food. Then came increase in tonnage and improvement in accommodations. Vessels operating under the Philippine flag even engaged in foreign trade.

War damage to water transportation in the Philippines was extensive. Some of the shortage was relieved by the transfer to the Philippines of about fifty ships under the Surplus Property Agreement. While totality in number of ships needed for the interisland trade has been approached, operation of these ships is not always conducive to comfortable travel. Complaints of dangerous passenger overloading and violations of accepted rules of maritime safety are frequently aired.

The history of the Manila Railroad Company reflects much the same experience as the Philippine road system and Philippine shipping.

---

[11] Data furnished by Isaias Fernando, Director of Public Works, on February 9, 1949, including a brief comment on pre-war and post-war public works.

Originally the Manila Railroad was British-owned and managed under a franchise granted by the Spanish Crown in 1887. In the old days a ride from Manila to Dagupan on the Railroad was an experience, and not always a happy one, which lingered long in the memory. Conditions later changed for the better. Particularly was this true after 1917 when the Philippine Government acquired ownership of the Railroad.

The lines of the Manila Railroad Company are entirely on the Island of Luzon. The main north line of the Railroad extends from Manila to San Fernando in La Union Province and the main south line from Manila to Legaspi in Albay Province. The laterals of the Railroad serve other regions.

Following the conclusion of the war, the Manila Railroad gradually acquired badly needed rolling stock. But all too much of its equipment is outmoded and dilapidated. Its ills are many. Its plight is sad. Under the circumstances the Railroad is operating as well as can reasonably be expected.

The Philippine Railway Company has operated lines on the Islands of Panay and Cebu. The Panay division was not seriously damaged, but the Cebu division was, during the war. The result has been that the former has continued operation, while the latter has made no attempt to do so.

Both railroad firms operate in the red.[12] The Philippine Railway has long been in financial difficulties; it now functions under receivers for the benefit of its bond-holders. The Manila Railroad also reports losses; ways and means to redeem bonds held in Great Britain which with operating loans have an aggregate face value of over ₱50,000,000 must be found. There is hope for the Manila Railroad if a realistic rehabilitation program is authorized.

A fourth method of transportation which could well afford to begin from scratch after the war was aviation. Commercial aviation had come to the Philippines before the war. Practically coincidentally with the inauguration of the Philippine Commonwealth in 1935, the China Clipper of the Pan American Airways had landed in Manila, and in so doing had initiated world wide service. But this and inter-island air service in reality merely marked entrance to the field. In contrast, shortly after the proclamation of the Philippine Republic in 1946, the Philippines was served by a number of airlines of domestic and foreign registry. The Philippine Air Lines, a domestic corporation, maintains modern local and foreign service.

---

[12] Manuel Vijungco, "Our Perennial White Elephant," *Manila Times*, December 8, 1948.

The Republic of the Philippines deemed aëronautics so important—and properly so—that a special bureau was established to supervise aviation in all its phases. The International Airport near Manila is the equal of any abroad. Compacts to attain equality of treatment and opportunity in flights have been entered into by the Philippines with the United States and other countries. The object is to make the Philippines the hub of transocean air travel between the Occident and the Orient.

Today the Philippine public has become air-minded. Air freight is also increasing. The result is that Philippine aviation is the prodigy of Philippine business.[13]

And so it has come about that the Philippines clings to the old while utilizing the new. The picturesque vintas of the Moros continue to sail the equatorial seas. The bull carts and carabao sleds of Filipino farmers plod slowly along the country roads. But by the vintas now pass fast and large water craft. By the bull carts and carabao sleds go the swift automobiles and passenger busses. Overhead fly modern passenger planes.

In the Philippines, whether by Moro vinta, carabao sled, motor bus, train, steamer, or plane, adequate transportation facilities are available. To the Philippines come the ships and airlines of the world bringing passengers and freight. From the Philippine docks and airfields pour forth outgoing travellers and the products of the land. The outlook for Philippine transportation of all vintages and kinds is favorable.

COMMUNICATIONS[14]

All of the transportation agencies—the roads, the ships, the trains, the planes, and the public utilities—are important factors in providing communications for the Philippines. In addition there are the cable, telegraph and telephone lines, and the radio broadcasting systems. All were heavily damaged during the war.

The Philippine Government takes a deep interest in the maintenance of the communication systems. The Bureau of Telecommunications operates a public telegraph and radio service.[15] The Department of Commerce and Industry supervises the privately owned radio stations of which there are a number. The National Government and some provinces operate telephone systems.

[13] "P. I. Aviation Progress Phenomenal," *Evening News*, December 11, 1948.

[14] Note Memorandum of Thomas Hibben on Philippine Economic Development, pp. 60-63, attached to the Report of the Joint Philippine-American Finance Commission. Mr. Hibben's Memorandum condenses a vast amount of pertinent material.

[15] Letter of F. Cuaderno, Director of Telecommunications, of November 27, 1948.

Notwithstanding the government's incursion into the communication field, private enterprise continues to be a major factor therein. The Philippine Long Distance Telephone Company provides long distance, radiophone, and teletype service to the important towns of the Islands and direct radiophone service with foreign cities and with ships at sea. The expansion of radio communication facilities for local and international service has been marked. A number of modern broadcasting stations are in operation.

Because of the high cost of replacement of the installations and the short supply, reconstruction of the telegraph, telephone and radio systems has proceeded slowly. An annoyance has been the looting of equipment. With normal operations realized, the further problems of expansion of communication facilities will claim attention.

CHAPTER XIX

ECONOMIC RESOURCES [1]

THE NATION'S WEALTH [2]

The total wealth of the Philippines is hard to estimate, and when estimated reaches such astronomical figures as to be beyond the comprehension of the common man. Possibly it would not be too far-fetched to say that ₱4,000,000,000 ($2,000,000,000) represents the valuation of the developed real estate; ₱2,000,000,000 ($1,000,000,000), the economic value of the public lands not taxed and not developed; ₱10,000,000,000 ($5,000,000,000), the "stumpage" value of the forests (the market value is ₱60,000,000,000); ₱2,000,000,000 ($1,000,000,000), the mines; ₱2,000,000,000 ($1,000,000,000), the manufacturing establishments, the fisheries, and the margin of economic intangibles and good will, in which are included an equable tropical climate, a strategic shipping position, and an adequate labor supply. An addition of these rough figures brings a grand total of

---

[1] The Report of the American Agricultural Mission to the Philippines, headed by Dr. Leland E. Call, Dean, College of Agriculture, Kansas State College, and assisted by Filipino associates, headed by Under Secretary Jose S. Camus, made in 1946, contains a factual survey of the conditions of agriculture in the Philippines. *International Agricultural Collaboration Series* No. 3, Washington, D. C., June, 1947. Of similar import is the technical Memorandum on Philippine Economic Development prepared by Thomas Hibben of the United States Department of Commerce for the Joint Philippine-American Commission, and attached to the report. Free use of the wealth of information brought together in these documents was made in the preparation of Chapter XIX. Catherine Porter, *Crisis in the Philippines,* contains a factual analysis of economic conditions in the Philippines as existing before the outbreak of World War II. Also see *Economic Problems of the Philippines,* by the Philippine Economic Association, Hon. Elpidio Quirino, President (1934).

[2] Hon. Paul V. McNutt, while Ambassador to the Republic of the Philippines, estimated the total "assessed value of the Philippines" before the war at ₱5,000,000,000. The '49 Philippines Business Guidebook, p. 187, gives the value of real property in 1948 as ₱3,500,000,000. Regarding a published statement that the market value of the timber in the commercial forests is ₱80,000,000,000, Director of Forestry Florencio Temesis writes: "The volume of standing timber in the Philippines is estimated at 1,096,083,672 cubic meters (approximately 464,739,476,900 board feet). The corresponding government forest charges on this timber, based on current rates, amounts to about ₱2,341,550,000 and the commercial value is approximately ₱58,092,434,000. Before the war the estimated *stumpage* value was 8 billion pesos, and as stumpage is generally figured as 10% of the market value, that is why possibly the market value is shown to be 80 billion pesos."

₱20,000,000,000 ($10,000,000,000). The latent resources of the Philippines are possibly ten times as great. On the minus side, it must be recorded that World War II destroyed much of the accumulated wealth of the Islands, which, however, is slowly being replaced.

This is an approximation of the wealth of the Philippines, but not necessarily of the Filipinos. The Filipinos have proved themselves poor traders. They produce; others distribute. They work; others gain. Hardly two percent of the population are foreigners, and yet this small percent handles eighty percent of the foreign trade and pays a large proportion of the taxes collected by the government. Of course, like all rules, there are exceptions to it. Toribio Teodoro, for instance, starting in the shoe business on a shoe-string capital of ₱200 in 1910, saw his modest shop grow to a ₱2,000,000 establishment in 1950. The names of other Filipino industrial magnates come to mind, but their number is not large.

The main sources of Philippine wealth are, in order of relative importance, agriculture, forestry, mining, fisheries, and manufacturing. The first three, namely, agriculture, forestry, and mining and the industries and products they represent can be said to be going concerns. Off-shore fishing, if properly exploited, can be as profitably carried on as it was before the war, when it was practically a Japanese monopoly. Industrialization described in previous pages under Finance is in the blueprint, government-fostered stage.

Actually, then the Philippines boasts considerable wealth. Potentially the Islands possess vast natural resources awaiting development. The problem is to transmute wealth into realistic cash.

AGRICULTURE [3]

The Philippines is essentially an agricultural country. Even with the emphasis being placed on lumbering, mining and manufacturing, the chief prop of Philippine prosperity will continue to be the products of a fertile soil.

The war disrupted the agricultural economy through enforced neglect of crops and loss of work animals. Even thus handicapped, the opportunities for the expansion of a basic industry are practically limitless. Of 14,000,000 hectares of potential farm land, only about one-half is under cultivation. Sparsely populated and naturally rich Mindanao beckons to land-grubbing pioneers.

---

[3] See Report of the American Agricultural Mission to the Philippines, pp. 10 et. seq.; F. G. Galang, "The Bureau of Plant Industry," and Lands Administrative Order No. 1.

Approximately half of the farms are owner-operated. The prevailing form of tenancy is *kasama* or share tenancy. The historic division in the rice-growing areas was one-third for human labor, one-third for animal labor, and one-third for the owner of the land. After the inauguration of the Philippine Republic, the Congress thereof provided for a seventy percent for the tenant, thirty percent for the owner, division, with the tenant furnishing the labor and the planting materials. But no law, no matter how lofty the purpose, can alter human nature. The cropper problem remains.

The Bureau of Plant Industry is geared towards the ultimate development of Philippine agricultural resources. Its activities are grouped into research, extension, and regulatory work, and the propagation and distribution of improved seeds and plant materials. Model farms and experiment stations are maintained.

The Bureau of Lands is charged with the duty of administering the public lands. A number of areas have been set aside for national parks. Other portions of the public domain have been thrown open for homesteading or lease. Experience has demonstrated that where unoccupied lands are surveyed and roads are opened, settlers soon follow. The National Land Settlement Administration has been established to afford supervision and to furnish services to homesteaders.

The most important agricultural products are rice, corn, *abaca* (hemp), sugar, copra, and tobacco. Conditions are also favorable for the growing of coffee, cacao and cotton. At one time considerable quantities of coffee were produced locally. Philippine-grown cacao has a fine flavor. Filipino farmers have not taken to the raising of cotton with any degree of enthusiasm, possibly because of too close association of the plant with Japanese propaganda. The catch of fish in salt water and inland ponds, generally and even judicially considered an agricultural product, helps to supply an adequate diet.

Rubber is only grown in driblets, although conditions are ideal for its production. American experts have reported that the climate of the Philippines is as favorable for rubber planting as that of Sumatra and the Malay Peninsula. It has been estimated that 5,000,000 hectares of land in the Philippine group are suitable for rubber culture. But we do not have to rely on theory. The experience of Dr. J. W. Strong and of a rubber company on the Island of Basilan, lying just off Zamboanga, has proved that rubber can be produced profitably.

The principal agricultural products, on which the maintenance of a balanced trade and economic stability depends, will be described briefly in succeeding paragraphs.

Rice—The Ifugao Rice Terraces

It remains for some gifted author to tell the story of rice in the Philippines. Properly narrated the work would depict the life of the Filipino people. Provided with an abundant rice crop, there is more money, more diversion, and more contentment in the land. With inadequate production of this staple food, there is woe, misery and discontent.

Rice, however, is not the sole basic food of the people. Enough corn can be grown for those who rely on it for subsistence. Camotes (a type of sweet potato) are also produced in certain regions. But the fact remains that the price of these, and other prime commodities, as well as the scale of wages, are geared closely to the price of rice.

Rice occupies the attention of the farmer and laborer more than any other one thing. Rice planting in the lowlands is an occasion for song, for love, and for neighborliness. To grow rice in the highlands, the Ifugaos have built the stupendous rice terraces which hang like gardens in the sky.

Palay, the unhusked rice, is grown all over the Islands more or less extensively. The five provinces comprising the greater portion of the central plain of Luzon and the plains of Cotobato of Mindanao are the regions most favorably adapted to rice growing on a large scale. In excess of 2,000,000 hectares of land are regularly planted to rice.

The normal production of rice is 55,000,000 *cavans* annually. Even this is not enough to meet the demands of an increasing population. Since liberation the situation has been aggravated by a lack of work animals and implements, destruction of irrigation systems, and lawlessness. The Philippine administration has been forced to buy rice in the world market wherever found available. To reduce the gap between production and consumption, the government has intensified mechanized growing of rice.

The planting season of rice is celebrated in the Philippines as corn husking is in the United States. Rice planting usually begins in the early part of June and ends in the latter part of August. Often it is made a community affair. The farmer supplies the eatables and his friends supply the man- and woman-power, for men and women work side by side in the fields. To the accompaniment of guitars and harmonicas and with song and laughter, the seedlings are made ready, the land is harrowed, and the rows of *palay* are planted. It is a golden opportunity for love-making, and needless to say youthful swains and their adored make the most of it.

On the precipitous slopes of the mountainous country of Northern Luzon between Bontoc and Kiangan with Banaue as the center, the Ifugaos have built a wonderful series of irrigated rice terraces that are among the great engineering works of the world.[4] The terraced rice culture found in Japan, Southeast Asia, and the mountains of Java sinks into insignificance in comparison. The rice terraces of the Ifugaos are the most extensive to be found anywhere in the world, rival the gigantic feats of engineering of the Incas of South America, and are as marvelous as the pyramids of Egypt. Reflect on these facts: the Ifugao terraces are chiseled in the steep mountainsides; the terraces are watered by ditches heading in the rivers miles above; the terraces are sometimes fifty feet in height; the terraces cover one hundred square miles; twelve thousand miles of stone support them; the walls are held in place without cementing material of any kind. So cunningly and securely have the retaining walls been made that despite the lack of binding material, they have withstood the shocks of earthquake and flood for two thousand years.

One evening during Easter week, the author stood on the veranda of the Rest House at Banaue and from that vantage gazed upon miles upon miles of rice terraces. A full moon accommodatingly lent its rays to bring out the splendor of the scene. Lights gleamed here and there in the grass-thatched homes of the residents. In the distance the drums beat for a *canao* in preparation. To mind came those other wonders of the Orient—the Great Wall of China, the gigantic bronze statue of Daibutsu of Japan, the Angkor Wat of Cambodia, the Taj Mahal of India, and the temple of Borobudur of Java—all stupendous and soul-stirring. Not one surpasses the rice terraces of the Ifugaos in the Philippines.

The next morning as the sun brought out more sharply the green of the growing rice and the immensity of man's handiwork, one reflected on these questions: Are the astounding irrigation systems of the Ifugaos an invention of their own? Their crude civilization would seemingly answer no. If not, what people introduced rice terraces worthy to be called the eighth wonder of the world?

The goal set by the Republic of the Philippines is to reach self-sufficiency in rice production with a comfortable margin to spare. There is no reason why, with a return to settled conditions, the Philippines cannot supply the local market and even have a surplus.

---

[4] A number of authors have painted word pictures of the Ifugao Rice Terraces. See Samuel E. Kane, *Life and Death in Luzon.* Governor Kane, having lived for years in close proximity to the Terraces, could best appreciate their grandeur and utility.

Manila Hemp[5]

Abaca of Philippine growth has long been known to commerce as "Manila Hemp." This was the magic name which first beckoned American ships to Manila. In those days the Manila Hemp industry was a virtual Philippine world monopoly. More recently keen competition, the absolute quantitative limitation of Philippine cordage exports to the United States, destruction brought about by the war and the ensuing neglect have brought about a confused situation.

Abaca is of indigenous origin. The Spaniards found the Filipinos cultivating the plant for use in spinning and weaving. The fiber is the product of the plant which to the uninitiated is indistinguishable from the banana plant. Various regions, as the Bicol provinces of Southern Luzon, the islands of Leyte and Samar, and portions of the island of Mindanao, are especially adapted to the growth of *abaca*. Davao, a province of Mindanao, where American and Japanese planters introduced scientific methods of production, became the leader in total output and in average yield per hectare. Before the war, close to 500,000 hectares in the Philippines were planted to *abaca* with an annual yield valued at ₱20,000,000.

The revival of the *abaca* industry at war's end was complicated by the fact that in Davao a large part of the production and processing had been in the hands of the Japanese. With dispossession of these enemies from their lands, some fields became overgrown and damaged and other fields were overstripped, while in some areas the plants were destroyed in order to grow food crops. The Davao plantations as such no longer existed. The distribution of the land to guerrillas untrained in *abaca* farming did not offer much encouragement for replanting in the Davao region.

Stabilization of the *abaca* situation on the pre-war basis has proved difficult of accomplishment. Overcutting, typhoons, and high Manila prices for other products were adverse factors. Under these conditions additional planting of fiber-producing areas was not an attractive investment. The output was far below normal.

The above problem has naturally claimed governmental attention. The Bureau of Lands and the former National Abaca and Other Fibers Corporation took over the management of the Japanese properties. Well financed business interests have agreed to develop 7,500 hectares of potential *abaca* land. Permanent tenure of land and renewed research under government direction, coupled with private initiative, would seem to offer a practical program.

---

[5] See Report of the American Agricultural Mission to the Philippines, p. 17.

The *abaca* industry can be saved. It can be because of favorable Philippine conditions for production, because a market is waiting, and because hemp prices are at a reasonably high level. The Philippines should not allow consumers to turn to Western Hemisphere-grown *abaca* and to sisal and other substitutes without a struggle.

Help for the Manila hemp ex-king came from ramie, a long despised poor relative. This plant was known to the ancient Egyptians and Chinese. It can be grown readily and extensively in the Philippines. The wonder fiber offers all sorts of possibilities in the manufacture of textiles. So while the output of *abaca* dwindles, ramie can take up the slack.[6]

Abaca is admitted free of duty to the United States. However, the American cordage interests succeeded in obtaining the insertion of a provision in the Philippine Commonwealth and Independence Act restricting importation of Philippine cordage to 3,000,000 pounds annually. A year later the quota was doubled to 6,000,000 pounds annually by special Congressional legislation. This figure was retained in the Philippine Trade Act of 1946.

Manila hemp thus occupies a relatively sheltered position in the United States, and other markets are available. But the good old days when the fiber was a world commodity, known to every skipper who sailed the seven seas, and to every farmer who harvested his grain, and when it was cock of the walk, will come no more. However, there is ramie.

SUGAR[7]

The rise and fall of Philippine sugar may not parallel the history of the Roman Empire, but in the smaller Philippine setting sugar has had similar ups and downs. In its heyday sugar dominated the economic life of the Islands. The industry had then to see its exalted position first deflated by crop-reduction programs and later nearly wiped out by war. The attempt under the Republic of the Philippines is to rebuild to the extent that sugar quotas can be filled in the American market and that the local consumer demand for refined sugar can be met.

The soil and climate of the Philippines are well adapted to the production of sugar. Reliable data disclose that sugar cane was cultivated nearly everywhere when the Spaniards entered the Islands.

[6] See Memorandum on Philippine Economic Development by Thomas Hibben, pp. 37, 38, attached to the Report of the Joint Philippine-American Finance Commission.

[7] Vicente G. Bunuan, Chief of the Philippine Sugar Quota Office, submitted a memorandum of facts.

It is even recorded that one hundred and thirty-two tons of sugar were exported to the United States in 1795. The middle of the nineteenth century was a particularly prosperous period for the Philippine sugar trade.

The sugar industry fell away with the implantation of American sovereignty. Then came free trade with the United States; came American and other capital to raise and mill Philippine sugar; came government financing of sugar centrals after the establishment of the Philippine National Bank. Sugar flourished. The use of improved varieties of cane, and more modern methods of cultivation and milling, raised year by year the amount of sugar exported, almost entirely to the United States. Sugar overtook all other products to become the leading export. With abundant labor, adequate capital, and the advantage of free entry to the American market, attractive profits were made. Unthinkingly, the Philippine money eggs were placed all in one basket.

In the six years immediately preceding the inauguration of the Commonwealth of the Philippines in 1935, the shipment of sugar to the United States more than doubled. The 1933-34 sugar crop of 1,600,000 short tons ranked the Philippines fifth in the world in the production of sugar. Pressure exerted by domestic-raised sugar beet and sugar cane interests in the United States and by American capitalists with large investments in Cuban sugar resulted in restricted quotas being assigned Philippine sugar pursuant to Congressional legislation. For crop reductions, the planters were given benefit payments out of the processing tax collected in the United States to compensate them for their losses.

While prior to the war sugar was the most important export item, it nevertheless faced a gloomy future in a glutted market. It was the expectation that with the passing of the transitory Commonwealth period, the American tariff wall would be raised against Philippine sugar. With local sugar consumption insignificant and with no available purchasers elsewhere, the loss of a preferential position in the American market offered slight chance for survival.

Before a wake could be held over the departed, disaster struck from another direction. During the occupation the Japanese evinced slight interest in the sugar industry except in the confiscation of machinery and equipment. The forty-one sugar centrals were either destroyed or damaged. Cane fields lay fallow. The fall of the sugar empire was complete.

Rehabilitation of the sugar industry was not easy. Some planters were financially incapable of putting their farms in shape. Centrals heavily damaged by the war were unable to obtain machinery replacements. Work animals for cultivation were scarce. Fertilizers were lacking. Yet definite progress was made. Year by year the output of sugar increased.

As a matter of fact the rehabilitation of the sugar industry moved ahead much faster than had been expected. Consolidation of milling capacity and sugar districts eliminated obsolete mills and low acreage. The Binalbagan-Isabela Sugar Company now operates the largest sugar central in the world. The Insular Sugar Refinery was reopened, which signifies that a steady supply of refined sugar at lower consumer cost will be available to meet domestic needs. Measured by the value of exportable sugar, the Philippine sugar industry may be said to be right back where it was before the war.

Philippine sugar available for export in 1948-49 was around 550,000 short tons, or more than double the preceding year. Full quota milling on a pre-war level will be reached in 1951 and succeeding years. In legal parlance, this means that in conformity with the Philippine Trade Act of 1946, until 1974, the total amount of Philippine sugar allowed annual entry to the United States will be 952,000 short tons, of which 56,000 short tons may be refined sugar. This means that ₱150,000,000 worth of the commodity will reach the American market.

Philippine sugar is once again on the rise. But once again it enters upon a period of anxiety due to labor difficulties, progressively increasing tariffs beginning in 1954, and uncertainty as to future trade relations with the United States.

Coconut Products [8]

The coconut products of the Philippines include copra (the dried meat of the coconut), coconut oil derived from copra, copra meal (a by-product of extraction), and desiccated and shredded coconut. The oil is used in the manufacture of soaps, oleo, and lard substitutes. Copra meal finds its way into cattle feed and fertilizers. Desiccated and shredded coconut meat is used in making candy.

It is not generally realized that the Philippines occupies the first place among the copra-producing countries and normally supplies one-third of the world's copra needs. While coconuts are grown in widely scattered areas, the industry is centered chiefly in Luzon. The district clustering around San Pablo City, south of Manila in Laguna and Quezon Provinces, is one immense grove of coconut

[8] See Report of the American Agricultural Mission to the Philippines, pp. 16, 17.

trees, approximately 2,500 square miles in extent. Within a radius of thirty miles of this city are more coconuts than in any other area of the same size anywhere. It has been estimated that one out of every three persons in the Philippines is dependent on the coconut industry.

Small damage was done by the fighting during the war to the coconut groves abounding in every province of the Philippines; in fact the number of coconut trees actually increased. On the other hand, the manufacturers of coconut products suffered severe losses. These companies, however, were able within a comparatively short period of time to reopen their Philippine plants. Included among the entities which resumed operations were subsidiaries of large American and foreign corporations. Rebuilding of processing facilities was undoubtedly hastened by the insatiable post-war market for coconut products.

Pre-war exports of copra averaged 330,000 tons per year. Post-war demands practicallly doubled the amount exported. The demand for coconut oil, coconut meal, and desiccated coconut revived more slowly. Then inordinately high prices, for instance copra selling at ₱40 to ₱65 in contrast to a former price of ₱6 to ₱8 per one hundred kilos in Manila, a glutted market, and the appearance of substitute products deflated the boom. Even the Philippine Republic was caught in the collapse of the market and suffered heavy losses.

The inoffensive coconut has had to bear the brunt of the same campaign which has been aimed at Philippine sugar. The dairy interests of the United States felt that coconut derivatives were unduly competing with American products. So the free entry of coconut oil was limited by the Philippine Commonwealth and Independence Act to 200,000 long tons in any one year. The ink was hardly dry on this law, when the American Congress proceeded to violate the basic principle underlying the measure by writing into the Revenue Act of 1934 a processing tax of three cents a pound on coconut oil. The millions of dollars representing the proceeds of the taxes returned to the Philippine Government constituted windfalls for the Commonwealth and aided the Republic appreciably in getting under way.

The Philippine Trade Act of 1946 fixes the absolute quota for coconut oil at the same 200,000 long tons annual rate. The amount of free coconut oil diminishes by 10,000 long tons annually beginning in 1955 until in 1974 zero is reached.

In 1949 the President of the United States acted to give Philippine copra and coconut oil a two-cent per pound advantage in the American market. This was accomplished by raising the processing tax on non-Philippine copra and coconut oil to five cents a pound while leaving the tax on the Philippine products at three cents. The restoration of the two-cent differential in favor of the Philippines gave that country virtually exclusive access to the American market.

A return to normal conditions has meant lower copra prices and correspondingly lower profits for all concerned. Yet even with increased competition from abroad, copra and its related products will find purchasers in the world market. One encouraging note is that copra is not dependent alone on trade with the United States; European countries need copra as well. Then, too, just as in the past, tariff limitations and excise taxes—not to speak of Philippine land taxes, and pests, diseases, and typhoons—have left the coconut industry in a bad way, so has it invariably bounded back in a spectacular manner to prosperity. Besides an untapped outlet is greater use of coconut by-products in domestic industry.

TOBACCO [9]

The tobacco plant was introduced into the Philippines from Mexico at the turn of the sixteenth century. Its cultivation became the oldest industrialized agricultural enterprise in the country. The Cagayan Valley in Northern Luzon was found to be especially adapted to the raising of fine grade tobacco. The Spanish regime fostered the industry, and at one time it was a government monopoly. Exports of tobacco products to the United States in any appreciable quantity are of comparatively recent date.

The tobacco industry suffered severely during the war. Planting was reduced. Warehouses and processing facilities were destroyed. Transportation was slow in resuming operations. The inevitable result was that in 1946 the production of cigars was at the rate of sixteen percent and of cigarettes at the rate of twenty-five percent of the pre-war volume.

Unfortunately the best grade of Philippine cigars are not known outside the Islands. The Philippine tobacco trade has had to be content with supplying the American market with leaf and scrap tobacco and cheap cigars.

Barriers to free access to the American market were erected in the Philippine Trade Act of 1946. An absolute annual quota was fixed at 200,000,000 for cigars and at 6,500,000 pounds for scrap tobacco. Beginning with 1955 the number of duty free cigars will be reduced by 10,000,000 each year until zero is reached in 1974, and for the

---

[9] Facts were taken from published statements by Vicente Formoso, General Manager of the National Tobacco Corporation.

same period the amount of duty free tobacco will be reduced at the annual rate of 325,000 pounds.

A curious commentary on the tobacco situation is that the balance of trade is decidedly in favor of the United States. The Philippine importation of tobacco products, chiefly cigarettes, increased by leaps and bounds. The conclusion of the war saw a threefold rise in the consumption of American-manufactured cigarettes due in great part to a developed taste for American brands. The Philippines was the largest foreign customer of United States cigarettes in 1948.

The statistics substantiate these statements and give a clear idea of the plight of the tobacco industry. Exports of tobacco products decreased from a yearly average of ₱10,000,000 before the war to ₱4,000,000 in 1947. Imports of tobacco products increased from a yearly average of ₱12,000,000 before the war to ₱44,000,000 for the indicated year.

The aim is to improve the quality and appearance of locally produced aromatic cigarettes. Self-sufficiency in the tobacco trade is being sought. The restoration of the market in Spain of tobacco leaf of Philippine growth may be expected.

FRUITS [10]

The Filipino, to give expression to his admiration for his favorite fruit, the mango, gallantly insists that it be called by the feminine, "mangga". Thus the mangga is crowned queen of all Philippine fruits. And it is deserving of this universal homage. Nowhere does the mangga attain such size and excellence of flavor as in the Philippines. The eating of the fruit can, however, become a messy business for the uninitiated.

The mangga grows on trees which are distinguished for their size, dignity and grace. When the trees line a road, they form a shapely domed bowl and furnish a deep shade. They will continue to bear fruit for as many as two hundred years.

More prosaically considered, mangga raising is financially profitable. In any one year ₱3,000,000 is the market value of the yield. The fruit is easily preserved by canning.

If the mangga is the queen of Philippine fruits, the banana, it has been said, should be proclaimed the princess. Its popularity and avail-

---

[10] The Institute of National Language gives the spelling of "mango" as "mangga". P. A. Rodrigo, Chief Horticulture Research Section, Bureau of Plant Industry, writes on "The Lowly Banana" is the *Philippines Free Press*, and Vicente Villamin, Filipino economist, on "The Neglected Banana" in the *Manila Daily Bulletin*. Both articles make out a good case for the banana.

ability place it in the royal family of the Island's fruits. Over seventy varieties of edible bananas are grown, but only five of them have commercial value. Practically every backyard boasts a banana tree. Camarines Sur alone devotes 16,000 hectares to this fruit. Mindanao is climatically ideal for the culture of the banana in large quantities.

Here, then, is a fruit which can be grown practically anywhere in the Philippines, which has high food value, and which should be even more a standard item of diet. Nor is this all. While 40,000,000 bunches with a value of ₱10,000,000 per year are produced, this does not begin to meet what should be normal domestic consumption. The potentialities of a foreign market in the Orient for the banana are limitless. It can be made another export crop to add to *abaca*, sugar, copra, and tobacco.

While, for obvious reasons, the mangga and the banana have been accorded the spotlight, it remains to be added that there are found in the Philippines possibly two hundred varieties of fruits. The citrus fruits are grown but do not compare in flavor to their Mediterranean and American cousins. A sizable pineapple industry has been developed in Mindanao and is back to the position that it occupied in the country's economy before the war. The mangosteen is a delicate and deliciously flavored fruit which thrives in Sulu. The malodorous durian, also a native of Moroland, is supposed to augment manly vigor, and to obtain the fruit many a bloody fight has been staged.

It would possibly not be out of place to add a word about the nuts of the Islands (the word "nuts" not being used in a slangy sense). Peanuts are grown for food rather than oil, although at one time they were an item of export. Pilinuts, rich in oil, are exquisitely flavored. Both peanuts and pilinuts, together with the cashew nuts, have commercial possibilities.

There does not appear to be any justifiable reason why the Philippines cannot supply its own market for fruits and nuts and have a sizable surplus available with which to develop foreign trade.

Livestock [11]

No one has ever been inspired to dedicate an ode to the carabao. Nor has anyone ever raised his voice in hosannas of praise of this animal. Yet the carabao, the same as rice, is symbolical of Philippine life.

---

[11] See Report of the American Agricultural Mission to the Philippines, pp. 20, 21. Facts were derived from an article "Accomplishments of the Bureau of Animal Industry for the Fiscal Year 1947-1948" by Director Vicente Ferriols.

The carabao or water buffalo is an ungainly creature with well-formed, evenly-set, and symmetrical-spreading horns. He is built on ponderous battleship lines. His gait is slow, his gaze mournful. A daily mud bath he demands, and his caretaker is careful to see to it that his carabao is permitted to perform his ablutions in a water hole. Like his master, the carabao is placid and easygoing. Yet slow as this beast of burden is, he performs an amazing amount of work. The carabao is more powerful than the horse and can move extraordinarily heavy loads on either a two-wheeled cart or sled.

Of all domesticated animals, the carabao is the most helpful and useful to the common *tao*. He is the indispensable beast upon which many families depend for a livelihood. Mr. and Mrs. Carabao are a source of food. The female of the species supplies the family with milk. Is it any wonder that the carabao should be considered the prized possession of his owner, and a friend of the family? And is but fair that the carabao should be the recipient of anxious care?

Slow-moving under ordinary conditions and with an even temper, at times the carabao becomes excited and charges rapidly and ferociously. For some reason, he is imbued with race prejudice and resents the presence of white men. While a small Filipino urchin can easily control a carabao, the animal is suspicious of a white person and is likely to display his instinctive antipathy.

Besides carabaos, other domestic animals which are raised in the Philippines include cattle, horses, sheep, goats, swine and poultry. Before the war the Islands had become nearly self-sufficient in the supply of work and beef animals. Cattle raising was extensively and successfully carried on in the uplands of Bukidnon, Mindanao, and other regions. Sheep could be seen placidly grazing in the fields of the Ilocos and Mountain Provinces. Goats, pigs and common fowls were found in the yards of practically every home. Fresh milk, however, except in small amounts was practically unknown.

The livestock population did not suffer losses from war damage to anywhere near the extent originally estimated. Carabaos were reduced in number from 3,000,000 to 2,000,000; cattle, from 1,300,000 to 800,000, and swine, from 4,300,000 to 4,000,000. These figures signify that while the numbers of pigs and poultry have been rapidly raised to their pre-war levels, the restoration of carabaos and cattle to make up the one-third loss will take more time. Replacements from India and Thailand have been received. The Congress appropriated ₱2,000,000 for the rehabilitation of the stock farms.

The 1949 view of the Bureau of Animal Industry is that there is not really a serious shortage of work carabaos in the Philippines.

Investigations conducted by the field personnel of the Bureau revealed sufficient animals in a majority of the provinces. A shifting of carabaos from regions where there is a surplus to regions where there is a shortage would stabilize production. Each hardworking farmer would then have a carabao with which to cultivate three hectares of land. The raising of sufficient beef cattle to supply the market will, however, take years. Similarly, it will be a long time before modern dairies, scientifically run, will be able to meet local demands for fresh milk.

The Bureau of Animal Industry has underway a worthwhile program of livestock improvement. Rinderpest, once the scourge of carabaos and cattle, has been eradicated through quarantine and immunization. Anthrax and other animal diseases have been largely suppressed by similar methods. The College of Agriculture, University of the Philippines, has begun a breeding program to better native stock.

The program planned for the livestock industry is modest. A sufficient number of work animals should be locally available to meet the needs of agriculture. Meat production at the level of self-sufficiency should be attained. Considering the domestic market, the favorable conditions for the expansion of beef cattle herds in Mindanao and the available cattle feed, this last goal should in time be reached.

FORESTS [12]

Compared with the great lumber-producing countries, the Philippines ranks first in regard to the ratio of forest to total land area, and sixth in forest extent. Philippine forests aggregate 17,000,000 hectares and cover fifty-nine percent of the land area. Nearly all of the forests are state-owned. The economic value of this vast national resource conservatively estimated reaches nearly unbelievable figures.

The stand of hardwood timber in the Philippines is the finest and largest in the world. In these forests appear vast numbers of stately and gigantic trees of great height. From them come the many varieties of wood for which the Philippines is famous. A trip to one of these forests cannot but be a source of wonder and delight.

The forests contain timber well adapted for general use. Narra of two shades, yellow and red, is particularly alluring. Camagon (ebony) is durable and valuable. Molave, ipil, and apitong are favorite woods for structural purposes. Tanguile and lauans, known

---

[12] Director of Forestry Florencio Tamesis answered a number of enquiries. See note 2 to this chapter.

abroad as "Philippine Mahogany," constitute the bulk of the lumber export of the Philippines. Pine is found in the higher altitudes. Rattan is abundant.

Lumbering was and is one of the important industries of the Islands. In 1941, it was estimated that 950,000,000 board feet were produced. Of this 750,000,000 were consumed locally with the remainder available for export. During the war there was considerable destruction of lumber mills, but with peace it was not long before operations were resumed. One company alone invested up to ₱6,000,000 of American capital in the exploitation of timber concessions.

Philippine requirements of lumber for reconstruction were naturally great. In fact for a time the emergency was so pressing that an embargo on the export of Philippine lumber was clamped on the industry. In 1949 the ban was lifted and unlimited exportation of lumber was permitted. To strengthen the confidence of foreign buyers in Philippine lumber, it will be inspected and graded before being sent out of the country.

Lumber production is on the upgrade. Pre-war capacity is being exceeded by 100,000 board feet a year. The increased domestic requirements are being met with a surplus left for export. In addition a ready foreign market can be found for the fine cabinet woods of Philippine origin and for rattan furniture, due to the excellent quality and workmanship of the Filipino furniture workers.

Before this topic is brought to a close, it would seem permissible to visit a Filipino home to view the use to which Philippine lumber is put.

The *sala* (reception room) has a floor of alternate strips of Philippine narra three feet in width and of Philippine ebony one foot in width. Polished as only a *muchacho* (boy) can polish floors on coconut husks or rags propelled by bare feet, the effect is most artistic and pleasing. The panels and ceiling of the room are of beautifully grained native lumber. A one-piece table nine feet in diameter is in evidence, for table tops this large are not uncommon. Antique pieces of Spanish furniture, really made by Filipino artisans of Philippine woods, complete the indoor picture. Around the house will likely be found the *cadena de amor* (chain of love), a climbing vine popular for decoration, the *dama de noche* (lady of the night), which opens its petals—but only at night—to laden the air with lovely fragrance, and the *sampaguita*, the adored and immaculate national flower.

The Bureau of Forestry is in charge of the forest wealth of the country. It has wisely adopted a policy of delimitation, protection and conservation. The forests are not sold, but are utilized under a lease system or exclusive concessions for stated periods. Forest reserves and national parks have been set aside and communal forests have been established. With regret it must be added that important segments of the Filipino people are engaged in the spoliation of their patrimony.

Associated with forestry in the Philippines in recent times are the names of Colonel Arthur F. Fischer, last American Director of Forestry, and of Florencio Tamesis, Filipino head of the Bureau under the Commonwealth and the Republic. A false sense of security induced by the large forest reserves should not undo the pioneering work of these competent and far seeing men. The United States is a bitter example of a nation that saw its forest heritage looted and wasted. Firm support of conservation of a rich resource, coupled with appropriations for reforestation and scientific investigation, will pay off in the long run.

MINING [13]

If a person had had the foresight—and the courage—to invest ₱2,000 ($1,000) in Benguet Consolidated Mining Stock along in 1910 or 1911, when the stock sold at twenty centavos (ten cents) a share, by 1940 his original stock augmented by stock dividends at market value and the dividends declared would have grown to a cool million dollars. The estimate leans to the conservative side.

Benguet Consolidated, the bonanza above mentioned, is a mining concern which operates near Baguio in the mountains of Northern Luzon. It also controls Balatoc (which means "gold" in the Igorot dialect), the most profitable mine in the Islands, and has drawn to itself other mines. In 1940 Benguet milled more than ₱1,000,000 ($500,000) worth of gold a month and earned the stockholders ₱8,000,000 ($4,000,000). The 1950 Benguet-Balatoc Mill had a capacity of 2,500 tons of ore a day.

Gold fever in the Philippines is no new disease. Primitive mining had been carried on centuries before Magellan discovered the Islands. In pre-Spanish times Luzon was called the "mountain of gold" or the "land of gold." As early as the third century A. D., the Chinese recorded mining activities in Luzon. The Spanish *conquistadores* were attracted by rumors of fabulously rich gold mines. Even the

---

[13] This section was originally read by the late A. F. Duggleby of the Benguet Consolidated Mining Company. Walter Robb, former editor of the *American Chamber of Commerce Journal* of Manila, described the mining situation in the Philippines in succinct fashion in the *Christian Science Monitor* of May 9, 1947.

Moro pirates came to claim the prize of gold. One story, fairly well substantiated, has it that Doña Panay, who sent a petition to the Queen of Spain asking for protection against these pirates, accompanied her petition with a life-sized hen and setting of eggs all in virgin gold.

Not long ago in developing the Lepanto Mine, pottery of pre-Ming 1368 China origin was found. Who taught the Chinese and the Igorots how to mine and the value of gold is an unfathomed mystery.

The 1933-38 period witnessed another rush for Philippine gold. These were the years when gold was repriced at $35 an ounce, when easy money received from sugar benefit payments sought investment, and when Spanish, British, and Chinese capital was attracted to the Philippine market. A spectacular stampede for mining claims resulted. Literally scores of mining corporations—over five hundred—were formed. While some of the companies proved failures, the feverish activities fomented a remarkable growth in gold production. As in all such booms, money was made and money was lost. The eventual collapse of the market left in its wake many victims of their own cupidity.

While the fortunes of Benguet and Balatoc have here been underscored, they are only two of a number of gold mines. Goldfields as widely distributed as Camarines Norte, Masbate, Surigao, and Mindanao are in process of development. Prior to the war Philippine mines yielded ₱100,000,000 worth of gold a year.

The mineral wealth of the Islands is not confined to gold. Iron ore is being mined in Camarines Norte; an iron deposit in Mindanao is estimated to contain one billion tons of ore. Lepanto is the largest copper mine in the Orient. Manganese mines are in production. Millions of tons of high grade, low cost chrome-aluminum ore are available. One chromite deposit at Masinloc, Zambales bids fair to develop into the world's largest single deposit of that mineral (one estimate is 10,000,000 tons), and is indicative of a chromite-bearing belt extending through almost the entire length of the Islands. Coal is mined but in inadequate quantities to meet domestic needs.

It will not escape notice that the Philippines encompasses abundant base metals needed for war material.

The Japanese chose to operate only the Lepanto Mine, in order to get copper for the metal-starved homeland. Practically every other mine in the Philippines was plundered for machinery and equipment. Actual losses run as high as ₱100,000,000 ($50,000,000). In general, however, owners found their mines in far better condition than they had thought would be the case.

Mining, particularly gold mining, was the last of the major pre-war industries to be rehabilitated. High cost and slow deliveries of machinery, increased expenditures for labor, government taxes, and delay in securing war damage payments were obstacles difficult to hurdle. As a consequence, five years after the conclusion of the war sees only five important producers of gold as against some twenty-five producers before the war. The marginal mines cannot afford to operate. The industry is only about twenty-five percent restored in point of value of ore mined. The Director of Mines estimates that it will be another five years before the Philippines can equal the pre-war gold output.

It should be understood that value of production is computed on the basis of the official price of gold at $35 per ounce. In the Philippine free market of the post-war era, gold actually sold at a price well above the American-set figure.

One interesting post-war development concerns the resumption of the quest, begun over thirty years ago, for "black gold." The existence of oil in commercial quantities in the Western Pacific oil belt in the neighboring islands leads experts in geology and paleontology to believe that similar deposits occur in the Philippines. Under the supervision of the Philippine Oil Commission, full scale exploration for oil by private entities is under way.

Three main groups dominate Philippine mining. One group is headed by canny Jan Hendrik Marsman, married to Mary Peterson, widow of the pioneer prospector Nels Peterson; Marsman has renounced allegiance to the Netherlands to become a Philippine citizen. Another group has as the directing genius of sprawling interests the aggressive Colonel Andres Soriano, successively a Franco adherent, a MacArthur aide, and a Philippine Cabinet officer. And the third group represents the life work of "Judge" John W. Hausserman, "the grand old man" of Philippine mining who presides over a mighty empire.

"Judge" Hausserman's—everyone affectionately and respectfully calls him "Judge"—luck, or maybe it was faith, has been phenomenal. In 1911 he was handed the thankless job of retrieving what he could from the bankrupt Benguet mining venture; he not only saved the mine but made it the financial prop of Philippine mining. In 1922 the fainthearted proposed that Benguet be dissolved and the cash reserve split among the stockholders; the "Judge" balked, saw a new strike materialize, and consolidated his position by the acquisition of a controlling interest in the rich Balatoc mine. In 1945, out of retirement on his peaceful Ohio farm, again came the "Judge" to pick up the pieces left by the marauding Japanese and fit them together into a going concern. "Judge" Hausserman may be in opulence the Gold King of the Philippines, who pays seventy-five percent of his income in taxes, but, in addition, in the Philippines he is one of the best liked private citizens, and in the United States he is the best known Manilian.[14]

Gold is one of the Philippines most valuable exports. Of all Philippine industries, it can best assure business stability. This does not mean that the Philippines can ever hope to displace the Witwatersrand region of South Africa as the chief gold-producing country in the world. It is sufficient that the Islands produce approximately as much gold as California or Alaska. For whatever happens to sugar, someone will covet Philippine gold—and also Philippine copper, chromite, manganese, and iron.

FISHERIES

Fishing has been, and once again can be, a major Philippine industry. Fresh and sun-dried fish form an important element of the food of the masses.

Fishing in the Philippines is carried on in various ways. Deep-sea fishing, formerly a successful business systematically conducted by the Japanese, offers alluring possibilities. Tuna canned under an American trade name was actually the product of the Philippines. Fishing along the coasts and in the rivers is by fish-traps and nets.

Fish are also raised on farms. The *semillas* (literally seeds or fry) are planted in the fish ponds. When grown they become the *bangos* or milkfish so popular with the people.

Perhaps a hundred boats are engaged in pearl-fishing in the waters around the Sulu Archipelago. The value of pearls sold to European buyers has amounted to as much as ₱1,000,000 a year. Very fine specimens are found by divers. Single pearls have brought as much as ₱25,000 in the open market.

The Bureau of Fisheries is a comparatively recent addition to the Government. It is devoting scientific knowledge and energy to giving an impetus to the fishing industry. The Fish and Wildlife Service of the United States Department of the Interior has cooperated in a fishing rehabilitation, development, and training program, with notable success. These agencies candidly concede that the Philippines is in its infancy in the industrialization of the fisheries. Their aim is to utilize the aquatic wealth wisely and profitably.

---

[14] See the human interest story on "Judge" Hausserman entitled "Return of the King" in the March 8, 1948 issus of *Time*.

LABOR [15]

The labor movement in the Philippines exemplifies tendencies similar to those found in the United States and other countries. There are workers uninterested in being organized, and there are labor unions ranging from conservative and corporation-dominated to radical and communist-infested.

The prejudice against Filipino labor which capital early displayed has largely disappeared. Employers now concede that the Filipinos do their jobs satisfactorily. Much of the results obtainable from the use of Filipino laborers depend on how they are handled. Treated fairly and firmly, they cause no trouble. Treated roughly or with too much intimacy, the laborers either become sullen or quit.

Wages in Spanish times were unbelievably low. The worker's pittance increased under joint American-Filipino propulsion to an extent that approached nearer to a decent living wage. Nevertheless, as late as 1939 an investigation conducted by the Department of Labor disclosed wages as low as twelve centavos (six cents) a day for women. In the same year the average daily wage of the agricultural worker was forty-four centavos (twenty-two cents); laborers in the mines averaged ₱1.39. The minimum wage law making ₱1.00 the daily minimum in the country districts and ₱1.25 in Manila was a step in the right direction. The standard of living in the Philippines, low as it was, was many times higher than in neighboring China and Malaya.

The impact of the war was felt most by the masses. The cost of living curve spiraled from a one hundred percent level in 1941 to seven hundred and fifty in 1945, to fall to four hundred and sixty in 1946. Wages nearly kept pace with living costs. The average daily wage of a skilled laborer in Manila rose from ₱2.34 in 1941 to ₱6.62 in 1946, and of a common laborer from ₱1.24 in 1941 to ₱4.21 in 1946. But such a situation was an invitation to unrest and unstable capital-labor relations. The lack or the high cost of necessities, plus a large family, plus non-employment, plus red fomentation were the factors which caused discontent among the masses.[16]

In 1949, it was estimated that one million individuals were unemployed. Yet even this figure was indicative of an increase in em-

---

[15] See Ramon Torres, *A Review of Labor Developments in the Philippines* (Manila, 1934). Aurelio Intertas, General President, U. O. E. F., writes on the subject "Let Us Organize Our 16,000,000 Co-Workers" in the February, 1949 Labor Bulletin.

[16] Tables prepared by the Bureau of Census and Statistics show the wages of laborers in industrial and commercial establishments in Manila for 1941, 1945, 1946, 1947, and 1948 and the cost of living index for a wage earner's family in Manila. The Bureau of Commerce publishes weekly changes in price level.

ployment. Along with it, a rise in the productivity of labor was registered. At the same time the cost of living had dropped one-third. The daily wages of the men employed in one of the Nation's best known mines were practically doubled by order of the Court of Industrial Relations. Labor was in a fairly favorable position.

The trade-union movement in the Philippines dates back to 1902. The struggle for a living wage was then begun. However, it was only in the '30's and '40's that labor became truly organized. There are now about nine hundred registered unions loosely confederated into larger organizations. They claim a membership of 2,000,000.

One of the oldest of the labor bodies is the *Federation del Trabajo*, with which the name of the late Joaquin Balmori is indelibly linked. Other labor organizations have included the *Federation Obrera de Filipinas* of the Visayas, the National Federation of Labor, the Association of Labor Unions, the K.K.M., and the *Magdaragat*. The National Confederation of Trade Unions in the Philippines was formed in 1948, with its aim the unification of labor.

The Congress of Labor Organizations, known as the CLO, was organized in 1945 while there was still fighting around Manila. This militant body is the counterpart of the American CIO. Bigger than the CLO is the Peasants Confederation, called PKM.

An investigation conducted by a committee of the Philippine Congress found that the CLO and the PKM had communist affiliations. The report emphasized that violence was deliberately provoked in labor disputes. The result has been that rehabilitation of pre-war enterprises has been hampered by the interference of labor leaders and by nuisance strikes.[17]

The Philippine Government has endeavored to be just to the proletariet. A separate Department of Labor has tried to protect the interests of labor, without, however, satisfying the labor leaders. The eight-hour labor law, the woman and child labor law, the workmen's compensation law, and the minimum wage law have been enacted to give labor its due. The representatives of the Department of Labor intervene to settle strikes and other labor disputes. When these efforts fail, the Court of Industrial Relations is available alike to capital and organized labor to decide industrial, tenancy and similar cases.

The ultimate aim of Philippine labor is political influence along with economic improvement. It will gradually gravitate into a radical

---

[17] F. L. Worcester, Manager of the Philippine Refining Company, in an article appearing in Manila papers on April 26, 1947 told in detail how the company's efforts to get reestablished were hampered by the interference of the C. L. O.

party—just how radical only time will tell—and will become bolder in its demands.

AGRARIAN UNREST [18]

The age old problem of peasant exploitation in the Philippines is no nearer solution today than it was in centuries long past. It was then, and is now, a struggle between the very rich and the very poor; between the very rich to continue to bask in luxury, and the very poor to get a living wage.

When the Spaniards arrived in the Philippines during the sixteenth century, they found there a people who were class conscious. The Chiefs exercised despotic authority. The subjects paid the Chiefs tribute out of the crops that they gathered. Change the titles of "chiefs" and "subjects" to modern equivalents, and it will be seen that the system is not much different in the Philippines of the present from what it was in the Philippines of the past. It smacked then of medieval feudalism. It still does.

The Spaniards parceled out large tracts of land to favorite Spanish *encomenderos*, and with the land went the people virtually as serfs. Recognition was also granted the Filipino Chiefs. The result was that *caciquism* survived and that on this feudal base was superimposed the *ilustrado* class who lived in a grand manner on their great estates. In theory the Laws of the Indies were protective to a high degree. Actually Spanish rule had benefited the lowest stratum of the masses very little.

The American regime that followed was acutely conscious of the rights of what has been termed the unrepresented minority of Filipinos. Civil Governor Taft journeyed to Rome to put over a deal with the Church for the purchase of the Friar Lands. These holdings were gradually sold to Filipinos in small parcels. Under American administrations liquidation of large estates proceeded spasmodically; laws protective of labor were enacted, and emigration to Hawaii and the undeveloped regions in the Island of Mindanao was encouraged. The plight of the submerged masses was well understood. Good intentions to right wrongs were not lacking. But the surface of the system of landholding, with its attendant evils, was barely scratched.

The promotion of social service to insure the well-being and economic security of all the people was recognized in the Philippine

---

[18] For a view of the broader aspects of Asiatic unrest see Robert Payne, *The Revolt of Asia*. The articles by Judge Quirino Abad Santos describe the Huk-PKM Problem.

Constitution as the concern of the State. The declaration of this principle, one of the unique features of the Constitution, was given specific reenforcement in another Constitutional provision that made it the obligation of the State to afford protection for labor and to regulate the relations between landowner and tenant.[19] The Filipinos understood better than any alien just what the trouble was and what had to be done to alleviate it.

The Filipino-controlled administration of President Quezon came on the scene, and with characteristic vigor took steps to enforce the Constitutional mandate. The President had been much impressed during a 1937 trip to Mexico by the Cardenas program of social justice, and returned home determined to accomplish as much for his own country. More big estates were acquired by the government and subdivided for sale to tenants and others. The National Land Settlement Administration came into being. Colonies, notably the Coronadal Valley Project in Mindanao, were sponsored. A minimum wage law was passed. Progress had been made. Nevertheless the lowly *tao* continued a man apart, restless in spirit and ready to follow any glib leader.

President Roxas' task in the infant Republic was not made easier by the troubles dredged up by war. The farmers of Central Luzon had resisted the Japanese invaders. They claimed to have fought 1,200 engagements and inflicted 25,000 casualties; included were spies and collaborators, and also innocent victims. The President found these people, with arms acquired by devious means and in a resistant mood, not easily susceptible to reason. Still President Roxas tried. His major contribution to a program of social reform was the securing of a tenancy law that provided for a crop division of seventy percent to the tenant and thirty percent to the owner.[20]

Assuredly an advance from the long sanctioned fifty-fifty division to sixty-forty and now to seventy-thirty was not unfair to the tenant. To go forward any farther would amount to land confiscation. Of course the success of the law depends on the effective advice and wise decisions of the attorneys and agents of the Tenancy Law Enforcement Division created in 1939 as one phase of the social justice program. That resolute enforcement of this law is needed was brought to light by Judge Quirino Abad Santos, one of the famous brothers, when he revealed that the seventy-thirty crop sharing law was being sabotaged by landlords.

---

[19] Constitution of the Philippines, Article II, sec. 5; Article XIV, sec. 6.
[20] Republic Act No. 34, approved September 30, 1946, amendatory of Act No. 4054, "The Philippine Rice Tenancy Act."

President Quirino inherited an unsolved social problem from his predecessor in office. He first tried magnanimity—and when that failed, force. Now he has announced that his purpose will be the formulation and implementation of a grand economic development program in which his chief concern will be the betterment of the masses. He may achieve something worthwhile. A reasonable supposition is that the overall problem will be passed on to his successor and to his successor's successor for consideration.

What, then, is the precise cause of agrarian unrest in the Philippines? To state, as we did in the beginning, that it is a struggle between the "haves" and the "have nots" is neither precisely accurate nor adequately specific. The primary reason for the problem is the never ending struggle for survival on the part of the poor. Hatred for their masters, jealousy of their affluence, and downright abuse by agents, thrives in such a soil. The effort may be misdirected. It may take the form of revolt against constituted authority. It may be made the dupe of mountebanks. It may follow strange gods to destruction. It may degenerate into out-and-out banditry. Behind all such manifestations are legitimate grievances.

Agrarian unrest in the Philippines is not confined to any one region. It is not in evidence at all among the forty to fifty percent of Filipino families who own their homes and land. The main seat of trouble lies north of Manila in Central Luzon in the fertile rice bowl and sugar producing region. There reside the tenant farmers who look to landlords, often absent and represented by agents, for help that all too often is not forthcoming. These tenants are sunk in a morass of mounting debt. To them flock the vulture usurers to gorge on the distress of the poor and ignorant.

It is feared that sympathy for the underdog has resulted in a one-sided picture of Philippine economy. Now there is nothing wrong in the aggressive individual accumulating property. That is the private enterprise system in action. The capitalist, become a landlord, may in turn assist the less fortunate to build homes and may look after his tenants as a good father cares for his children. The tragedy of the process is that as the landlord either by inheritance or initiative becomes richer, an increasing proportion of the people become landless.

It is easier to describe the Philippine feudal problem dating back to pre-Spanish times than to offer a ready made solution for that problem. It is trite to state that life rooted to the soil with private ownership is the best bulwark against radicalism. Yet it is on that platform that a long range program must be built. The thousands of hectares of uncultivated land must be made available for homesteads.

More, and yet more, *haciendas* must be acquired and broken up for resettlement.

Too many people live in the wrong places in the Philippines. Too few people live in the right places. The jig-saw puzzle consists of getting the too many in the wrong places to move to the right places. That means government encouragement and assistance must be extended to attain a more even distribution of the population. Along with that policy must go private pioneering that scoffs at hardship.

Other phases of the general topic "Agrarian Unrest" will be discussed in a succeeding chapter under the headings "The Huk Headache" and "The Communistic Invasion."

CHAPTER XX

THE PLEASURE LOVING PHILIPPINES

ATHLETICS [1]

The Filipino Nation is sport-minded. The Filipino individually is an enthusiastic sportsman. Be it at the makeshift cockpit, at the prize-fight ring, or at the magnificent Rizal Memorial Field, he is vociferously present. Of the few primitive games which still persist, *sipa*, a form of kickball, is one which was played long before the Philippines was influenced by foreign customs. But most of the athletic contests of today are importations from the United States.

The governing body for athletics is the Philippine Amateur Athletic Federation, which corresponds to similar organizations in the United States and other countries. Its current President is Jorge B. Vargas, and its Executive Secretary, experienced National Physical Director Dr. Regino R. Ylanan. The Federation is busily engaged in fostering athletics and athletic tournaments. A National College of Physical Education has been organized.

The development of athletics has been a cardinal part of the educational program for the schools. Filipino youth responded nobly to instruction. Baseball, soccer football, basketball, volleyball, tennis, swimming, and track events are popular. Cold weather games, like American football, are not played, being unsuited to the Philippine climate.

The public schools hold annual regional and national contests. Interrupted by the war, beginning with 1949 these meets began again to function normally. The Bicol Meet of Southern Luzon, which is converted into a great social event, is the best known regional meet. The National Interscholastic Games organized by the Bureau of Public Schools Athletic Association bring together public school athletes from all over the country.

The Rizal Memorial Field in Harrison Park in Manila, which was thrown open to the public to usher in the Tenth Far Eastern Olympic Games, is the Orient's finest playground center, and is modern in every way. All sports have adequate playing fields and stands. The various

---

[1] Information was furnished by the National Physical Director, Dr. Regino R. Ylanan.

stadia furnish a fit setting for Filipino athletic activities and international competition.

THE OLYMPIC GAMES

The Philippines has joined in competition in athletic contests with other nationals whether regional or world-wide in scope.

The Philippines furnished the impetus for the organization of the Far Eastern Athletic Association in 1913. Regularly every two years thereafter, the Oriental Olympics were held alternately in the Philippines, Japan, and China. The athletes of these three countries met in a great sporting event in all the standard contests. Under Japanese pressure, the Association was dissolved in 1934 and was expanded into the Amateur Athletic Association of the Orient. This organization in turn disappeared with the war. The post-war successor took form in the Asian Games Federation, organized in Delhi, India, in 1949, with the Philippine Republic a member. Games will be held on strictly amateur lines every four years in even years between the Olympic games.

The Philippines has sent athletes to engage in world Olympic competition. While the points won have been few, needed experience has been gained. Simeon Torribio, later to become a Congressman, was twice a high jump winner for the Philippines. In the XIV Olympiad held in London, the Philippines had to be content with the two points won by weight-lifter Rodrigo del Rosario. Possibly the Philippines would be justified in laying claim to a half interest in petite Vicki Manalo Draves, Olympic Diving Champion, whose father was a Filipino.

FAVORITE SPORTS

In certain branches of athletics the Filipinos have tended to be more proficient than in others. This was particularly true of boxing in the '20's and '30's. Filipinos then establshed themselves as the gamest of game fighters. Their shifting, slashing attack made them prime favorites with the crowd. Pancho Villa died the world champion in the fly-weight class when he fought his last fight with an infected jaw. Little Dado and Small Montaño, likewise in the fly-weight division, and Ceferino Garcia, middleweight boxer, were other less renowned Filipinos who annexed world titles in the ring.

Unfortunately, Filipino fighters of this calibre are virtually extinct. A combination of high government taxes in the Philippines and unscrupulous promoters have been the undoing of Philippine boxing.

There is a Boxing Commission, but it does not appear that the Commission can do much to improve the situation. Of course what is needed is instruction for willing youngsters and businesslike conducting of contests.

The Manila Bay Baseball League functions in that area. Baseball is played from November to May, or mostly during the time when it is not played in the United States. Filipinos make snappy fielders and speedy base runners, but lack the physique to become home run clouters.

The game of golf attracts cosmopolitan enthusiasts. Larry Montes, a former caddy and more recently the professional of the Wack-Wack Golf and Country Club adjacent to Manila, is a ten-time Philippine Open Champion.

Tough little ponies are bred in Batangas and other provinces and engage in short-distance running races. The big events are associated with the holding of the Philippine Charity Sweepstakes.

Tennis has its addicts, both masculine and feminine. The Ampon family—father, son and daughter—are the reigning dynasty. Felicisimo Ampon the younger, known as the "Mighty Atom," is Philippine Champion; the diminutive giant killer has given a good account of himself in international competition.

Basketball has gained the favor of the public, just as it has in the United States. So likewise have soccer football, swimming, jai-alai, and other sports.

COCKFIGHTING

If any one sport can be called the national sport of the Filipinos, it is cockfighting. This is a pastime indigenous to the Islands which was fostered by the Spanish Governors. More recent policy leaned toward eventual extermination of cockfighting, but as the power of the cockpit trusts made this not feasible, endeavored to curtail it as much as possible. In 1949 a move in the other direction was taken when cockfighting was legalized in Manila.

Notwithstanding governmental preachments, cockfighting continues to be the favorite sport of the masses. Restricted to Sundays and holidays, crowds gather on those days in the nipa-thatched arenas. In the heat, the people mill with excitement as bets are made and won or lost.

The owner of a game-cock is wont to tend it well and possibly more tenderly than any living object of his household, wife and children not excepted. It is a common sight to see a Filipino with a game rooster carried carefully under his arm, or to find him in front of his home training his bird for a coming fight. Yet it is a curious fact that the Philippines must import eggs.

HUNTING[2]

A hunter can prove his right to be initiated into the thirty-third degree of sportsdom by shooting a tiger in India, a lion in Africa—or a timarau in the Philippines. The timarau is a buffalo of a species which is only found on the Island of Mindoro in the Philippine group. A savage beast possessed of a notoriously bad temper, it is as elusive in a wild country as it is savage. Its habit is to attack man ferociously.

The great mammals of adjacent Borneo and Sumatra and of Asia, as the elephant and orang-utan, are lacking in the Philippines. Besides the timarau, the only other big game is the wild carabao, still to be found in the Archipelago. The carabao is no relative of the caribou of Canada. The finding of the wild species of the carabao is not easy. For this reason, the suspicion will not down that tame carabaos have been driven in front of the line of fire of high government officials, there to be sacrificed on the altar of Philippine hospitality.

Two kinds of crocodiles of sizable dimensions frequent the streams and lakes of the Islands. In one small lake on an island in San Bernardino Strait more than five hundred crocodiles were counted at one time. General Aguinaldo once bagged one in Pampanga Province eighteen feet long, eight feet around, and weighing 3,000 pounds, and this was by no means the largest in the Islands. A few crocodiles are maneaters, as post mortems have disclosed.

Snakes, both venomous and harmless, of a variety of species are found. A python has been known to swallow whole a fully grown deer. Water snakes are hunted for commercial purposes.

Snipe-shooting rivals that in any community in the world. In the same class are the wild ducks. The monkey-eating eagle has been encountered in the mountainous regions of Mindanao and in other places in the Philippines; it is the largest bird which preys on other living animals for food. Wild hogs are abundant, and deer are found in nearly all parts of the Islands. The mouse deer of the small island of Balabac is no deer at all, but is closely related to the pig. The mouse deer is only about sixteen inches long and eight inches high.

To avoid the extermination of wild animals, it has been necessary for the Government to establish closed seasons.

---

[2] See Dean C. Worcester, *The Philippines, Past and Present*, Hayden edition of 1930, Ch. XXVII.

FISHING

Philippine bodies of water encompass a fisherman's paradise. Think of catching a forty-pound tanguingui, or sailfish, or a fifty-pound pompano, or a one hundred-pound barracuda. These are but samples, for 2,000 species of fish, most of which are edible, are found in Philippine waters, and some fish have not even been classified. A favorite with epicureans for its delicious flavor is the lapu-lapu, of which twenty-four known species exist in the Philippines. As Philippine waters teem with fish, they can be caught in incredible numbers. Which is no fish story.

It is unnecessary to state for the benefit of Izaak Waltons that these are salt-water fish. They are caught on a trolling line or with rod and reel. That is, fish are caught legitimately, but illegally they are killed by explosives.

Fishing is more than a sport in the Philippines. It is an important industry.

THE DANCE

The Philippines is no straight-laced Quaker settlement. Sundays are not long-faced Puritan Sabbaths. In the Philippines life is one long procession of good times. Sundays and holidays, of which latter there are a medley of religious and Filipino anniversaries, seem specially designed for a hasty appearance at early mass, to be followed by diversions of all sorts.

Folk dances have not entirely lost favor. The stately *rigodon de honor*, an importation from Spain, opens formal balls. But it is the modern dance that is most popular.

The dance is the favored means by which the Filipinos enjoy themselves. Clubs, from the fashionable Kahirup to far less pretentious organizations in the remotest towns, exist for the sole purpose of holding balls. The problem of the universities is to keep the number of dances which the students organize within reasonable bounds. A wedding, a baptismal party, or a reception for a visitor are eagerly seized upon to provide opportunities for longer indulgence in the favorite pastime.

As if this were not enough, cabarets exist all over the Islands. In these establishments, the native *bailarinas* (dancing girls) prove as engaging hostesses as the taxi dancers of America. For a modest fee per dance, the *bailarinas* will trip the light fantastic in every known variation. They will also flirt with suitors with direful consequences when jealousy is inflamed to passionate deeds. The money made by these girls of a night is by no means insignificant.

Santa Ana Cabaret in Manila makes the claim that it is the largest in the world. To its hospitable doors come nocturnal wanderers of all classes—an American sailor to exhibit the latest Broadway step, a tired husband to dally with the brown girls, a Filipino clerk to dance sedately, and a society matron to climax a night of frivolity. A slender line divides the *bailarina* side from the society side, and a still slighter line divides the bad from the good. For the colonel's wife and the sergeant's sweetheart are sisters under the skin.

Possibly the impression has been given that life in the Philippines is one interminable fox-trot. Not quite that. Serious business gains attention. And other diversions are available. Yet it is the dance which adds spice to life in the Philippines.

CARNIVALS AND FIESTAS

The Mardi-Gras of the Orient was formerly the Manila Carnival, held annually on historic Wallace Field in Manila during the month of February, when the climate of the Islands is at its best.

The Manila Carnival was first staged in 1908, inspired by the buoyant exuberance of Colonel George T. Langhorne of the United States Army, a brother of Lady Astor. Annually thereafter the Carnival city took form under the supervision of the Director General, customarily popular Arsenio N. Luz. The Carnival became one great dance, a thousand *fiestas* combined in one.

The war offered little encouragement to frivolity. The Carnival disappeared. It only came back in 1948-49 in the modest guise of the Boys Town Carnival and Fair and a veterans-sponsored Carnival. Yet anyone familiar with the Philippines can safely hazard a guess that the Manila Carnival combined with an industrial exhibition will return in all its glory.

On a smaller scale Carnivals are held in provincial cities. Iloilo offers an example of one artistically and financially successful.

Annually every municipality also celebrates the anniversary of its patron saint. It is signalized by an impressive high mass in the morning and a brilliant religious procession in the evening.

The celebration has its lighter side. It is a homecoming and town-visiting day, a miniature carnival, and a town *fiesta* all in one. Every home of the municipality is hospitably thrown open. All guests are fed bountifully. Orchestras are present, and dancing is indulged in until even the most ardent devotee is satisfied. As the dates of the *fiestas* rarely coincide, they combine to make a great circle for the display of neighborliness.

BEACHCOMBERS

In the Philippine tropics, life is easy, too easy. The unaccustomed languor of the climate and indulgence in large quantities of native liquor lessen the moral fiber of the white man. Time lies heavy on his hands. There is every temptation to slack. The tempters are the twin consolations of liquor and women. A squalid shack. A slatternly female. A mongrel dog. A bottle of gin. How readily a man can raise a thirst. For him "there aren't no ten commandments."

These are the weaklings who have been taken in by the tropics and who live upon the poorer class of native women. There are not many of them in the Philippine North Seas, not as many as in the South Seas. But the breed exists, to the annoyance of better-behaved compatriots who bestir themselves as much East of Suez as West of Suez, and to the cynical amusement of Filipino onlookers.

The American Association organized in 1949 will do what it can to assist the worthwhile cases and to get the ne'er-do-wells out of the country.

FILIPINO MOVIES

There is no prospect of Hollywood's premier position in the motion picture industry ever being threatened by Philippine-produced films. Capital, equipment, and technical perfection are lacking. All too many plots repeat a stale and established pattern.

Nevertheless Filipino movies fill a void acceptably in the local amusement field. They are produced in Tagalog by Filipino directors, are based on Filipino stories, and have Filipinos for actors. The resultant films are shown in theatres throughout the Philippines and in Hawaii where there is a large contingent of Filipinos.

Producers have banded together in the Motion Picture Association of the Philippines. Other people connected with the industry have grouped themselves into the Motion Picture Guild of the Philippines. The five major companies engaged in the business have shown marked technical improvement since liberation. English versions of stories with local settings have been successes.

One interesting sidelight is that Filipino pictures have been made in Hollywood, the Hollywood way. Big shots in the movie capital have been favorably impressed with the performances of Filipino actors and actresses.

CHAPTER XXI

DEFENSE AND PUBLIC ORDER

Defense Agreements

The various Chiefs of the U. S. Military Advisory Group to the Philippines have told the Filipino people not to worry about external aggression. They have recommended that major efforts be devoted to securing internal peace. Nevertheless military and diplomatic strategists consider the Philippines in the first line of defense. This latter view was authoritatively confirmed by Secretary of State Dean Acheson in a policy-making address delivered in 1950.

For the mutual protection of the Philippines and the United States, a Military-base Agreement was signed in Manila on behalf of the two countries on March 14, 1947. One week later an Agreement on Military Assistance to the Philippines was executed. Both pacts were entered into pursuant to explicit authority granted by the Congress of the United States and the Congress of the Philippines.[1] Important steps had been taken to provide for the national security of the two countries.

Agreements on these subjects were only reached following firm but friendly negotiations. The United States slashed the number of bases originally listed and yielded to the request of the Philippine Government that no bases be established in centers of population. Corregidor Island, which for fifty years symbolized American military might, and along with it Fort McKinley, Nichols Airfield and Fort Santiago, as well as other American establishments, were to be turned over to the Philippine Government. The United States was allowed two years within which to vacate a number of installations in Manila and elsewhere. (The transfer to the Philippine Government was mainly effectuated in 1949.) On the other hand, the United States was granted rights over a series of bases for ninety-nine years. In the interest of international security, any of the bases may be made available to the Security Council of the United Nations.

The Agreement on Military Assistance to the Philippines supple-

---

[1] Joint Resolution of the Congress of the United States of June 29, 1944; Joint Resolution of the Congress of the Philippines of July 28, 1945.

Major General Mariano N. Castañeda, Commanding General of the Philippine Armed Forces; Mrs. Aurora A. Quezon; Major General Rafael Jalandoni, Rtd., Mayor of Iloilo; and Brigadier General Alberto Ramos, Chief of Constabulary.

mented the Military-base Agreement. The Philippine Republic received military equipment and naval vessels from the United States Army and Navy. The Philippine Army's training program was aided by American officers. The groundwork was laid for the active participation of the Philippines in military operations. The attack upon Korea in 1950 led President Truman to direct that military assistance to the Philippines be accelerated.

The Philippines and the United States were taking no chances in preparedness for future eventualities, whatever their form and extent.

THE UNITED STATES ARMED FORCES IN THE PHILIPPINES

Americans can take justifiable pride in the record, extending over half a century, made in the Philippines by the Armed Forces of the United States.

In the early insurrectionary days the United States Army was forced to keep large bodies of men in the Philippines. After military government ceased, the number of soldiers was kept at a minimum. In the years preceding World War II, approximately 10,000 troops were maintained in the Islands, of whom somewhat more than half were Philippine Scouts. The troops were stationed in seven garrisons which together constituted the Philippine Department.

The Philippine Scouts were a unit of the United States Army in which the enlisted men were carefully selected Filipinos and the officers Americans and Filipinos. A number of these Filipino officers had received their training at West Point. The Scouts made good soldiers. The discipline, deportment and marksmanship of the Scouts were often favorably commented upon by their commanding officers.

The disbandment of the famed Philippine Scouts in 1948-49 was a mistake. The armed forces, both American and Philippine, available for defense were small enough without further depletion. And here were nearly 30,000 well trained professional soldiers as proud of their fighting unit as are the Marines.

The Scouts bring to a close a long record of fine service. Some who are American citizens were received into the regular force of the U. S. Army. Others were absorbed into the Philippine Army. The majority simply dispersed into civilian life. All the Scouts retired with honor.[2]

The names of Philippine-trained Army officers who achieved distinction in both World Wars read like an Army register. The meteoric career of General of the Army John J. Pershing received its

---

[2] Hanson W. Baldwin, Military Editor of the *New York Times*, January 20, 1949.

original impetus in combat with the Moros, when President Theodore Roosevelt raised Pershing from Captain to Brigadier General. The name and fame of General of the Army Douglas MacArthur were intimately associated with the Philippines from the days when his father was Military Governor of the Islands until he defeated the Japanese, liberated the Philippines, and passed on to Japan to revolutionize that feudal country. General of the Army Dwight D. Eisenhower had served in the Philippines in 1935-39 as Assistant Adviser of the Military Mission that helped establish the Philippine Commonwealth's defense plan. General Walter Krueger was the hard-bitten soldier who, with a Philippine background and from a private, rose to command the Sixth Army in the reconquest of the Philippines.

The history of the United States Navy in the Philippines followed about the same pattern as that set by the Army. In other words, naval stations were maintained at Cavite and Olongapo. Most of the civilians employed by the Navy were Filipinos. The Asiatic fleet customarily spent the winter season in Philippine waters.

The Navy has given at least three names to Far Eastern history: Perry, who opened Japan to contact with the outside world; Dewey, who brought the Philippines within the ken of America; and Halsey, who wiped the Japanese armada off the sea.

The Philippine station was always of interest to the Army and Navy. Assignment to the Philippines was usually welcomed by officers and their families. The social life at the posts was alluring; in prohibition days the non-prohibition Philippines had its advantages; and the fascinating Orient lay at the Philippine threshold.

The standard maintained by the Armed forces in the Philippines, except in the hysteria provoked by victory over the enemy at the end of the Second World War, has been high. Understandingly the Army and the Navy, and with them in later years the Air Force, have done their jobs with creditable thoroughness. All branches of the service were brought in close contact with the Filipino people, and the unswerving policy was one of friendly cooperation. The officers of the higher ranks were not afflicted with race prejudice; it was only in the junior grades and among the feminine contingent that astigmatic color lines occasionally were drawn.

This is not the place to carry on the narrative through the battles of World War II to victory and peace. Suffice it to say, in inadequate words, that it constituted a glorious chapter in American history, a saga of unrivaled heroism.

With the Philippines a Republic, the status of the Armed Forces of the United States—Army, Navy and Air—changed. Their contingents are now in the Philippines by mutual agreement between the Philippines and the United States.

The United States Army has consolidated its principal military establishment at Fort Stotsenberg and nearby Clark Field in Pampanga Province in Central Luzon. The Clark Field Air Base is expected to dominate all the south China coast, Malaya, Thailand, and the Netherlands Indies. Certainly, this is quite a change from pre-war days when the Negro 9th Cavalry was stationed at Fort Stotsenberg. The United States Navy maintains operating areas at Subic Bay, Zambales, Sangley Point, Cavite, and elsewhere.

The basic policy of the Armed Forces of the United States stationed in the Philippines continues to stress tolerance and helpfulness.

THE ARMED FORCES OF THE PHILIPPINES[3]

With the inaguration of the Philippine Republic, the Armed Forces of the Philippines had to be completely reorganized. This task was accomplished under the efficient direction of Colonel Ruperto Kangleon, the Secretary of National Defense and the guerrilla hero of the Leyte campaign. He was ably aided by the then Chief of Staff Major General Rafael Jalandoni, and by American advisers specially assigned pursuant to the Agreement on Military Assistance.

The Philippine Army of the Commonwealth of the Philippines was called into the service of the United States prior to the outbreak of World War II. The Filipino rank and file served with distinction on Bataan and Corregidor, and, after those reverses, in scattered units throughout the Islands. The Philippine Army remained under the administrational control of the United States Army until a few days before the proclamation of the Philippine Republic in 1946.

The Filipino officers in command were confronted with the problem of demobilization which was kept up until the Army was pruned down to about 35,000 officers and men. Included in the process was the elimination of undesirable elements. On the other hand, care and treatment for disabled veterans were provided. At the same time attention had to be given to the organization of military districts and the reestablishment of the Philippine Military Academy and the Philippine Ground Force School. Training was augmented by instruction of designated students in American institutions.

A Philippine Naval Patrol was planned on a modest scale. A nu-

---

[3] Facts were taken from the Annual Report of the Chief of Staff, AFP for 1948. Executive Order No. 308 by the President of the Philippines, dated March 30, 1950, reorganized the Armed Forces.

cleus of a maritime establishment was begun with the help of the United States Navy. The Revenue Cutter Service and the Lighthouse Service were transferred from the Bureau of Customs to the Naval Patrol. The Philippine Nautical School was rehabilitated and has turned out Filipino cadets. Filipino cadets have made a particularly good showing in the U. S. Merchant Marine School at San Mateo, California.

An air force was established. This was necessarily small, not alone on account of the cost involved, but because defense bases were presumably adequately manned by American personnel. A flying training program was carried on.

As reorganized and functioning in 1950, the major commands of the Armed Forces of the Philippines are the Philippine Constabulary, the Philippine Army, the Philippine Navy, and the Philippine Air Force. The Armed Forces have an overall complement of 40,000, if the Philippine Constabulary be included. Four military areas have been established. ROTC training has begun. Universal military training has made some progress.

The Commanding General (called the Chief of Staff) is the head of the Armed Forces. A general Military Council advises the Secretary of National Defense. Headquarters of the Armed Forces have been set up in commodious Camp Murphy near Manila.

One disagreeable but necessary obligation of the Philippine Armed Forces has been to judge the foe who had outraged the Filipino people. The National War Crimes Office[4] was constituted to try the Japanese war criminals. Eleven Military Commissions were organized. Of the suspects, about eighty have been given the death penalty. But it remains to be said that the Filipino Commissions leaned over backwards to be fair to erstwhile enemies. Many Japanese prisoners, according to American officers, received lighter sentences at Filipino hands than they would if Americans had handled their cases. Yet countless Filipinos suffered beyond words to express.

It had been the popular impression that under the Military Base and Military Assistance Agreements the United States was committed to defend the Philippines in case of attack. That would also seem to be the logical deduction. The American Secretary of State cleared the atmosphere when in a 1950 policy address he announced that "an attack on the Philippines could not and would not be tolerated by the

---

[4] Executive Order No. 68 established a National War Crimes Office. Letter of Attorney Felix Cajulis of November 30, 1948 furnished facts relative to the activities of the Office.

United States." The doubts concerned the extent to which the United States would go in making good her legal and moral promises, and the place the Philippines was to fill in the Pacific security scheme.

The vital question according to the viewpoint of the Philippine Command was: Does the United States intend to defend her bases in the Islands to the limit of her capacity, or will she abandon them in order to effect a withdrawal to her inner ring of defenses? The ambiguity compelled the Philippine Armed Forces to prepare plans, ranging from one in which maximum assistance from the United States is assumed to one in which no assistance is received. The United States should give unequivocal assurances relative to what positive military action may be expected from her, if and when the Philippines is again drawn into war as a result of the presence of American forces there. Another Bataan and another Corregidor are not attractive prospects.

It would appear that what the Philippines needs is a compact, hard hitting, well equipped Philippine Army. It can have it if the Philippine Scouts be made the nucleus of the army. Backing it can be adequate naval patrol vessels and a stronger air force. Thus organized, the Armed Forces should be capable of performing their primary missions, which are handling internal disorder of any proportions and taking an effective part in the defense of the homeland.

The Philippine Constabulary[5]

An Insular police force has been maintained in the Islands under varying nomenclature for a long time. The record made by this semi-military organization has been spotted with bad marks and excellent marks.

The Spaniards supported a body of men, known as the *guardia civil*, in the Philippines to apprehend evildoers. This group was cordially detested. The problem confronting the American administration was to provide a police force to keep public order which, unlike the *guardia civil*, would not terrorize the people. The answer was found in the Philippine Constabulary.

The Philippine Constabulary during this period was a general

---

[5] The annual report of the Chief of Constabulary was used. Exact words were lifted from a special release prepared for the author. John R. White, *Bullets and Bolos* is a stirring account of the activities of the pre-war Constabulary. A later book is that of Major Emanuel A. Baja, *Philippine Police System and its Problems* (Manila, 1933).

police force under military discipline. It was commanded by a distinguished list of officers. A number of the American officers who won renown for themselves and their country in World War I had received their training in the Philippines—men of the stature of Generals Harbord and Bandholtz. Major General Basilio J. Valdez, a skilled Philippine physician who served in the French Army in World War I, became Chief of Constabulary and later Chief of Staff of the Philippine Army in World War II.

The Constabulary was engaged in numerous important campaigns. In the performance of multitudinous, and frequently less spectacular, functions, the force won deserved fame.

This was the fine organization which the Japanese took over to make of it the instrument of attempted conquest. The reputation of the Constabulary reverted to the odor of *guardia civil* days. Nor did conditions improve very much when, after the defeat of the invaders, the Philippine Army formed the Military Police Command. This was an unsatisfactory arrangement because the Provost Marshal General became responsible to two different departments, National Defense and Interior. Recognizing the anomalous situation, President Roxas, by an executive order effective in 1948, abolished the Military Police Command and in its place revived the pre-war Philippine Constabulary. It was made distinct and separate from the regular army. Subsequently President Quirino delimited the functions of the Constabulary to purely police duties, leaving suppression of dissidence and rebellion to the Armed Forces. In 1950 the Philippine Constabulary was formally absorbed into the integrated Armed Forces in order to achieve unification of command.

General headquarters of the Constabulary are maintained at Camp Crame, Quezon City, so named in honor of Brigadier General Rafael Crame, the first Filipino to command the force. The revitalization of operational activities for greater efficiency was accomplished by re-organization into zonal commands.

The personnel of the Constabulary was raised from 6,000 authorized before the war to a strength of 12,000 men. This force was for a time complemented with an additional 8,000 men on temporary detail from the Armed Forces of the Republic. The serious peace and order situation which has prevailed since liberation more than warranted the increase. However, as a part of the plan to effect better coordination of the nation wide campaign to cope with disorder, the Constabulary eventually reverted to its pre-war status in functions and number.

Since liberation of the Philippines from the Japanese, the Constabulary has engaged in putting down armed resistance not only in Moroland as before the war, but also in Central and Southern Luzon where the Huks, a communist-led outlaw organization, has perpetrated a reign of terror and violence for some time. Hundreds of Constabulary lives have been lost, and millions of pesos worth of arms and supplies have been spent in the attempted suppression of this rebellious group. The Constabulary was only partially successful in decimating the Huk forces and in driving them to the mountains.

Added to this post-liberalization problem is the existence of small outlaw bands in many provinces. These bands were resistance groups during the enemy occupation, which after liberation refused to turn in their weapons to the authorities. Fortunately, some of them have been rounded up. More than 200,000 firearms have been confiscated, but double that number are loose in irresponsible hands.

MUNICIPAL POLICE

The municipal police forces constitute one of the most serious weaknesses in the whole governmental structure. This statement errs on the side of leniency.

Every city and municipality possesses a police force at the head of which is a chief of police. Cities like Manila and Baguio have had, and again can have, well organized police departments. Elsewhere, and particularly in the smaller municipalities, the police are riddled with politics. The municipal Mayor is prone to consider policemen as his personal servants or agents. The police departments become veritable dumping grounds for political protégés and favorites who are untrained in the work they are expected to perform.

The policeman's pay is grossly inadequate. Some of them have been known to receive as little as six pesos a month. Even at ₱100 a month a living wage is lacking. The situation is ready-made for rampant corruption and odorous scandals.

Reformers have tilted their lances in favor of doing away with a rotten police system, without success. An experiment with a State Police Force begun by the Commonwealth Government in 1936 had to be abandoned two years later.[6] The failure meant a victory for local self-government but not for efficient keeping of the peace and the apprehension of malefactors. Petty politics had again claimed its spoils.

The Government is alive to the danger incident to allowing unfit

---

[6] State Police Force created by Commonwealth Act No. 88 of October 26, 1936. Act No. 88 repealed by Commonwealth Act No. 343 of May 23, 1938.

persons to perform the duties of protecting life and property. The technical assistant to the Government on police matters urges revitalization of police forces.[7] The N. B. I. is training specially selected police officers.

What more can be done to improve law enforcement by the local governments, remains for someone better informed to say.

CRIME[8]

Law enforcement in the Philippines has passed through a series of stages. First there was the initial period in the early days of American occupation, characterized by brigandage and lawlessness. Next followed tranquil years only broken by occasional mercantile swindles, opium raids, and Moro outbreaks. During this period the statement could truthfully be made that Manila residents had less to fear from criminals than the people of any city anywhere, and that one could travel safely throughout the length and breadth of the Archipelago. This was a situation too good to last, for beginning in the '30's the curve of criminality began to move upward to reach an all-time high in post-war scorn of the law.

The prevalence of crime in the Republic of the Philippines is readily explainable. The war placed weapons in many hands and induced slight respect for authority. The aftermath of the war brought in its wake high cost of living, government scandals, and mass restlessness. While conditions gradually adjusted themselves, it will be a long time before normalcy prevails.

Civilization masquerading as Mars, the God of War, had brought with it hangers-on of uncertain character. Moving among the naturally peace-loving Filipino people were gangster bands, plying their trade of robbery and violence in passable imitation of the American type of the breed. Greed extended its hand into government funds to extract its toll, and smaller fingers filched from private owners. Petty thieves emulated their more showy brothers to the annoyance of householders. The handouts needed to expedite action in certain government offices, while not exactly criminal, were certainly nuisances.

Statistics disclose that the most prevalent crimes in the Philippines are against property. In 1946, a total of six hundred and thirty-nine

[7] Speech of Delfin Batacan before the Manila Rotary Club on January 13, 1949.

[8] Facts were obtained from the annual report of the Bureau of Prisons for 1948 and in a personal conference with Alfredo M. Bunye, Superintendent, New Bilibid Prison. See Justice Ignacio Villamor, *Criminality in the Philippines* (Manila, 1909).

prisoners found guilty of such offenses were committed to the Bilibid and San Ramon penal institutions; in 1948, the number was 1,711. Crimes against persons were likewise on the rise during the same period, the homicide figures growing from two hundred and thirteen in 1946 to nine hundred and thirty-five in 1948.

Credulity and superstition are also important factors in Philippine criminology. The barrio people have proved gullible victims of fake prophets.

Verdicts of death are authorized in the Philippines. Great care is taken to avoid a miscarriage of justice in this class of cases. The law requires the elevation of the record to the Supreme Court for review whenever the death penalty is imposed in the trial court, and the concurrence of eight of the eleven members of the high Court.

The Spaniards gave the Islands a Penal Code which even for its time was antiquated and which Spain has discarded in favor of more modern legislation. The code made the law an arithmetical process. The judge had no discretion. The penalty for the higher crimes was denominated *cadena* (chains), as *cadena perpetua* (perpetual chains). Little by little the Spanish Penal Code has given way to more humane measures, such as a Revised Penal Code, an indeterminate sentence law, and a probationary system.

The Spanish penal system was as defective as its penal laws. The American forces liberated countless Filipino prisoners incarcerated for unknown crimes or still awaiting trials after years of delay. Gradually the dark dungeons were sealed and conditions improved in Bilibid Prison located in the center of Manila.

The present penal system is far ahead of the one which it succeeded, as tested by the generally accepted principles of penology and as testified to by well qualified prison experts. The institutions under the administration of the Bureau of Prisons are the New Bilibid Prison in Muntinlupa not far from Manila; the Correctional Institution for Women; the San Ramon Colony and Penal Farm near Zamboanga; the Iwahig Colony and Penal Farm on the Island of Palawan; and the Davao Colony and Penal Farm. Vocational training of inmates is emphasized. Under way is an industrial and agricultural program intended to make the penal colonies self-supporting. Major Eriberto Misa, Director of Prisons, who passed away in 1949, was the man who made prison life bearable and who initiated these practical and humanitarian policies.

The prison system is complemented by the provincial and municipal jails. Possibly "complemented" is too complimentary a word to use. Probably "handicapped" would be nearer the truth. The sanitary equipment of these jails is deficient. Prisoners are frequently allowed their freedom and are permitted to sleep at home. One enterprising provincial governor who had been authorized to use prisoners to construct a road gave a dance in their honor at which they passed delightful hours with the village belles.

It needs to be repeated that the Filipinos are innately peaceful. This admirable quality should help greatly to bring about tranquillity.

THE HUK HEADACHE [9]

Unsettled conditions in the post-war Philippines were ideally fitted to irresponsible agitation, lawless banditry, and armed revolt. The Huk-PKM associations that sprang up were the lineal descendants of the *Colorum, Tangulan,* and *Sakdalista* movements, and these in turn were but the modern manifestations of age old grievances.

The *Colorum* uprising in Northeastern Mindanao in 1923-24 was suppressed by a Constabulary expedition that killed some one hundred and thirty-five of the fanatics. The *Tangulan* outbreak in Northern Luzon in 1931 met a similar fate. The *Sakdalistas* organized in 1930-31 by Benigno Ramos, a disgruntled minor employee of the Philippine Senate, among the discontented masses in the provinces close to Manila, set a pattern of subversive agitation and sedition that was even more serious.

The biggest surprise of the 1934 elections was the showing made by the *Sakdalistas.* Before the elections, even the name *Sakdalistas* was unknown to the public. Then the results were published, and everyone was astounded to learn that the *Sakdalistas* had elected two representatives to the Legislature, one provincial governor, and a number of municipal officials.

A year later came another unwelcome surprise. Labor Day, which in the Philippines coincides with May Day, annually causes apprehension due to the fear of excesses. In 1935, that apprehension would naturally be expected to be increased because of the near approach of the date for voting on the Constitution, against which there was opposition. A carefully prepared *Sakdal* plot to seize the Government by force broke out in riots at three points. Municipal buildings were seized, property was destroyed, private citizens were molested, and constituted authority was defied. Before the Constabulary could

---

[9] The articles by, and interviews with, Judge Quirino Abad Santos contain first hand information on the controversial subject of the Huks. Judge Abad Santos is a former member of the Agrarian Commission and a former legal adviser of the Huks. Current Manila press reports were used. *Hukbong Mapagpalaya Ng Bayan,* is known as *Hukbalahap* in its abbreviated form, or merely as *Huk.*

put down the revolt, over a hundred *Sakdalistas* and a few Constabulary men had been wounded or killed.

For a brief period the grievances of the peasant farmers of Central Luzon were partly channeled into democratic conduits. They accepted the leadership of the scholarly Pedro Abad Santos of Pampanga Province and voted the Socialist ticket. In 1940 he was defeated for the Governorship of his province, but polled 33,000 votes against the 40,000 received by the *Nacionalista* incumbent of the office. This was a remarkable showing in view of the fact that nearly fifty percent of the Santos followers were not qualified voters because of illiteracy.

In the meantime the *Sakdal* Party had been rejuvenated under the name of *Ganap*. The *Sakdal-Ganap* group of Benigno Ramos became a fifth column for the Japanese. Countless other persons, however, formed resistance units to fight the invaders.

The *Hukbalahap* was formally organized in 1942. It boasts of a commendable record of harassment of the Japanese.[10] However, other activities that came to the notice of the United States Army during the war denied the Huks the benefit of guerrilla recognition. With the war over, they became the headache of the Filipino administration. The Huks now call themselves the Peoples Liberation Army.

It is, of course, impossible to more than roughly estimate the membership of the allied Huk-PKM associations. One intelligence report affirmed that in two provinces alone (Nueva Ecija and Pampanga) 110,000 individuals were affiliated with the two organizations, some from choice, some by chance, and others because of compulsion. Their habitat is Central and Southern Luzon. In this region fear and insecurity of property have curtailed the production of badly needed agricultural products.

The Huk movement is a purely local undertaking.[11] Nevertheless, there is a strict adherence to the Communist line. The Huk leaders, among them Luis Taruc, are avowed members of the Communist Party.[12] Their goal is the implantation of communism in the Philippines and the overthrow of the regularly constituted government by armed force.

The story of the Huk-PKM associations reveals a government within a government. It is well organized, with economic, political and military aims. The authority of the Republic has been repeatedly challenged. A number of towns have been invaded by the Huks.

---

[10] Memorandum to General MacArthur and President Osmena submitted by "Luis M. Taruc, Commander in Chief Hukbalahap."

[11] Statement of Judge Quirino Abad Santos, *Philippines Free Press*, July 3, 1948.

[12] Luis Taruc's letter in the *Manila Times* of August 13, 1948.

Military patrols have been ambuscaded. Engagements with the government forces have been fought with varying results. Ultimately, the Huk menace, originally socialist-inspired, and later communist-motivated, degenerated into common banditry. In one year, according to the Chief of Constabulary, the Huks got from Central Luzon peasants ₱12,000,000 worth of rice and ₱1,200,000 in cash.

Pedro Abad Santos and Luis Taruc, the two chief exponents of present day peasant grievances, were opposites in temperament, beliefs and methods.

Abad Santos was the elder brother of the heroic Chief Justice, and was made of the same stern fibre. He was an experienced lawyer, and a socialist zealot, who honestly believed that the only solution to mounting agrarian unrest lay in the immediate expropriation and subdivision of Church and private estates. Abad Santos died without seeing his hopes for the betterment of the poor realized.

Luis Taruc, a protégé of Abad Santos, was also Pampanga-born. After graduation from high school, he became secretary of the General Union of Workers. From labor leader to elected Member of the House of Representatives, to top Huk Commander was an easy transition. Taruc's co-leader has been Castro Alejandrino and his collaborator Mateo del Castillo, head of the PKM. In these men is personified the spirit of protest.

Government policy for the solution of the Huk problem understandingly followed a wavering course. Appeasement through conferences was first tried. When this line failed, enforcement of the law was attempted. Bombastic announcements that at last the Huk menace had been stopped once and for all were made, only to have the ubiquitous Taruc and his followers thumb their noses at the agents of the law. Finally government patience was exhausted. On March 6, 1948 President Roxas formally outlawed the Huks. He supported his charges with a mass of evidence gathered by government agencies.[13]

Not long after, Vice President Quirino was catapulted into the Presidency. With a realization of the difficulties involved in an attempt to uproot Hukism through force alone, the new President reverted to negotiations with the Huk leader with a view to his surrender under a grant of amnesty to him and his followers. Taruc did, indeed, present himself personally to President Quirino on June 21, 1948 with a token number of arms. Amnesty was immediately proclaimed.

The dramatic surrender of the rebellious Huk chieftain was a surprising climax to protracted negotiations. Taruc was escorted by

---

[13] Printed press statement of 32 pages of President Roxas released on March 6, 1948.

plane to Manila, was whisked to Malacañan, and there gave his personal pledge of recognition of the authority of the government. The President forthwith signed the amnesty proclamation. The President of the Republic and the leader of the dissidents exchanged handclasps in token of amity. It was generally conceded that President Quirino conducted himself with dignity and that Taruc responded in a quiet, modest manner.

The surrender of the supreme commander of the Huks merely signified a temporary truce. Taruc lived comfortably in Malacañan Palace or elsewhere. The Huks were provided with a vacation for recuperation, so to speak. The amnesty offer expired on August 15th without the Huks surrendering their arms. Taruc slipped away to join his followers in the hills. From his hideout, he wrote a letter to a Manila paper in which he asserted that Russia is "the ally" of the Filipinos, and openly urged Filipino peasants to support Russia's policy in Asia. Benevolent amnesty was a fiasco.

Let no one delude himself into believing that peace and order have come to the Philippines. Hardly a day passes but that the public is regaled with newspaper headlines of the Huks swooping down on a town, sacking it, and departing with loot and captives. As one of the countless instances of this brand of lawlessness, in early 1949 an estimated three hundred Huks attacked the important town of Orani, Bataan under cover of darkness. In a wild orgy of murder, pillage and arson, sixteen peaceful citizens were killed, numerous others were injured, and some seventy houses were burned and gutted, rendering about four hundred people homeless.

The acme of wanton and pointless tragedy came on April 28, 1949 when Mrs. Aurora A. Quezon and party, while on a trip to Baler, the birthplace of the late President, to unveil a historical marker and to participate in the inauguration of the local hospital, were treacherously ambuscaded by a band of well armed Huks. Slain and robbed were Mrs. Quezon, "the most revered woman in the Philippines," her daughter Maria Aurora, her son-in-law Felipe Buencamino Jr., and others. Even as a shocked nation mourned, there came a renewed determination to suppress the bands which perpetrated the incredible crime. But that retribution would not be brought about easily was made evident, when a few days after the tragedy, while government forces were engaged in tracking down the savage killers, Huks descended on Sibul Springs and ravaged that peaceful health resort. The year 1950 saw an even more serious threat to peace and order by rampaging bands who flaunted their armed strength before the police and Constabulary and even the army in towns close to Manila.

The Huks have a legitimate cause of land reform to champion, but they are going about securing a redress of grievances in an illegitimate, treasonable way.[14] A permanent solution of a basic problem will take time, patience, understanding, and persuasion. In the meantime the purpose of the Huks remains the overthrow of the Government and the establishment of their own Communistic State. Consequently force must be met by force. There is no alternative.

The Communist Invasion [15]

Communism exists in the Philippines. It would be strange if this were not so. Nearby are Indonesia, Malaya, Indo-China, Burma, and Korea, where the pattern of events has long indicated a communistic upheaval. Even closer is China, where the harassed Nationalists have fought a life and death and losing struggle with the communistic hordes of "the Peoples Republic." Farther away are Siberia and the Union of Soviet Republics, where Filipinos have been indoctrinated with the principles of Marx and Lenin. Distant in mileage but with modern communications easily bridged is the communistic organization in the United States, that is said to direct the activities of the Communist Party of the Philippines.

The extent and the nature of ties with Russia are of course shrouded in the secrecy in which the agents of communism operate. It is known that the Philippine immigration authorities have carefully screened Russian residents, and that a number of them have been deported as undesirable aliens. It is also known that Chinese with unsavory radical antecedents have suddenly cropped up in the Islands. Indirect connections between the Filipino Huks and Moscow have been established by Philippine Army operatives through the seizure of documents and hammer and sickle flags. It is even reported that submarines have been seen to surface near the coast in isolated regions, to land arms and equipment and to bring in technicians.

Communism thrives on poverty and ignorance. As a consequence it found a virgin field for propaganda in certain parts of the Philippines. The type of Philippine-adopted communism is but another manifestation of the restlessness of the spirit that brought thousands of credulous Filipinos into the folds of the *Colorums*, the *Tangulans*,

---

14 Restrained American views were revealed in editorials "The Use of Force," *Manila Daily Bulletin,* April 15, 1948, and "Patriotism or Demagoguery," *Louisville* (Kentucky) *Courier Journal,* July 4, 1948.

15 See preceding notes and Maximo Giron, *Report on Communism in the Philippines* (Manila, 1946).

the *Sakdalistas*, the *Ganaps*, and the *Hukbalahaps*, all in nature fanatical and subversive organizations.

As early as 1932-33 the Supreme Court of the Philippines, in a series of decisions in which all the members joined, declared the Communist Party of the Philippines to be an illegal association.[16] The constitution and bylaws of the party quoted by the Court disclosed its ideals and aims, among them to establish in the Philippines a Soviet government under the proletariat. A number of party members were found guilty of the crime of sedition. Notwithstanding these judicial precedents, the Communist Party is allowed to operate freely in the Philippines.

About the time of the inauguration of the Philippine Republic, the Congress of the Philippines was confronted with the problem of alleged communistic activities with special reference to election terrorism in Central Luzon. An Un-Filipino Activities Committee of the lower House, headed by Member Cornelio T. Villa-Real, conducted an exhaustive investigation. The Committee reported "that there is a deliberate plot to create a revolutionary situation here, similar to that which existed in Russia in 1917, in order to enable a militant minority to capture the powers of government." The Committee then proceeded to describe the Communist Party in the Philippines. It found this party an integral part of a world-wide revolutionary movement. "It seeks," said the Committee, "the overthrow of the form of government established by the Constitution of the Republic of the Philippines." The Committee continued to expose communism and to combat its spread.

The findings of the Un-Filipino Activities Committee were supported by the testimony of a number of well informed officials, among them the N. B. I. Director, the Chief of the Armed Forces intelligence division, and the former head of the Philippine Constabulary, who led the military phase of the campaign against communism for over two years, and who subsequently became the respected Commanding General of the Armed Forces. The latter, Major General Mariano N. Castañeda, stated bluntly that the Communist Party in the Philippines is the political front of the militant Huk organization. He revealed that the local communists and Huks are getting financial aid from foreign sources and from local Chinese supporters.

The number of communists in the Philippines and the elements that make it up can, of course, only be guessed at. Secretary of Labor Primitivo Lovina's estimate is that half a million persons in the Philip-

[16] Evangelista *v.* Earnshaw, 57 Phil. 255; People *v.* Evangelista, 57 Phil. 354; People *v.* Capadocia, 57 Phil. 364; People *v.* Feleo, 58 Phil. 573.

pines are party members or sympathizers. The hard shell of fanatics is there, and around it is a fringe of fellow travelers who would as readily take part in any other similar cause.

The Huk and PKM leaders readily admit sympathy with communism; their lawless acts constitute indisputable proof of their treasonable purposes. The CLO is a radical labor organization closely associated with the communistic camp. The Democratic Alliance, it is charged, is communistic-tainted, but this the President of the Alliance denies.[17] The danger is that all of these ramifications of communism and near-communism will be welcomed into partnership by some democratic group, and from the inner circle of sham respectability will undermine the whole government's foundation to its destruction.

The top Filipino communist is Mariano P. Balgos, the secretary-general of the Communist Party of the Philippines. The dossier of Balgos discloses that he is a labor leader who holds the rank of Major General in the Huk organization, as the political commissar. He has been most vocal in espousing the tenets of the party line. Balgos and Guillermo Capadocia, another communist leader, have declared that in case of trouble, they and their fellows will side with the Red Army and sabotage the war effort of the democratic Philippines. Balgos and Capadocia joined the Huks in their hideouts shortly after the 1949 election.

Communism will be a potential threat in the Philippines as long as misery and discontent provide a breeding place for it to work on. It is significant that communism is weakest in countries like Mexico and Argentina, where social reform is most advanced. Communism, or something akin to it, is strongest in the Far East region of spawning millions in close proximity to the Philippines. It will be no easy matter to contain communism and stem its spread.

These facts carry a moral for the Philippines. Use the strong-arm method when forced to do so when revolt impends. Otherwise, to quote the words of a former President of Venezuela: Satisfy the "longing for justice and well-being that torments the popular soul with practical, positive, and concrete achievements, and thus remove it from the seduction of Marxist promises."

---

[17] Judge Jesus A. Barrera in a statement made to the press on May 31, 1947 and appearing in the *Manila Chronicle* of that date.

CHAPTER XXII

PUBLIC WELFARE

THE PUBLIC SCHOOLS[1]

On August 23, 1901, Manila capitulated a second time, and on this latter occasion to some six hundred American school teachers who arrived on the Transport *Thomas*. These pioneer teachers spread out over the Islands like an army of occupation and peacefully conquered the youth who were avid for education. Their advance-guard had been soldiers called from the ranks to teach, who, within three weeks after the capture of Manila, had opened seven schools in the city. The public school system begun by the military was permanently established under the School Law enacted by the Philippine Commission.

The executive control of the Bureau of Public Schools is centralized in the Director. The entire responsibility for the conduct of the school work rests directly upon him. The powers of the Director are tremendous: the disbursement of over thirty percent of the annual appropriations of the National Government, the development of educational policies for the entire school system, and the marshaling of thousands of teachers and millions of pupils. To administer efficiently this educational empire, the Director must depend on a system of detailed supervision extending in a direct line from his office to the division superintendents of schools and right down to the classroom teachers.

In the hands of capable Directors, the powers lodged in the directorate have been used to the best advantage. American educators like Dr. David P. Barrows, later to become President of the University of

---

[1] Under Secretary of Education Esteban R. Abada checked the copy. Dr. Luther B. Bewley, Educational Adviser to the President of the Philippines, offered valuable suggestions. Representative authorities on the subject of the schools include the following: Monroe, *Survey of the Educational System of the Philippine Islands* (1925); Report of the Quezon Educational Survey Committee (1936); Encarnacion Alzona, *A History of Education in the Philippine Islands* (Manila, 1932); Antonio Isidro and others, *Education in the Philippines* (Manila, 1939), a commemorative volume to celebrate the silver anniversary of the College of Education, University of the Philippines, and containing 18 monographs on as many phases of Philippine education; J. R. Hayden, *The Philippines, A Study in National Development*, Part Three (New York, 1942); Benigno Aldana, *The Educational System of the Philippines* (Manila, 1949); and Gilbert S. Perez, *From the Transport Thomas to Sto. Tomas* (Manila, 1949).

California, laid the foundation of the Philippine public school system. Dr. Luther B. Bewley, the last American Director of the Bureau, occupied the position for nineteen years undisturbed by political changes, and when he did relinquish the office to a Filipino successor, only did so to pass to the equally important post of Educational Adviser to the President of the Philippines.

The Bureau of Public Schools has been allowed to perform its normal functions with little interference from above. The Secretaries of the Department of Education have not always been educators, and so, wisely, they have limited their supervision to support of policies developed by the experienced schoolmen who have headed the Bureau. Dr. Alejandro Albert, for two decades Undersecretary of the Department, cooperated modestly but effectively in the adaptation of progressive ideas to Philippine educational needs. Dr. Gabriel R. Mañalac, Prudencio Langcauon, Esteban R. Abada, and Dr. Cecilio Putong, were worthy successors.

The Filipino participation in the direction of the Bureau of Public Schools naturally became increasingly important, until today it is all important. Camilo Osias, Columbia-educated, became the first Filipino division superintendent; he later won further distinction in education and politics. Celedonio Salvador was the first Filipino Director. He was an able administrator and was serving at the head of the Bureau at the outbreak of the Pacific war. Benito Pangilinan, more recently the Director, is a straight thinking administrator who is striving to recoup the losses due to war, to reestablish education on a firm basis, and to give his country the best system possible under available appropriations.

Dr. J. R. Hayden, who knew whereof he spoke because of experience gained in the office of Secretary of Public Instruction, has pointed out that the development of an educational system for the Philippines has resulted in a never completely satisfactory answer to the question of quality or quantity.[2] It was desired to meet basic educational objectives; to do so, standards in instruction had to be maintained. It was desired to enroll all the Filipino children of school age; to attempt to do so, facilities for school work had to be strained to the limit and standards had to be lowered.

Instruction was formerly provided in the primary schools which gave a four-year course, in the intermediate schools which provided a three-year course, and in schools on the secondary level which offered courses of four years. Although a total of eleven years of

2 J. R. Hayden, *The Philippines, A Study in National Development*, Ch. XVIII.

schooling did not err on the side of over-education, in 1940 a law was enacted which authorized a reduction of the elementary course (primary and intermediate grades) from seven to not less than five years. What actually resulted was the elimination of the seventh grade, thus further reducing the required years of instruction from eleven to ten. Quality had been sacrificed so as to place the primary and intermediate courses of instruction "within the reach of the largest number of school children," to quote one of the objectives of the law.

The Bureau of Public Schools also maintains special national schools which offer courses on the junior college level. The Philippine Normal College in Manila provides facilities for teacher training; seven other collegiate normal schools are located in regional centers, and one normal school in the provinces operates on a secondary level.

The Philippine School of Arts and Trades in Manila places emphasis on vocational training; and there are two large trade schools in the provinces financed by the National Government that have similar aims. In addition there are two vocational high schools, one in Manila and the other in Aparri, Cagayan, and twenty-two provincial trade schools in operation.

The Central Luzon Agricultural College at Muñoz, Nueva Ecija, is the best known of the agricultural schools. At present there are in operation four other regional agricultural schools that are financed by the National Government. There are also eleven special national agricultural schools and eleven rural high schools maintained by the local governments.

One of the problems constantly confronting the school authorities has been the acquisition of school sites and the construction of school buildings. They have never been able to meet the demands of an expanding enrollment. With the destruction of war added to an already complicated situation, the standardized building program has had to be modified to meet emergency conditions. With war damage funds, reconstruction of buildings to house the schools goes on apace. Until this program is farther advanced, classes must continue to be held in makeshift structures.

The legislative body has at all times provided generously for the public schools. The first Act passed by the Philippine Assembly in 1907 appropriated ₱1,000,000 for the building of rural schools. Another outstanding legislative enactment set aside ₱30,000,000 for the operation and extension of the elementary schools. The regular annual expenditures for educational purposes have totaled over twenty percent of all insular, provincial, and municipal income.

The percentage total carried by the National Government has

tended to increase under the Commonwealth and the Republic, because of the execution of educational policy laid down in the Constitution and auxiliary laws, by which financial responsibility for the primary grades was assumed by the National Government. Thirty percent of the national budgets have been devoted to education. In proportion to income, the Philippines expends more for the encouragement of the means of education than Latin American and Far Eastern Nations—more even than the United States.

Filipino youth has responded magnificently to the call for educations. Before the inauguration of the Philippine Commonwealth, approximately 1,300,000 pupils were enrolled in the schools, public and private. Under the impetus of the expansion of the school system that thereafter occurred, enrollment reached the 2,000,000 mark. During the ghastly four years of the Occupation, attendance dropped eighty percent. In the years since liberation, not alone has this lost ground been regained, but school attendance has more than doubled. Enrolled in the Philippine Schools in 1949-50 were over 4,000,000 students.

These cold figures do not tell half the story. Filipino parents make all kinds of sacrifices so that their children may be educated. Juan in the field and his good wife Maria in the house may be putting away in a bamboo tube a peso today and two pesos tomorrow to send to Juan, Jr., in the big city, who is studying to be a *medico* (doctor). The pity of it all is that strain as much as the Government may to obtain more money to devote to education, and save as much as parents may to educate their offspring, there still remain out of school thousands of children of school age. It will be a long time before combined government and private resources will be sufficient to assure every Filipino child an education.

Filipino children make good students. At this point recall the handicap they are under. First they must learn to speak, read and write a foreign language before they can proceed with their studies. Notwithstanding this tremendous obstacle, Filipino boys and girls are ambitious to learn. So long as the Filipino pupils are able to find justness and firmness in their teachers, they show better discipline than American children. In intelligence the Filipino students compare favorably with any other nationality.

The public schools are staffed by over 70,000 teachers. It is to be doubted if half of them have gone beyond high school. Enrollment in the normal schools has steadily decreased. The reason why more young people are not attracted to the teaching profession is not far to seek. Salaries paid teachers have been so low as to offer little inducement to the ambitious to follow such a career. Before the war, the average monthly salary of elementary municipal teachers was about ₱52.00 ($26.00). The increases granted teachers since liberation have not kept pace with living costs, with the result that thousands of experienced teachers have been driven by necessity to seek more lucrative employment. However, standardization of teachers' salaries in 1948 and 1949 helped to undo an injustice to these poorly paid employees.

Those in executive authority, the various Governors General and Secretaries of Public Instruction under the Government of the Philippine Islands, the President and the Secretary of Instruction under the Philippine Commonwealth, have presented a common front against the intrusion of politics into the schools. It came, therefore, as something of a shock to find the Secretary of Education of the Republic (not the actual incumbent of the office) publicly stating his conviction that teachers should take part in politics. This announcement would appear to be a repudiation of the portion of the Constitution which prohibits Civil Service employees (teachers) from engaging directly or indirectly in partisan politics. This attitude on the part of the highest educational authority at that time resulted in untold harm to the educational system.

Opinions differ on whether the public school system of the Philippines has proved to be a failure or a success. Repeatedly expert advice has been sought in an effort to point the way to improvements in the system.

In 1925 a Commission of nine American educators, under the Chairmanship of Dr. Paul Monroe of Columbia University, a schoolman with an international reputation, made a careful survey of Philippine education. The Monroe Commission found things to praise and matters to condemn. Particularly noteworthy, because of direct application to present day conditions in the schools of the Philippines, was the Commission's sharp comment on the appalling elimination of pupils in the lower grades. "The mass of Filipino pupils do not stay in school long enough to develop for permanent use even the rudiments of an education," read one sentence in the Commission's report. Nevertheless as a general conclusion, Dr. Monroe in 1935 declared that "The present system of education in the Philippines is one of the best in the world."

It was natural for the Filipino leaders, when they obtained control of the governmental machinery in the same year in which the laudatory statement about their educational system was made, to want to have it reexamined from the Filipino view-point. There resulted three bodies, a committee appointed by the Commonwealth President in 1935, a joint executive and legislative committee named in 1939, and a more permanent organization, the National Council of Education, created in 1936, all designed to adapt the educational system to the needs of the Nation and to advise on policies and reforms. Republic Act No. 176, which became a law in 1947, created a National Commission on Educational, Scientific, and Cultural Matters. The Commission supersedes the National Council of Education. Dr. Gabriel Manalac, an experienced educator and rightly looked up to as a model of integrity, is Chairman of the Commission, an assurance that its powers and duties will be performed competently.

The year 1949 saw still another survey of the Philippine educational system. At the request of the Philippine Government, it was conducted by the United Nations Educational, Scientific and Cultural Organization (UNESCO) consultative educational mission to the Philippines. Dr. Floyd Reeves, Dean of the College of Education, University of Chicago, headed the body. The mission worked on the principle that education should concern itself not only with instruction of the pupils, but with the broader purpose of promoting the social, economic and cultural life of the people. If the mission can succeed in laying a proper emphasis on goals for Philippine youth it will have been worthwhile. At present the Philippines abounds with professionals. The Philippines lacks technicians in the trades, manufacturing, transport, and related pursuits.

The 1940 Law sanctioned certain changes in the educational system with which few can quibble. For instance, the law decreed that no child shall be admitted to the public schools except on condition that he shall remain in school until he shall have completed the primary courses. This provision of the Educational Act was strictly enforced prior to the outbreak of the war. Since liberation, little attention, if any, has been given to compulsory education. The law further made effective the provision in the Constitution that the Government shall provide at least free public primary instruction, by making the National Government responsible for financing elementary education.

The debatable parts of the 1940 Act were those which in effect eliminated Grade VII, and which authorized the holding of two complete single sessions a day. In an effort to provide for quantity education, quality education had been so dangerously sacrificed as to arrive at a minus result. The horrendous consequence was that most of the pupils did not stay long enough in the crucial elementary grades and did not learn enough under the abbreviated session plan while enrolled to emerge literate. Few learned to speak, read and write either English, Tagalog, or their own dialect, and those who did were mostly the well-to-do who could afford to continue their studies.[3]

It was pertinently observed that this school system created two classes: the adequately educated rich, and the half educated poor. No wonder that an aroused citizenry, backed by teacher and parent opinion, demanded a return to the levels obtaining before 1940. The provisions of the Educational Act of 1940 enforcing the double single session not only resulted in lowering standards, but the additional burden that was placed on the already overworked teachers caused many of the most efficient ones to leave the service.

Occasional attacks on the Philippine educational system have in the main only served to bring out the general excellence of the administration of the public schools and to strengthen the faith of the people in it. A complete answer to many of the aspersions cast on the Bureau of Public Schools is that the same reflections apply as well to education in the United States and other countries. Except that within the foreseeable future not enough money can be found to guarantee every child an opportunity to obtain the rudiments of an education, all other defects would seem to be within the competency of the authorities to remedy.

By way of final comment it can be said that American and Filipino educators have done a good job, that the teachers deserve unstinted praise for the sacrifices they have made and for the splendid work they have done, that the Filipino students constitute a fine body, and that the Philippine educational system has proved to be a prime factor in nation building.

THE UNIVERSITY OF THE PHILIPPINES [4]

The year 1949 found the University of the Philippines established in its new home in Diliman, Quezon City.

The transfer from the cramped Manila campus to the vast, rolling plain northeast of Manila was decided upon in 1938. This was the recommendation of President Edward C. Elliott of Purdue University and Dean Paul C. Packer of the University of Iowa, who surveyed the University in that year and whose views met with the strong endorsement of Commonwealth President Quezon. War's heavy hand disrupted the plan and laid low the artistic University buildings in Manila. But with peace came the transfer of two hundred buildings of

---

[3] See the critical article by Teodoro M. Locsin, staff member in the *Philippines Free Press* of May 29, 1948.

[4] Pertinent data was made available by President Bienvenido M. Gonzales. See Encarnacion Alzona, *A History of Education in the Philippine Islands*, Ch. XXI.

various sizes on the Diliman site to the University by the American Government and war damage payments in the amount of ₱10,000,000 permitting of a large scale construction program.

For obvious reasons the College of Medicine, the Institute of Hygiene, and the College of Nursing will remain in Manila. The College of Agriculture and the College of Forestry will continue in Los Baños. The Cebu College and the Iloilo College will function in their respective localities.

The University of the Philippines is the capstone of Philippine education. Founded in 1908 by an Act of the Philippine Legislature[5] drafted by Secretary of Public Instruction Shuster, it was to be expected that the state university in the Philippines would conform to the American pattern in organization and methods. In other words, the University of the Philippines was intended to occupy a place in the Philippine system of public education similar to that of the pioneer State University in Michigan, whose graduates have most influenced the development of its Philippine counterpart.

The governing body of the University of the Philippines is a Board of Regents composed of members either *ex officio*, including the Secretary of Education as Chairman, or appointed by the President of the Republic; four of the appointive members are selected from among the University alumni. At the head of the University is a President with customary powers, except that he does not preside over meetings of the Board of Regents. The University Council consists of the President and all instructors in the University holding the rank of professor, associate professor, or assistant professor; this body exercises authority over the academic affairs of the institution.

The student body totals 7,000, which taxes the facilities of the University to the limit. The enrollment is not large when compared with the numbers registered in private universities, but suffices if the purpose of the State institution be kept in view. For it should, as it does, set the standard in scholarship for others to emulate.

Based on past pleasant association with the Filipino students of the University, which was renewed for the academic year 1948-49, the author can affirm without reservation that they possess an innate capacity for intellectual achievement, make great personal sacrifices to acquire the knowledge essential to entrance into the professions, and are a well mannered body of ambitious young men and women. Their handicaps are ten or eleven instead of twelve years prior school-

[5] Act No. 1870, enacted on June 18, 1908, subsequently amended. *The Code of the University of the Philippines of 1946* contains the University Charter and rules and regulations passed by the Board of Regents and the University Council.

ing and an inadequate preparation in English. A minority of them fall prey to the temptations of a big city.

The reputation of any institution of higher learning is made by its graduates. Tested in this manner, the University of the Philippines can claim unrivaled success. Graduates of the University hold sixty percent of the country's positions of leadership. Its alumni largely became responsible for the destiny of the fledgling Philippine Republic. Among them were numbered Presidents, Congressmen and Senators, Justices of the Supreme Court, and Cabinet officers. The list could continue on and on into public and private life.

For the University to be in fact the highest seat of learning in the Philippines, the research output of its faculty must match the needs of the Republic. Individual University Professors have indeed been responsible for original investigations of great value. Yet it remains true that the promotion of work of this nature along scientific lines has hardly begun.

The University of the Philippines has had seven Presidents, two Americans and five Filipinos. Dr. Murray Bartlett, the first head of the institution, made up in earnestness and conscientious effort for any lack of marked executive ability. Dr. Bienvenido M. Gonzales, the actual President, is a product of the University, and has an understanding of its problems. He is endowed with a tough mind and an independent character.

It could be said of all the past University Presidents that they were only too happy to retire to more congenial and less exciting labors. The University of which each was the symbol was the target of unremitting attacks. The prime reason for this situation was the close association of the faculty members and the students with contemporary politics, and the injection of outside influence into the University. At the time of the enactment of the Hare-Hawes-Cutting Act by the Congress of the United States, the University was divided into two political camps, one militantly *Pro* and the other aggressively *Anti*.

If the University is to serve its purpose, it must be so administered that personal or party politics are kept from entering its portals. The University of the Philippines can have either a bright or a dismal future, depending on the quality of its leadership and the extent of its support.

The year 1955 should see a resurgent University of the Philippines spread out over a campus of nearly five hundred hectares, the largest of its kind in the world. Permanent buildings will have been erected and will be in use. A University town will have arisen. Fifteen thousand faculty members and students will live there. It is to be hoped that scholarship will have kept pace with the emergence of the magnificent physical plant.

THE UNIVERSITY OF SANTO TOMAS AND THE PRIVATE SCHOOLS

The oldest university ever under the American flag is not Harvard in Cambridge but Santo Tomas in Manila. Hoary with age and tradition as Harvard is, Santo Tomas is by a quarter of a century the older. The Royal and Pontifical University of Santo Tomas, to give Santo Tomas its official title, was founded in 1611 by the Most Reverend Miguel de Benavides, third Archbishop of Manila. The University has had a continuous existence during all the years of Spanish, American, and Filipino control.

Conservatism, as possibly should be expected from a Catholic-founded school, has marked the career of Santo Tomas. It was established for the children of Spaniards only, but later admitted Filipinos. For some years after American occupation, Santo Tomas was not very enthusiastic about the new regime, and continued to make use of antiquated educational methods. Suddenly the Dominican fathers who constituted the faculties of Santo Tomas about-faced, revised their curricula, admitted women to their halls, and erected new buildings on a campus on the outskirts of Manila.

The University of Santo Tomas is now modern in every way. Its various colleges and schools afford opportunities for Filipino youth to obtain religious and secular instruction. Many of the best known Filipinos are Santo Tomas graduates.

Prominence has been given to the University of Santo Tomas because of its age and renown. However, it is but one of many Catholic-backed schools. San Juan de Letran, San Beda College, De La Salle College, and Ateneo de Manila rank high in preparatory and secondary education for boys. Particularly has the Ateneo of the Jesuits ever been forward looking. By working unreservedly in harmony with the Philippine Government and by adherence to high academic standards, the Ateneo need not shrink from comparison with the private schools of any land. In 1949 Ateneo transferred to a spacious site in Quezon City, near the University of the Philippines.

The Catholic-fostered girls' schools of Manila offer both well planned preparatory and collegiate courses. Among the best known are Santa Isabel (the oldest), Assumption, Holy Ghost, Santa Catalina, Santa Theresa, St. Mary's and Sta. Scolastica.

The Protestants have likewise entered the educational field with encouraging results. Silliman University founded in 1901 by the

Presbyterian Board of Foreign Missions and located in Dumaguete, Oriental Negros, is one of the five great mission schools in the world. Indelibly associated with the rapid growth of Silliman and its fine influence for good are the names of Dr. D. S. Hibbard, the founder, of his successor, Dr. Roy H. Brown, and of the more recent head of the institution, Dr. Arthur L. Carson. Central Philippine College at Iloilo is sponsored by the American Foreign Mission Society.

In Manila are found a number of non-denominational universities. These private institutions include Adamson University, Arellano University, Centro Escolar University, Far Eastern University, Manila Central University, National University, University of the East, University of Manila, and the Philippine Women's University. All are coeducational except the last named, which is exclusively for women. The quality of the instruction offered in the Universities above listed tends to fluctuate from the very good, of a qualified and conscientious if poorly paid professor, to the very bad, of the irregular and careless faculty member.

The educators who founded and headed these private universities have numbered national figures. For instance, Mrs. Francisca Tirona Benitez, President of the Philippine Women's University for approximately thirty years, has devoted her life and talents to providing education for useful womanhood.

American boys and girls may enroll in any public or private school in the Philippines. In addition, there is in Manila the American School operated especially for the benefit of the children of American and foreign residents. The school offers courses from kindergarten through high school under American teachers.

There are literally hundreds of private schools, colleges and universities scattered over the Islands. The Director of Private Schools exercises general supervision over them. It has been the set purpose of Dr. Manuel L. Carreon, the Director, to maintain proper levels of instruction. This has been no easy task considering the post-war lack of educational facilities and competent teachers, and the rush on the part of youth to resume their schooling. In the face of all handicaps, the number of private schools and the enrollment therein exceed that of pre-war days. The Far Eastern University, for instance, had an enrollment in excess of 25,000 for the school year 1949-50, which was double its pre-war registration.

Unfortunately there is an unpleasant side to the private school picture. Some of these institutions are run solely for profit and for profit inordinately high. The only excuse for their existence is to make money for the owners. The students are heartlessly exploited.

Instruction is deficient, constructive scholarship is lacking, and diplomas are easily obtainable from the "degree factories." The graduates acquire degrees but not educations.[6]

The Director of Private Schools should wage an unrelenting battle to reform or eliminate the private-adventure schools. Aside from these unworthy participants in education, the remaining private schools of all types have a definite and important place in the Philippine educational system.

LITERACY [7]

A fundamental purpose of the government, oft announced, has been to develop a literate body politic. How successful the authorities have been in their efforts to reach this goal may best be understood when it is realized that literacy in the Philippines is higher than in any former European colony in the Orient, many Latin American, and some European, countries. On the other hand, the Philippines suffers by comparison with Sweden where illiteracy has a percentage too small to be measured.

The exact ratio of literacy and illiteracy is difficult of determination for the Philippines. The 1903 Census showed that forty-four and five-tenths percent of the population over ten years of age could "read" in some language. The 1918 Census disclosed forty-nine and two-tenths as able to "read." The 1939 Census estimated that forty-eight and eight-tenths percent of the population ten years or over "read and write."

How seriously the Filipinos have tackled the problem of the elimination of illiteracy is shown by their strengthening of the Office of Adult Education before the war. This is now a firmly established entity in the Department of Education. Its program to "raise the general intellectual level of the common *tao*" is ambitious, but of course can only be partially realized.

Through the efforts of the Department of Education, literacy in the Philippines is being lifted to perhaps fifty-five percent. However, mere figures mean little. In addition to being able to "read and write," people should have an understanding of the printed word.

---

[6] Dr. H. H. Bartlett, University of the Philippines visiting Professor from Michigan in 1947 gave his views on private colleges and universities in the Philippines, and his remarks were highly critical. Dr. Bartlett maintained that "Education in the Philippines is fast becoming a commodity to be bought and sold in the black market of private schools." Answers came from Alfredo Q. Gonzales and Pedro T. Orata who attempted to show that all is not dark on the Philippine educational front.

[7] Facts taken from the Philippines '49 Business Guidebook, p. 187, which places Philippine literacy at 50 percent.

Whether the estimate of literacy be over eighty percent for Manila and less than twenty percent for two southern provinces, with the general average for the Philippine Republic resting somewhere between fifty and sixty percent, the moral is clear. The Philippines cannot long house a contented people half literate and half illiterate.

ENGLISH AND A NATIONAL LANGUAGE[8]

A complicated question for which the Republic of the Philippines must find an answer is: What shall be the national and official language of the country?

It is not a new problem. The Spaniards faced it in ages long past, and temporized by affording an opportunity for a comparatively few Filipinos to become familiar with the language of Castile. The Americans faced it half a century ago, and instinctively and out of necessity declared English to be the basis of education in the schools and an official language of the administration. The Filipinos faced the age old problem, when in 1935 they came to adopt a Constitution, and sanctioned a trilingual compromise amongst those favoring English, or Spanish, or a dialect as the national language.

Fortunately the Filipinos have a flair for languages, and are natural polyglots. The truth is every educated Filipino is compelled by circumstances to be a linguist. Commonly he needs and uses three languages—English, Spanish, and a dialect—and in addition Tagalog, if that is not his dialect. He requires a knowledge of English for governmental work, business transactions, national conventions, and intercourse with Americans, Europeans, and others. He prefers to avail himself of Spanish in formal social gatherings. His dialect comes to him from his parents and is used in the home, in conversations with neighbors, and in political campaigns.

The Filipinos, as history shows, were possessed of written languages before the coming of the Spaniards. The difficulty then was that there was no national unity, and this meant the propagation of numerous dialects. As many as ninety dialects are spoken in the Islands. The most important of them are Tagalog (most generally understood), Visayan, Ilocano, Bicol, Pampango, and Pangasinan. All are chiefly of Malay-Indonesian origin, which means that while the user of one dialect is unable to understand the user of another dialect, he can readily learn the language of the other group. The

---

[8] This section was originally read by Dean Francisco Benitez of the College of Education, University of the Philippines. The Monroe Educational Survey of the Philippines of 1925 discusses the language problem, pp. 24 *et. seq.*, 127 *et. seq.*

dialects are no longer pure, for in them have been incorporated Sanskrit, Chinese, Spanish, and even English loan words.

Because of linguistic difficulties, it has been necessary for the Filipino people to make use of a foreign language as a common medium of communication. Formerly that language was Spanish, and it still is to a diminishing extent. Now the most important official language is English to a steadily increasing extent.

The American Government in an early and far reaching decision made English the medium of all instruction in the schools. While this action was bitterly assailed at the time, in result it ultimately became the greatest single factor of unification. From the first, English was used exclusively in the executive departments. The development of English as a court language was retarded when special consideration was shown the Spanish-speaking members of the bar, but nevertheless it has steadily gained favor there. Ninety-five percent of the cases in the Courts are tried in English; ten of the eleven Supreme Court Justices prepare their opinions in English. In the Philippine Legislature some time elapsed before any elected member addressed the house in English. At present it is not unusual for English and Spanish to be employed interchangeably in debate, with English the customary and Spanish the occasional medium.

Many more Filipinos use English than Spanish or a dialect. The 1939 census revealed that twenty-seven percent of the people could speak English. On the basis of the present population, well over 7,000,000 have an understanding of English. This number tends to increase because of better opportunities for those acquainted with the English tongue, because all but a negligible few of the candidates take civil service and other examinations in English, and because of the cumulative advantage of the entire process. Contrasting the language situation in the Philippines with that in the rest of the world, it will not escape attention that following the United States and England the Philippines ranks high among the English-speaking countries.

On account of deficient instruction, especially in the lower grades of the schools, Filipino-used English cannot be expected to improve. The result is a type of spoken English unlike that heard in the United States. As reported by the Monroe Educational Commission, Filipino English has "an accent, tonal expression, and rhythm that are thoroughly Malay." However, that finding furnishes no basis for criticism. If the language of the Filipinos in whatever form is sufficiently English to furnish a common medium of conversation and understanding, the public interest will be served.

Two observations, in connection with the implantation of English in the Philippines, are indicative of the reasons why there was sentiment favoring a national language other than English. The first and obvious point was that English was a language foreign to the Islands. The second reason was that English is not, and probably never will be, the language of the Filipino home. Nationalist pride demanded, as reflected in the Constitution, that steps be taken toward the development and adoption of a common national language based on one of the existing native languages. [9]

The Government of the Commonwealth moved rapidly to make the Constitutional mandate effective. The Institute of National Language was created. It recommended the adoption of Tagalog as the basis of the national language. On December 30, 1937, the President proclaimed Tagalog the national language. In 1940, the Filipino national language was declared by law to be an official language of the Philippines, effective coincidentally with independence on July 4, 1946.

The decision to make Tagalog the national language was originally accepted by the other linguistic groups without much protest. However, after every public school began to teach Tagalog, the anvil chorus was sounded. It has been asserted that instruction in Tagalog arouses little interest among students in non-Tagalog regions, that the children find it hard to learn, that they get better grades in English than Tagalog, and that the Tagalog taught in the schools is not the Tagalog spoken at home. Government efforts to spread the use of Tagalog throughout the Islands have met with little success.

The language situation is not akin to the many-tongued Tower of Babel, but it is most confusing. It may also be highly detrimental in effect on pupils made the guinea pigs for linguistic experiment. Tagalog is the national language. English and Spanish are also official languages. May the outcome not be that Filipino students will leave school unable to speak, read and write any language—Tagalog, English, Spanish, or their own dialect?

The question last phrased bids us return for another look at the school curriculum. Eighty percent of the pupils are enrolled in the elementary grades. Might it not be advisable to make the basis of instruction during the first three years the dialect of the region, with very little English taught? If the majority of these students then leave school, they will at least be literate in one language. Those students who continue can begin to stress English more and more as they ad-

---

[9] Constitution of the Philippines, as amended, Article XIV. sec. 3.

vance toward collegiate training. Such a solution may present disadvantages, but at least it worked out fairly well in the village schools of the nearby Netherlands Indies. And it is practical.

The problem presented by the diversity of languages in the Philippines cannot readily or finally be solved. But it can be reexamined in the light of advancement of national unity and maintenance of essential foreign relations, by setting the goals at attainment of literacy in the vernacular and the retention of English as an official language.

HEALTH [10]

The triumph of American medical science over nature in the construction of the Panama Canal is known to all. The victory over disease was as complete in the Philippines, but has not been so well advertized to the world. In the succeeding paragraphs the highlights of the Philippine health story will be sketched.

Sanitary conditions in the Philippines were deplorable at the time of the American occupation. The standard of living was appallingly low. Infant mortality reached an enormous figure. The death rate was so high that the population was at a standstill. Smallpox was regularly carrying off thousands of persons. Asiatic cholera came in epidemic waves and was much feared. The City of Manila, although the capital and metropolis, possessed no sewage system; a huge moat encircled the Walled City, and was filled with stagnant water and sewage wherein bred countless numbers of mosquitoes. In all the Archipelago there was not one modernly equipped hospital.

In the ensuing years from 1898 onward, changes so wonderful as hardly to be comprehended were wrought in the field of public health. The man to whom prime credit is due for these accomplishments was Dr. Victor G. Heiser, originally Passed Assistant Surgeon, United States Public Health and Quarantine Service. He occupied the two positions in the Philippines of Chief Quarantine Officer and Director of Health from 1905 to 1915. Even after leaving these posts, Dr. Heiser, because of his association with the Rockefeller Foundation and the International Health Board, kept in contact with Philippine health problems.

Director of Health Heiser developed an organization which transformed the Philippines, formerly a plague spot, into the best sanitated country in the Orient. Acting for the Rockefeller Foundation, he

---

[10] Dr. E. B. Salud conferred with the author in 1949. See Victor G. Heiser, *An American Doctor's Odyssey* (New York, 1936).

later aided in the improvement of public health education and cooperated with the Philippine Government in the scientific study of malaria, one of the most destructive and the most widespread of all tropical diseases. The activities of the Rockefeller Foundation were terminated in the Philippines in 1935.

The program of the Bureau of Health was executed in the field by many competent men and women. One of the doctors, respected by his chiefs and best liked by the Filipinos, among whom he labored in Iloilo and elsewhere, was Dr. Gilbert I. Cullen. It was said of him that he could do more things well than anyone in the Islands. He also knew how to get results without offending Filipino feelings. More recently Dr. Cullen has been associated with the Quarantine Service.

In time practically all the personnel in the Philippine Health Service were Filipinos. The Directors of Health numbered worthy leaders like Dr. Jacobo Fajardo. The College of Medicine, University of the Philippines, and the Philippine General Hospital came to have, as Deans and Directors, physicians of the stamp of Dr. Antonio G. Sison.

The more recent medical setup is similarly no less competent. Dr. Felipe Arenas is a Director of Health with a background of valuable experience, as is Dr. T. Elicano, Director of Hospitals. In fact the Philippines can point with pride to a long line of physicians and surgeons. It is one of the professions in which the Filipinos most excel. The records made by these fine men and women individually and collectively are highly creditable.

The war dealt a severe blow to health conditions in the Philippines.[11] Nevertheless, the Philippine Archipelago remains one of the cleanest countries in the Far East, surpassing in this respect China, India, and Malaya, and rivaling Japan. The Philippine sanitary system in general withstood the impact of war to constitute a model for the Orient. Manila and its environs have been provided with pure water. Virulent epidemics, particularly diseases found in the tropics, have been stamped out. Cholera, that dread scourge which formerly swept away thousands, is now unknown. Smallpox, similarly dreaded, through wholesale vaccination has been checked; during 1948 one lone case brought from abroad caused a scare.

The birth rate in the Philippines is about thirty-two per one thousand, and the death rate about twelve per one thousand. This means that the birth rate in the Islands equals that of India and Japan and is

---

[11] Dr. Gumersindo Sayago, Argentina representative on the UNWHO Medical Mission to the Philippines.

half again higher than that of the United States.[12] Unfortunately, infant mortality in the Philippines of one hundred and fourteen per one thousand is appallingly high, in fact higher than in other countries, barring China. Nevertheless, it is heartening to note that this infant mortality rate has dropped radically since 1904, to be more exact over sixty percent. The death rate in the Philippines is lower than for many Oriental and Latin American countries, but is higher than in the United States.

Satisfactory health conditions obtain in the Philippines as shown by 1947 and 1948 downward trends in death and infant mortality rates.

Hospital facilities are available in all parts of the Philippines. In Manila are the Philippine General Hospital, conceded to be the best-equipped hospital in the Orient, and the recently organized North General Hospital. Near Manila are the Quezon Institute for tubercular patients, which is receiving strong governmental support, and the National Psychopathic Hospital for the mentally diseased. The Institute of Malariology trains students in the science of controlling one of man's most dreaded diseases. Nearly eighty Government hospitals are found throughout the Islands.[13]

Wonderful as the results have been, much work lies ahead for the medical authorities. Tuberculosis, malaria and other diseases continue to take their deadly toll. To combat tuberculosis, the "number one killer" in the Philippines, a nation-wide immunization campaign was undertaken in 1949. Babies die because of beri-beri due to maternal malnutrition. Intestinal parasites sap the strength of thousands of Filipinos.

The carefree life of the Islands is conducive to longevity. Every once in a while the death of a man or woman one hundred years of age, one hundred thirty years of age, and so on, is reported. Some of these cases have been proven to be authentic. They go to show that if persons born in the Philippines can be properly nurtured at birth, and thereafter can avoid epidemic diseases, they are placed under ideal conditions which permit them to live to ripe old ages.

All in all, the protection for health afforded in the Philippines, through the original initiative of American officials and later developed

[12] Population Bulletin of the Population Reference Bureau incorporating statistics reported to the United Nations. India, birth rate 28.0; death rate 21.6. Japan, birth rate 29.0; death rate 18.1. United States, birth rate 21.5; death rate 10.4. Dr. Felipe Arenas, Director of Health, in a letter of March 15, 1949 furnished corresponding Philippine figures for 1948—birth rate 32.03; death rate 12.98; infant mortality rate 114.43.

[13] Data furnished by Dr. T. Elicano, Director of Hospitals.

by Filipino officials, can be said to be one of the most notable accomplishments of the last half century.

QUARANTINE [14]

An indispensable partner of the Health Service is the Quarantine Service.

The Philippines is so situated geographically as to be in constant danger of infection from abroad. The Quarantine Service stands guard against the introduction into the Islands by vessels or aircraft of dangerous communicable diseases, which, having gained entrance, might develop into epidemics with great loss of life. These duties have been performed efficiently and successfully by well disciplined ofcers.

The Quarantine Service has been in operation continuously in the Philippines since American occupation. Before the independence of the Philippines, this work operated under the supervision of the U. S. Public Health Service. Shortly after the inauguration of the Republic, a basic law was approved which provided for the organization of the Bureau of Quarantine. A commissioned corps of officers trained in all phases of quarantine service was formed. Quarantine stations are in operation in Manila and other important entry points. The Director of Quarantine is Colonel Rufino Abriol with long experience in this class of work.

As in the past, the U. S. Public Health Service is cooperating in the rehabilitation and development of its counterpart in the Philippines. Brigadier General Howard F. Smith has been in charge of the U. S. Public Health Service in this part of the world. He retired in 1950 after almost forty years of tireless public service dedicated to fighting disease in the Philippines.

HANSEN'S DISEASE [15]

"Unclean! Unclean!" So cried frightened people in Biblical times at the unfortunate lepers. Thus stigmatized have been social pariahs who happened to contract a repulsive disease, and who were cast out

[14] Statement on Quarantine furnished by the Director of Quarantine. See Victor G. Heiser, *An American Doctor's Odyssey*. Note Philippine Rehabilitation Act of 1946, as amended by the Act of Congress of July 2, 1948.

[15] This section was originally read by Dr. H. W. Wade of the Leonard Wood Memorial for the Eradication of Leprosy. The medical term "Hansen's Disease," after Dr. Gerhard Hansen, Norwegian physician who in 1879 discovered the bacillus which causes the disorder called leprosy, is favored in order to banish as much as possible the terror-ridden words "leprosy" and "lepers" from the language.

to die, in all ages and lands. The Philippines has proved no exception. The Filipinos have been as seriously afflicted with the disorder as other peoples among whom it is prevalent. One leper to every thousand of the inhabitants is a condition to send fear to the hearts of everyone.

In Spanish days, Filipino lepers along with the insane were confined in San Lazaro Hospital in Manila; that is, some of the lepers were housed there, while thousands of them were permitted to roam about the country. The Americans came and recognized the imperative necessity of isolating the lepers.

Culion, an island on the edge of the China Sea, was selected for a leper colony as early as 1901 by Secretary of the Interior Worcester. The colony was opened five years later. Dr. Heiser and others went about the Islands in a "leper ship," collected the active cases, and placed them in the care of trained physicians and nurses in Culion. This task was done as a part of the day's labor in as kindly a manner as possible, but it was a tragic task. In spite of many difficulties, Culion Leper Colony grew to be the largest of its sort anywhere.

Governor General Wood, himself a physician, took a personal interest in this humanitarian work. On his initiative, Dr. H. Windsor Wade was transferred from the chair of pathology at the University of the Philippines to Culion, and its staff of doctors and nurses was enlarged. General Wood frequently visited the island, and these visits and the improvement of conditions that followed gave moral support to the inmates and encouragement to those who labored to advance scientific knowledge of the disease. Culion became the Island of Hope.

But this was not enough. New victims of the disease resisted detection and transfer to the colony. Governor General Wood approved a plan to liberalize the system through the establishment of regional leprosaria, where suitable cases could be kept within reach of their families. He also endorsed an appeal to the American public, made by Dorothy Paul Wade, the wife of Dr. Wade, for a special fund to intensify research and in this way extend the great work carried on by the Government. When Governor General Wood died before the plan had materialized, this fund was fittingly made a memorial to him, with Dr. Wade as Medical Director. The activities of the Leonard Wood Memorial now touch and affect the efforts against leprosy throughout the world.

With the Filipinos in control of the administration, action was taken to relieve a condition most often complained of—exile to Culion. There was already in existence the Eversley Childs Treatment Station at Cebu, said to be the most attractive leprosarium in the world; seven other regional treatment stations were established. The Central Luzon Leprosarium at Tila, Rizal, was also placed in operation.

The doctors and nurses engaged in service to these wards are making real sacrifices. At least four Filipinos have gained international recognition for their scientific investigations of leprosy. Dr. Casimiro B. Lara, Chief of the Culion Colony, is their worthy colleague. The Sisters of St. Paul de Chartres have dedicated themselves to the care of the unfortunate. Mother Damien is a French nun who has devoted forty years of her life to lightening the days of the lepers of Culion; she was one of five persons who in 1949 were cited for unselfish service to the Filipino people.

Hansen's disease (leprosy) is believed by scientists to be only feebly communicable. While no cure has been found, victims have benefited from the chaulmoogra oil and the promin, a sulfa drug, treatments. The disorder has been so arrested in thousands of cases in the Philippines, that every year many patients are returned to their homes, free from symptoms of active disease.

Step by step advances are being made toward the solution of the leprosy problem, one of the most baffling in medical science. The Philippines is contributing a major share.

SOCIAL SERVICE [16]

The Philippines has evidenced the phenomenon of a people who not long ago adopted a fatalistic attitude toward misfortune, lacked incentive for community progress, and then made the advancement of the public welfare a paramount plank in the drive for social justice and amelioration.

The Philippines was the locale of another contrasting scene during the Harrison administration of the Islands. While this period signalized retrogression in health service, coincidentally a worthwhile public welfare program was initiated. On the foundations thus laid, succeeding Governors General built, until the governmental objective became the relief of distress due to any cause.

The Filipino-controlled Commonwealth and Republic not alone continued the policies of their American predecessors, but went forward to new accomplishments. Appropriately enough public welfare became a part of the broader-conceived program of social justice. Under the Commonwealth Government social services were ex-

[16] This section was originally read by Dr. Jose Fabella, Commissioner of Health and Welfare, subsequently Secretary of Health and Public Welfare. Mrs. Asuncion A. Perez sent in copies of pertinent literature, which was freely used.

panded. Particular attention was given the care and treatment of the sick and the relief of those suffering from public disasters. Puericulture Centers and National Charity Clinics were founded.

A unique and particularly praiseworthy institution is Welfareville, a little city designed to help the unfortunate, located not far from Manila. Within its confines have been established the Home for Orphans and Destitute Children, for Mentally Defective Children, and for Non-leprous Children of Leper Parents, the Home for the Aged and Infirm, the Philippine Training School for Boys, and the Philippine Training School for Girls. There the orphans, the destitute, and the infirm are given homes. There wayward boys and girls are trained and offered another chance.

The Republic of the Philippines has a well-coordinated organization to supervise and assist public welfare. The various educational and health offices are important factors in help afforded the people. However, most of the agencies for social betterment are united under the Social Welfare Commission.

Under the Republic, the Bureau of Public Welfare was dissolved and made the nucleus of the Social Welfare Commission. Its main functions are child welfare, public assistance, and coordination of all public and private social work. The War Relief Office is still another branch of the Commission. The Action Committee on Social Amelioration was created to meet emergency conditions in the provinces of Central and Southern Luzon where dissident elements have caused disorder.

The man who more than any other was responsible for the success of the social service program in the Philippines was Dr. Jose Fabella. He organized the Bureau of Public Welfare, and in 1941 became the first Secretary of Health and Public Welfare. His worthy successor in this field was Mrs. Asuncion A. Perez, Commissioner of Social Welfare. Mrs. Perez, with a full life devoted to assistance to the unfortunate, was particularly well qualified to handle this important branch of government service.

Up to this point we have dwelt on the Government's part in welfare work. Private agencies have proved as helpful. The Rotary Clubs, the Lions Clubs, the Junior Chambers of Commerce, the Anti-Tuberculosis Society, *Gota de Leche,* the Young Ladies Association of Charity, the Y.M.C.A., the Y.W.C.A., the Boy Scouts, the Girl Scouts, the Philippine Band of Mercy, and the Philippine American Guardian Association, are among the one hundred and seventy-five or more organizations which have been active in community service. One Community Chest Drive a year coordinates their overlapping appeals in Greater Manila. A step in the right direction was taken in 1949 when leading agencies grouped themselves into the Federation of Welfare Agencies.

The Red Cross for obvious reasons is the best known of the privately financed public welfare organizations. A charter was granted the Philippine chapter of the American Red Cross in 1917. From that date until abolished by the Japanese, the chapter rendered valuable service to the people in disaster relief and school dental clinics. Reconstituted in 1945, the Red Cross was nationalized on April 15, 1947 and accorded recognition by the International Red Cross. Mrs. Aurora A. Quezon, widow of the late President of the Philippines, lent the weight of her name to a worthy cause by accepting the post of Chairman of the Philippine National Red Cross. On her death, former Justice Manuel Lim was elevated from Vice-chairman to Chairman of the organization.

It is a good omen for the Philippines that governmental help united with private effort to advance the public welfare.

CHAPTER XXIII

RELIGION

Paganism

The people of the Philippines are predominantly Roman Catholics in religion. Close to eighty percent of the entire population adhere to this faith. The Filipino Independent Church, composed of the *Aglipayanos*, accounts for another ten percent, the Mohammedans for four percent, the Protestants for over two percent, and the rest are pagans.

The primitive religion of the Filipinos was Anism, a sort of ancestor worship. Then arrived the banner of Islam, and it swept triumphantly over the Islands of Mindanao and Sulu to the south. The spread of Mohammedanism was stayed by the coming of the Spaniards, who baptized the people *en masse* as Catholics. After the Philippine Revolution the schism from Rome of the Filipino Independent Church occurred. Finally, with the American flag came the Protestant missionaries. That is a tabloid sketch of religious history in the Philippines.

But we were to speak more precisely of paganism. The early Filipinos were in their way intensely religious. They worshipped the spirits of departed ancestors represented by *anitos* (idols). They believed in fate and were fond of myths and whispered stories. They were full of taboos and superstitions. Their most omnipotent God, if one may use the word reverently in this connection, was called by the Tagalogs "Bathala" and by the Visayans "Lauon." That the religion of these early Filipinos did not satisfy their spiritual hunger was shown by the ease with which they yielded to Mohammedan and Catholic missionary effort.

Pagan beliefs still exist, but to a steadily lessening degree. Even under the veneer of Mohammedanism and under the pageantry of the other religions, superstition is to be found. Every sign foretells that this or that will happen. The *antinganting* (talisman) of medallions or amulets with pictures of saints is carefully guarded because it is thought to endow its possessor with god-like attributes.

Mohammedanism [1]

Mohammedanism was introduced into the Philippines over five centuries ago. In 1380 there came from the Moluccas to Sulu one Makdum, a noted Arabian judge, who was successful in gaining adherents to the Mohammedan religion. Raja Baguinda and Abu Bakar continued the work of their predecessor and gave further impetus to the growth of Mohammedanism in the Sulu Archipelago. Then to the great Island of Mindanao went the conqueror, Sharif Mohammed Kabungsuwan, who claimed to be a descendant of the prophet Mohammed, to convert the people there. Only the timely arrival of the Catholic priests on the scene blocked the onward and upward march of Islam through the Philippines. The adherents of Mohammedanism, now called Moros, form a respectable part of the Philippine community and offer a problem in assimilation and attraction.

Mohammedanism is the most militant of religions. The Moros believe in one God whose prophet is Mohammed, and their holy writing is the Koran. They are a compact unit who resent bitterly any intrusion into their religious practices and are extremely sensitive to any slur, real or fancied, on their faith.

This does not mean that the Moros are orthodox Mohammedans, for, as a matter of fact, they are lax in the observance of its rituals and precepts. Nevertheless the prohibitions of pork and alcoholic beverages are generally observed. So also do the men claim the right of plural wives. The fanaticism of the Moros is most feverishly displayed when one of their number becomes a *juramentado* or runs *amuck*, slashing promiscuously everyone in his path.

The spiritual head of the Moros in Sulu is nominally at least the Sultan of Sulu. Elsewhere the other sultans and datus retain considerable power over religious questions. Quite a number of Moros have made the journey to Mecca and are entitled to use the title of "Hadji." In 1948 one thousand Philippine Moros headed by Congressman Hadji Mohamad Amir Bin Mindalano made the holy pilgrimage.

The Roman Catholic Church [2]

The growth of the Roman Catholic Church in the Philippines is closely interwoven with secular history. When Magellan, in his heroic

---

[1] See Dr. Najeeb M. Saleeby, *Studies in Moro History, Law, and Religion* (Manila, 1905).

[2] This section was originally read by Father Henry C. Avery, S. J., Rector of the Ateneo de Manila. See Rev. Louis L. R. Morrow, *A Short History of the Filipino People* (Manila, 1936). The secretary to the Archbishop of Manila courteously checked certain statements on January 29, 1949.

effort to sail around the world, came to Cebu, the wife of Rajah Humabon was the first member of a long line of Filipino royalty to be baptized a Catholic. When the equally notable expedition of Legaspi and Urdaneta arrived from Mexico in Cebu, the niece of Tupas, a petty ruler of Cebu, was made a Catholic. Wholesale baptisms occurred, and the conversion of the Filipinos in the following years is an achievement without a parallel in history.

The Church hierarchy in the Philippines exercised incalculable influence. The power of the bishops on occasion was even greater than that of the Spanish Governors General. The religious orders were represented in the Philippines. The Church, and with it some of the religious orders, in time acquired by state grant or pious legacy vast and valuable estates for mission work. Churches and convents, well constructed and situated, sprang up throughout the Islands.

Much was done by the priesthood for the moral and intellectual development of the people. The reverend parochial priest played an important part in practically every branch of the municipal government and in the lives of the people. In many municipalities the memory of some good *padre*, truly a father to his flock and their kind benefactor, is still cherished. To the everlasting credit of the Catholic Church stands the conversion of practically an entire people, and a conscientious effort to supply that people with the Christian religion and to better their conditions in many and varied ways.

In the course of time it cannot be gainsaid by anyone that the friars as a class became unpopular. Exactly what the causes of this antagonism were need not be gone into in detail, but probably the bitterness arose largely because of the priests becoming the symbols of foreign domination, with real or imaginary oppression. Also what has been described as the "vexed and delicate question" of the morality of the friars need not detain us, except to observe that it would be strange if in a far country like the Philippines an occasional priest might not be tempted by earthly considerations. The Filipinos themselves were inclined to be tolerant and to condone any slip from grace on the part of the priests. Whatever the causes of the hostile feeling, when the Americans arrived the Filipinos were ready to go to the extreme of confiscating all Church properties and of banishing the Spanish priests.

During the past five decades, the breach between the people and the Church has been healed. The great mass of the people belong to the Catholic Church. Hardly a prominent Filipino can be mentioned who was not at least baptized a Catholic. The ordinary Filipino is loyal to his Church and the Church satisfies his religious nature. This is particularly true because of the ceremonies of the Church and its religious processions in which hundreds participate carrying lighted candles and singing hymns. Probably as a class the women are more devout than the men. The anomaly is found among some of the men of their joining the Masonic fraternity and at the same time retaining loose connections with the Church.

The Catholic Church has gradually changed its attitude with reference to the political situation. It is commonly believed that the Clarke Amendment to the Jones Law, which would have granted quick independence to the Philippines, was defeated through the intervention of Cardinal Gibbons. Since then, however, the dignitaries of the Catholic Church have freely announced their sympathy with Filipino aspirations and apparently have lost their fear of excesses aimed at the Church under an independent Philippines. The principal economic problem of the Church relates to the large landed estates which it possesses and the agitation of the tenants for the ownership of the land.

A number of holy shrines are found in the Philippines. Stories of the miraculous powers possessed by these hallowed relics are current. They are highly venerated.

The Vatican is represented in the Philippines by an Apostolic Delegate. The Philippines is divided into two archdioceses, Manila and Cebu. Irish-born Archbishop Michael J. O'Doherty, long the respected primate *de facto* of Catholicism in the Islands, died in late 1949, and was succeeded by Archbishop Gabriel M. Reyes of the diocese of Cebu. The Archbishops of Manila and Cebu and most of the more than twenty bishops are Filipinos. The standing of the Philippines in the Roman Catholic World was shown by the choice of Manila for the holding of the Twenty-third International Eucharistic Congress in 1937.

THE FILIPINO INDEPENDENT CHURCH [3]

The history of the Filipino Independent Church, the followers of which are commonly called *Aglipayanos*, is encompassed by the biography of the late Supreme Bishop Gregorio Aglipay.

This leader of his church and of a large segment of the people studied for the priesthood and was ordained a Catholic priest. Father Aglipay was excommunicated when during the Filipino uprising against Spain, he headed a movement bent on refusing to recognize any foreign element in the Catholic Church in the Philippines. Gen-

[3] See Louis C. Cornish, *The Philippines Calling* (Philadelphia, 1942). The author is Honorary President of the Filipino Independent Church.

eral Aguinaldo named him Vicar General of the Filipino Army, and he stayed with the insurrectionist forces until their capitulation.

Ecclesiastical councils met under Father Aglipay's Presidency. In 1902 the Filipino Independent Church was proclaimed. The following year Father Aglipay was consecrated *Obispo Maximo* (Supreme Bishop). He held this position continuously until his death in 1940 at the age of eighty.

To the same extent that the Catholic Church in the Philippines is Spanish in background, and that the Protestant Churches are of American origin, is the Filipino Independent Church intended to be a Church of the Filipinos, by the Filipinos, and for the Filipinos.

This indigenous Church was born of Philippine nationalism. The dialects are used in conducting the services except in the saying of the Masses. Lay heroes like Rizal have been canonized. The *Aglipayano* priests are allowed to marry and are encouraged to participate actively in politics. Bishop Aglipay set the example for his followers by taking a bride unto himself in his later years, by assuming a commanding position on political issues, and by expressing himself freely on current questions.

Originally a schismatic church, the Filipino Independent Church retains a portion of the colorful liturgical service of the Catholic Church. Except in form the Independent Church is, however, farther away from Rome than Protestantism. Science has been daringly fused with religious liberalism. Rapprochement with the modernistic Unitarian Church of America resulted.

The Filipino Independent Church has set the number of its adherents as high as 4,000,000, but the census records a smaller number. The Church finds its strongest support in the Ilocano provinces. Numerically strong, the Church is financially weak. It has no imposing edifices, for the courts uniformly decided that Philippine Churches belonged to Rome, and has found no rich benefactors to endow the Church liberally. More serious weaknesses have been the lack of proper training for the clergy, and of intensified efforts to retain the interest of the young people.

In line with the desire of the Filipino Independent Church to obtain recognition by the Anglican Communion, the Board of Bishops of the Protestant Episcopal Church in 1947 approved the request of the Philippine Church that its bishops be consecrated by Episcopal prelates. This meant not union or merger but adoption of an Episcopalian-type of church organization.

The death of Bishop Aglipay engendered a protracted controversy, unbecoming for churchmen, as to who was the lawful head of the Church. It was left for a lay agency, the courts, to render decision, which has been done with inconclusive results.

The Filipino Independent Church, while having lost the inspiration of its progenitor and while facing serious internal problems, should hold its own.

THE PROTESTANT CHURCHES[4]

In a Roman Catholic, *Aglipayano*, Mohammedan country like the Philippines, the Protestant Churches can hardly expect to compete on equal terms. It is significant, however, that between the 1918 census and the 1948 census, the membership of the Protestant Churches had quadrupled. Approximately 600,000 persons are affiliated with Philippine Protestantism. Its influence far exceeds the number of worshippers.

The American forces were hardly settled in the Philippines when Bishop James H. Thoburn of the Methodist Episcopal Church came from India to preach the first sermon ever delivered by a Protestant missionary in the Philippines. A month later, on April 21, 1899, Dr. and Mrs. James B. Rodgers of the Presbyterian Church arrived, and thirty-odd years later were still active. The Protestant Episcopal Church in 1902 elected the Reverend Charles H. Brent to be Bishop of the Philippines, and he became internationally renowned. In 1949 the Golden Jubilee of Protestantism in the Philippines was reverently observed.

The honor roll numbers the late Reverend George W. Wright, popular General Secretary of the General Assembly of the United Evangelical Church of the Philippines, and other zealous American missionaries. The American Board of Foreign Missions in 1915 sent Dr. Frank C. Laubach to the Philippines, and there among the Moros he devised a system of reading by adults that thereafter took him into the farthest corners of the world. Prominent Filipinos who have shown the way toward Protestant unity include Dr. Jorge Bocobo, former President of the National Christian Church and later President of the Philippine Federation of Evangelical Churches, and Bishop Enrique C. Sobrepeña of the United Church of Christ, long a leader in Protestant circles.

The Protestant Churches have had to meet the problem of over-

---

[4] See Frank C. Laubach, *The People of the Philippines: Their Religious Progress and Preparation for Spiritual Leadership in the Far East* (New York, 1925). The 1948 merger of the Protestant Churches was described by L. O. Ty in the *Philippines Free Press* of June 12, 1948. The Golden Jubilee of Protestanism was highlighted in the *Sunday Times* of February 20, 1949.

lapping activities. They have done so sensibly by cooperative union. In 1901 the Evangelical Union was formed and proceeded to divide the Islands among the missions. This was followed by other efforts to accomplish church unification, which culminated in 1948 in the organization of the "United Church of Christ in the Philippines." The churches thus merged were the United Evangelical Church of the Philippines organized in 1929, the Philippine Methodist Church, and the Evangelical Church in the Philippines. The United Church of Christ has nearly a thousand local congregations in different sections of the country.

Not affiliated with the United Church of Christ are the Protestant Episcopal Church and the Seventh Day Adventists. The Episcopalians have confined their evangelistic efforts to the non-Christians. The pagans and Moros have been afforded educational opportunities for betterment by the Episcopal Mission and the Moro Educational Foundation. The Episcopalians and the Seventh Day Adventists maintain well equipped and administered hospitals and a sanitarium, open to all persons irrespective of creed.

Christian education is mentioned in another connection. It need only be said here that it was spearheaded by Silliman University. The Union Theological Seminary of Manila is an interdenominational school established for the training of young men and women for the ministry.[5]

The Protestant Churches have a distinct place in the religious life of the Philippines. That place will be filled, it would seem, to the extent that Protestant unity can be maintained and the churches converted into a national institution.

SEPARATION OF CHURCH AND STATE[6]

Under Spanish rule, the State and the Catholic Church were united in the Philippines. With the coming of the democratic regime of the Americans, the separation between State and Church was made real and absolute. That principle was carried over into the Philippine Commonwealth and Republic by the Filipinos, who in their freely adopted Constitution prohibited the enactment of any law respecting the establishment of religion. No sentiment exists for any deviation from this sound policy.

The Philippine Constitution is zealous in guarding religious liberty

---

[5] Dr. Albert J. Sanders, President of the Union Theological Seminary, furnished data on the post-war status and activities of the Seminary.

[6] See J. R. Hayden, *The Philippines, A Study in National Development*, Ch. XXIII, for a discussion of religious instruction in the schools.

and equality. At the same time the Constitution commanded the schools to develop courses in character building and citizenship. "Optional religious instruction shall be maintained in the public schools as now authorized by law," continued the Constitution.[7]

As in other vital subjects where difference of viewpoint obtained, the fathers of the Constitution compromised opinions. In this respect they were in good company. The applicable law which the Constitution ratified was in turn the brainchild of Civil Governor Taft, and a compromise. As embodied in the Administrative Code, teachers in the public schools were prohibited from teaching or criticizing the doctrines of any church or religious denomination, or from attempting to influence the pupils for or against any church or religious sect. But the law permits a priest or minister to teach religion for one half hour three times a week, in the school building, to those public school pupils whose parents or guardians desire it and express their desire therefor in writing.[8]

The above described plan, as indicated, was a compromise of a delicate question which probably pleased no one. It also presents a situation fraught with potential danger. It is easy to charge the school authorities with lukewarmness toward providing facilities for religious instruction. As readily could a too zealous teacher step out of the bounds of pedagogical religious neutrality. It is noticed, however, that a large gain has resulted in the number of pupils enrolled in the religious classes.

---

[7] Constitution of the Philippines, Article 3, sec. 1, clause 7; Article XIV, sec. 5; Aglipay v. Ruiz, 64 Phil. 205.

[8] Revised Administrative Code, secs. 927, 928.

CHAPTER XXIV

PHILIPPINE CULTURE

FILIPINO ATTAINMENTS

Culture — civilization — humanism — aesthetics are elusive words. They can include little or much. Thinking practically, let us appraise Philippine culture by outlining the characteristic attainments of the Filipino people in contrast with other peoples.

The story of primitive man's advancement in the Philippines would be interesting to tell, but need not now concern us. It must be presumed that human progress in ages long past went through the same evolutionary processes here as elsewhere.

On the coming of the Spaniards, they found a people with a culture of their own. This had been made possible not only because of innate ability but because of the effect of Hindu contacts. On the tree of the indigenous civilization the Spanish conquerors engrafted a Latin civilization. The influence of Spain was marked and was particularly commendable in giving to the people the Christian religion. The Americans came and brought with them an entirely different culture which aided in the progress of the Islands, especially in educational, economic, and political ways. Thus Native, Hindu, Spanish, and American civilizations—in other words, Oriental and Occidental civilizations—have combined to make a localized Filipino civilization.

At present it can positively be asserted that there is in the Philippines an advanced state of national and social well-being, which is after all the criterion of culture. Moreover, the Filipino people are in a position to accept the contributions of both the East and the West and to adapt the importations to indigenous conditions.

One sterling factor in Philippine life is the importance of the Filipino family in the community. The average Filipino is very much attached to his home. No better basis for a stable society could be found than this laudable characteristic.

Another factor equally important is the fine type of Filipino womanhood. Philippine women occupy a unique place in society in comparison with other women of the Orient. They are not only accorded respect by the male sector of the Philippines, but in some instances, as in the display of practical business sense, are accepted as on an even higher level than that of their menfolk.

In other portions of this volume reference has been made to the Filipino's universal thirst for education; to the Philippines' standard of literacy which is higher than in many nations; to the growth of nationalistic unity; to the Filipino's capacity for self-government, and to experience in statecraft. These and other Filipino attainments must be taken into account in appraising Philippine culture. Further manifestations in the same field are next discussed under the topics of Philippine Literature, Philippine Classics and Near Classics, Science, Art, Music, and Public Opinion.

Philippine Literature [1]

A description of the development of Philippine Literature divides into five eras, which may be called pre-Spanish, Spanish, Revolutionary, Spanish-Filipino, and American-Filipino.

Unfortunately, misplaced missionary zeal has deprived us of the privilege of having knowledge of all but a scanty few of the documents which had been prepared in the Philippines before the coming of the Spaniards. But we do know that long before the Spanish conquest the ancient Filipinos had a literature written in native characters. The manuscripts of these early Filipinos reflected the simple activities of their lives and consisted principally of maxims, proverbs and songs (*kundimans*). Even today the Ifugaos possess a great epic poem known as the "hud-hud," which requires more than twenty-four hours to sing.

Then came Spain, and, as Rizal once remarked, the laws, customs and culture of the people were all changed by a single stroke of the pen. Native talent in writing thereafter received scant encouragement from the Spaniards. Practically all of the books printed in the dialects were of a religious trend or romantic and fantastic stories. Standing out like mountain tops over valleys were the names in this era of Tomas Pinpin, Francisco Baltazar, and Jose Rizal. Tomas Pinpin, who lived in the first half of the seventeenth century, was the father of Philippine printing. Francisco Baltazar, known as Balagtas, of a somewhat later period, became the poet and philosopher of the Philippines. And then, as if to usher in the glories of the twentieth century, came Jose Rizal, the most eminent author of his race.

Balagtas was the most prolific bard the Philippines has ever pro-

---

[1] A standard work is that by Teofilo del Castillo y Tuazon, *A Brief History of Philippine Literature* (Manila, 1937). See the notes to Chapter VI.

duced. But his fame rests largely on *Florante At Laura*, the single work of widest popularity. *Florante At Laura* is a narrative poem with a dramatic trend. It has been termed the masterpiece of Tagalog literature. Translations have been made into the Visayan, Pampango, and Bicol tongues, and Professor George St. Clair has brought out a commendable version in English. Balagtas is conceded by all to be the national poet of the Filipinos.

Jose Rizal's novels were *Nole Me Tangere* and *El Filibusterismo*. These two works in literary construction were perhaps not so much novels as social documents. They were a series of realistic pictures of Philippine life under Spanish rule. In the sense that Mrs. Stowe's "Uncle Tom's Cabin" was literature were Rizal's books masterpieces. William Dean Howells, a discriminating critic, pronounced Rizal's *Nole Me Tangere* the greatest book written in any language in fifty years. Assuredly its appearance constituted a landmark in the development by the Filipinos of their own literature.

Rizal gave his final message to his dearly beloved fatherland in the beautiful poem, *Mi Ultimo Adios*, written some nights before his martyrdom. No one can translate these verses without tragic loss, but a number of attempts at English versions have been made. One of the first was made by an Italian, Zanoni Volpicelli; and another, it is interesting to note, was rendered by a Japanese, Dr. Y. Mikami. The most widely known version is the one done by an American, Dr. Frank C. Laubach. The poem represents the Philippines in "The Poetry of Freedom," an anthology of the world's poetic expression in the struggle for liberty.

The Philippine Revolution naturally encouraged writing and was attended by the issuance of State papers of more or less intrinsic value. Major J. R. M. Taylor translated and compiled the insurgent records, but the work was left in the form of galley proofs in the archives of the War Department at Washington. General Emilio Aguinaldo's account of the Revolution appeared in his *Reseña Veridica de la Revolucion Filipina* ("True Version of the Philippine Revolution"), which was written by him and corrected by one of his advisers. Apolinario Mabini, the premier of the Revolutionary Government, afterwards wrote *La Revolucion Filipina* ("The Philippine Revolution"), and Felipe G. Calderon, the author of the Malolos Constitution, brought out his *Mis Memorias Sobre La Revolucion Filipina* ("My Memories of the Philippine Revolution"). These works are valuable because they furnish source material, but do not shine with literary brilliancy.

What has been termed with questionable right the Golden Age of Literature in Spanish overlaps the Spanish and American regimes.

Then appeared Dr. Trinidad H. Pardo de Tavera, the Filipino philologist and scholar, a master of Spanish; Epifanio de los Santos, the indefatigable researcher, acknowledged savant, and brilliant writer; Teodoro M. Kalaw, the careful historian; and Justice Ignacio Villamor, industrious statistician, famed criminologist, and distinguished essayist. The works of these great Filipinos were characterized by an authoritative use of Spanish, although they were also acquainted with English and other languages, by a distinct trend toward the expression of nationalistic feelings, and by a sincere desire to encourage the development of Philippine Literature.

What shall we say of the American-influenced era? We are too near to events to offer a convincing critique of Filipino literature in English. The best that can be done is to describe the impression that the writers have made on one reader.

The years before World War II in the Philippines permitted greater latitude in the development of literature because of freedom of speech and press. The output was plentiful and in some instances promising. But all too many of the short stories and poems, and even the more pretentious works, were superficial and lacked point or purpose. A possible exception was Dr. Rafael Palma's prize winning biography of Jose Rizal, which gains added importance on account of the admirable 1949 translation from Spanish into English by Justice Roman Ozaeta under the supplied title, "The Pride of the Malay Race."

Life in the United States brought recognition to a number of Filipino writers. Jose Garcia Villa won fame for his short stories and poems. Edward J. O'Brien sponsored the statement that Villa's *Footnote to Youth; Tales of the Philippines; And Others*, places him "among the half dozen short-story writers in America who count." Anthologies of the best American poetry include selections from his works. Villa's later versification, "Have Come, Am Here," introduces an original method of rhyming called "reversed consonance."

Carlos Bulosan also made a reputation for himself as a writer in the United States, as did Marcelo de Gracia Concepcion and others. Bulosan's *The Laughter of My Father* is a well known story. More pretentious is a personal narrative, *America Is In The Heart*. This book traces the odyssey of a Filipino from his modest Binalonan home in the Philippines, through his trials and tribulations in the Pacific Coast States of the United States. The Bulosan style is easy. The work is a worthwhile contribution to literature.

The war inspired a number of notable books. President Manuel Quezon started his memoirs, only to be interrupted by death. Published posthumously, with additions by intimate associates, under the title *The Good Fight*, the book has value as an historical document. General Carlos P. Romulo added to his fame as a journalist by authoring a series of books, of which *I Saw The Fall of The Philippines* is most dramatic in appeal.

It was left for a young law student, Stevan Javellana, in a first novel, *Without Seeing The Dawn*, to produce what the critics call a story "worthy to become a classic."[2] Why? The title was inspired by a passage in Rizal's *Nole Me Tangere*. The book carries on from where that great Filipino left his crusade, to reveal the people of the Philippines as they lived in a typical village before and during the last war. Why? Because Javellana's style is light and vivid and his characters are real and true to life. Jose Garcia Villa, famous in his own right, welcomes Javellana into the inner circle, with words of commendation for *Without Seeing The Dawn* as follows: "A work of very great power . . . a Philippine Classic. It is genuine, very genuine indeed."

Stevan Javellana's success points the path for other Filipino writers to tread.

Philippine Classics and Near Classics

When novelist John Erskine was called upon to preside over the improvised American Army University of Beaune in France after World War I, the idea occurred to him to make it possible to read the Great Books themselves, instead of reading about them. The idea caught on and eventually spread to the University of Chicago in the United States, where Chancellor Robert M. Hutchins organized and headed "The Great Books Foundation." All over the United States "Great Books" Clubs are meeting regularly, with members trying to discover what these books have to teach people now.

Another educator, Dr. Charles W. Eliot, after a long and fruitful life as President of Harvard University, and as a good American citizen, approached the problem of popularizing the Great Books from another angle. He sponsored the Harvard Classics. On a five-foot shelf he placed the masterpieces of all time.

It would hardly seem impertinent to attempt in a smaller way to interest people generally in reading the Great Books which have to do with the Philippines. There may be among the written words applied to the Philippine scene not Great Books like the Bible or those produced by Plato, Cervantes and Shakespeare. Granted. Still there may be listed books on and for the Philippines that have survival value.

---

[2] John Cournos in a review for the *New York Sun*.

The National Library, now become the Bureau of Public Libraries, has done a worthwhile job in taking the initiative in the acquisition of valuable collections of *Filipiniana*. While the vandalism of war obliterated the home of the Library, a portion of these irreplaceable manuscripts and all of the archives were salvaged. Included among the archives are 11,000,000 pieces of historical documents covering the entire period of Spanish rule in the Philippines, not to be found anywhere else in the world.

A major contribution to knowledge was the publication by the Library of a series of important documents on Philippine history. The late Director of the Bureau of Public Libraries, Eulogio B. Rodriguez, faithfully carried on a work well begun by his illustrious predecessors. The latest venture in this category was a book entitled "Japanese War Atrocities in the Philippines."

In 1949 the Congress of the Philippines approved a measure which will provide a free circulating library for practically every town in the Philippines. It was money well spent. The Nation has shown an avidity for education, which means the reading of good books. The people who need books but are least able to procure them will be given access to them.

In any survey of Philippine books, one is compelled to start with Spain in the Philippines. As a beginning, it would appear not out of place to include the Italian Antonio Pigafetta's *Primo Viaggio Intorno Al Mondo* ("First Voyage Around the World"), which is a journal by a participant of Ferdinand Magellan's near circumnavigation of the world, including his appearance in the Philippines.

The literature on the Philippines in Spanish is extensive, as is disclosed by that monumental work, Blair and Robertson, *The Philippine Islands*, where fifty-five volumes are needed to encompass the translations of documents and books of historical importance concerning the Philippines. Of these strictly Spanish descriptions of the Philippines, it is everywhere conceded that the most reliable is the first by Chief Justice Antonio de Morga, *Sucesos de las Islas Filipinas* ("Events of the Philippine Islands"), which work gains additional prestige because it was considered of enough importance to warrant an English translation by Lord Stanley and because of an edition brought out by Rizal. The articles on the Philippines prepared by the Catholic Fathers were numerous, but here again it is generally admitted that *Estadismo* by Joaquin Martinez de Zuñiga, O.S.A., an illustrious member of the Augustinian Order, is the best because characterized by a charming style and careful observation. Foreign writers on the Philippines were not lacking during the Spanish regime, but it is conceded that the book by the German naturalist Feodor Jagor, *Reisen in den Philippinen* ("Travels in the Philippines"), is outstanding because the author was a keen and trained scientific observer.

Coming now to the American occupation of the Philippines, our task of selection is not made difficult by paucity of materials to select from, but is complicated by the very fact that there has been so much produced on the Philippines. However, the arrival of the American fleet under the command of Commodore George Dewey in Manila Bay on May 1, 1898, and the naval battle which followed, had about the same relative importance as the arrival of Magellan and later of Legaspi had in Spanish times; one "discovered" the Philippines for Europe, and the other "discovered" the Philippines for America. In the latter instance, we are fortunate in having a first-hand account written by the commander of the American squadron under the title, *Autobiography of George Dewey, Admiral of the Navy.*

The books by former Governors General W. Cameron Forbes, Francis Burton Harrison, Henry L. Stimson, and Theodore Roosevelt, Jr., each approaching the subject from a different viewpoint, have much to commend them. Without doubt, however, the fairest works to all concerned were those produced in incomplete form by James Alfred Le Roy in *The Americans In the Philippines.* More recently scholarship of a high order was displayed by former Vice Governor Joseph Ralston Hayden in *The Philippines: A Study In National Development.* In the line of sustained biography was Austin Craig's *Rizal's Life and Minor Writings.* Dr. Craig devoted a lifetime to research on the lineage, life and labors of the Filipino author and patriot.

The purely Filipino element in Philippine Literature was formerly blunted by repression, and more recently has been handicapped by having to be expressed in alien tongues. The first Filipino masterpiece in point of time came from the facile pen of the bard and philosopher Francisco Baltazar (Balagtas) under the title *Florante At Laura.* In the name of the greatest of all Filipino authors, Dr. Jose Rizal, stands the patriotic novel *Noli Me Tangere* and the tender elegy, *Mi Ultimo Adios.* Probably the best historical account so far produced by a Filipino was that written by the Sublime Paralytic, Apolinario Mabini, *La Revolucion Filipina* ("The Philippine Revolution"). It is a pity that nothing can readily be selected from the works produced by the Filipino scholar Dr. Trinidad H. Pardo de Tavera, by the Filipino savant Epifantio de los Santos, by the Filipino historian Teodoro M. Kalaw, and by the Filipino statistician Justice Ignacio Villamor.

With some hesitation we are led to extend recognition to three

Filipino authors of the present. This may be a mistake because our viewpoint may be out of focus. However, we take our stand for Carlos P. Romulo's *I Saw the Fall of the Philippines*, because it has historical value; Carlos Bulosan's *America Is In the Heart*, because it clutches at hearts and minds in vivid description of a Filipino's progress through prejudice to find happiness; and Stevan Javellana's novel *Without Seeing the Dawn*, because it is, in truth, a minor classic.

In short, out of the plethora of books so laboriously written on and for the Philippines, only fourteen are placed among the elect. Seven have been written in English, four in Spanish, one in Tagalog, one in Italian, and one in German. Of the authors, six were Filipinos, four Americans, two Spaniards, one Italian, and one German.

A place is waiting other classics in Philippine Literature. There is room for autobiographies by the famous, and for notable works in the fields of fiction, poetry and history.

The selections here attempted of Philippine Classics and Near Classics for a shelf of books on and for the Philippines—with which selections everyone is privileged to disagree—are the following:

1. Antonio Pigaffeta, *Primo Viaggio Intorno Al Mondo* ("First Voyage Around the World").

2. Antonio de Morga, *Sucesos de las Islas Filipinas* ("Events of the Philippine Islands").

3. Joaquin Martinez de Zuñiga, *Estadismo*.

4. Feodor Jagor, *Reisen in den Philippinen* ("Travels in the Philippines").

5. *Autobiography of George Dewey, Admiral of the Navy*.

6. James Alfred Le Roy, *The Americans In the Philippines*, with an introduction by William H. Taft.

7. Joseph Ralston Hayden, *The Philippines: A Study in National Development*.

8. Austin Craig, *Rizal's Life and Minor Writings*.

9. Francisco Baltazar, *Florante At Laura*.

10. Jose Rizal, *Noli Me Tangere* ("The Social Cancer," with introductions by Epifanio de los Santos and the translater Charles E. Derbyshire) and *Mi Ultimo Adios* ("My Last Farewell").

11. Apolinario Mabini, *La Revolucion Filipina* ("The Philippine Revolution").

12. Carlos P. Romulo, *I Saw the Fall of the Philippines*.

13. Carlos Bulosan, *America Is In the Heart*.

14. Stevan Javellana, *Without Seeing the Dawn*.

Science [3]

Scientific research in the Philippines has had its ups and downs. Fostered during the major portion of the American administration of the Islands, eventually agencies entrusted with scientific investigations dissipated their energies in uncoordinated efforts and were allowed to disintegrate. The curve again began to move slowly—very slowly—upward in the Filipino-controlled Commonwealth and Republic.

Only the lights and shadows of an abstruse topic can here be depicted in broad outlines.

When one thinks of science in the Philippines, he automatically associates the idea with the Bureau of Science. This unique institution was established in 1905 by American administrators, who assembled in one organization activities of a laboratory nature. In the course of time the number of uses to which the Bureau was put were greatly expanded. Behind the Bureau stood a sympathetic government, and it received Federal and private encouragement. The Bureau of Science was a well-rounded scientific institution.

When mention is made of the Bureau of Science, there is necessarily brought to mind the name of its founder, Dr. Paul C. Freer. From Freer, the eminent chemist, to Dr. William H. Brown, the eminent botanist, and the last American Director of the Bureau of Science, not a long period of time was spanned, but it was sufficient to permit of noteworthy researches by scientists associated with the Bureau.

It needs to be repeated that the implantation of scientific work in the Islands was a comparatively recent development. Just as the Spanish regime was characterized by a crusade for the spread of the Christian faith among the people, so the coming of the American regime gave impetus to the advance of science along lines adequate to meet modern requirements. Fifty years ago life in the tropics was extremely hazardous due to rampant diseases. The early American scientists, with unremitting toil and untold sacrifices, made fundamental investigations which helped check the heavy tolls of tropical epidemics such as cholera, smallpox, malaria, and dysentery. These inroads of epidemics were then considered acts of God, similar to great upheavals of nature. The rapid advances in health and sanitation have made Philippine life enjoyable and comparable in safety

---

[3] This section was originally read by Dr. A. S. Arguelles, Director of Science. See report of the American Agricultural Mission to the Philippines, *International Agricultural Collaboration Series*, No. 3, June, 1947, pp. 31 *et. seq.*

with that in countries in the temperate zone. With the stabilization of public health, attention was thereupon directed to researches in technical industries, forestry, mining, agriculture, and fisheries.

Not all of the scientific output of the Philippines was monopolized by the Bureau of Science. For instance, there were investigations of tropical diseases by the United States Army, of leprosy by the Bureau of Health and the Leonard Wood Memorial, and of rinderpest by the Bureau of Agriculture and its successor, the Bureau of Animal Industry. The list could be continued to include the University of the Philippines, the Bureau of Forestry, the Bureau of Plant Industry, and other branches of the government.

Many names have been associated with science in the Philippines. Two of them, the one Filipino and the other American, should at least be mentioned. Dr. Leon Ma. Guerrero, to whom death came in 1935, was the famed and foremost Filipino botanist. Dr. H. Otley Beyer won international renown for his researches in the fields of ancient Philippine and Oriental history. Dr. Beyer, with unremitting care and unruffled patience, assembled the largest and finest collection of tectites in the world. He is head of the Anthropology Department and of the Museum and Institute of Archaeology and Ethnology in the University of the Philippines.

The dark side of the picture is that the government has failed at times to furnish adequate support to science. Brilliant men have been lost when any kind of encouragement would have kept them. Some of these scientists went from the Philippines to better and more responsible posts. As late as 1933 the Bureau of Science was practically dismembered and its various units scattered hither and yon. Fortunately in 1934 a sagacious department secretary put the pieces of the Bureau together again. Commonwealth President Quezon soon after rectified some of the earlier mistakes of policy.

The Philippine Constitution provides that "The State shall promote scientific research and invention." The National Research Council was created to promote and coordinate research along scientific lines. The Institute of Science as its operating agency represented a faint effort to make a basic principle more than a piece of paper. The Director, Dr. A. S. Arguelles, was a scholarly scientist. His co-workers were well trained. The Institute properly backed could have played a vital role in the defense of the health of the people and in the economic development of the Nation. Instead, shortly before the clock struck twelve to usher out the year 1950, the President signed an executive order that once again, and probably finally, broke up the Institute of Science and transferred its divisions to other agencies.

ART[4]

The Philippines occupies a secure place in the world of art. The Filipino, whether as a surgeon performing a complicated operation, as a painter putting beauty to canvas, as a sculptor carving in wood or modeling in clay or bronze, or as an architect sketching the plans of a memorial, is endowed with skilled hands and artistic temperament. Taking cognizance of the self-evident talents of the Filipinos, the development of the fine arts both in Spanish and American times and at present has been encouraged. Unfortunately, because of their contact with western civilization, the expression of art among the Filipinos is mainly imitative. This is frankly admitted by the Filipinos themselves.

Juan Luna and Felix Resurreccion Hidalgo were the first Filipino painters to rise above mediocrity to win international reputations. Their paintings are treasured in European galleries and in Manila. They were in many ways the antithesis of each other, for while Luna reveled in strength and fire, Hidalgo's work reflected melancholy and languor.

Luna's masterpiece was the "Spolarium," which won several prizes and was at last sold to the City of Barcelona, Spain. Another well-known Luna painting was "The Blood Compact." The latter now greets the eye as one ascends the grand staircase in Malacañan Palace in Manila. Hidalgo's paintings include "Oedipus and Antigone" and "Las Virgenes Cristianas Expuestas al Populacho."

Modern painting is not without its master. The premier figure is Fernando C. Amorsolo, the Director of the School of Fine Arts of the University of the Philippines. Amorsolo is by all odds the most widely recognized Filipino painter at home or abroad. He is deserving of such popular favor and esteem.[5]

Amorsolo has been the target of scathing criticism. It is said that he lacks vision, feeling, growth. At the same time all must concede that he is the most genuinely Filipino artist. Genre is his forte. Amorsolo has been able to catch the spirit of everyday scenes among his countrymen and make them live on canvas. He is the first painter to interpret faithfully the brilliant color and sunshine of the Philippine tropics. If among the canvases are portrait or landscape daubs

---

[4] Director of Fine Arts Fernando C. Amorsolo supplied notes on "Art in the Philippines." See Ignacio Manlapaz, "*Filipino Art,*" appearing as an Appendix to Maximo M. Kalaw's *Philippine Social Science* (Manila, 1933) and Raymundo C. Banas, *Brief Historical Sketches of Philippine Catholic Churches* (Manila, 1937).

[5] The articles by Francisco Arcellano and Aurelio S. Alvero in the Manila press of November, 1948 can be noted.

to meet patronage demands, the great painter can be forgiven for claiming monetary rewards for his efforts.

Another enthusiastic modernist is Victorio Edades. He has executed several beautiful murals with the help of younger artists. Carlos Francisco has become his foremost follower.

Filipino sculptors have likewise executed beautiful works of art. In pre-Spanish days, the Filipinos carved their idols, and even today a recrudescence of this talent may be seen in the primitive but nevertheless pretty objects made by the mountain peoples. The town of Paete, Laguna, has long attracted attention on account of the ability of its residents in sculpture. The carvings in the churches made by Filipino artisans were symphonies of beauty.

The most distinguished Filipino sculptor is Guillermo T. Tolentino, who is an assiduous and productive worker in his chosen field. His masterpiece is the monument to the Filipino patriot Andres Bonifacio. The Bonifacio monument is far superior to the more pretentious mausoleum to Rizal on the Luneta in Manila, which is the world's ugliest national monument and which the irreverent refer to as a bottle. And speaking of monuments, the one honoring Miguel Lopez de Legaspi and Andres de Urdaneta, overlooking the Luneta and Manila Bay, which was put in place soon after the American occupation, still surpasses all others in the Philippines in appropriateness of location and design.

The most typical expression of Philippine art is to be seen in the hundreds of old and beautiful churches which are found scattered over the Islands. They are solid structures which have defied the elements and destructive earthquakes. Mainly of Byzantine and early Renaissance architecture, the lines of these churches are simple and their interiors satisfying in religious appeal. The imposing churches stand as monuments to untold sacrifices of the craftsmen who were responsible for their creation.

Foremost among Philippine churches is the San Augustin Church and Convent, one of the Philippines' most ancient structures, located in Manila's Walled City. Completed as it now stands at the beginning of the sixteenth century, miraculously it has escaped the ravages of man and nature. Even the Battle of Liberation left it only slightly damaged. Possibly one reason for its sturdiness is the foundation, which is said to be egg-shaped. Another reason is its retaining walls and buttresses, which average thirteen feet in thickness. But the most remarkable feature of the Church is the ceiling of solid, hewn stone. In the sacristy between the altar and the vestry the terms for the American occupation of Manila were signed. In the Church below the stone flagging lie buried the remains of Legaspi and others of Spain's noblest dead.

Utility more than beauty was the aim in the construction of most business and public buildings in the Philippines of the modern era. A standardized type in cold cement was cheaper and more practical than variegated expressions of the architect's vision. The exceptions were a few apartment and office structures, the pillared halls of the University of the Philippines along classic lines, the Posts, Finance and Legislative Buildings, and the Metropolitan Theatre. The four last named, located not far apart in Manila, were the children of Juan M. Arellano, the Filipino architect, himself an artist of no mean repute, who in spite of the handicaps imposed by unfeeling sponsors, yet managed to adapt native architectural motifs to modern uses.

War was no respecter of buildings in laying low the bad, the mediocre, and the good. Some of these structures will remain rubble. Others will undergo improvised repair. And others will be rebuilt on former sites or elsewhere. The decision to have Quezon City the capital makes possible the erection there of beautiful Government and University buildings. The opportunity thus provided can either be met with architectural creations of distinction, or the reverse can be the outcome. Knowing the Filipinos' appreciation of the fine arts, it can be expected that neither money nor effort will be spared to provide the Philippine Republic with a Capital and a University that will reflect honor on the new State.

Music[6]

The Filipinos are gifted musicians. From the earliest era to the immediate present, and in every part of the Philippines, and in whatever country Filipinos may be found, they will invariably make known their fondness for music. All the peoples of the Islands have delighted in giving expression to the yearnings of their souls by means of folk-songs and dances.

In recent times, Filipino music has assumed modern methods of expression. During the Philippine Revolution at the beginning of the century, Julian Felipe composed the music and Jose Palma wrote the words in Spanish of the Philippine National Hymn, commonly re-

---

[6] Professor Ramon Tapales, Director of the University of the Philippines Conservatory of Music, conferred with the author and furnished important data. See Justice Norberto Romualdez, *Filipino Musical Instruments and Airs of Long Ago* (Manila, 1931) and Francisco Santiago, *The Development of Music in the Philippine Islands* (Manila, 1931).

ferred to as "Aguinaldo's March." Although the European influence in the Philippine equivalent of the "Star Spangled Banner" is noticeable, the anthem possesses a martial air and rhythm which is peculiarly appealing.

The Constabulary Band, organized in 1904 and trained by Colonel Walter H. Loving, an American Negro with exceptional talent, is world famous. The band has not only established itself as a successful local organization, but has gone on foreign tours and met with the plaudits of world audiences. It participated in the St. Louis Exposition in 1904, attended the inaugural ball of President Taft in 1909, and took part in the Panama-Pacific Exposition in San Francisco in 1915. Major Antonio Buenaventura capably wields the baton over the First Armed Forces Band (formerly the Constabulary Band).

The Manila Symphony Society took form in the 1930's. It organized a symphony orchestra composed mainly of Filipino musicians, that gave annually a series of concerts to capacity audiences. During the war, thanks to the vigilance of Mrs. Trinidad F. Legarda, the beautiful and enthusiastic President of the Symphony Society, the orchestral instruments were thoughtfully and ingeniously buried to hide them from the enemy. Following liberation of the Philippines, the instruments reappeared, and concerts were resumed, with American soldiers constituting a portion of the appreciative audiences. Others who participated in the production of good music included the late Dr. Alexander Lippay, who organized the orchestra, and his successor Dr. Herbert Zipper, expatriate of a German prison camp, later the conductor of the Brooklyn Symphony. Bernardino F. Custodio is the present conductor of the Manila Symphony Orchestra.

Not to be outdone, the City of Manila has created the Municipal Symphony Orchestra. The Orchestra conductor is Ramon Tapales, talented Director of the University of the Philippines Conservatory of Music. Besides concerts given locally, the Orchestra concluded a successful tour which took it to China, Guam, and Hawaii. Federico Elizalde organized the Manila Little Symphony, possibly the finest musical ensemble in the Philippines.

An ever-increasing group of musicians educated in Europe and the United States form an important factor in the progress of music in the Philippines. Conspicuous among them were Jovita Fuentes, a soprano who in the role of Madame Butterfly and other operatic parts had a remarkable career abroad, and Luisa Tapales, who triumphed in the opera of Paris. The unexpected commentary is that Miss Fuentes had to pretend she was a Japanese in order to secure recognition for her talents, and her experience, sad to relate, has not been the exception but the rule for other Filipina singers. Also conspicuous among Filipino musicians was Jose Mossesgeld Santiago, known to the world of opera as Santiago Font, who was the first Filipino to make successful appearances in La Scala Theater of Milan, the most exclusive operatic institution of Italy. Ernesto Vallejo, talented violinist, was murdered by the Japanese.

After the war Enya Gonzalez and Conchita Gaston won musical fame in the United States. So likewise did Dalisay Aldaba, well known Filipina diva with a successful concert tour of the United States to her credit. The thirteen-year-old pianist Nena del Rosario made her debut in New York City in 1948. The group of young musicians is very promising.

PUBLIC OPINION

"There is no public opinion in the Philippine Islands." So it has been asserted on sundry occasions. But this affirmation will bear reexamination, for, like most sweeping statements, it includes more than strictly conforms to fact.

What is true is that the Filipino people do not constitute a reading public to anywhere near the extent of the Americans or the British, or, to make a rather unkind comparison, the Japanese, who at all hours and in all manner of public places are engrossed in newspapers, magazines or books. What is also true is that those in the Philippines who form national sentiment, like political leaders and journalists, are comparatively few, and that the persons who do evince an interest in what the political leaders and journalists are saying or writing are not as numerous as they should be.

It should also be remarked that the authorities who once decried the lack of public opinion in the Philippines did so to evoke opposition to Philippine independence. The last two decades have seen a remarkable development in the publication of newspapers and other periodicals. Since independence came to the Philippines, to an increasing extent the people feel a sobering sense of responsibility, and accordingly take more interest in current events and scrutinize more closely the actions of their representatives.

The press is without question the most powerful organ for shaping public opinion.[7] In the Philippines the influence of the press has made steady progress. The first genuine newspaper, in the nature of a gazette of the High Government of Spain in the Philippines, was pub-

---

[7] See Carson Taylor, *History of the Philippine Press* (Manila, 1927) and Jesus V. Valenzuela, *History of Journalism in the Philippine Islands* (Manila, 1933).

lished in Manila on August 8, 1811. *El Comercio*, founded in 1863, long appearing in Spanish, survived the change of sovereignty. The journal of Philippine propaganda in Spain was *La Solidaridad*, established by Graciano Lopez Jaena in Barcelona in 1889, in which appeared the articles of Marcelo H. del Pilar and other Filipino patriots.

After American occupation of the Philippines, numerous periodicals made their bows to the public, only for varying reasons to depart the scene unheralded and unsung. The *Manila Daily Bulletin* and the *Philippines Free Press* launched in the days of the Empire were notable exceptions. Both have sailed the turbulent journalistic seas with amazing success from those far off times down to the present.

The *Manila Daily Bulletin*, the Philippines' oldest operating newspaper, began publication in 1900 as a shipping sheet. In 1912 it became a full fledged newspaper of general circulation. Carson Taylor was the founder of the *Bulletin*. He remained its publisher for fifty years. Bombed out during the war, the resourceful newspaperman staged a comeback with a paper of heightened influence and circulation. Under Mr. Taylor's inspiration, the sole remaining American daily has enjoyed the favor of the reading public—Americans, Filipinos and others—because of high standards consistently maintained.

The *Philippines Free Press* was taken over by Scottish-born R. McCulloch Dick in 1908. Not long after, he brought into the inner sanctum of the *Free Press* as business manager the popular and versatile F. Theo. Rogers. Together the Dick-Rogers combination, with the help of able Filipino and American associates, made the weekly the "Bible of the Filipinos." This feat was accomplished by careful proof reading, by insistence on the use of correct English, by taking an independent and courageous stand on vital public questions, and by the composition of editorial masterpieces. The influence for good of the *Philippines Free Press* on the development of young Filipinos, who in due course become older Filipinos, cannot be over estimated.

Before the outbreak of war, the principal newspaper publishers in Manila were Madrigal's *DMHM*, Taylor's *Bulletin*, and Roce's *TVT*. The *DMHM* newspaper plant was destroyed, but in 1949 the *Philippines Herald* resumed publication. The *Bulletin* office, likewise demolished, went into temporary eclipse. The *TVT* papers chose collaboration and became the mouthpiece of the Japanese. In contrast, underground newspapers, mimeographed or clandestinely printed, succeeded in disseminating information under conditions fraught with peril. The *Liberator* was a resistance newspaper of this dauntless type.

Following liberation, the *Free Philippines*, a U. S. Government organ, started publication while shells were still bursting over Manila.

Other periodicals soon followed, over fifty it has been estimated, most to fold in a few months, the rest to survive for a more normal life. Economic forces have now stabilized conditions among the Philippine press.

The circulation of periodicals entered as second-class mail matter reveals the extent and language of publication.[8] The facts disclosed by the 1949 figures of the Bureau of Posts show two hundred and fifty-one publications entered as second-class mail matter, as compared to three hundred and forty-five in pre-war days. Three-fourths are accounted for by one hundred and nineteen English-language and by sixty-five English-Native dialects publications. Thirty-eight, or one-seventh of the total, appear in a single native language and only seven in Spanish and seventeen in English-Spanish.

Sixteen daily newspapers (more or less, as new dailies begin publication and others abandon the field) are published in Manila. This is nine less than appeared before the war, but eight out of the nine are non-existent Spanish papers. On the other hand, the sixteen circulate daily 50,000 more copies than the former twenty-five (before the war, 251,018; in 1949, after the war, 308,379). The *Manila Times* alone claims an average net paid circulation daily in excess of 80,000.

An analysis of the above statistics shows that English is most widely read. The native languages are a respectable second, while Spanish is a poor third. If the reading habit be made the criterion of public opinion, then Manila and its environs are by all odds the center of Philippine culture. The upper class naturally constitutes the main financial support for publications, but an encouraging note is that the reading habit has developed among the middle class. Finally, if one were to add still more statistics, they would show a remarkable growth in the circulation of all kinds of periodicals in the Philippines.

The Philippines has been particularly fortunate in the quality of its periodicals. Associated with the Philippine press have been men and women of the highest repute. In addition to Taylor, Dick, and Rogers already mentioned, the roll call continues with the names of Jose Romero Salas, long the Spanish dean of Philippine journalism; Banker Martin Egan and his talented wife Eleanor Franklin Egan, formerly connected with the *Manila Times;* Frederick O'Brien, cosmopolite of South Sea Island fame; Bill Lewis or, to give him his British title, Sir Willmott Lewis of the Washington Bureau of the *London Times;* Walter Robb, former editor of the *American Chamber of Commerce Journal;* A. V. H. Hartendorp, erudite publisher of

---

[8] Director of Posts Juan Ruiz submitted a comparative statement on the number and circulation of second-class mail publications.

the same Journal; Fernando Ma. Guerrero, famed Filipino poet and editor; and General Carlos P. Romulo, Pulitzer prize winning editor of pre-war days. Names more recently to be reckoned with in the publishing field include Ramon Roces, David Boguslav, and the Lopez Family.

The news service and the articles, for which these and other men and women were responsible, were of immense variety and number. A famous editorial which nearly produced a governmental revolution was Frederick O'Brien's satire on "Why the Fly Climbs Up the Window Pane." Another editorial with a similar bite was *El Renacimiento's* allegorical "Birds of Prey," which lampooned Secretary of the Interior Worcester. The owners and editors of the nationalist daily were assessed damages, which amounted to confiscation of the newspaper plant, and on conviction for libel received prison sentences. After judgment was confirmed by the Supreme Court of the United States, the author who had appeared as counsel for the government in the criminal case took the initiative in obtaining pardons for the accused.

One of the richest gifts of the American people to the Filipino people consisted in making effective the guaranty of freedom of speech and press. Notwithstanding this careful safeguarding of a right dear to the people, the Philippines has a strict libel law. Prosecutions in attempted vindication of name and honor have been altogether too frequent. The tendency of the appellate courts in dealing with these cases has been to adopt a tolerant attitude, and to deal lightly with offenses which fall under the libel law.

One way by which public opinion is formed in the Philippines is not by the written word but by the spoken word. The Filipino politicians are fluent and eloquent speakers. They find large and appreciative audiences ready to listen to them even in the remote *barrios*. What is said at these meetings then passes on from mouth to mouth and is further discussed at gatherings of the elders in the vicinity. It is believed that the importance of this method of making public opinion has not been sufficiently appreciated, and that it exists to a remarkable extent in the Islands.

When, therefore, the statement is made that there is no public opinion in the Philippines, the matter is overstated. More correctly it can be said that public opinion to an ever increasing extent does exist and does exert an influence on the government through an alert press, public discussion, and the ballot. The purpose of all should be to develop a healthy public opinion by elevating and protecting the organs and agencies by which it is formed.

CHAPTER XXV

THE PHILIPPINES TOMORROW[1]

FILIPINO CAPACITY FOR SELF-GOVERNMENT

The President of the United States in proclaiming the independence of the Philippines on July 4, 1946 did so on the premise: "The people of the Philippines have clearly demonstrated their capacity for self-government." The people there mentioned—the Filipinos—are of the Malay race. The independence which the Filipinos achieved under American auspices took form in the Republic of the Philippines, the first Malayan State democratically founded of either the ancient or the modern world.

Was the President justified in making so sweeping a statement in favor of the right of the Filipino people to govern themselves?

Writers who set themselves up as experts on Malaysia would likely disagree. They are apt to stress the inability of the Malays to govern one another. According to these authorities, Malay culture is unstable, and is hostile to the development of those unities and loyalties from which a nation can be welded. Typical of this viewpoint is A. R. Colquhoun in the work *The Mastery Of The Pacific*, cited approvingly by other authors, in passages reading: "No Malay Nation has ever emerged from the hordes of that race, which has spread over the islands of the Pacific. Wherever they are found they have certain marked characteristics, and of these the most remarkable is their lack of that spirit which goes to form a homogeneous people, to weld them together."[2]

Applying general principles specifically to the Philippines, authorities belonging to the skeptical school of thought question the ability of the Filipino people to maintain a democratic form of government.[3]

---

[1] "The Philippines Tomorrow" was one of the subjects covered in the 48th anniversary number of the *Manila Daily Bulletin*.

[2] A. R. Colquhoun, *The Mastery of the Pacific*, p. 122 (1902) cited approvingly by Dean C. Worcester, *The Philippines, Past and Present*, Hayden edition of 1930, pp. 672, 673; E. Alexander Powell, *Asia at the Crossroads*, pp. 280, 281 (1922); and D. R. Williams, *The United States and the Philippines*, p. 50 (1924). Claude A. Buss in *The New World of Southeast Asia*, p. 375 (1949) points to the Malays as not democratically minded.

[3] Woodhern E. Remington, *Cross Winds of Empire*, p. 230 (1941). Sir Hugh Clifford's conviction "of the utter inability of the Malays to govern one another with anything approaching wisdom, justice, or honesty" is quoted at pp. 84, 85.

Former Governor General Stimson emphasizes "the Malay tendency to backslide." As a consequence the date of independence of the Philippine Republic found the distinguished statesman torn "by both fear and hope."[4]

Statements like the foregoing serve to reflect in a narrower sense the sentiments of those who flaunt the God-given superiority of the white man over the brown man, the yellow man and the black man. Even as broadminded a journalist as William Allen White in referring to Cuba, shortly after the conclusion of the Spanish-American War, was moved to proclaim that "Only Anglo-Saxons can govern themselves."

In the case of the Filipino Malays, it must be recognized that patronizing Spaniards and uninformed Americans have not dealt kindly or fairly with the inhabitants of the Philippines. American members of Congress, in the excitement of debate, have used language in referring to the Filipino people which only served to underscore the ignorance of the speaker. It is slight consolation to recall that a similar warped attitude of mind was reflected in ante-Revolutionary days in the United States when Englishmen were wont to term the Americans "egregious cowards," to ridicule their manners and ways of living, and to prophesy that if Great Britain abandoned the colonies they would soon sue for succor.

Happily the capacity of the members of a race for self-government is not determined by the virulence of the epithets thrown at them or by race prejudice. Facts offered in a detached manner in the court of public opinion become the determining factors. Moreover, these facts should be given direct application to conditions in the Republic of the Philippines and a modern setting in the middle of the twentieth century. Thus judged, the Filipinos have given the lie to their detractors by concrete accomplishments.

The statements last made signify that we need not linger long over ancient history. In passing it is merely necessary to recall the former Malayan Empires of Sri-Vishaya and Madjapahit, with boundaries reaching to the Philippines. It might also be that the Mayas of North America and the Incas of South America with their high civilizations were of Malay extraction. Nor is the theory not without support that the Malays were near kin of the Iberian type of the Mediterranean peoples and so partners in the building of the ancient civilizations of Egypt and Chaldea.

Once again endeavoring to get closer to our problem: At the time

[4] Annual Report of Governor General Stimson for 1928; Henry L. Stimson and McGeorge Bundy, *On Active Service in Peace and War*, pp. 127, 151 (1948).

of Spain's arrival in the Philippines, the natives had a culture comparable to that of peoples of the same time in other lands. What we now refer to as Filipinos were living in groups ruled by chiefs, with occasional loose confederations. The enlarged family was the main unit of society. The Spaniards, taking advantage of this lack of cohesiveness, expanded it to form municipalities clustering around the town *plazas*.

It was to a Philippines in which national consciousness was gradually emerging that the United States came in 1898. Respect for the family and adherence to the communal group were admirable qualities, but they did not make for national unity. To consolidate districts speaking different dialects into a nation was the problem that confronted the Filipinos and the Americans alike, as the former strove to attain statehood and as the latter encouraged these legitimate aspirations.

The Filipinos and the Americans could and did build on the legacy left by the Spaniards. Spain's great contribution was the gift of a common religion. The Philippines is the only Christian nation in the Orient. The effect of religious practices on the masses under the leadership of the Princes of the Catholic Church has been to foster respect one for another. It has constituted a telling force in the attainment of unity.

The United States during the half of a century of its association with the Philippines set a pattern in colonial administration entirely new in the history of the world. For the first time, a great and powerful country like the United States, having a small and weak country like the Philippines under its control, agreed of its own free will and accord to permit the Filipinos to move forward step by step in self-government until independence was attained. The Americans fulfilled their promise. The Filipinos cooperated wholeheartedly in making an ideal realistically workable.

American policy meant in practice that democratic principles as known in the United States were transplanted to the Philippines. The growth of democratic thought was there rapidly fostered through the schools, the ballot, and actual experience in the art of government. The Filipino took direct part in the development of his own land. He has given ample proof that the man of Malayan blood can and will cooperate with his fellows for a common purpose.[5]

Out of necessity English was made the language of administration

---

[5] Fay-Cooper Cole, *The Peoples of Malaysia* (1945). A favorable view of the "great ability in self government" shown by the Filipinos.

and the basis of instruction in the schools. In results it has meant an official language which has done much to unify the Islands.

The universal craving for education, which strains the facilities of the schools to the limit, indicates that culture should continue to develop in many ways. The Philippines has a higher standard of literacy than many nations. The fine type of Filipino womanhood is an added asset.

It must be admitted that currents pound upon the national organization which tend to undermine unity. Regional and dialectic rivalries exist. Class distinctions—the rich oppressing the poor, the poor jealous of the rich—occur. Intrusive foreign elements causing them to be set apart are present. Mostly these matters engender disputes in the nature of family quarrels. They are no more accentuated than in the United States.

It must also be admitted that democracy in the Philippines has its weaknesses. It would be expecting over much of a people to have them learn all the lessons of representative government in half a century. In the Orient the man—the strong leader—is the one who counts and who is followed. If representative government in the Philippines works differently behind a democratic front than in the United States, it need not be accepted as a fatal weakness. Conditions in the two countries are radically divergent. Basically the Filipinos are a homogeneous people, with common ties and common problems, who are proud to live under a constitutional government.

On the adverse side Filipino unity is actually threatened from three directions: Moro troubles, Capital-Labor difficulties, and Huk-Communistic revolt. The Moro problem need not become acute if governmental policy of tactful consideration for the Moros' religion and usages is continued. Capital and Labor differences follow the same pattern everywhere, and in the Philippines require the same application of good sense and fair dealing to arrive at settlement. The Huk-Communistic threat can be met from two directions—by settling the poor on land, and by energetic stamping out of any attempt to overthrow the government and set up by force an alien type of ideology. No one of the problems is insoluble.

In synthesis, an appraisal of those factors which work for or against national unity leads to the definite conclusion that the affirmative greatly overbalances the negative and that even the most intricate of the problems can be solved by statesmanlike planning. It is submitted that the Filipino people have demonstrated a capacity for self-government which has properly permitted them to establish a Christian Democratic Malayan State.

WILL THE FIRST MALAYAN REPUBLIC SURVIVE? [6]

It would be presumptuous to answer this question with a categorical "Yes" or "No." The judgment of history will perforce have to be awaited. Yet, assuredly, the Malayan Filipinos should be given a fair chance to maintain a Republic of their own creation.

Several factors in the situation are reassuring.

The reins of government have not fallen into untried hands. Quezon and Osmeña were competent leaders. So likewise was Roxas, the first President of the Republic. President Quirino and his advisers are experienced in statecraft. Recently they have shown a fuller understanding of the complexities of finance and economics. The approach to their tasks of the officials chosen by the people is one of sobriety and earnestness, marked by a commendable disposition to take a realistic view of the problems that confront them. Radical and fundamental changes in governmental organization and practices and strange methods are not seriously contemplated.

The responsible leaders have at their command notable blessings. We will itemize a few of the most important. In the first place there is a people mainly Christian in religion, athirst for education, and wanting an honest, efficient administration of their affairs. In the second place there are the rich resources of the Islands, as a whole merely scratched—a fertile soil producing salable rice, corn, hemp, sugarcane, and tobacco; great tracts of hardwood timber; equally large areas of coconut- or fruit-producing trees; and large deposits of minerals of all descriptions scattered over the Islands. In the third place, all can be reasonably confident that rehabilitation will proceed and that finances will stabilize.

While the foregoing furnishes a strong foundation for the Republic, yet there are serious problems to be faced. The export trade must be carefully nurtured and watched. The Huk menace, on the one hand, must be tolerantly handled to wean away the unwary, and, on the other, must be met head-on to strike down elements planning the overthrow of the Government. Indefensible extravagance, rampant graft, addiction to nepotism, and electoral terrorism, place the entire people in an unfavorable light and must be sternly cast out of the temple of the Republic.

The Republic of the Philippines, close in time to 1951, possesses many assets working for success, but has to admit to undermining

---

[6] Readable and stimulating is Felix Keesing, *The South Seas in the Modern World* (New York, 1945). Also see Ralph Coniston, *The Future of Freedom in the Orient* (1947) and Lennox A. Mills and Associates, *The New World of Southeast Asia* (1949).

influences. Put into the form of an equation, the problem might be presented like this:

Assets: 1. People, approximately 20,000,000; 2. Religion, ninety percent Christians; 3. Democracy, training and experience; 4. Language, unifying English in general use; 5. Culture, proficient in the arts and sciences; 6. Resources, so vast as to be beyond specification; 7. Aid, furnished by the United States; 8. Stability, not as yet dangerously threatened by any outside source; 9. Leadership, tested and generally not found wanting; 10. Future, prospects favorable for 100,000,-000 people living in a prosperous land.

Liabilities: 1. Divisions, regional and dialectic; 2. Divisions, religious between the Moros and pagans and the Christians; 3. Divisions, economic with the common man demanding land to cultivate and the right to live decently; 4. Divisions, political not rising above narrow partisanship to take the longer view; 5. Divisions, seditious seeking to establish a Communistic State; 6. Weakness, over dependence on the United States; 7. Weakness, countenancing extravagance, graft, nepotism, and election frauds; 8. Weakness, the war's aftermath of devastation and demoralization; 9. Weakness, proximity to larger, crowded lands; 10. Weakness, a symbolic show window of democracy with shoddy articles on display.

Add the assets and the total goes beyond human comprehension. Utilization of the resources to the fullest extent depends on careful planning. Add the liabilities and they, in truth, do indicate a "tendency to backslide." But divisions among the people can be avoided and indicated weaknesses can be remedied by mature, courageous action. The outlook is not discouraging.

Senator William E. Borah, on the floor of the United States Senate, in announcing his vote in favor of the Hare-Hawes-Cutting Independence Bill, uttered these words: "I know, Mr. President, that whenever independence is granted, there will be a risk. I am aware that the Filipino people may stumble and fall. But knowing full well that whenever independence is given these same things may—I should almost say must—happen, I am not willing longer to deny them a chance to work out their own salvation." That is an honest statement of the American viewpoint. "A risk" is to be incurred by the Filipino people. Permit them to take it and try their luck. It is up to the Filipinos to sink or swim.

Let us take a closer look at the two major "risks" of the Philippine Republic—one internal and the other external.

The current of unrest and dissatisfaction flowing over the world carrying with it demands for a new setup for the common man has not bypassed the Philippines. Manifestations of it are seen there every day. Discontent exists and will continue to exist, and defiance of the government is in evidence and will continue to plague the government, to the detriment of economic development and political normalcy, unless energetic measures are taken.

The *Manila Chronicle* in a forthright editorial of March 15, 1950 pleaded with the Government to consider first things first. "Let it solve the one and only problem which holds the key to everything. Let it solve the peace and order problem, and the rest will follow." A blunt statement of actualities!

The ultimate success of Philippine independence will depend in great measure upon the ability of the Filipinos to evolve an economic existence in the new state of affairs in which they find themselves. Will the Philippines be able to survive economically?

The economic future of the Philippines is far from hopeless, in fact, it is bright. It is doubtful if actual hunger to any considerable extent will ever exist in the Islands. In the tropics wants are few and readily satisfied. The family system is well intrenched, and the caring for needy relatives is assumed as a matter of course.

Aside from these locally self-evident truths, there are larger aspects to be considered.

The Philippine Trade Act of 1946 threw open the American market with complete fairness to 1954, and after that date to 1974 with diminishing consideration. But it should be recalled that the Philippines produces hemp, copra and sugar which the United States needs. And no one can take away the Islands' lumber and minerals without paying for them. An extension or a modification of the Philippine Trade Act which will permit the Philippines to continue to have access to the American market for a very considerable volume of Philippine products, and which will allow access to the Philippines for American merchandise, is feasible, for the reason that it would be mutually advantageous.

With normal conditions returning to the world, the Philippines can look to Asiatic and European countries to buy an increasing amount of Philippine products. If you add to this trade the tapping of heretofore hidden resources like rubber and oil and the growing of ramie, and add to this the implantation of an industrialization program, the economic picture becomes tinged with brighter colors. To consolidate the facts, they mean that the economic future of the Islands requires careful and measured thought.

The second major "risk" has international aspects. Placed as the Philippine Islands are near the center of the stage of the Far Eastern drama, it is likely that the Republic will continue to be involved in delicate foreign relations. At this point let us consider a few of its varied phases.

First, as to America's attitude toward the Philippine Republic. The lessons of World War II, and in particular the amazing development in aerial warfare, have wiped out provincial isolationist sentiment in the United States. It is indeed one world, and the United States cannot evade living in this troubled world. The Far East is a primary front, and the democratic Philippines is a part thereof. For the United States to abandon a friendly ally under such conditions is unthinkable.

The United States and Soviet Russia are in reality Oriental neighbors who are playing for the high stakes of national survival. As a consequence, there is little or no desire on the part of the American public to evade responsibility in the Philippines. Common decency demands that the United States express its gratitude in a practical manner to the thousands of Filipinos who suffered and died because of alignment with the forces of democracy. This means cooperation with the Philippines in rehabilitation, trade and culture. The retention of American military and naval bases in the Islands should signify that President Roosevelt's "solemn pledge" to the people of the Philippines that their independence will be "established and protected" will be fulfilled.

Philippine-American relationship thus entered into naturally presents two views. One is that it frees the Philippines from fear of aggression on the part of any power. The other view is that it makes the Philippines a partner of the United States, and if war should break out between the United States and Soviet Russia, the Philippines, because of association with the United States, would be drawn into the war. This is not as bad as appears at first hand. All the nations of the world are being compelled to choose sides, either on the Democratic team or the Communistic team, and the Philippines is no exception. Even if a third World War should occur, the Philippines is not so located as to be a likely battleground.

The spectre of China—of nearby Formosa in unfriendly hands— frightens the Filipino people. The Philippines lives within the shadow of the largest nation on earth and also the most congested and the most impoverished. Immigration pressure from China is unremitting. Peaceful infiltration of the Chinese goes on apace. It is met by anti-Chinese agitation on the part of the Filipinos. The attention of the Chinese giant is presently too much centered on a civil war and domestic problems to give a look to the pinpricks from the Philippines. In the future, however, a united and communistic-tinged China under ambitious leadership would bear careful watching. It would behoove a sagacious Philippines not to permit overcharged nationalist jealousy of the Chinese to overreach itself to endanger Philippine-Chinese amity.

There remains a Japan beaten down to her knees, but potentially either a friend or a foe. In course of time, Japan will be freed from American military administration and will enter into normal relations, diplomatic and mercantile, with other states. The pressure of a Japanese population with a cry for land will again be heard. If the Yellow Peril is to be avoided, the Philippines will have to forget bitterness involving Japanese atrocities, will have to renew intercourse with Nippon, and will have to accept the democratically-indoctrinated Japanese as equals. The fate of the Filipino people is inexorably involved with that of other Oriental peoples, among which the Japanese are numbered.

The external relations of the Philippines can be expected to pivot on close association with the United States, to include the fostering of trade with all nations, and to stress mutual understanding with close neighbors. Back of all policy will be support of the United Nations as the instrument of peace. And fortifying the whole will be compact, well trained, and modernly equipped armed forces.

The chances are good for the Filipinos to prove that they have capacity for self-government. The chances are equally good for the Filipinos to set the world aright about the Malay race, by not only establishing the first Malayan Republic, but by making it a going concern. Subject to the vicissitudes that beset every land, the Filipino people should be able to maintain their Republic an equal in all respects among the free nations.

The prophets of doom may again be proved wrong. Forecasts of the "collapse" or "overthrow" of the Philippine Government, like predictions of typhoon weather, may not materialize. It should be the prayer of everyone that the Republic of the Philippines shall succeed.

Mabuhay

When the popular hero returns in triumph, the people shout *Mabuhay*. When the orator reaches his frenzied climax, the listeners join in *Mabuhay*. When the glasses are raised in salute, the toast is *Mabuhay*. The time honored Philippine expression is a word of the Tagalog dialect and means "Here's How," "Cheerio," "Salud," "Aloha," and all the words of joy, love and good luck rolled into one.

To the Republic of the Philippines, *Mabuhay!*

INDEX